EASTERN CHRISTIANITY

EASTERN CHRISTIANITY

- A Reader -

Edited by J. Edward Walters

WILLIAM B. EERDMANS PUBLISHING COMPANY

GRAND RAPIDS, MICHIGAN

Wm. B. Eerdmans Publishing Co.
4035 Park East Court SE, Grand Rapids, Michigan 49546
www.eerdmans.com

27 26 25 24 23 22 21   1 2 3 4 5 6 7

ISBN 978-0-8028-7686-7

Library of Congress Cataloging-in-Publication Data

Names: Walters, J. Edward, editor.
Title: Eastern Christianity : a reader / edited by J. Edward Walters.
Description: Grand Rapids, Michigan : William. B. Eerdmans Publishing Company,
   [2021] | Includes bibliographical references and index. | Summary: "A collection
   of significant Syriac, Armenian, Georgian, Arabic, Coptic, and Ethiopic Christian
   texts in English translation, along with informative introductions"—Provided by
   publisher.
Identifiers: LCCN 2021019880 | ISBN 9780802876867
Subjects: LCSH: Christian literature, Early—Arab authors. | Christian literature,
   Early—Armenian authors. | Christian literature, Early—Coptic authors. | Chris-
   tian literature, Early—Ethiopic authors. | Christian literature, Early—Georgian
   authors. | Christian literature, Early—Syriac authors. | Christian literature,
   Early—Translations into English.
Classification: LCC BR60 .E275 2021 | DDC 270.2—dc23
LC record available at https://lccn.loc.gov/2021019880

To the many scribes, readers, archivists, and librarians
who have preserved these texts.
Most of their names have been forgotten,
but their contributions have not.

CONTENTS

Contents

ILLUSTRATIONS

Each illustration appears at the beginning of the chapter to which it belongs.

Chapter 1: Syriac

The beginning of Narsai's mēmrā on Canaanite woman. Chaldean Cathederal, Mardin MS 60.19, fol. 204r (HMML project number CCM 00578). Image courtesy of Chaldean Cathedral, Mardin, Turkey, and the Hill Museum & Manuscript Library. Published with permission of the owners. All rights reserved.

Chapter 2: Armenian

The beginning of Grigor of Narek's *Book of Lamentation*. Armenian Patriarchate of Istanbul, Azgayin Matenadaran, Istanbul, Turkey, MS 131, fol. 3v (HMML project number APIA 00131). Image courtesy of the Armenian Patriarchate of Istanbul, Azgayin Matenadaran, Istanbul, Turkey, and the Hill Museum & Manuscript Library. Published with permission of the owners. All rights reserved.

Chapter 3: Georgian

A loose folio containing Georgian liturgical chants; this manuscript is also a palimpsest with two erased layers of earlier Syriac texts. Saint John's University, Collegeville, MN, Hill Museum & Manuscript Library Special Collections, MS Frag. 32 (HMML project number SJRB 00154). Image courtesy of the Hill Museum & Manuscript Library. Published with permission of the owners. All rights reserved.

Illustrations

Chapter 4: Arabic

The beginning of Ḥunayn Ibn Isḥāq's *How to Discern the True Religion*. Fondation Georges et Mathilde Salem, Aleppo, Syria, MS Ar 238, fol. 85r (HMML project number GAMS 01040). Image courtesy of Fondation Georges et Mathilde Salem, Aleppo, Syria; Chaldean Cathedral Mardin, Turkey, and the Hill Museum & Manuscript Library. Published with permission of the owners. All rights reserved.

Chapter 5: Coptic

The beginning of the *Anaphora of Saint Thomas the Apostle*. Bibliothèque nationale de France, Paris, France, BnF copte 129.20, fol. 123r. Image courtesy of the Bibliothèque nationale de France. Published with permission of the owners. All rights reserved.

Chapter 6: Ethiopic

Part of the *Letter of Eusebius to Carpianus* in the Ethiopic Abba Gärima gospels. Abba Gärima I, Ǝndā Abba Gärima Monastery, Tigray Province, Ethiopia. Image courtesy of Michael Gervers (2004).

ABBREVIATIONS

CSCO   Corpus Scriptorum Christianorum Orientalium. Leuven: Peeters, 1903–.

GEDSH   *The Gorgias Encyclopedic Dictionary of the Syriac Heritage.* Edited by Sebastian P. Brock, Aaron M. Butts, George A. Kiraz, and Lucas Van Rompay. Piscataway, NJ: Gorgias, 2011 (online at http://gedsh.beth mardutho.org).

LXX   Septuagint

MH   *Matenagirkʿ Hayocʿ* (*Armenian Classical Authors*). Vols. 1–15: Antelias, Lebanon, 2003–2010; vols. 16–21: Erevan, Armenia, 2012– (some volumes online at https://matenadaran.am).

RIÉ   *Recueil des inscriptions de l'Éthiopie des périodes pré-axoumite et axoumite.* Vol. 1, *Les documents*, and Vol. 2, *Les planches*, by É. Bernand, A. J. Drewes, and R. Schneider. Paris: Boccard, 1991. Vol. 3, *Traductions et commentaires*, part A, *Les inscriptions grecques*, by É. Bernand. Paris: Boccard, 2000. Vol. 3, *Traductions et commentaires*, part B, *Les inscriptions sémitiques*, by A. J. Drewes, revised by Manfred Kropp, edited by Manfred Kropp and Harry Stroomer. Äthiopistische Forschungen 85/ De Goeje Fund 34; Wiesbaden: Harrassowitz, 2019.

PREFACE

J. Edward Walters

T he story of the rise and expansion of the Christian movement in the Roman Empire, at least in its basic contours, is generally well known. The movement began as a Jewish sect in Roman-occupied Palestine and ultimately grew into a distinct, albeit diverse, collection of communities that spread across the whole Mediterranean world. These communities eventually became numerous and distinct enough that they drew the attention of their Roman neighbors and even local magistrates, occasionally resulting in social persecution and even violence. Ultimately the Roman Empire officially sanctioned the suppression of the Christian movement, first under Emperor Decius in the middle of the third century and even more intensely in the final decade of the third century under Emperor Diocletian. Then, somewhat ironically, Christians would emerge from the Great Persecution of Diocletian as inheritors of the very empire that tried to exterminate them. And, even more ironically, within a century the formerly persecuted would become the persecutors: a Christian Roman Empire that violently suppressed both Jews and adherents of traditional Greco-Roman religions.

It is at this point, with the rise of Constantine, that the story of Christianity becomes entangled with the political history of the Mediterranean world. The continuity of the late Roman Empire, even as the political center of the empire shifted from Rome to Constantinople, allowed Christianity to flourish, and even the changing demographics of central and northern Europe resulting from migrations from the east provided opportunities for Christian communities to take root in new places. This growth of Christianity throughout Europe is generally thought to coincide with its demise elsewhere, as armies expanded from the Arabian desert to the west across North Africa and to the north and east across lands that previously belonged to the Roman and Persian (Sassanian) Empires. Jerusalem itself, the birthplace of the Christian movement, was brought under

Muslim authority, as were other cities, like Alexandria and Antioch, that had been significant sites of Christian presence and authority.

The story of Christianity then continues as a history of Western Christendom, often contrasted with the Islamic empires to the east. The developments of medieval Christianity in Europe are certainly not isolated from Eastern influences (as evidenced by the translation and religious exchanges in the Iberian Peninsula or by the influence of John of Damascus on Thomas Aquinas), but aside from the study of the Crusades, the history of Christianity in Europe is often studied in isolation, with the effect that "history of Christianity in Europe" has become synonymous with the "history of Christianity." There are certainly exceptions to this rule, as some historians try to increase awareness of the global reach of Christianity in the premodern period.[1] Yet, despite such efforts, many people—even many historians of Christianity—remain unaware of the other stories of Christianity, the stories not rooted in the Roman Empire and not based in the lands that would come to be known as Europe.

The general lack of awareness concerning Eastern Christian communities in Europe and North America is certainly rooted in the colonialist history of the West as European Christianity came to be seen as part of the foundation of "Western civilization." As such, it is the westward expansion of Christianity that received the most attention. Additionally, the status of Christianity as part of Western civilization naturally resulted in the glorification of the sources for Christianity preserved in the preferred "classical" languages of Western civilization: Greek and Latin. Thus, even sources from within the Roman Empire and of equal antiquity and significance for the history of Christian communities as some contemporary Greek and Latin literature remain understudied and undervalued because they were written in Syriac, Armenian, or Coptic.

The end result of the exclusively Western-focused study of Christianity is that general knowledge about non-European Christian communities from late antiquity through the medieval period is woefully impoverished, primarily because

---

1. It can be difficult to find church history or history-of-Christianity survey textbooks that discuss premodern Christianity outside of the European/Mediterranean context, but there are a few notable exceptions that should be highlighted: Dale T. Irvin and Scott W. Sunquist, *History of the World Christian Movement*, vol. 1, *Earliest Christianity to 1453* (Maryknoll, NY: Orbis Books, 2001); Samuel Hugh Moffet, *A History of Christianity in Asia*, vol. 1, *Beginnings to 1500* (Maryknoll, NY: Orbis Books, 2008); and Robert Louis Wilken, *The First Thousand Years: A Global History of Christianity* (New Haven: Yale University Press, 2012). For primary source materials, the global nature of early and medieval Christianity is also reflected in John W. Coakley and Andrea Sterk, *Readings in World Christian History*, vol. 1, *Earliest Christianity to 1453* (Maryknoll, NY: Orbis Books, 2011). A broader popular treatment may also be found in Philip Jenkins, *The Lost History of Christianity: The Thousand-Year Golden Age of the Church in the Middle East, Africa, and Asia—and How It Died* (New York: HarperOne, 2008).

the sources for the study of these communities remain difficult to access. After all, the history of Christianity, like other historical disciplines, is reliant upon sources, both material and literary. As a result of the political developments briefly described above, scholars and historians had much more access to the sources for the study of Western Christianity. The written sources for Eastern Christianity exist in equal, if not greater, number, but they suffer from lack of access, both physically because the manuscripts often reside in more difficult to reach libraries and linguistically because the sources for Eastern Christianity require language training beyond what is offered at many institutions of higher learning.

It is precisely this problem—the lack of access to relevant sources—that the present volume attempts to address. This volume certainly cannot solve the problem entirely, as no single anthology could possibly hope to provide comprehensive access to the complex living traditions of Christian faith and practice across multiple linguistic and theological traditions. Indeed, the history and sources of the communities and language traditions represented in this book— Arabic, Armenian, Coptic, Ethiopic, Georgian, and Syriac—can be as distinct from each other as they are from the Latin tradition. As such, the present volume offers not a comprehensive survey, but a series of windows into these traditions, through which readers can learn more about the distinctives of each language tradition and the people who wrote, read, and preserved these texts.

As a final note, it is important to clarify how the term "Eastern Christianity" is being used in this volume. Frequently when Christianity is divided into Eastern and Western halves, the West is roughly equivalent to the Latin-speaking tradition in Europe that would come to be known as the Roman Catholic Church (and, subsequently, of course the Protestant traditions), and the East is regarded as Greek-speaking Christianity, associated with the Byzantine Empire, which would come to be known as the Greek Orthodox Church, including the other autocephalous Orthodox traditions related to the Greek tradition (Russian Orthodox, Serbian Orthodox, Bulgarian Orthodox, Romanian Orthodox, etc.). By contrast, the language traditions included in the present volume are often called the Oriental Orthodox churches—that is, those traditions found in the East that have not been in communion with the other Eastern Orthodox churches since the fifth century.[2] The present volume does not use the common terminology "Oriental Orthodox" because of the problematic history of the use of the term "oriental" in Western scholarship to refer to anything different from Western customs and traditions. Instead, the term "Eastern Christianity" is used, even

---

2. Though even in this volume there are exceptions, as the Georgian tradition ultimately came to be aligned with the Greek Orthodox Church, as discussed in the introduction to chap. 3.

though this volume does not represent all of the traditions that might be considered part of Eastern Christianity. Most notably, this volume does not include writings from the Greek Orthodox tradition. The omission of Greek sources is in no way meant to devalue the importance of the Byzantine tradition of Christianity or to exclude it from the category "Eastern Christianity." Thus, the term "Eastern Christianity" is used in this volume not as an essentialist category that includes and excludes specific traditions, but as a broadly inclusive category that is meant to reflect the diversity of Christian communities that developed to the east and south of the Roman/Byzantine Empire.

From its inception, the Christian movement idealized itself as a global phenomenon. Followers of Jesus were directed to "go into all the world, making disciples" (Matt 28:19–20). By all accounts, Christians were remarkably successful in this endeavor, and Christianity quickly became a global movement, spreading from Jerusalem to the West and to the East. The story of the spread to the West is already well known, and hopefully the sources and resources included in this volume will help document the rest of the story.

INTRODUCTION

J. Edward Walters

I t would be impossible to provide an in-depth survey of the history of Eastern
Christianity in the span of just a few pages to serve as an introduction to
this volume. The history of Christianity's spread to the East and the stories
of its survival amid enormous political, social, and religious change over time is
just as complex, nuanced, and interesting as the story of Christianity in Europe.
As such, this introduction serves not as a comprehensive survey, but as an in-
vitation to you, the reader, to immerse yourself in texts that may, at first, seem
unfamiliar, to learn names that are difficult to pronounce, let alone remember,
and to hear the voices of Christian communities that are not often included in
historical surveys of Christianity. The texts contained in this volume cover a large
geographic area and span a significant time period, so it can be easy to lose the
way. The following guide is meant to help orient you, providing a map of sorts
as you begin your journey.

Mapping the Territory of Eastern Christian Literature

Generally, when one thinks of the "map" of early Christianity, cities like Jerusalem and Syrian Antioch are on the eastern side of that map, and the Christian
movement expands westward from there, through Asia Minor into Europe to the
north, and through Egypt to North Africa to the south. The texts in this volume
require us to zoom out and refocus that map so that Jerusalem and Antioch are
in the center of the frame. They also require us to learn new place names, like
Ḥirta, Ḥimyar, Beth Lapaṭ, Hatsʻeakkʻ, Narek, and Atripe, and confront unfamiliar terrain. As we explore this terrain, we encounter new people, Christian
saints, martyrs, authors, and even kings whose names we may not recognize:
ʻEzana, Pawla, Habo, Abū Qurrah, Christophoria, Eznik, Grigor, and Theodore

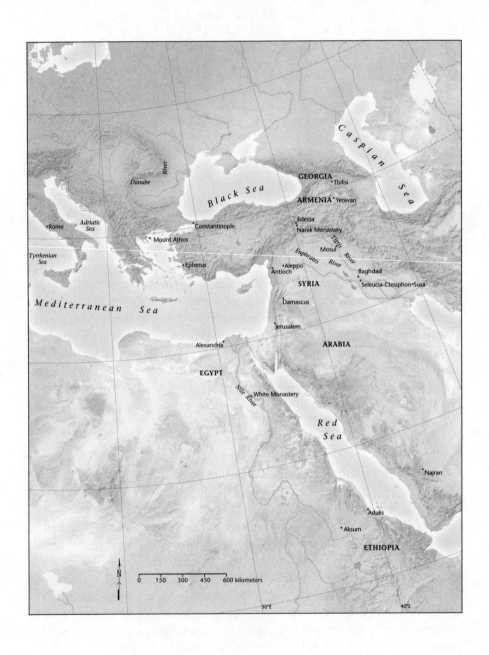

bar Koni, to name just a few. Even amid the newness, however, careful readers will find in these unfamiliar texts familiar themes and threads that run throughout Christian literature, which serve as signposts to guide them. The following suggested themes may provide helpful paths to follow.

Beginnings/Origins

Throughout Christian literature there is an interest in the question of origins, which is perhaps most readily observed at the border of canonical and noncanonical New Testament literature. That is, Christians were intrigued by origin stories, whether of Jesus's birth (e.g., the canonical birth narratives and the various "infancy gospels") or more broadly the origins of the Christian movement in various places and the people who brought it there (e.g., Paul's missionary journeys in the canonical Acts and the various similar stories in apocryphal Acts literature). It is no surprise, then, that as Christianity continued to expand into new territories and new language groups these new Christian communities were interested in their own origin stories. The *Doctrina Addai*, for example, provides a legendary account of the arrival of Christianity in the city of Edessa, and thus the origin of Syriac Christianity. The Ethiopic inscriptions pertaining to ʿEzana and the story of the Christianization of Ethiopia by Frumentius likewise shed light on the origins of Christianity in Ethiopia. The Armenian *Life of Mashtotsʿ* invites readers to reflect on the origins of the Armenian alphabet and thereby on the origins of Christian literature in the Armenian tradition. It can often be difficult to sort fact from fiction in such accounts, but regardless of historical merit, the popularity of such stories helps modern readers understand the concerns of ancient communities.

Interpreting the Christian Tradition: Scripture and Theology

One of the more readily identifiable themes that readers will encounter in this volume is that of biblical interpretation. From the very origins of the movement, Christians self-identified with respect to a corpus of texts that they considered authoritative, beginning with the corpus they would come to call the Old Testament and expanding over time to include a complementary New Testament. Subsequently, Christians throughout late antiquity and the medieval period wrote essays, treatises, books, and multivolume commentaries on biblical works. They also wrote and delivered homilies, which provide fascinating windows into the ways that biblical interpretation was performed for Christian audiences. The homilies of Jacob of Serugh and Narsai of Nisibis, for example, show how two late ancient Syriac authors creatively engaged their biblical source texts and gave those texts new meanings through their delivery. The Armenian *Teaching of Saint Grigor* and Anania of Narek's *On This Transitory World* provide interesting examples of the developing Armenian tradition of biblical interpretation. Likewise, in the anonymous Arabic *Commentary on the Pentateuch* and the Coptic writings of Shenoute, John of Paralos, and Pseudo-Cyril of Alexandria, we see how other authors engaged with biblical texts and with prior patristic commentary traditions as they sought to explain the biblical texts in new contexts. Several texts in this volume also deal with the topic of the translation, not only of Scripture, but other early Christian theological and liturgical texts, such as the Armenian *Life of Mashtots'* and the Georgian *Lives of John, Euthymios, and George*.

As with the writings of the Greco-Roman world, there is no sharp division between biblical and theological works in Eastern Christianity, and many of the texts above are also examples of theological reflection and development. As Christianity took root in new environments and then survived as the environments around it changed, Christians also had to confront new theological challenges. We see this in the Christian-Muslim dialogue texts like the Arabic *Disputation of Abraham* and Christian didactic literature like Abū Qurrah's argument *That God Is Not Weak* and Theodore bar Koni's *Scholion*. We also see this theme in texts like the Ethiopic *Book of the Trinity*, in which Christians made internal arguments about orthodoxy and heresy within the Christian tradition. In the writings of Ephrem the Syrian, Grigor of Narek, and Nersēs Shnorhali, we also see biblical and theological reflection delivered in a poetic medium.

Asceticism, Hagiography, and Martyrdom

Across all language traditions of premodern Christianity, one of the largest bodies of literature that Christians produced and read deals with the overlapping categories of hagiography and asceticism.[1] The late ancient Christian literary world was fascinated by the concept of the "holy man,"[2] and the rigid demands of the ascetic life came to define the concept of holiness. The *Martyrdom of Mīles* provides one example of such a traveling holy man who practiced ascetic denial and performed miracles. Although we should not imagine that most "regular"

1. For a broader view of this literature in early Christianity, see Susan Ashbrook Harvey, "Martyr Passions and Hagiography," in *The Oxford Handbook of Early Christian Studies*, ed. S. A. Harvey and D. G. Hunter (Oxford: Oxford University Press, 2008), 603–27.

2. Peter Brown, "The Rise and Function of the Holy Man in Late Antiquity," *Journal of Roman Studies* 61 (1971): 80–101.

Christians subjected themselves to such strict ascetic practice, the popularity of this literature helps us understand the ways that regular Christians perceived the world around them. Such texts mediated access to holy people, and thus to the divine holiness that was mediated through their exemplary lives. This hagiographic tradition can also be seen in the Syriac translation of the *Life of Mary of Egypt* and in the various Georgian *Lives* translated in this volume. A specific subset of hagiography also deserves special mention: stories of the martyrs. As much as Christians valued the stories of a holy life lived, they perhaps valued even more the stories of a holy life ended by violent means. These stories of death, including the martyrdoms of Mīles and Shushanik, and the related stories of the relics and bones of martyrs and saints, provide further evidence of the ways that Christians across many different historical contexts performed their own piety in proximity to their holy heroes.

Closely related to the subjects of asceticism and hagiography, Eastern Christian communities also produced a significant amount of literature relating to monastic communities. Such literature was translated and retranslated and often expanded as it circulated through various communities. Several of the texts included in this volume attest to the different monastic traditions that developed in diverse geographic locations. In particular, the Georgian accounts of John the Iberian, Euthymios the Athonite, and George the Athonite provide a significant amount of information about monastic practices, including devotional and religious life, translations of holy texts, and travel from one monastery to another. Likewise, the Coptic texts of Pachomius, Shenoute, and the *Encomium on Macarius* offer glimpses of the Egyptian monastic traditions. Scholars who work with hagiographic, ascetic, and monastic literature will find many familiar themes throughout these works in this volume.

Encounters with Religious Others

As Christians spread to the east, they also encountered and interacted with various religious "others" as neighbors, including those familiar from the Mediterranean world like Jews, Manicheans, and "pagans," but also others who are less commonly found in histories of Christianity, like Zoroastrians. The Zoroastrian context emerges in the Georgian *Martyrdom of Saint Shushanik*, and there is a particular focus on the eradication of paganism and pagan shrines in the Syriac *Doctrina Addai* and the Georgian *Life of Porphyry of Gaza*. Ephrem's *Hymns against Heresies* deals with communities who complicate the question of early Christian identity in the Syriac tradition: Marcionites, Bardaisanites, and Manicheans. The excerpt of Eznik of Koghb's *Refutation of the Sects* included in this volume also takes up the topic of local pagan beliefs in Armenia prior to the arrival of Christianity. Ultimately, of course, Eastern Christian communities were among the first to experience rule by the Islamic caliphates, and these communities were forced to adapt in various ways as a result of their interactions with Muslim neighbors. Furthermore, while there was certainly tension and even violence in Christian-Muslim relations over time, the (Western) history of the Crusades often overshadows the everyday reality of religious interactions between Christians and Muslims. The dialogue genre that became common for Syriac- and Arabic-speaking Christians, such as the *Disputation of Abraham*, offers an intriguing example of the ways that Christians came to define themselves and articulate their theology within an Islamic context. Such texts also provide a necessary counterbalance to imperialist narratives of Western Christians "liberating" holy sites under Muslim control. Three other texts, the Syriac *Scholion* of Theodore bar Koni and the Arabic texts of Theodore Abū Qurrah and Ḥunayn Ibn Isḥāq, serve as examples of Christian theological reflection in Islamic contexts. The Arabic *Miracles of Saint George* also provides a fascinating window into interreligious interaction in popular piety.[3]

Christianity and Political Power

The final theme that readers will recognize in this volume is that of the relationship between Christianity and political power. In many ways, the history of Christianity in western and central Asia is the opposite of that in Europe, where, after the fourth century, Christianity became entwined with political leadership. Many early Syriac and Armenian Christians, for example, found themselves participating—willingly or not—in border wars between the Roman and Persian Empires. Other Christians, such as the Ḥimyarite martyrs on the southwestern corner of the Arabian Peninsula, became victims of sociopolitical maneuvering. Still many others lived well beyond the border under the authority of the Sassanian Persians, and they were forced to negotiate their Christian identities within a sociopolitical context that was indifferent, if not openly hostile, to their existence. Several texts in this volume speak to the Sassanian context, including the Syriac *Martyrdom of Mīles* and the Georgian *Martyrdom of Saint Shushanik*. Furthermore, each of the linguistic traditions in this volume encountered, either directly or indirectly, the Arab conquests and Islamic caliphates that were

---

3. For a much broader survey of Christian piety and religious practices in the Islamic context, see Jack Tannous, *The Making of the Medieval Middle East* (Princeton: Princeton University Press, 2018).

established soon thereafter. The themes of martyrdom continue, as can be seen in the Georgian *Martyrdom of Habo*, but as mentioned above, such instances of violence do not tell the full story of Christian-Muslim relations. Indeed, although there were Christian martyrs under Islam,[4] many Christians adjusted to life under Islamic rule and even contributed to the social, cultural, and intellectual life of their societies.[5] The Ethiopic tradition, however, stands out in this volume as an exception in this regard, because, as evidenced by the early inscriptions and texts about the conversion of the Aksumite kingdom, the region of Ethiopia became a Christian kingdom, and it maintained that status over time, even as political dynasties around it changed.

The themes covered here are only a few examples of the paths that could be followed through this volume. It is important at the outset to remember that the texts translated here serve as an introduction to each linguistic tradition. Many more texts could be selected to represent these diverse traditions, so the texts included here are meant to give readers a small sample of the richness of each tradition and invite them to further study. Each chapter includes a bibliography that will help interested readers find their way to new resources as they continue the journey.

4. For treatment of this topic, see Christian C. Sahner, *Christian Martyrs under Islam: Religious Violence and the Making of the Muslim World* (Princeton: Princeton University Press, 2018).

5. For further literature, see J. J. van Ginkel, H. L. Murre-van den Berg, and T. M. Van Lint, eds., *Redefining Christian Identity: Cultural Interaction in the Middle East since the Rise of Islam*, Orientalia Lovaniensia Analecta 134 (Leuven: Peeters, 2005); Sidney H. Griffith, *The Church in the Shadow of the Mosque: Christians and Muslims in the World of Islam* (Princeton: Princeton University Press, 2008); R. G. Hoyland, *Seeing Islam as Others Saw It: A Survey and Evaluation of Christian, Jewish, and Zoroastrian Writings on Early Islam*, Studies in Late Antiquity and Early Islam 13 (Princeton: Darwin, 1997); and Michael Philip Penn, *Envisioning Islam: Syriac Christians and the Early Muslim World* (Philadelphia: University of Pennsylvania Press, 2017).

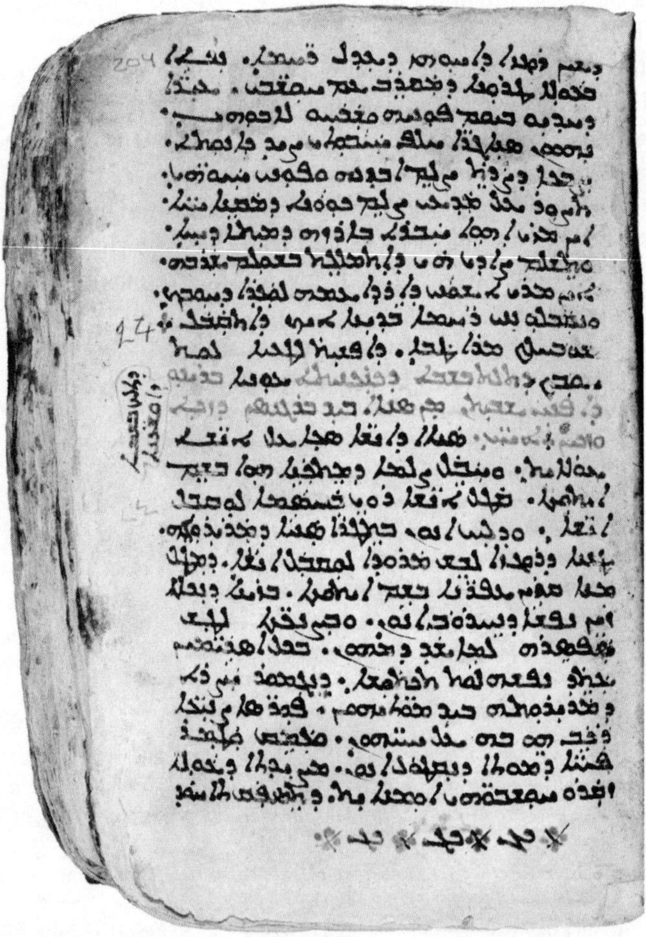

1

SYRIAC

Introduction and Bibliography by J. Edward Walters

Traveling east and slightly north from Syrian Antioch, ancient travelers would have come to the magnificent city of Edessa in the kingdom of Osroene, which occupied a strategic location on the Roman-Parthian (and later Roman-Sassanian Persian) border.[1] Edessa was a cosmopolitan city, located along a major east-west trade route, and well known as a home to many gods and the diverse peoples who were devoted to them.[2] Although the sources are difficult to trust as straightforward records, it seems that Edessa served as a gateway for early Christian expansion to the east.[3] Edessa was also the home of the dialect of Aramaic known as Syriac, which would become the primary literary language for Christianity in Mesopotamia for several centuries.[4] Further to the east, not far from Edessa lay the city of Nisibis, an ancient fortified city that is perhaps most well known as a territory lost by the Roman Empire in the aftermath of the defeat and death of Emperor Julian at the Battle of Samarra in 363 CE. As a result of the treaty signed by Julian's successor, Jovian, the Persian King Shapur II, who had failed on three previous siege attempts against Nisibis,

---

1. The modern-day location of Edessa is Urfa (or Şanilurfa), in southern Turkey, not far from the Syrian border. See Thomas A. Carlson et al., "Edessa," in *The Syriac Gazetteer* (online at https://www.syriaca.org/place/78).

2. For more on Edessa's religious context, see H. J. W. Drijvers, *Cults and Beliefs at Edessa* (Leiden: Brill, 1980).

3. The *Doctrina Addai*, excerpts of which are included in this volume, provides one of the crucial—albeit inflated—accounts of the arrival of Christianity in Edessa. For a general introduction, see Amir Harrak, "Was Edessa or Adiabene the Gateway for the Christianization of Mesopotamia?," in *The Levant: Crossroads of Late Antiquity: History, Religion, and Architecture*, ed. Ellen Bradshaw Aitken and John M. Fossey (Leiden: Brill, 2014), 165–80.

4. For a description of Classical Syriac, see Aaron Michael Butts, "The Classical Syriac Language," in *The Syriac World*, ed. Dan King (London: Routledge, 2019), 222–42; and Butts, "Syriac Language," in *GEDSH*, 390–91.

took control of the city without having to destroy its walls, while the Christian community in Nisibis was forced to relocate across the Roman border, namely back to cities like Amida and Edessa.[5]

Among those Christians who were exiled from Nisibis was a theologian and poet who would come to be known as Ephrem the Syrian.[6] Ephrem's influence on the Syriac traditions of Christianity cannot be overstated. His theology permeates the Syriac liturgies, and his unique expressions and turns of phrase are echoed throughout later Syriac authors. His signature composition style, a metrical structure known as a *madrāšā* (frequently translated "hymn" but perhaps more accurately rendered "teaching song"), became a standard genre of Syriac literature.[7] In both prose and poetic compositions, Ephrem is also one of the most significant Syriac sources for three teachers who would ultimately come to be regarded as heretics by Christians, but who also had significant communities of followers in Ephrem's time: Bardaisan, Marcion, and Mani.[8] These texts serve as valuable witnesses—albeit one-sided, polemical witnesses—to the beliefs and practices of these communities in the fourth century.

Ephrem also had a significant impact on the development of biblical exegesis in the Syriac tradition, as his poetic teaching songs displayed a unique creativity with interpretation, sometimes in the form of invented dialogue for biblical characters.[9] This style of poetic exegesis allowed Syriac authors to creatively

---

5. For a collection of primary source documents pertaining to this event, situated within the broader context of the fourth-century Roman-Persian wars, see Michael H. Dodgeon and Samuel N. C. Lieu, eds., *The Roman Eastern Frontier and the Persian Wars, AD 226–363: A Documentary History* (London: Routledge, 1991), 201–36.

6. One of the best general introductions to Ephrem the Syrian is Sebastian P. Brock, *The Luminous Eye: The Spiritual World Vision of Saint Ephrem the Syrian* (Collegeville, MN: Cistercian, 1992); see also Jeffrey Wickes, *Bible and Poetry in Late Antique Mesopotamia: Ephrem's Hymns on Faith* (Oakland: University of California Press, 2019); and Kathleen McVey, *Ephrem the Syrian: Hymns* (New York: Paulist, 1989).

7. Ephrem's works were collected into cycles of thematically similar content and preserved as collections such as *Hymns on Faith, Hymns on Virginity, Hymns on Paradise*, and *Hymns against Julian*. The final cycle mentioned here is significant because Ephrem describes in some detail his anger at Julian, both for his attempted revival of the pagan gods and for his actions that resulted in the loss of Nisibis.

8. Two of Ephrem's *Hymns against Heresies* are included in this volume.

9. For a collection of several examples of this creative exegetical genre in English translation, see Sebastian P. Brock, *Treasure-house of Mysteries: Explorations of the Sacred Text through Poetry in the Syriac Tradition*, Popular Patristics Series 45 (Yonkers, NY: Saint Vladimir's Seminary Press, 2012); see also Brock, "Syriac Dispute Poems: The Various Types," in *Dispute Poems and Dialogues in the Ancient and Medieval Near East: Forms and Types of Literary Debates in Semitic and Related Literatures*, ed. G. J. Reinink and H. L. J. Vanstiphout, Orientalia Lovaniensia Analecta 42 (Leuven: Peeters, 1991), 109–19.

embody characters, often giving voice to figures—especially women—who are relegated to silence in the biblical text itself.[10] It is also likely that at least some of these poems were performed by women in liturgical settings.[11] Later Syriac authors also continued to develop their own form of poetic meter for biblical interpretation and homilies. In particular we may mention authors like Jacob of Serugh and Narsai of Nisibis, who each perfected the syllabic homily for their own exegetical purposes. Although his name is certainly not commonly known among historians of Christianity, it is estimated that Jacob of Serugh has the third largest surviving corpus of homilies from early Christianity across all languages, behind only John Chrysostom and Augustine of Hippo.[12]

These two authors, Jacob and Narsai, are notable for another reason: though their careers overlap, they represent two distinct emerging traditions of Syriac Christianity that put them on opposite sides of a significant theological dispute that forever altered the ecclesiastical context for Syriac Christians. The impetus for this change was, of course, the christological disputes set off by Nestorius, the bishop of Constantinople, who infamously argued that Mary, the mother of Jesus, should not bear the title *theotokos* ("God-bearer" or "Mother of God") because, according to Nestorius, such a title unnecessarily collapsed and confused the divine and human natures of Christ. Nestorius soon found himself the object of significant backlash, led by Cyril of Alexandria. The resulting controversy spawned not one, but two councils: the Council of Ephesus (431) and the Council of Chalcedon (451). It would be impossible to summarize these complicated events in this short introduction, but the following points are pertinent to Syriac Christianity.[13]

The key issue at stake in the two councils was the question of the human and divine natures of Christ and what language was appropriate for describing them. One side of the debate, represented by Nestorius and his deceased teacher,

---

10. For example, see the dialogue of the Canaanite woman in Narsai's homily and that of Eve in Jacob of Serugh's homily in this volume.

11. See Susan Ashbrook Harvey, "Singing Women's Stories in Syriac Tradition," *Internationale kirchliche Zeitschrift* 100 (2010): 171–89; Harvey, "2000 NAPS Presidential Address: Spoken Words, Voiced Silence: Biblical Women in Syriac Tradition," *Journal of Early Christian Studies* 9 (2005): 105–31; and Harvey, "Performance as Exegesis: Women's Liturgical Choirs in Syriac Tradition," in *Inquiries into Eastern Christian Worship: Selected Papers of the Second International Congress of the Society of Oriental Liturgy Rome, 17–21 September 2008*, ed. Bert Groen, Steven Hawkes-Teeples, and Stefanos Alexopoulos, Eastern Christian Studies 12 (Leuven: Peeters, 2012), 47–64.

12. Philip Michael Forness, *Preaching Christology in the Roman Near East: A Study of Jacob of Serugh*, Oxford Early Christian Studies (Oxford: Oxford University Press, 2018), 23–24.

13. For a broader survey of the controversy, see Frances M. Young with Andrew Teal, *From Nicaea to Chalcedon: A Guide to the Literature and Its Background*, 2nd ed. (Grand Rapids: Baker Academic, 2010).

Theodore of Mopsuestia, argued that Jesus's human and divine natures remained distinct (and thus they were called dyophysites, meaning "two natures").[14] The other side, represented by Cyril of Alexandria and his supporters, argued that it was heretical to distinguish too sharply between the natures because it implied not just two natures, but two "persons" in Christ. The theological statement produced by the Council of Chalcedon attempted to resolve this issue with a conciliatory position that Christ is "acknowledged in two natures . . . in one person and one hypostasis."[15] While the ratification of this formulation at the council did succeed in giving Christians a new theological articulation, it failed to convince everyone. In fact, not only did the new statement not pacify the dyophysites who were loyal to Theodore and Nestorius, it also sparked a reaction from the opposite end of the spectrum: the miaphysites, who argued that the "in two natures" language of the Chalcedonian formula misrepresented the Christology of Cyril of Alexandria (who had died in 444, several years before the council). The miaphysite position argued, contra both Nestorian dyophysites and Chalcedonian dyophysites, that the union of divine and human natures in the incarnate Christ did not permit anyone to speak of them as distinctly two natures in the person of Christ; thus, they argued for one united nature after the incarnation (subsequently they were called miaphysites, meaning "one nature").[16]

Thus, in the aftermath of the Council of Chalcedon, there were three distinct confessions: (1) those who supported and affirmed Chalcedon, primarily made up of Christians within the bounds of the Roman Empire, (2) the non-Chalcedonian dyophysites (who are often called "Nestorians"), who were primarily located in Persia, and (3) the miaphysites, who were concentrated in the eastern Mediterranean, stretching from Egypt, through Syria, and into Armenia. Throughout the sixth century, these distinct theological positions hardened in

14. For an excellent survey of these issues particularly relating to the Syriac context, see Sebastian P. Brock, "The 'Nestorian' Church: A Lamentable Misnomer," *Bulletin of the John Rylands University Library of Manchester* 78 (1996): 23–35. For a collection of primary sources in translation pertaining to Nestorius's predecessors, Theodore and Diodore, see John Behr, *The Case against Diodore and Theodore: Texts and Their Contexts* (Oxford: Oxford University Press, 2011).

15. For the full acts of the Council of Chalcedon with helpful commentary and context, see *The Acts of the Council of Chalcedon*, ed. Richard Price and Michael Gaddis, Translated Texts for Historians 45 (Liverpool: Liverpool University Press, 2005).

16. Although the terms "monophysite" and "miaphysite" are confused and used interchangeably, they are actually two distinct positions, with the former referring to the unique expression of Eutyches of Constantinople, who argued that the human and divine natures *combined* to create a new, distinct nature (hence *mono-*, meaning not just "one," but "unique, only"). The distinction, then, is that miaphysites argued for an indivisible union of natures, whereas the monophysite position represented a mixture of the natures.

opposition to each other, forming distinct communities of Christians with separate leadership and hierarchical structure. Thus the end result of this controversy was the origin of several unique Christian church organizations that were not in communion with one another: (1) the Chalcedonians (who would separate later into the Byzantine Greek Orthodox and Roman Catholic traditions), distinguished by the affirmation of the Council of Chalcedon, (2) the Assyrian Church of the East (the non-Chalcedonian dyophysites), and (3) the various miaphysite confessions that formed among linguistically diverse communities: Syriac Orthodox Church, Armenian Orthodox Church, Coptic Orthodox Church, and Ethiopian Orthodox Church. Thus, after the fifth century, Syriac authors are universally designated by which tradition they represent: West Syriac (Syriac Orthodox), East Syriac (Assyrian Church of the East), or Melkite (i.e., the Syriac and later Arabic speakers who supported Chalcedon).[17] Mention should also be made of the Maronite tradition, which is another branch of early Syriac Christianity distinct from the East and West Syriac churches who remained in communion with the Chalcedonian tradition. Maronites remain as a distinct tradition today, concentrated in Lebanon.[18] As time went on, there were further geographic and theological fragmentations of these branches.

The geographic dispersion of Syriac-speaking Christians meant that individual communities faced very different political situations, even at contemporaneous times. For example, while Christians in the Roman Empire enjoyed the ascendance of Christian political power with Constantine and his successors, Christians in the Sassanian Empire remained a religious minority who were often at odds with their political leaders. As a result of these circumstances, the martyrdom genre became a significant feature of Syriac literature, resulting in a sizable corpus known as the *Persian Martyr Acts*.[19] Historians of Christianity are likely very familiar with the persecutions associated with the Roman Emperors Decius and Diocletian, but comparatively far less is known about the persecution associated with Shapur II or Yazdagird I.[20] At the same time, it is also important to

17. The term "Melkite" comes from the Semitic root *mlk* (noun "king"; verb "to rule"); thus, the Melkites were those who were loyal to the Roman king through their support of Chalcedonian theology. Melkites are also known as Arab Orthodox, Rūm Orthodox, or Antiochian Orthodox. For a collection of translated texts from this tradition, see Samuel Noble and Alexander Treiger, *The Orthodox Church in the Arab World, 700–1700: An Anthology of Sources* (Dekalb: Northern Illinois University Press, 2014).

18. See Joseph P. Amar, "Maronite Church," in *GEDSH*, 270–71; and Shafiq Abouzayd, "The Maronite Church," in *The Syriac World*, ed. Dan King (London: Routledge, 2019), 731–50.

19. For one example of such a text, see the *Martyrdom of Mīles*.

20. For a recent assessment of the persecution associated with Shapur II, see Kyle Smith, *Constantine and the Captive Christians of Persia: Martyrdom and Religious Identity in Late Antiquity* (Oakland: University of California Press, 2019).

remember that there were Syriac-speaking Christians *within* the Roman Empire, as evidenced both by the existence of the Melkite tradition mentioned above and by many miaphysite Christians finding themselves persecuted as heretics by their own emperor, Justinian.[21] It is often tempting to collapse "Syriac Christianity" with something foreign to the context of the Roman Empire, but this erases communities who existed as both Romans and Syriac Christians. Moreover, as seen in the *Letter on the Ḥimyarite Martyrs* (translated in this volume), Syriac-speaking Christians well beyond the borders of the Roman and Persian Empires were involved in geopolitical schemes that ultimately resulted in persecution and death. Despite these trying political situations, Christianity flourished in the Sassanian Empire and beyond, as communities spread and episcopal sees proliferated.[22] For example, despite a narrative of antagonism with the Sassanian rulers, Seleucia-Ctesiphon, the Sassanian capital, became a significant episcopal see, ultimately serving as the seat of the catholicos of the Church of the East[23] and the site of the earliest known synod of the Syriac tradition, the Synod of Isḥaq (410).

As evidence of their continued flourishing, Christians found a place in the royal courts of the Sassanians, the Umayyads, and the Abbasids, and they came to play a pivotal role in the translation of texts from Greek and Syriac into Arabic.[24] And, while the Muslim caliphates conquered the lands of the Sassanian Empire, while Islam uprooted Zoroastrianism, and while Arabic slowly but surely replaced other regional languages, Syriac-speaking Christians retained many of their distinct practices, including the use of Syriac as a liturgical language.[25]

In addition to sociopolitical and theological divisions, Syriac Christians also came to define themselves over and against religious others as well: Jews, pagans (i.e., adherents of traditional and local gods in various places), Manicheans, Zoroastrians, and—ultimately—Muslims. It is not surprising, then, that these other religious communities occupy a constant place in Syriac Christian literature, both as foils and as real theological opponents.[26] The eradication of pagan-

21. See Volker L. Menze, *Justinian and the Making of the Syrian Orthodox Church*, Oxford Early Christian Studies (Oxford: Oxford University Press, 2008).

22. For a treatment of the ways that Syriac Christians negotiated their identities in the Persian context, see Richard E. Payne, *A State of Mixture: Christians, Zoroastrians, and Iranian Political Culture in Late Antiquity* (Oakland: University of California Press, 2015).

23. Marcia C. Cassis, "Seleucia-Ctesiphon," *GEDSH*, 365.

24. For a short introduction, see Sebastian P. Brock, "Greek, Syriac translations from," in *GEDSH*, 180–81.

25. One intriguing product of the encounter between the Syriac and Arabic languages is the practice of writing Arabic-language texts in Syriac script, also known as Arabic Garshuni, which is attested in thousands of manuscripts from the Middle East.

26. For more on Jews and Christians in Syriac literature, see Aaron M. Butts and Simcha

ism and destruction of pagan temples plays an important role in origin stories for Syriac Christianity, such as the *Doctrina Addai*, and anti-Jewish rhetoric shows up throughout many forms of Syriac literature, including the *Letter on the Ḥimyarite Martyrs*, in which a Jewish king sets off a persecution of Christians within his kingdom. It is also not surprising that, following the advent of Islam, Syriac Christians produced a rather large corpus of writings that explicitly discusses Islamic theology and Christian-Muslim relations.[27]

Syriac Christians also produced a large body of ascetic and hagiographic literature. In the earliest period of Syriac Christianity, a unique expression of asceticism arose that was not directly influenced by the Egyptian monastic movement.[28] Even by the time of one of the earliest surviving Syriac corpuses, the *Demonstrations* attributed to Aphrahaṭ the Persian sage (dated 337–45 CE), there is already an established group of ascetics known as the *bnay qyāmā*, the "children of the covenant."[29] These ascetics, unlike their Egyptian contemporaries, were not removed from society and living as hermits in remote locations; rather, it seems that they lived alongside other lay Christians and were distinguished only by their rigid practices of denial, namely virginity.[30] By the fifth century, writings from the Egyptian and Greek monastic contexts had begun to be translated into Syriac, which influenced both the practices and literature of Syriac ascetic communities, including the proliferation of hagiographic lives, many of which exist in Syriac as translations from Greek[31] or as native Syriac compositions. Regardless of language of origin, though, it is clear from the size of the surviving corpus in Syriac that hagiographies and devotion to saints came to be a particularly significant expression of piety in the Syriac context.[32]

Gross, *Jews and Syriac Christians: Intersections across the First Millennium*, Texts and Studies in Ancient Judaism 180 (Tübingen: Mohr Siebeck, 2020).

27. An excerpt of one such text, by Theodore bar Koni, is translated in this volume. Many other texts are published in Michael Philip Penn, *When Christians First Met Muslims: A Sourcebook of the Earliest Syriac Writings on Islam* (Oakland: University of California Press, 2015). For more on Syriac Christians and Islam, see Penn, *Envisioning Islam: Syriac Christians and the Early Muslim World* (Philadelphia: University of Pennsylvania Press, 2017); and Sidney H. Griffith, *The Church in the Shadow of the Mosque: Christians and Muslims in the World of Islam* (Princeton: Princeton University Press, 2012).

28. The classic work on this topic is Arthur Vööbus, *A History of Asceticism in the Syrian Orient: A Contribution to the History of Culture in the Near East*, 3 vols., CSCO 184, 197, 500 (Leuven: Secrétariat du CSCO, 1958, 1960, 1988).

29. Aphrahat, "Demonstration 6: On the Bnay Qyama," in Adam Lehto, *The Demonstrations of Aphrahat, the Persian Sage*, Gorgias Eastern Christian Studies 27 (Piscataway, NJ: Gorgias, 2010), 169–98.

30. For more description and bibliography, see Robert A. Kitchen, "Bnay Qyāmā, Bnāt Qyāmā," in *GEDSH*, 84–85.

31. Such as the *Life of Mary of Egypt* included in this volume.

32. For a comprehensive resource on Syriac hagiography, see *Qadishe: Guide to the Syriac*

The topic of translations of Greek writings is also significant for the issue of the transmission and reception of biblical writings in Syriac. The Gospels were likely one of the earliest corpuses to be translated from Greek to Syriac, which is all the more significant given that there were at least three distinct versions of the Gospels in Syriac by the fourth century: (1) the Diatessaron of Tatian, (2) the "Old Syriac Gospels," and (3) the Peshiṭta.[33] The last of these, the Peshiṭta, became the authoritative version of the Bible over the course of the fourth and fifth centuries,[34] despite the Peshiṭta New Testament lacking several books that had come to be accepted in the Greek canon: 2 Peter, 2–3 John, Jude, and Revelation. These latter books were later translated into Syriac, likely in the sixth century, as part of a broader Greek-to-Syriac translation movement, and they ultimately came to circulate as part of Syriac biblical manuscripts.[35] As Greek translations into Syriac increased in the fifth and sixth centuries, attitudes with respect to translation theory and practice also shifted,[36] resulting in yet two more Syriac New Testament translation projects: the Philoxenian revision and the Harklean version.[37] The latter of these, named after its translator, Thomas of Harkel, is a hyper-literal translation that attempts, as much as possible, to render a word-for-word Syriac translation of the Greek New Testament. And there were many other translations of biblical and parabiblical materials as well. There is a significant body of apocryphal literature in Syriac,[38] including some works that exist only in Syriac and Arabic translations, such as 2 *Baruch* (also known as the *Syriac Apocalypse of Baruch*) and 4 *Ezra*, and other works for which the Syriac text is a significant textual witness, such as the

---

Saints, ed. Jeanne-Nicole Mellon Saint-Laurent and David A. Michelson (online at https://www.syriaca.org/q/index.html); see also Mellon Saint-Laurent, "Syriac Hagiographic Literature," in *The Syriac World*, ed. Dan King (London: Routledge, 2019), 339–54.

33. The best introduction to the Bible in Syriac is Sebastian P. Brock, *The Bible in the Syriac Tradition*, Gorgias Handbooks 7 (Piscataway, NJ: Gorgias, 2006).

34. The translations of the Peshiṭta Old Testament and Peshiṭta New Testament were distinct translation projects; they just came to circulate together as "the Peshiṭta" version.

35. It is still quite common to find Syriac biblical manuscripts that lacked these books, even long after they were translated into Syriac.

36. For a short introduction, see Sebastian P. Brock, "Aspects of Translation Technique in Antiquity," *Greek, Roman, and Byzantine Studies* 20 (1979): 69–87, reprinted in Brock's *Syriac Perspectives on Late Antiquity* (Aldershot, UK: Ashgate Variorum, 2001).

37. For more on the Philoxenian revision, see J. Edward Walters, "The Philoxenian Gospels as Reconstructed from the Writings of Philoxenos of Mabbug," *Hugoye: Journal of Syriac Studies* 13 (2010): 177–249. See also George A. Kiraz, *Comparative Edition of the Syriac Gospels: Aligning the Sinaiticus, Curetonianus, Peshitta, and Harklean Versions* (Piscataway, NJ: Gorgias, 2004).

38. See Muriel Debié, Alain Desreumaux, Christelle Jullien, and Florence Jullien, eds., *Les apocryphes syriaques*, Études syriaques 2 (Paris: Geuthner, 2005).

Infancy Gospel of Thomas.[39] The Septuagint column of Origen's Hexapla was also translated into Syriac, known as the Syro-Hexapla, and this version remains one of the most important witnesses to Origen's monumental work.[40]

The genres and titles mentioned above comprise a significant percentage of surviving Syriac works, yet even these works scarcely scratch the surface of surviving Syriac literature, which also includes translations of important classical works of philosophy, medicine, science, historical works and chronicles, patristic writings (both translated and native Syriac), grammars and linguistic resources, and a vast body of liturgical materials that testifies to Syriac enduring (even today) as, primarily, a liturgical language. The Syriac literary culture also continued to thrive throughout the medieval period. Indeed, some scholars refer to the eleventh–thirteenth centuries as a period of renaissance for the Syriac tradition.[41] Two particularly important and prolific authors from this period are worth mentioning for their significant contributions to the Syriac tradition: Patriarch Michael the Great and Gregory Bar 'Ebroyo.[42] Michael wrote a monumental historical work that incorporates excerpts of many earlier historical works in Syriac, some of which have not survived otherwise,[43] and Bar 'Ebroyo is the author of dozens of works of theology, philosophy, grammar, and history.[44]

The vast majority of Syriac literature was copied and preserved at Syriac monasteries and churches. Many Syriac ecclesiastical leaders were educated at monastic schools, such as the School of Edessa, which was shut down in 489 CE by the Roman emperor Zeno,[45] and subsequently the School of Nisibis, founded by Narsai.[46] Beyond this school environment, the study and preservation of Syriac texts took place primarily within the monasteries. Thousands of Syriac

39. Tony Burke, *The Infancy Gospel of Thomas in the Syriac Tradition*, Gorgias Eastern Christian Studies 48 (Piscataway, NJ: Gorgias, 2017).

40. For an interesting historical note on the Syro-Hexapla in Syriac, see the translation of Timothy I's *Letter 47* in this volume.

41. Herman G. B. Teule, "Renaissance, Syriac," in *GEDSH*, 350–51.

42. The latter is also frequently known as simply Barhebraeus or by his Arabic name Grigorios Abū al-Faraj.

43. See Dorothea Weltecke, "Michael I Rabo," in *GEDSH*, 287–90.

44. See Hidemi Takahashi, "Bar 'Ebroyo, Grigorios," in *GEDSH*, 54–56.

45. Though, as Adam Becker argues, there is some question about the existence of a "school" of Edessa, as all of the sources for this school are from a later period; Becker, "Edessa, School of," *GEDSH*, 139–40.

46. For a brief introduction, see Adam Becker, "Nisibis, School of," *GEDSH*, 311–12; see also Becker, *Fear of God and the Beginning of Wisdom: The School of Nisibis and Christian Scholastic Culture in Late Antique Mesopotamia* (Philadelphia: University of Pennsylvania Press, 2006); and Becker, *Sources for the Study of the School of Nisibis*, Translated Texts for Historians 50 (Liverpool: Liverpool University Press, 2008).

manuscripts, dated from the fifth century all the way to the twentieth century, survive, testifying to an active scribal and literary culture. In the West Syriac tradition, the region of Tur ʿAbdin (near Mardin, Turkey) was home to many monasteries, including the famous Dayr al-Zafaran, longtime residence of the Syriac Orthodox patriarchate. The cluster of monasteries in Tur ʿAbdin became a hub of manuscript copying and preservation. In the East Syriac tradition, monasteries in Mosul, Karka d-Beth Slok (Kirkuk), and Alqosh became important sites of manuscript production.[47] It should also be noted that there are a significant number of early Syriac manuscripts that were preserved at the Deir al-Surian monastery in Egypt, thanks in large part to an industrious monk named Mushē of Nisibis, who traveled through Mesopotamia, purchased and collected manuscripts, and brought them back to Egypt.[48]

As a final point, it is worth reflecting on the state of Syriac Christianity as a living heritage, divided as it is across multiple confessional identities. To begin with, the three early branches of Syriac Christianity that have their origins in the fifth century still remain to this day in the form of the Maronite Church, the Assyrian Church of the East, and the Syriac Orthodox Church. The latter two traditions, however, also have multiple offshoots, which can be quite confusing. First, it is significant to note that East Syriac Christian missionaries took Christian teachings along the Silk Road as far as India and China at least as early as the sixth century, if indeed not much earlier.[49] Although Syriac Christianity persisted in China until it was expelled in the fourteenth century, it took root and thrived in India under the authority of the Assyrian Church of the East. Following the arrival of Jesuit missionaries in the early modern period, though, the picture of Syriac Christianity in India is much more complex, with multiple splits and newly formed organizations (often with overlapping names) who practice distinct rites.[50] Catholic missionary activity in the early modern

47. Images of manuscripts from these important locations, and many others, have been digitized and are available for viewing through the Hill Museum & Manuscript Library.

48. For more information, see Monica J. Blanchard, "Moses of Nisibis (fl. 906–943) and the Library of Deir Suriani," in *Studies in the Christian East in Memory of Mirrit Boutros Ghali*, ed. Leslie S. B. MacCoull (Washington, DC: Society for Coptic Archaeology, 1995); and Sebastian P. Brock, "Without Mushê of Nisibis, Where Would We Be?: Some Reflections on the Transmission of Syriac Literature," *Journal of Eastern Christian Studies* 56.1–4 (2004): 15–24.

49. The Syriac apocryphal work known as the *Acts of Thomas* places the origins of Christianity in India in the first century with the arrival of the apostle Judas Thomas. For more on the spread of Syriac Christianity into central Asia and China, see Mark Dickens, "Syriac Christianity in Central Asia," and Hidemi Takahashi, "Syriac Christianity in China," both in *The Syriac World*, ed. Dan King (London: Routledge, 2019), 583–623, 624–52.

50. A very accessible and thorough treatment of this topic is István Perczel, "Syriac Christianity in India," in *The Syriac World*, ed. Dan King (London: Routledge, 2019), 653–97.

Middle East also produced a number of changes in Syriac ecclesiastical organization, most notably the creation of the Chaldean Catholic Church (which split from the Assyrian Church of the East and joined in communion with the Roman Catholic Church) and the Syriac Catholic Church (which split from the Syriac Orthodox Church and joined in communion with the Roman Catholic Church). Finally, it is worth noting that primarily because of the turbulent events of the early twentieth century in Turkey and Armenia, known in Syriac as the *Sayfo* ("the sword"),[51] significant diaspora communities of Syriac heritage are spread around the world.

The Syriac traditions of Christianity are diverse and vibrant witnesses to the ways that Christianity has adapted to different circumstances throughout time. Syriac literature is rich and expansive, and the following translated texts provide only a cursory introduction to the Syriac heritage. The bibliography below will hopefully provide interested readers with more resources for further study.

Bibliography

Barsoum, Ignatius Afram. *The Scattered Pearls: A History of Syriac Literature and Sciences*. Translated by Matti Moosa. 2nd rev. ed. Piscataway, NJ: Gorgias, 2003.

Baumstark, Anton. *Geschichte der syrischen Literatur, mit Ausschluss der christlich-palästinensischen Texte*. Bonn: Marcus & Webers, 1922.

Becker, Adam H. *Fear of God and the Beginning of Wisdom: The School of Nisibis and Christian Scholastic Culture in Late Antique Mesopotamia*. Philadelphia: University of Pennsylvania Press, 2006.

Beggiani, Seely. *Early Syriac Theology, with Special Reference to the Maronite Tradition*. Rev. ed. Washington, DC: Catholic University of America Press, 2014.

Briquel-Chatonnet, Françoise, and Muriel Debié. *Le monde syriaque: Sur les routes d'un christianisme ignoré*. Paris: Les Belles Lettres, 2017.

Brock, Sebastian P. *The Bible in the Syriac Tradition*. Gorgias Handbooks 7. Piscataway, NJ: Gorgias, 2006.

———. *A Brief Outline of Syriac Literature*. Kottayam, India: Saint Ephrem Ecumenical Research Institute, 1987.

———. *Fire from Heaven: Studies in Syriac Theology and Liturgy*. London: Variorum, 2006.

———. *An Introduction to Syriac Studies*. 3rd ed. Piscataway, NJ: Gorgias, 2017.

———. *The Luminous Eye: The Spiritual World Vision of Saint Ephrem the Syrian*. Collegeville, MN: Cistercian, 1992.

51. For a brief introduction, see Sebastian P. Brock, "Sayfo," in *GEDSH*, 361.

————. *Studies in Syriac Christianity: History, Literature, and Theology*. Aldershot: Variorum, 2001.

————. *The Syriac Fathers on Prayer and the Spiritual Life*. Collegeville, MN: Cistercian, 1987.

————. *Syriac Perspectives on Late Antiquity*. Aldershot: Variorum, 1984.

Brock, Sebastian P., Aaron M. Butts, George A. Kiraz, and Lucas Van Rompay, eds. *The Gorgias Encyclopedic Dictionary of the Syriac Heritage*. Piscataway, NJ: Gorgias, 2011 (online at https://gedsh.bethmardutho.org).

Brock, Sebastian P., and Susan Ashbrook Harvey. *Holy Women of the Syrian Orient*. Rev. ed. Berkeley: University of California Press, 1987.

Butts, Aaron M. *Language Change in the Wake of Empire: Syriac in Its Greco-Roman Context*. Winona Lake, IN: Eisenbrauns, 2016.

Butts, Aaron M., and Simcha Gross. *Jews and Syriac Christians: Intersections across the First Millennium*. Texts and Studies in Ancient Judaism 180. Tübingen: Mohr Siebeck, 2020.

Carlson, Thomas A. *Christianity in Fifteenth-Century Iraq*. Cambridge: Cambridge University Press, 2018.

Doerfler, Maria, Emanuel Fiano, and Kyle Smith, eds. *Syriac Encounters: Papers from the Sixth North American Syriac Symposium, Duke University, 26–29 June 2011*. Eastern Christian Studies 20. Leuven: Peeters, 2015.

Fiey, J.-M. *Jalons pour une histoire de l'église en Iraq*. CSCO 310. Leuven: Secrétariat du CSCO, 1970.

Griffith, Sidney H. *The Church in the Shadow of the Mosque: Christians and Muslims in the World of Islam*. Princeton: Princeton University Press, 2008.

Harvey, Susan Ashbrook. *Asceticism and Society in Crisis: John of Ephesus and the Lives of the Eastern Saints*. Berkeley: University of California Press, 1990.

————. "Theodora the 'Believing Queen': A Study in Syriac Historiographical Tradition." *Hugoye: Journal of Syriac Studies* 4 (2001): 209–34.

Heal, Kristian S. "Catalogues and the Poetics of Syriac Manuscript Cultures." *Hugoye: Journal of Syriac Studies* 20 (2017): 375–417.

————. "Corpora, eLibraries, and Databases: Locating Syriac Studies in the 21st Century." *Hugoye: Journal of Syriac Studies* 15 (2012): 65–78.

Healey, John F. "The Edessan Milieu and the Birth of Syriac." *Hugoye: Journal of Syriac Studies* 10 (2011): 115–27.

King, Daniel, ed. *The Syriac World*. London: Routledge, 2019.

Kiraz, George A. *Malphono w-Rabo d-Malphone: Studies in Honor of Sebastian P. Brock*. Piscataway, NJ: Gorgias, 2008.

Labourt, J. *Le christianisme dans l'empire perse sous la dynastie Sassanide (224–632)*. Paris: Lecoffre, 1904.

McVey, Kathleen. *Ephrem the Syrian: Hymns*. New York: Paulist, 1989.

Mellon Saint-Laurent, Jeanne-Nicole. *Missionary Stories and the Formation of the Syriac Churches*. Oakland: University of California Press, 2015.

Murray, Robert. *Symbols of Church and Kingdom: A Study in Early Syriac Tradition*. Rev. ed. London: T&T Clark, 2004.

Murre-van den Berg, Heleen. "Generous Devotion: Women in the Church of the East between 1550 and 1850." *Hugoye: Journal of Syriac Studies* 7 (2007): 11–54.

———. *Scribes and Scriptures: The Church of the East in the Eastern Ottoman Provinces (1500–1850)*. Eastern Christian Studies 21. Leuven: Peeters, 2015.

———. "Syriac Christianity." Pages 249–68 in *The Blackwell Companion to Eastern Christianity*. Edited by Ken Parry. Oxford: Blackwell, 2017.

Payne, Richard E. *A State of Mixture: Christians, Zoroastrians, and Iranian Political Culture in Late Antiquity*. Oakland: University of California Press, 2015.

Penn, Philip Michael. *Envisioning Islam: Syriac Christians and the Early Muslim World*. Philadelphia: University of Pennsylvania Press, 2017.

———. *When Christians First Met Muslims: A Sourcebook of the Earliest Syriac Writings on Islam*. Oakland: University of California Press, 2015.

Possekel, Ute. *Evidence of Greek Philosophical Concepts in the Writings of Ephrem the Syrian*. CSCO 380. Leuven: Secrétariat du CSCO, 1999.

Shepardson, Christine. *Anti-Judaism and Christian Orthodoxy: Ephrem's Hymns in Fourth-Century Syria*. Washington, DC: Catholic University of America Press, 2008.

Smith, Kyle. *Constantine and the Captive Christians of Persia: Martyrdom and Religious Identity in Late Antiquity*. Oakland: University of California Press, 2019.

Van Rompay, Lucas. "Past and Present Perceptions of Syriac Literary Tradition." *Hugoye: Journal of Syriac Studies* 3 (2000): 71–103.

———. "Syriac Studies: The Challenges of the Coming Decade." *Hugoye: Journal of Syriac Studies* 10 (2011): 23–35.

Walker, Joel. *The Legend of Mar Qardagh: Narrative and Christian Heroism in Late Antique Iraq*. Oakland: University of California Press, 2006.

Weitzman, M. P. *The Syriac Version of the Old Testament*. Cambridge: Cambridge University Press, 2005.

Wickes, Jeffrey. *Bible and Poetry in Late Antique Mesopotamia: Ephrem's Hymns on Faith*. Oakland: University of California Press, 2019.

Wilmshurst, David. *The Ecclesiastical Organisation of the Church of the East, 1318–1913*. CSCO 582. Leuven: Secrétariat du CSCO, 2000.

Wood, Philip. "Syriac and the 'Syrians.'" Pages 170–94 in *The Oxford Handbook of Late Antiquity*. Edited by Scott Fitzgerald Johnson. Oxford: Oxford University Press, 2012.

1. The *Doctrina Addai*

Introduction and translation by J. Edward Walters

The *Doctrina Addai* is likely a fifth-century CE composition, but it purports to contain details about the earliest period of Syriac Christianity. It narrates the arrival of Christian teaching in the city of Edessa, modern Urfa, Turkey, and the geographic origin of the Aramaic dialect known as Syriac. The story does not lack for flair; not only does it place the origin of Edessene Christianity in the time of the apostles, it even includes a letter from Abgar, the local king of Edessa, to Jesus of Nazareth, who responds and personally promises to send one of his followers to Abgar. Of even more intrigue than the letter, though, is the detail that one of Abgar's envoys painted a picture of Jesus, which led to a lively early Christian tradition about the *mandylion* or image of Edessa. Moreover, the *Doctrina Addai* is not the only witness to the letter and the image, as Eusebius also describes them and even claims to have seen and transcribed the letter personally (*Ecclesiastical History* 1.13.5–22). The pilgrim Egeria also claims to have seen the letter from Jesus to Abgar (*Itinerarium Egeriae* 19). This legendary account would not only place the Christianization of Edessa in the time period of the apostles, it would also make Edessa the first Christian kingdom with the conversion of King Abgar and much of the city.

The narrative of the text begins with Abgar, king of Edessa, learning about Jesus's healings and miracles through diplomatic correspondence with a Roman procurator named Sabinus, who was presumably given authority over Palestine and the surrounding regions. Having learned of this miraculous power, Abgar wrote to Jesus directly to ask him to come to Edessa to heal him. Abgar's envoys deliver the letter to Jesus and monitor his activities so that they can report back to Abgar. In response to Abgar's request, Jesus sends his regards through the envoys but promises to send one of his apostles. Following Jesus's death, an apostle named Addai, named as one of the "seventy-two apostles,"[1] was sent to Abgar at the behest of Judas Thomas. When Addai arrived, he stayed at the home of a local Jew named Tobias, a detail that some extrapolate as a possible historical kernel of truth, not for the timeline, but for the means by which

---

1. This is a reference to the seventy apostles, or seventy-two apostles according to a textual variant, mentioned in Luke 10:1.

Christianity may have spread to the east: through networks of Jewish communities.

Once Addai arrives in Edessa, he heals Abgar and preaches a sermon before the whole city, ultimately resulting in the conversion of the city and the construction of a new church, funded by Abgar himself. Addai's lengthy discourses in the text reflect a clearly post-Nicene theological position, which suggests that the text was not written prior to the fourth century. The text exaggerates the antiquity of Christianity's arrival in Edessa, likely as an attempt by Edessene Christians to establish the city of Edessa as the most important site of early Syriac Christianity.[2] The text is also preserved in Armenian and Ethiopic translations.

Bibliography

Text and Editions

Cureton, William, ed. *Ancient Syriac Documents Relative to the Earliest Establishment of Christianity in Edessa and the Neighbouring Countries, from the Year after Our Lord's Ascension to the Beginning of the Fourth Century.* London: Williams & Norgate, 1864.

Howard, George. *The Teaching of Addai.* Society of Biblical Literature Texts and Translations 16/Early Christian Literature Series 4. Chico, CA: Scholars Press, 1981.

Phillips, George, ed. *The Doctrine of Addai, the Apostle, Now First Edited in a Complete Form in the Original Syriac, with an English Translation and Notes.* London: Trübner, 1876.

Studies

Brock, Sebastian P. "Eusebius and Syriac Christianity." Pages 212–34 in *Eusebius, Christianity, and Judaism.* Edited by Harold W. Attridge and Gohei Hata. Studia Post-biblica 42. Leiden: Brill, 1992.

Desreumaux, Alain. "La Doctrina Addaï: Le chroniqueur et ses documents." *Apocrypha* 1 (1990): 249–68.

Drijvers, Han J. W. "Facts and Problems in Early Syriac-Speaking Christianity." *Second Century* 2 (1982): 157–75.

---

2. For an overview and summary of the text and an extensive bibliography, see Jacob A. Lollar, "Doctrine of Addai," *e-Clavis: Christian Apocrypha* (online at https://nasscal.com/e-clavis-christian-apocrypha/doctrine-of-addai).

Drijvers, Jan Willem. "The Protonike Legend, the Doctrina Addai, and Bishop Rabbula of Edessa." *Vigiliae Christianae* 51 (1997): 298–315.

Griffith, Sidney Harrison. "Christianity in Edessa and the Syriac-Speaking World: Mani, Bar Daysan, and Ephraem; the Struggle for Allegiance on the Aramean Frontier." *Journal of the Canadian Society for Syriac Studies* 2 (2002): 5–20.

———. "The Doctrina Addai as a Paradigm of Christian Thought in Edessa in the Fifth Century." *Hugoye: Journal of Syriac Studies* 6 (2003): 269–92.

Harrak, Amir. "Was Edessa or Adiabene the Gateway for the Christianization of Mesopotamia?" Pages 165–80 in *The Levant: Crossroads of Late Antiquity: History, Religion, and Architecture.* Edited by Ellen Bradshaw Aitken and John M. Fossey. Leiden: Brill, 2014.

Mellon Saint-Laurent, Jeanne-Nicole. *Missionary Stories and the Formation of the Syriac Churches.* Oakland: University of California Press, 2015.

Ramelli, Ilaria L. "Possible Historical Traces in the Doctrina Addai." *Hugoye: Journal of Syriac Studies* 9 (2006): 51–127.

<hr />

TRANSLATION

The Teaching of the Apostle Addai

The letter of King Abgar, son of King Ma'nu, which he sent to our Lord in Jerusalem, after which the apostle Addai came to Edessa, and what he declared in the good news of his preaching, and those things he said and commanded to those who received the hand of priesthood from him when he departed from this world.

In the year 343 of the kingdom [of the Greeks][3] and in the reign of our lord Tiberius, the Roman Caesar, and in the reign of King Abgar, son of King Ma'nu, in the month of Tishri[4] before the twelfth day, Abgar Ukkama sent Maryahb and Shmeshgram, nobles and honored men of his kingdom, and also Hannan, the official archivist with them, to the city called Eleutheropolis (and in Aramaic: Beth Gubrin), to the honored Sabinus, son of Eustorgius, a procurator of our lord Caesar. He had authority over Syria, Phoenicia, and Palestine and over the

---

3. That is, 32 CE.
4. October.

whole region of Beth Nahrin.[5] They brought him letters concerning matters of the kingdom. When they arrived, he received them with joy and honor, and they were with him for twenty-five days. He wrote a reply to the letters for them, and he sent them to King Abgar.

When they left him and traveled and went along the road toward Jerusalem, they saw many people who were coming from far away so that they could see the Messiah, because the news of his wonders and deeds spread to remote places. When Maryahb, Shmeshgram, and Hannan the archivist saw those people, they also went with them to Jerusalem. And when they entered Jerusalem, they saw the Messiah, and they rejoiced with the crowds who were accompanying him. They also saw the Jews, who were standing and crowding around, thinking about what they might do to him. For they were distressed, because they had seen a multitude of their people confessing him. They were there in Jerusalem for ten days, and Hannan the archivist wrote down everything that he saw the Messiah do, and also the rest of what happened there before they departed.

They traveled and came to Edessa, and they came before King Abgar, their lord, who sent them. They gave him the reply to the letters that they brought with them, and after the letters had been read, they began to narrate before the king everything that they had seen and everything that the Messiah had done in Jerusalem. Then Hannan the archivist read before him everything that he wrote and brought with him. When King Abgar heard [these things], he was astonished and amazed, as were his nobles who stood before him. And Abgar said to them: "These mighty deeds are not of a human, but of God, because there is no one who can give life to the dead except God alone." Abgar himself wanted to cross over and go to Palestine so that he might see everything that the Messiah was doing with his own eyes. But because he was not able to cross the territory of the Romans (because it was not his), lest this matter result in hateful contention, he wrote a letter and sent it to the Messiah through Hannan the archivist. He departed from Edessa on the fourteenth of Adar and entered Jerusalem on the twelfth of Nisan,[6] on the fourth day of the week. He found the Messiah at the house of Gamaliel, the leader of the Jews, and the letter was read before him, which was written thus:

Abgar Ukkama, to Jesus, the good physician, who appeared in the area of Jerusalem: greetings, my lord. I have heard about you and your healing, that you heal not by medicines or herbs, but by your word you heal[7] the blind, cause the lame to walk, purify the lepers, and cause the deaf to hear. And the spirits, the

5. That is, Mesopotamia.
6. Adar = March, and Nisan = April.
7. Literally, "open the blind ones"

lunatics, and the tormented ones, you heal through your word. You also raise the dead! When I heard about these great wonders that you have performed, I resolved that either you are God who has come down from heaven and done these things, or you are the Son of God, because you do all these things. Because of this, I wrote, requesting that you come to me, while I show reverence to you, so that you might heal my sickness, as I believe in you. I have also heard this: that the Jews plot against you and pursue you, and also that they desire to crucify you, planning to harm you. I have one small and beautiful city, suitable for both [of us] to dwell peacefully.

When Jesus received the letter at the house of the chief priest of the Jews, he said to Hannan the archivist:

Go and say to your master who sent you to me: "Blessed are you who, although you have not seen me, have believed in me, for it is written about me that those who see me will not believe in me, but those who do not see me will believe in me.[8] Regarding what you wrote to me, that I should come to you: the thing for which I was sent here is now completed, and I am taking myself up to my Father who sent me. And when I have gone up to him, I will send to you one of my disciples so that he may heal your sickness and cure you. And he will restore everyone who is with you to eternal life. Your city will be blessed, and no enemy will conquer it ever again."

When Hannan the archivist saw that Jesus had spoken to him thus, and because he was the king's artist, he took the opportunity to paint a portrait of Jesus with choice colors, and he brought it with him to his master, King Abgar. And when King Abgar saw the portrait, he received it joyfully and placed it with great honor in one of his palaces. Then Hannan the archivist narrated to him everything that he had heard from Jesus, for he had recorded his words in writings.

After the Messiah had ascended to heaven, Judas Thomas sent the apostle Addai, who was one of the seventy-two apostles, to Abgar. And when Addai came to the city of Edessa, he resided in the house of Tobias bar Tobias, the Jew, who was from Palestine, and he was heard about throughout the whole city. One of Abgar's nobles, whose name was Abdu bar Abdu, and who was one of the princes who sat kneeling before Abgar, came and spoke about Addai: "Look, an envoy has come, and he resides here, the very one whom Jesus sent word to you about him: 'I will send to you one of my disciples.'" And when Abgar heard these things, the mighty deeds that Addai had done and the marvelous healings

---

8. This quotation is similar to John 20:29, but it is not a direct citation.

that he had performed, he resolved and confirmed that truly he was the one about whom Jesus had sent word: "When I ascend to heaven, I will send one of my disciples to you, and he will heal your sickness." Abgar sent and called for Tobias and said to him: "I heard that a certain powerful man came and resides in your house. Bring him to me, [so that] perhaps a good remedy of healing might be found for me through him."

Tobias rose early the next day, and he took Addai the apostle and brought him to Abgar, although Addai already knew that he was sent to him by the power of God. When Addai came up and approached Abgar, whose nobles were standing with him, during his approach toward [Abgar], a wondrous vision appeared to Abgar from Addai's face. As soon as Abgar saw that vision, he fell down and worshiped Addai. A significant shock seized everyone who was standing before him, for they did not see that vision that had appeared to Abgar. Then Abgar said to Addai: "Truly you are a disciple of Jesus, that mighty wonder-worker, the Son of God, who sent word to me: 'I will send to you one of my disciples for healing and life.'" Addai said to him: "Because you have believed from the beginning in the one who sent me to you, this is why I have been sent to you. And if again you believe in him, everything you believe in will be yours." Abgar said to him: "I have believed in him so much that I wanted to lead an army to go and destroy the Jews who crucified him, but it is part of the kingdom of the Romans, so I refrained because of the peace treaty that stands between me and our lord Caesar Tiberius, like my forefathers." Addai said to him: "Our Lord completed the will of his father, and when he completed the will of his begetter, he was lifted up to his father, and sat with him in glory, he who was with him eternally." Abgar said to him: "I also believe in him and in his father." Addai said to him: "Because you believe thus, I place my hand upon you in the name of the one in whom you believe." As soon as he placed his hand upon him, he was healed from the injury of his disease, which he had for a long time. Abgar marveled and was astounded that just as he had heard about Jesus—his working and healing—so also could Addai heal in the name of Jesus without any medicine. Likewise regarding Abdu bar Abdu: he had gout in his feet, and he brought his feet near [Addai]; he placed his hands upon them and healed him, and he no longer had gout. And even throughout the whole city, he performed great healings and displayed marvelous feats of power.

Abgar said to him: "Now that everyone knows that you have done these marvelous deeds through the power of Jesus the Messiah, and we are marveling at your deeds, therefore I request of you that you tell us about the arrival of the Messiah (how it happened), about his glorious power, and about those wondrous things that we have heard that he did, those things that you saw along with the rest of your companions." Addai said to him:

Regarding this I will not hesitate to preach, it is for this very reason that I was sent here: to speak and teach everyone who wants to believe like you. Tomorrow, gather the whole city for me, and I will sow the word of life in it through the proclamation that I will preach before you about the arrival of the Messiah (how it happened), about his glorious power, about the one who sent him (and why and how he sent him), about his power and his wondrous deeds, about the glorious symbols of his arrival, those which he spoke about in the world, and about the accuracy of his proclamation, how and why he diminished himself and humbled his exalted divinity in the body that he took on, and was crucified and went down to the place of the dead, and broke open the border that had never been opened, and made the dead come alive by his death. He descended alone, and he ascended with many to his glorious father, whom he was with forever in one exalted divinity.

Abgar commanded that they give silver and gold to Addai. Addai said to him: "How is it possible for us to take something that is not ours? Look, whatever belonged to us, we have abandoned it just as it was commanded by our Lord that we should have no bags or wallets, but while carrying crosses on our shoulders, we were commanded that we should preach his gospel throughout the whole creation—that which the whole creation felt and suffered in his crucifixion, which happened for us and for the salvation of all people."

[Omitted: a brief description of the content of Addai's preaching, and Addai recounting the story of Queen Protonice and the finding of the true cross.]

On the following day, Abgar commanded Abdu bar Abdu, who had been healed from a cruel sickness of the feet, to send out a herald and call throughout the whole city that everyone—men and women—should be gathered at the place called Beth Tabara, a spacious area of the house of Avida son of Abd-naḥad, so that they could hear the teaching of the apostle Addai, how he taught, in whose name he healed, and by what power he performed these signs and did these marvels. For when he healed King Abgar, only the nobles who stood before him saw it, when he healed with the word of the Messiah. Many physicians had not been able to heal him, but a foreign man healed him through the faith of the Messiah.

And the whole city—men and women—was gathered, just as the king had commanded. And Avida, Labbu, Ḥaphasi, Bar-Kalba, Labubna, Ḥesrun, and Shmeshgram stood there along with their companions who, like them, were princes and nobles of the king, and all the commanders and soldiers, and people who crafted with their hands, and Jews and pagans who were in the city, and foreigners from Soba and Ḥarran, and the rest of the inhabitants of the whole area of Mesopotamia—they all stood there so that they could hear the teaching of Addai, for they had heard that he was a disciple of Jesus, who was crucified in Jerusalem, and that he performed healings in his name. And Addai began to speak to them as follows:

Listen, all of you, and consider what I am saying before you, that I am not a physician with medicines or herbs of human craft; rather, I am a disciple of Jesus the Messiah, the physician of troubled souls and savior of the coming life, the Son of God who came down from heaven, clothed himself in a body, and became human, and [who] gave himself and was crucified on behalf of all people. And while he was hanging on the wood, he darkened the sun in the sky, and when he entered the tomb, he was revived and came out from the grave with many others. And those who guarded the grave did not see how he came up from the grave, but the watchers of the heights were the proclaimers and announcers of his resurrection. If he had not willed it, he would not have died, because he is the lord of the final death. If it had not pleased him, likewise he would not have clothed himself with a body, for he is the fashioner of the body. For the will that lowered him to birth from a virgin also brought him down to the suffering of death, and he humbled the greatness of his exalted divinity, he who was with his father forever and ever, he about whom the prophets spoke previously through their symbols—they depicted images of his birth, his suffering, his resurrection, his ascension to his father, and his seating at the right hand.

Look, he is worshiped from the heights and the depths,[9] he who has been worshiped eternally. For although his appearance was that of a human, his power, his knowledge, and his authority were of God, as he said to us: "Thus the Son of Man is glorified, and through him God glorifies himself"[10] by mighty deeds and marvels and by his honored position at the right hand. His body is the purified purple garment of his glorious divinity through which we are able to gaze upon his invisible lordship. Therefore, we preach and proclaim this Messiah Jesus, and with him we glorify the Father and we extol and worship the Spirit of his divinity, because we were commanded as such by him, that we should baptize and pardon those who believe in the name of the Father, the Son, and the Holy Spirit.

The prophets of old also said thus: "The Lord our God has sent us and his Spirit."[11] And if I say something that is not written in the Prophets, the Jews who stand among you and listening to me will not accept me. Likewise, if I mention the name of the Messiah over those who have sicknesses and diseases, yet they are not healed by this glorious name, they will not believe, adoring [instead]

9. Or "by those above and those below."
10. John 13:31.
11. Cf. Isa 48:16.

the work of their hands. If, however, these things that we say are written in the books of the Prophets and we can demonstrate mighty deeds of healing upon the sick, no one will look upon us without discernment regarding the faith that we preach, that God was crucified on behalf of all people. If there are those who do not want to be persuaded by these words, let them come to us and reveal their thoughts to us so that, like a disease in their mind, we might offer a remedy for the healing of their wound.

For even though you were not present during the time of the Messiah's suffering, the sun was darkened, and you saw it. Learn about and consider the very terrible event that took place in the time of his crucifixion, he whose good news has flown throughout the whole earth through the signs his disciples, my companions, have performed throughout the whole earth. And those who were Hebrews, who had known only the Hebrew language since birth, today they speak every language, so that those from far away might hear and believe like those who were near, for it was he who confused the languages of the stubborn ones in this region before us; he is the same one who teaches the true and certain faith today through us, defective and miserable people from Galilee of Palestine. For even I, whom you see, am from Paneas,[12] whence the Jordan River flows. I was chosen along with my companions to be a preacher of this good news, which has resulted in the glorious name of the venerated Messiah resounding throughout every district.

So then, let no one among you harden their mind from the truth or let their intelligence become distant from certainty. Do not be taken into captivity following thoughts of destructive error, which are full of the dread of bitter death. Do not be seized by the wicked customs of your ancestral paganism, and do not distance yourselves from true and certain life, which is in the Messiah. For those who believe in him are those who are faithful before him, he who came down to us in his compassion in order to rid the earth of pagan sacrifices and idolatrous libations, so that created things are no longer worshiped, but that we worship him and his Father and his Holy Spirit. For just as my Lord commanded me, I am preaching and proclaiming the good news. I cast his silver on the table before you, and I sow the seed of his word in everyone's ears; those who are willing to receive, the good reward of confession belongs to them; but as for those who are not persuaded, I shake the dust of my feet upon them, as my Lord told me.

So, my beloved, turn away from wicked ways and hateful deeds and be turned toward him with a good and pleasing will, just as he has turned toward you in his compassion and abundant mercies. Do not be like the previous generations that are passed, for, because they hardened their minds from the fear

12. Paneas is more famously known as Caesarea Philippi.

of God, they have received punishment openly so that they might be disciplined and so that those who come after them might tremble and fear. For the whole reason that our Lord came to the earth was to teach and show that at the end of the created order, a resurrection of all people will take place. And in that time, their manners of life will be depicted upon their persons, and their bodies will become pages for records of justice, and there will be no one there who does not understand the writing, for everyone will read out the records of their book on that day, and they will take the calculation of their deeds with the fingers of their hands. So even the uneducated ones will know the new writing and the new language, and no one will say to their companion: "Read this to me," because the one teaching and one instruction will rule over all people.

So let this concern be depicted before your eyes, and do not let it pass from your mind, because if it should pass from your mind, it does not pass justly. Beg mercy from God, that he might forgive you for the hateful rejection of your paganism, for you have abandoned the one who created you upon the face of the earth, the one who causes the rain to fall and his sun to rise over you, and you worship the things he made instead of him. For the idols and carved statues of paganism, and any created thing that you trust and worship, if they had sense-perception or understanding, on account of your worshiping and honoring them, it would be right for them to receive your kindness, for you carved and formed them, and you affixed and fastened them with nails so that they would not be shaken. For if the created things that you honor perceived your honors before them, they would complain, crying out to you: "Do not worship your associates who, like you, were made and created, because created, made things should not be worshiped, for they should worship their creator and glorify the one who created them." And as his grace shelters the stubborn here, so the time is coming when his justice will be avenged there for those who deny.

For I see this city, which is completely full of paganism, which is opposed to God. Who is this Nebo, a made idol that you worship? or Bel whom you honor? Look, there are some among you who worship Bath Nical, like the people of Harran, your neighbors, and [those who worship] Taratha, like the people of Mabbug, and [those who worship] the Eagle, like the Arabs, and [those who worship] the sun and moon, like the rest of the people of Harran who are like you. Do not be taken captive by the rays of light of the luminaries or the star of radiance. Cursed before God is everyone who worships created things. For even if there are among the created things some who are greater than their companions, they are still associates of their companions, as I have said to you. For this is a bitter disease that has no cure, that creatures should worship creatures and that created things should glorify their companions. Just as they are not able to stand by their own power, but through the power of the one who created them, so also are they not able to be worshiped with him or honored with him. It is blasphemy against both of them: against the created things when they are worshiped, and against the creator when the created things are regarded as partakers with him, they who are alien to the nature of his being. For the whole prophecy of the prophets, and also the preaching of we who come after the prophets, is this: the created things are not to be worshiped along with the creator, and likewise that people should not be bound in the yoke of corrupt paganism. It is not because created things are seen that I say they should not be worshiped, but because everything that is made is a created thing, whether visible or invisible. This is a bitter impiety, that the glorious name of divinity be placed upon [the created thing]. For it is not created things, like you, that we preach and worship, but the Lord of created things.

The earthquake that shook them at the cross testifies that everything that is made hangs and stands by the power of its maker, he who existed before the world and [before] created things, he whose nature is incomprehensible, because his nature is invisible, and he is sanctified with his father in the heights above because he is Lord and God eternally. This is our teaching in every place and every region, and thus we have been commanded to preach to those to listen to us, not by force, but by true teaching and by the power of God. The signs that were done in his name testify about our faith that it is true and trustworthy. Consent, then, to my words and receive what I have said and am saying before you. And because I do not seek your deaths, I will magnify the caution before you: receive my words well and do not disregard them. Come near me, you who are distant from the Messiah, and you will be near the Messiah. Instead of erroneous sacrifices and libations, now bring to him sacrifices of thanksgiving.

What is the great altar that was built for you in the middle of this city? And [who] are those going and coming, making offerings upon it to demons and sacrificing on it to evil spirits? If you do not know the Scriptures, does nature not clearly teach you that your idols have eyes, yet they do not see? Yet you who see with eyes and do not comprehend this, you are also like those who do not see or hear, and vainly urging your voices [that are] worthless to deaf ears, although they are not blamed for not hearing, because by nature they are deaf and silent. And the blame that hides in you is your justice, for you do not want to comprehend, not even in this thing that you see. For the darkness of error that covers yours minds does not allow you to possess the heavenly light, which is the understanding of knowledge.

So then, flee from things that are made or created, as I have told you, [things] that are called gods in name only, although they are not gods in their nature, and come near to the one who is, in his nature, God, eternally and forever, and who was not made like your idols, nor a created thing, nor fashioned like the images in which you boast. For although he clothed himself with this body, he was God along with his father. The created things, which trembled at his death and were terrified by the suffering of his death, testify that he is the one who created the created things. For it was not on account of a human that the earth shook, but on account of the one who spread out the earth upon the waters; and it was not on account of a human that the sun darkened in the heavens at the cross, but on account of the one who made the great lights; and it was not by a human that the righteous and just were raised, but by he who gave authority over death from the beginning; and it was not by a human that the veil of the Jews' temple was ripped from end to end, but by the one who said to them: "Look, your house is left desolate."[13] For unless they who crucified him knew that he was the Son of God, they would not have proclaimed the desolation of their city, nor would they have caused woes to fall upon themselves. And even if they wanted to disregard this confession, the terrible events that happened at that time would not have allowed them. For look, even some of the children of the crucifiers have now been made preachers and proclaimers of the good news, along with the apostles, my companions, throughout the whole region of Palestine, and among the Samaritans, and in the whole region of the Philistines. And the idols of paganism are deemed worthless, yet the cross of the Messiah is honored. The peoples and created things confess God, who became human.

[Omitted: a brief section that repeats many of the themes already mentioned.]

For everything that we say before you, we say as a gift that we have received from our Lord. We teach and show you that you can acquire salvation and not destroy your spirits in the error of paganism, for the heavenly light has raised itself upon creation, and he is the one who chose the ancestors, the just ones, and the prophets, and he spoke with them through the revelation of the Holy Spirit. For he is the God of the Jews, who crucified him, and also the erring pagans—they also worship him even without knowing it. For there is no other God in heaven or on earth, and confession goes up to him from the four regions of the earth. So, now your ears have heard something that they had not heard, and likewise your eyes have seen something they had never seen. Therefore, do not become unjust to what you have heard and seen. Push aside the rebellious mind of your ancestors, and set yourselves free from the yoke of sin that rules over you through libations and sacrifices before statues. Be concerned with your perishing lives and about your useless head bowing, and acquire the new mind, which worships the maker and not the thing that is made, the one who is represented in it, an image of truth and certainty, believing and being baptized in

13. Matt 23:38.

the glorious trifold names of the Father, of the Son, and of the Holy Spirit. For this is our teaching and our proclamation.

For it is not in many things that they believe the truth of the Messiah. And those who want to be convinced of the Messiah, you know that I have repeated my words many times before you so that you might learn and comprehend the things that you hear. And we will rejoice because of this like a farmer in a blessed field, and our God will be glorified by your repentance toward him. And while you live in this, we who counsel you about this will not be denied a blessed reward for this. Therefore, I am confident that you are a blessed land, according to the will of the Lord Messiah. Because of this, instead of the dust of my feet, which we were told to shake off against a city that did not receive our words, look, today I shake off upon the door of your ears the words of my lips, for the coming of the Messiah is depicted in them, that which has happened, and also what is about to happen: the resurrection and revival of all people, the separation that will occur between the believers and the deniers, and the blessed promise of joys that are coming, which those who believed in the Messiah, who worshiped him and his exalted Father, and who confessed him and his Spirit of divinity will receive. And now it is right for us to end our present speech. Let those who received the word of the Messiah remain with us as well as those who wish to participate with us in prayer, and then they will go to their homes.

And the apostle Addai rejoiced in this, when he saw that many people of the city stood with him, and there were a few who did not remain in that moment; but a few days later, these same few also received his words and believed in the good news of the preaching of the Messiah. And when the apostle Addai had said these things before the whole city of Edessa, King Abgar saw that the whole city rejoiced in his teaching, men and women equally, and they said to him: "True and faithful is the Messiah who sent you to us." And [Abgar] also rejoiced greatly at this while praising God, that as he had heard about the Messiah from Hannan, his archivist, so also had he seen the marvelous mighty deeds that the apostle Addai had done in the name of the Messiah.

And King Abgar also said to the apostle Addai:

Just what I sent to the Messiah in my letter to him, and what he sent to me also, and I have received from you today, thus I will believe all the days of my life, and I will remain, glorifying in these things, because I know that there is no other power in whose name these signs and marvels are done except by the power of Messiah, whom you proclaimed in truth and certainty. So now I worship him, I and my son Ma'nu, and Augustina and Queen Shalmath. So, build a church wherever you want, a meeting place for those who believed and who will believe in your words. And as it was commanded to you by your Lord, you will minister confidently. As for those with you who are teachers in this good news, I am prepared to give them great gifts so that they will not have any other work aside from ministry. And whatever you need for the construction expenses, I will give it to you without regard. Your word will have authority and dominion in this city, and without anyone else, you may gain access to me freely in my honored royal palace.

And when King Abgar went to his royal palace, he rejoiced, he and his nobles along with him—Abdu, Garmai, Shmeshgram, Abubai, and Meherdath, along with the rest of their companions—at everything their eyes had seen and their ears had heard. And in the joy of their hearts, they also praised God, who had turned their minds to him, rejecting the paganism in which they had stood, and confessing the good news of the Messiah. And when Addai built the church, they offered vows and gifts in it, they and the people of the city. And there they served for the rest of their lives.

[Omitted: the story continues describing Addai's work within the city, including more conversions and details about people in Edessa. Abgar later exchanges letters with the Roman Emperor Tiberius, and Abgar requests that Tiberius punish the Jews in Palestine for killing Jesus. Addai also travels to other cities and builds churches and makes another lengthy speech similar to the one included above. Ultimately, Addai and his closest companions are killed by one of Abgar's sons, who succeeded him as the king in Edessa.]

2. Ephrem the Syrian, *Hymns against Heresies* 3 and 53

Introduction and translation by Jeffrey Wickes

The two following works derive from Ephrem's *Hymns against Heresies*, a collection of fifty-six hymns in which Ephrem articulates a polemic against, primarily, Bardaisan, Mani, and Marcion. The hymns are interesting because of their unique intermingling of the characteristics for which Ephrem is generally known—his symbolic theology of names, his anti-Arianism and anti-Judaism, his awareness of the important function of hymnody in pedagogy, and his coupling of musical poems with difficult philosophical and theological ideas. As is typical of the Syriac hymn (*madrāšā*), both of these pieces would have been sung (they have melodies and refrains), both use the stanza as their organizing unit, and both are metered, in this case according to five-syllable hemistiches (though *Hymn 3* intersperses a three-syllable hemistich).

Ephrem sings against some basic ideas that he associated with Bardaisan, namely, that, though God is one, there exist a range of intermediate, quasi-divine beings who created the world, and that the world is now governed not only by God, but also through Zodiac signs, horoscopes, seasons, and the planets. Whatever Bardaisan actually taught, Ephrem alleges in these hymns that he connected with the one God five other beings corresponding to the four elements (air, fire, water, and light), to which he added the dark, and that he denied the resurrection of the body. (The cosmological and anthropological systems that Ephrem ascribes to Bardaisan vary somewhat from work to work and, as he makes clear in 53.3–4, he tended to address the details of Bardaisan's thought as tersely as possible.)

Ephrem presents Bardaisan's cosmology as nothing more than a crude polytheism. He does this by developing a particular theory of names, one that is similar to a theory he deploys in other hymns against those thinkers who presented Christ as subordinate to God (so-called Arians). While in his polemics with Arians, Ephrem would draw a far more nuanced picture of the relationship between names (divine and human) and the things to which they refer, in these hymns he traces an indissoluble link between two central divine names (Being and Essence), and the divine substance to which they refer. While it is difficult to communicate in translation, the Syriac terms for "Being" (*îtyâ*) and "Essence" (*îtûtâ*) both derive from the same Syriac verb "to be" (*'ît*). Importantly, these words serve as calques on the Hebrew divine name YHWH (Exod 3:14), and that is why, for Ephrem, they are so crucially linked to the oneness of God. (In fact, Ephrem will accept that while "God" can be pluralized as "gods," conceding the evidence of Ps 82, the divine name "Being" can never be. Thus, Bardaisan's idea that there is one God but many beings contradicts the evidence Ephrem finds in the Bible.)

Ephrem is known for his tendency to link seemingly disparate ideas and objects in an often rapid-fire manner. In these hymns, we see this same poetic framework tilted in a heresiological direction. In the first eight stanzas of *Hymn 3*, Ephrem brings together Bardaisan, Mani, and Marcion—none of whom saw themselves or their thought as genetically related—based on their shared polytheism (as he polemically identifies it). Having established this critique of all three, he then suddenly shifts, in stanza nine, to a polemic against Arians and Jews, which unites these two groups at the opposite end of the theological spectrum, insofar as they refuse to identify Christ and the Holy Spirit as God. (Note his continued collapse of Arians and Jews throughout 3.9–12.) It is in *Hymn 53*, moreover, that we find the detail that Bardaisan articulated his cosmological ideas in hymnic form, even writing 150 psalms in imitation of David. Though no such hymns remain, there is a long tradition that identifies Ephrem's desire to combat Bardaisan as the crucial factor that led him to develop his own hymnody. This is one of the few places in Ephrem's authentic corpus where he gestures toward such a link.[1]

Bibliography

Text and Editions

Beck, Edmund. *Des Heiligen Ephraem des Syrers Hymnen contra Haereses.* CSCO 169–170, subsidia 76–77. Leuven: Durbecq, 1957.

Ruani, Flavia. *Hymnes contre les heresies.* Bibliotheque de l'orient Chretien. Paris: Les Belles Lettres, 2018.

---

1. On Ephrem's representation of Bardaisan, see H. J. W. Drijvers, *Bardaisan of Edessa* (Assen: Van Gorcum, 1966).

Studies

Beck, Edmund. *Ephräms Polemik gegen Mani und die Manichäer im Rahmen der zeitgenössischen griechischen Polemik und der des Augustinus.* CSCO 391, subsidia 55. Leuven: Secrétariat du CSCO, 1978.

TRANSLATION

Hymns against Heresies 3

According to the melody "Judge of the Nations."

3.1   Let us admonish the deniers as we would thieves,
       since the wealth that they have stolen calls out against them—it can
           speak.
       They stole names and put them on a thing that has no self-existence.
       They have repeatedly put the name "God" on
       the idols they have worshiped, so that through [God's] titles
       beings that have no self-existence have come to be worshiped and
           named [as God].

       Refrain: Blessed is he by whose Scriptures the children of error are
           refuted!

3.2   Being did not create all [things] from "beings,"
       nor is there an "Essence" that might be sent for the purpose of
           creating.
       Though "Being" is the name of the Lord of "beings,"
       his name is never divided against him.
       Using created beings, [the deniers] have torn and divided his name,
       for they have divided his Essence between five powers.

3.3   [They say:] "The name 'beings' connotes equality, in that among
           [beings] there is not
       one older or younger." In that case, neither is there among them
       one stronger or weaker, for the identical name
       makes all of them equal in every way.

So, all must be either good or just,
and cannot be both created and creator.

3.4   Bardaisan has bound himself with Marcion, while also trying to loose
        himself
[by saying:] "There cannot be two gods,
for the substance of that name [God] is one, namely, [the substance]
        of God."
He has wandered astray, beaten by his own weapon.
If there are not "gods," he is beaten, for neither are there "beings,"
for the substance of the name is one, namely, [the substance] of
        Essence.

3.5   If he proclaims one God, let us proclaim one Being,
for there is only one God, just as there is one Being.
He is one in both of these [names]—"Being" and "God."
In one name, all of him is understood.
Since [Bardaisan] has refused to place another god beside God,
it would be foolish if, alongside Being, we placed five [beings].

3.6   Because of the six sides [of the earth], he has numbered six beings.
He established four beings corresponding to the four sides [of the
        earth];
he established one [more] in the deep and another in the height.
Marcion counted [only] two gods!
"Beings" and "gods" are refuted by the single Power,
whose godhead they have made a stranger, and whose Essence they
        have cut into pieces.

3.7   The error of the Greeks was disseminated through Bardaisan
when he taught that from beings [God] created all and ordered all.
The lie of the Hindus acquired power through Mani
when he introduced two powers at war.
Marcion further named three principles.
They have increased the gods, so let them be without a god.

3.8   The children of error have been rebuked for stealing from the
        one [God]
names that they put on a thing with no self-existence.
In the Son, the names [God and Son] are mingled without division.
Marcion and Bardaisan bear witness [to this]:

even though they are divided, they are the same as concerns his
     begetting,
for they confess that he is God, yet do not deny that he is also Son.

3.9   Who would not confess this true Son,
     especially when even tares[2] proclaim his birth?
     Shall we be shamed by the deniers who yet do not deny his birth?
     Who would not weep and repent,
     seeing the outsiders who believed without investigating,
     while gazing upon those inside who were not sated even when they
          were exiled?

3.10   Yet not even the Jew investigated secret things,
     though hidden deep within his writings are luminous things.[3]
     Investigation is that which, when he incited it, blinded him with its
          smoke.
     [The investigator] will praise the Holy Spirit without arguing,
     but when he is asked to give an account, he denies, and when he is
          completely defeated [in debate], he blasphemes.
     Their crown is death; their armor destroys hope.

3.11   When [the Jew] denied the Son, the entombed came forth
     from their tombs and refuted him there.[4] Here, if someone denies
     the Spirit, [saying] that he is not [God], the Scriptures will
          confound him,
     for the Spirit is the Spirit from the Lord's mouth,[5]
     and the Spirit is with him. If there were a time
     when he was without the Spirit, let them demonstrate [this] without
          controversy.

3.12   And instead of [admitting] that it was appropriate for him to create
          through his Son,
     they taught that when [God] created, [it was] through that [Spirit] who
          created with him.
     It was she who ordered with him the heavens and created things.
     Therefore, they have gone and denied the Son and have rejected him.

2. On "tares" as a name for Ephrem's opponents, see Matt 13:24–30.
3. Cf. Deut 29:29.
4. Matt 27:51–54.
5. Cf. Ps 33:6 and John 20:22.

They boast about the other maker, she who helped him.
Because they have sent truth far away, they have found shame.

3.13 I have learned and acquired the faith that you are one in your Being.
I have heard and I have affirmed that you are the Father in your only
  begotten.
I have been baptized triply in the name of the Holy Spirit.
I have learned the truths of all of them,
so that, as your riches are scattered, your treasure cannot be
  investigated.
Praises to you from all who have become aware that you are human.

The end.

Hymns against Heresies 53

To the tune "The Sect of Bardaisan."

53.1 Brothers, I have always believed in one Being.
I have recognized that he is only one, though I have not perfectly
  understood
how his nature exists. If for a thousand years someone
would contemplate to discover more through his debating,
this alone he would find: he is, and nothing more.

Refrain: Glory to the one Being through his beloved!

53.2 Just like our brothers the deniers, our race is from Adam
and our family is from Eve. I have marveled at how they have made
companions for the true Being. For though our family is the same
as Adam, who is from dust, we have a Father who lives,
in whom our group has been separated from every denier.

53.3 To recount before you their narrative would be a loss,
for the healthy ear would be pained by their words.
Since your hearing is the path for the sound of the true one,
which, upon entering, sealed the gates of your ears,
[the sound of their narratives] is hated, for falsehood cannot enter his
  dwelling place.

53.4   Yet, see how love will forcefully compel you
        to endure, my brothers, a recounting of their words
        about beings and hindrances, stars and horoscopes,
        a body that is from the evil one, which will experience no resurrection,
        a soul that is from seven, and the rest (let us not say more).

53.5   [Bardaisan] crafted hymns and mixed in melodies.
        He constructed psalms and introduced meters.
        He divided the melodies between measures and balances.
        He offered to the simple bitterness alongside sweetness,
        [as well as to] the sick, who did not choose healthy food.

53.6   He desired to look to David, to be adorned with his beauty,
        to be praised like him. One hundred and fifty psalms
        he even constructed. He abandoned [David's] truth, my brothers,
        but imitated his number, for David did not sing
        the song of the deniers, whose lyre lies.

53.7   David did not refer to "beings," as [Bardaisan] did,
        since there is only one Being. The name "Being," therefore,
        destroys the names of "beings," for they have no self-existence.
        If their names were the same, their natures would be the same.
        By [Bardaisan's] own account, my brothers, their teaching is defeated.

53.8   Look at how he was afraid to equate the natures
        of the beings that he named. Yet see how he presumed
        to equate their names. Both [ideas] are terrifying
        to those that have discernment. Just as it is not fitting
        for natures to be equated, neither is it [fitting] for names.

53.9   Error did not provide an opportunity for its preachers
        to examine and consider that when they proclaim "beings,"
        [these beings] share a single name. On that basis alone,
        the nature of all of them must be one. "Being" is only one,
        for it is entirely consistent with itself, in both name and nature.

53.10   All things, my brothers, that have been created make up creation.
        Though the name is the same, the natures [of created things] are
                different
        according to the creator's will. The creator, who renders things

both different and the same, has rendered different the natures and
     made same
the names of beings who do not possess his reasons.

53.11   Moses is our witness, for he did not name any other
with the name "Essence." They were called "gods,"[6]
not "beings." Let us learn through the name [God]
the knowledge of his bounty, and let us declare through the name
     [Being]
the weight of his Essence, so that they will confess both.

53.12   To Moses he revealed the name, for he called himself Yhwh,
which is the name "Essence." He did not ever call
another by this name, in the way that with his [other] names
he gave titles to many things. In the one name that he kept [for
     himself],
let us declare that he alone is Being and there is no other.

53.13   And though all of his names are glorified in majesty
and are worthy of praise, this name that he kept
for the glory of his Essence, the evil one has envied
and urged the deniers to give the name to beings.
[Bardaisan] has propped up idols with [God's] name and beings with
     his title.

                                     The end.

6. Cf. Ps 82:6.

3. *Martyrdom of Mīles, Abursam, and Sinay*

Introduction and translation by J. Edward Walters

The *Martyrdom of Mīles*, like many hagiographic works, is a collection of acts or deeds that concludes with a martyrdom. This text circulates along with a number of other Syriac martyrdom texts, which are collectively known as the *Persian Martyr Acts*. This particular hagiography is told through short episodes of Mīles's travels and the miracles he performs in various places. Thus, Mīles here plays the role of the traveling holy man. It may seem curious that someone who is named a bishop would come to be known primarily as an itinerant, but the story of Mīles provides an easy answer. Mīles's narrative begins with his elevation to the position of bishop of Susa,[1] but after his efforts in the city are thwarted for some time, he curses the city and leaves. The reader is informed that, not long after Mīles's departure, the city of Susa (also called Elam in the text) was destroyed by an unnamed Persian king. Thus, the bishop without a city sets off on a journey that takes him as far as the desert of Scetis in Egypt and to such renowned cities as Jerusalem and Nisibis. In many ways this story is typical of the hagiographic genre, but there is one episode in the story of Mīles that is of particular interest to broader issues of early Syriac Christianity: his encounter with an infamous bishop of Seleucia-Ctesiphon, Pāpā bar Aggai.

The *Martyrdom of Mīles* describes the encounter from a particular vantage point, presenting Pāpā as an arrogant bishop who overstepped the power of his office and Mīles as the humble holy man who challenges Pāpā's authority.[2] In their dramatic encounter, Pāpā strikes a gospel book that Mīles has placed before him, resulting in Pāpā immediately being stricken with divine punishment. There is, however, an alternate version of these events. In the early fifth century, there was a meeting of Syriac bishops known as the Synod of Dādishoʻ (424 CE), and the synodal rec-

---

1. In Syriac, Susa is also known as Shushan.

2. The nature of this encounter leads some scholars to conclude that Pāpā must be the errant bishop against whom "Demonstration 14" in the corpus *Demonstrations* of Aphrahat the Persian Sage is directed. For an English translation, see Adam Lehto, *The Demonstrations of Aphrahat, the Persian Sage*, Gorgias Eastern Christian Studies 27 (Piscataway, NJ: Gorgias, 2010), 305–60.

ords of this meeting include a different version of the encounter between Mīles and Pāpā.[3] In this story, Pāpā is presented as "holy" and "faithful," whereas Mīles is presented as a rash judge of character who stirs up others to falsely accuse and depose Pāpā. Interestingly, while this account is clearly sympathetic to Pāpā, it also tells the story of Pāpā striking the gospel book and, as a result, being struck with some kind of physical malady. These two accounts make it difficult to accurately assess the historical figure of Pāpā and the seemingly turbulent period of his bishopric (ca. 327–35 CE).

The precise date of the composition of the text is unknown; however, it must have been quite early because the names Mīles, Abursam, and Sinay are found in the list of "Eastern martyrs" who are named in BL Add. 12,150, which is dated to 411 CE (the oldest dated Syriac manuscript). Furthermore, the Greek historian Sozomen, who composed his *Ecclesiastical History* in the first half of the fifth century, recounts many of the details precisely as they are found in the *Martyrdom* narrative (*Ecclesiastical History* 2.14). The earliest witness to the text is BL Add. 14,654, which is thought to be a fifth- or sixth-century manuscript.[4] Thus, we can reasonably date the story of Mīles's martyrdom to the early fifth century, while also allowing that it may not have reached its final written form in Syriac until the sixth century (depending on the dating of BL Add. 14,654).

Bibliography

Text and Editions

Bedjan, Paul. *Acta Martyrum et Sanctorum*, vol. 2/pp. 260–75. Leipzig: Harrassowitz, 1891.

Studies

Brock, Sebastian P. *The History of the Holy Mar Ma'in, with a Guide to the Persian Martyr Acts*. Persian Martyr Acts in Syriac: Text and Translation 1.

3. The Syriac text of the records of this synod were published in Jean Baptiste Chabot, *Synodicon orientale ou recueil de synodes nestoriens* (Paris: Imprimerie Nationale, 1902), 45–53 (Syriac text), 285–98 (French translation); see also the German translation in O. Braun, *Das Buch der Synhados oder Synodicon Orientale* (Amsterdam: Philo, 1900), 44–59. I am indebted to Kyle Smith for sharing his as-yet-unpublished English translation of this text with me.

4. William Wright, *Catalogue of Syriac Manuscripts in the British Museum Acquired since the Year 1838* (London: Gilbert & Rivington, 1872), 3.1081.

Piscataway, NJ: Gorgias, 2008 (an indispensable resource for the *Persian Martyr Acts*).

Smith, Kyle. *Constantine and the Captive Christians of Persia: Martyrdom and Religious Identity in Late Antiquity*. Transformation of the Classical Heritage. Oakland: University of California Press, 2019.

———. *The Martyrdom and the History of Blessed Simeon Bar Ṣabbaʿe*. Persian Martyr Acts in Syriac: Text and Translation 3. Piscataway, NJ: Gorgias, 2014 (an important survey of issues pertaining to the persecution of Shapur II).

TRANSLATION

Martyrdom of Mīles, Abursam, and Sinay

Martyrdom of Mīles, bishop of Susa, of Abursam the priest, and of Sinay the deacon, at the beginning of the persecution.[5]

Even if I am not sufficient to speak, even if I am not adequate to narrate, my soul is sad for I am not able to magnify the mighty deeds of the great ones for their glories. And my mind is weary because I am not able to glorify the glories of the glorious ones for their mighty deeds. For behold, their signs whisper to me about their marvels, and their wonders indicate their amazements. For behold, their virtue appears to me in its truth, and their adornment awaits me in its labor. Their love enflames me through its actions. Behold, their faith writes to me through them in its victory. Their endurance gazes and inscribes me upon them in their victory. Behold, their death makes me meditate upon them through its suffering, and their blood interprets for me and instructs me through its sprinkling. Behold, their memory forgets the debts of the beloved, and their remembrance causes the stains of a friend to be forgotten. Behold, they reveal for him the thoughts of the mighty ones of the Divinity, and the ideas of the mighty ones of humanity pass before. For their virtue narrates through its rightness, giving counsel to me, and their glory declares its decorum, persuading me. Their course

---

5. This martyrdom text, like a handful of others, is not assigned a specific year, though the phrase "beginning of the persecution" implies that it should be dated to the early years of the Great Persecution of Shapur II. There is a significant debate in secondary literature about precisely when the persecution began, but generally it is dated between 340 and 343.

shows its moderation, commanding me, and their toil makes its measure known, giving counsel to me. Behold, their spring increases and becomes strong in my mind, and its ample departure has no defect in my speech. Behold, it fills me and overflows its course, yet the firm banks do not open for a channel. Behold, the pen contends with me in its movement because the writings detract from their greatness, and the parchment accuses me with its silence because the letters diminish their glories. But let the reader sit in thought, and let the hearer consider with discernment, because although we are not set as equal to their glories, nevertheless we are equal to write their truth.

[Omitted: a brief section in which the author continues extolling the virtues of martyrs in general.]

The election of the blessed Mar Mīles happened thus: he was from the place of the Raziqaye,[6] and he was chosen[7] in his childhood to serve the king of the land. But grace did not abandon him, this vessel of wonder, that he should be terrestrial like anyone, but rather directed him that he might obey the heavenly king like a heavenly angel. He was brought in through his faith to baptism, and a vision was revealed to him by the Holy Spirit, that in this path of discipleship to the Messiah, he should remain in virginity, a constant fast, and assiduous vigil, contending with and moderating his body. And in the teaching of God, his soul proceeded and became wise, and the great gate of new life in the providence of God was opened to his mind. The life-giving word boiled up and poured forth in his heart and kindled like a burning flame in his bones.[8] And he was not able to wait in that place where he was instructed, because the plentiful gain he was preparing that he might become.

He departed from the city of Beth Lapaṭ[9] and went down to the city of Elam (i.e., Susa),[10] in which there was a Shoshan fortress.[11] And every day he was teaching and making demonstrations to its inhabitants through the Holy Word

6. Beth Raziqaye is "a diocese of the Church of the East, south of the Caspian Sea"; see Thomas A. Carlson, "Beth Raziqaye," in *The Syriac Gazetteer* (online at http://syriaca.org /place/38).

7. Literally, the word here means "sealed" or "imprinted."

8. Perhaps an allusion to Jer 20:9.

9. Beth Lapaṭ, the ruins of which are located near modern-day Dezful, Iran, was a significant ecclesiastical center "whose metropolitan bishopric ranked second after that of Seleucia-Ctesiphon"; Sebastian P. Brock, "Beth Lapaṭ," in *GEDSH*, 72.

10. The name Elam (Syriac: *'īlām*) was used as an alternate name for the region/diocese of Beth Huzaye, but the word "Elam" was also used to represent the city of Susa. For more on the confusion regarding Elam as a geographic marker, see D. T. Potts, *The Archaeology of Elam: Formation and Transformation of an Ancient Iranian State* (Cambridge: Cambridge University Press, 2004), 1–9.

11. The fortress here is perhaps a reference to the biblical story of Esther (see especially Esth 9:1–12).

and true preaching. When he had toiled with exhaustion and affliction for three years and became weary, step by step in his love for the church of God, he was prepared for the bishopric. He was appointed by the hand of Gadyahb, bishop of the city of Beth Lapaṭ,[12] he who was also crowned in the famous martyrdom that was directed against the Messiah. And in these years when he was there, the blessed Mīles became wearied; this city did not grant anything for the rest for God or for him, and he often endured her afflictions up until they stoned him in its marketplace and dragged him outside. And every day he was struck with blows, yet he endured. And when he saw that [the city] clung to idolatry and Zoroastrianism, he left it alone and departed. And on the day that he left from it, he scraped it off [his feet][13] and said: "Because you do not want to be built or completed in perfection, from the calm a forceful destruction and speedy desolation will rise against you. Your exalted buildings will be thrown down, and your haughty inhabitants will be scattered." And three months after his departure, the nobles of the city offended the king, and he sent three hundred elephants, and they ruined its habitations and killed all its inhabitants.[14] They made it like a plain, and they sowed it with crops until today.

That holy one went to Jerusalem, with nothing on him except a gospel book in a bag. And from there he went down to the city of Alexandria because of the report about the blessed Ammonius,[15] disciple of Antony, head of the penitents. He was there for two years, visiting the brothers and their monasteries in the desert. And when he returned to his native dwelling place, he found a man, a certain mourner[16] who was dwelling alone in a cave. And when they stood in prayer for

12. Gadyahb of Beth Lapaṭ is mentioned briefly by Anton Baumstark, *Geschichte der syrischen Literatur, mit Ausschluss der christlich-palästinensischen Texte* (Bonn: Marcus & Webers, 1922), 30, though only in reference to the present text. Not much else is known about him.

13. This seems to be the implication of the Syriac verb *lṭʾ* here, referencing (but not quoting precisely) Jesus's admonition in Matt 10:14 that his disciples "shake the dust off their feet" of any city that does not receive them.

14. This destruction of Susa by elephants is also attested by a later Arabic source (Ḥamza al-Isfahānī, *Kitāb taʾrīkh sinī mulūk al-arḍ waʾanbiyāʾ*), though this source depicts the destruction as retaliation for the city revolting against Shapur II and says nothing of Mīles or his curse; see Richard Frye, "The Political History of Iran under the Sasanians," in *The Cambridge History of Iran*, vol. 3.1: *The Seleucid, Parthian, and Sasanian Periods*, ed. E. Yarshater (Cambridge: Cambridge University Press, 2000), 136. The Greek historian Sozomen also mentions the destruction by elephants (*Ecclesiastical History* 2.14), but his account appears to be entirely reliant upon the martyrdom narrative of Mīles (though it is unclear in what form Sozomen had access to this story). There is some dispute over the extent of Shapur's destruction among archeologists who have explored the layers of ancient Susa; see Potts, *Archaeology of Elam*, 428.

15. This figure, known variously as Ammonius, Ammon, or Amoun, is a widely attested Egyptian monk; cf. Sozomen, *Ecclesiastical History* 1.14.

16. In Syriac the word *abīlā* ("mourner") is another term for an ascetic.

the second time in the morning, immediately they saw a great vision of a serpent that was summoned, and its appearance was hideous and very frightful, and it was thirty-two cubits long. It began to enter the cave, according to its custom, because it dwelled there. But the blessed Mīles, when he saw it, was not alarmed or afraid; rather, he was comforted, and he extended his hand toward it and said to it: "Cruel serpent and enemy of humanity, why do you dare force us out while you enter in? For now, look: the spear of the Lord will tear you open from end to end as a marvel." And immediately the entire serpent swelled up and burst open from its head to its tail. Mīles spoke to that brother and asked him: "Have you seen this serpent before now?" And he said to him: "It regularly dwells in this cave, and also I [have dwelled] in it for a time and it has not harmed me in any way." The blessed Mīles reproved him greatly and said to him: "Since God established his verdict of enmity between humanity and the serpent,[17] why do you trust the enemy and exist with it in one dwelling place?" Then he departed from there for another place.

That blessed one traveled and came to the city of Nisibis, where he found a church that had been built by the hands of Bishop Jacob.[18] And when he had seen that great and excellent man and his glorious, adorned building, he stayed there a short time. Then he went down to Ḥadyab,[19] and from there he sent to [Jacob] no small amount of silk fabric according to the expenses of the house.[20]

He then went down to Beth Aramaye,[21] and became involved in a great dispute with the Bishop of Seleucia-Ctesiphon, who was called Pāpā bar Aggai.[22] And [Mīles] saw that [Pāpā] had become haughty over the bishops of the places who had gathered there according to his judgment. Likewise he was also arrogant over the priests and the deacons of his city. And [Mīles] recognized the pride of the man who was over them and his fall from God. He stood in the midst and said to him: "Why do you dare elevate yourself over your brothers and cause strife among your members gratuitously and without cause like a godless man? Is it not thus written: 'Whoever would be first among you, let him be a servant to you.'"[23]

17. Gen 3:15.
18. That is, Jacob of Nisibis, the first known bishop of the city; see J. P. Amar, "Yaʿqub of Nisibis," in *GEDSH*, 433.
19. That is, Adiabene; Thomas A. Carlson, "Adiabene," in *The Syriac Gazetteer* (online at http://syriaca.org/place/993). See also A. Harrak, "Adiabene," in *GEDSH*, 10–11.
20. Jacob is unnamed here, but the text seems to be implying that Mīles sent these fabrics back to Jacob, presumably for the decoration of the church building.
21. That is, the region around the Persian capital city Seleucia-Ctesiphon in modern-day central Iraq. See Lucas Van Rompay, "Beth Aramaye," in *GEDSH*, 70–71.
22. See the introduction to this text for a brief discussion of Pāpā and the historical significance of this encounter.
23. Matt 20:27.

Pāpā said to him: "You would teach me these things, fool, as if I do not already know them?" And immediately [Mīles] drew near and placed the gospel that was in his bag on the table before him and said to him: "If you do not wish to learn what is mine from me because it is from a human, you will surely be judged by this gospel of our Lord that is placed before your external eyes because you do not see its command with the hidden eye of your knowledge." Pāpā, in a wicked passion, raised his hand in anger, slapped it down upon the gospel, and said: "Speak, gospel, speak!" The holy Mīles was shaken; he ran and lifted the gospel, kissed it, and placed it before their eyes. And in a loud voice, he said to the hearing of that whole assembly: "Because you have been so audacious in your pride with the living words of our Lord, behold, his angel reaches out, and he will strike you upon your side and cause it to shrivel. And there will be fear and terror for many. You will die from this, but you will remain as a sign and a wonder." And immediately the likeness of lightning came down from heaven and struck him and shriveled his side.[24] And he fell down upon one of his sides in unspeakable torment for twelve years (and he died in this affliction). And fear and trembling came upon the whole assembly.

From there he went to the place of Maishan,[25] to a certain solitary man who dwelled in the desert. A difficult wound had occurred to the lord of that place and it grieved him for two years, and when it was reported to him that Mīles had come there, he sent and requested that he should come to him. Then he said to the one who spoke: "Go, and when you enter, say in a loud voice: 'Mīles says: In the name of Jesus the Nazarene, be healed, get up, and walk.'" And thus this was done, and that man was completely healed. He got up and went to his house,[26] and he glorified God. He and the inhabitants [of his house] and many others became disciples because of this sign. Likewise, they brought to him a certain young man who had a spirit of lunacy upon him, and he had been tormented by it from his childhood. As soon as [Mīles] saw him, he prayed and made a sign in the name of Jesus, and that spirit departed from him, and it did not come upon him again. And many more things like these were performed by his hand in that place, according to the glory of God.

From there he went to the place [called] Beth Raziqaye and entered a certain village in which there was a certain great woman, whose limbs had all been

24. The language of "shriveling" or "withering" of Pāpā's side suggests that he endured some kind of partial paralysis.

25. Maishan is located in the region of southern Iraq "south of Kashkar and northwest of Baṣra"; Thomas A. Carlson, "Maishan" in *The Syriac Gazetteer* (online at http://syriaca.org/place/123).

26. The reading "to his house" is suggested by Bedjan in a footnote, whereas the text says "he got up and went to him," Paul Bedjan, *Acta Martyrum et Sanctorum* (Leipzig: Harrassowitz, 1891), 2:268n3.

paralyzed by a difficult sickness for nine years, and when the news was reported where he was staying, they lifted her up, held her, and brought her there to him. He gazed at her and saw that she was afflicted, because she was greatly beseeching him. Then he said to her: "Are you a believer in the one God—that is, the only one who is able to heal you?" She said to him: "I am a believer in the Lord—that is, the one God alone, and there is no other except him." Then he stood, prayed, took her hand, and said to her: "In the name of the God in whom you believe, stand up and walk, and you will recover from your sickness." And immediately that woman was healed from her sickness, and she stood up and went to her house. And there was rejoicing throughout that whole village. And in that same village, two men came to him so that one of them might call his companion to testify regarding a theft of something. Mīles said to the one who took the oath: "Oh my son, do not testify falsely and deny your companion in this whole matter." But he did not listen to him, and he hastily testified. Then the blessed one gazed at him and said to him: "Now if you have testified truthfully, go confidently, and your house will be well, but if not you will be clothed with the leprosy of Gehazi.[27] And when you are put to shame, you will go forth from here." And immediately that man became completely leprous, and great fear came on that whole village, and many there were converted from paganism.

He departed from there and went to another place, and two brothers went with him as an escort. They came upon a large river, and it hindered them for a day because it did not allow passage on foot. Then he persuaded those brothers, standing up and praying, and he released them so that they could return to their place. So they departed from him quickly, while watching him [to see] what he would do or how he would cross. He stood up and prayed, and he walked upon the river and crossed, and his shoes didn't even come loose from his feet. And he happened to be in a certain village, and he found there a male priest speaking on the matter of adultery. [Mīles] called to him and accused him in the church and said to him: "Confess, my son, even if this matter applies to you. Engage in repentance before God, because he is merciful and will forgive you. Do not be rash, for you are not sanctified that you should serve before him, lest his justice suddenly destroy you." That man persisted and said to him: "Alas, my lord, I have not sinned, yet you speak poorly of me, for I am falsely accused in this matter." Then, he acted rashly and lifted the Book of David, and he stood on the *bema*[28]

---

27. The phrase "leprosy of Gehazi" refers to the biblical account of Gehazi, a servant of the prophet Elisha, who attempted to cheat Naaman the Syrian after Elisha had healed him from leprosy. In the story (2 Kgs 5:19–27), once Gehazi's deception is made known, Elisha curses him with the leprosy of Naaman, leaving his skin "white as snow."

28. The *bema* is a raised platform at the front of the nave in front of the sanctuary that was prominent in Syriac church architecture. For more information, see Marica C. Cassis, "The

so that he might sing. And something like the palm of a hand came down upon him from the sanctuary and struck him on the face. He fell down immediately and died. And great fear came upon that whole place. In that same village, they brought to him a certain child, who from birth had crawled on his knees because his feet were distorted from his legs. And when [Mīles] saw him, he stood up and prayed, and he took him by the hand and said to him: "In the name of Jesus the Nazarene, stand up and walk." And immediately he set straight his feet, his legs were made straight, and he was cured; he stood up and walked. That child who was healed was ten years old.

Concerning the signs and the healing of sicknesses that, by the power of God, were performed by his hand, we are not able to write all of them because they were too numerous. But we proceed briefly to hasten toward the great sign of his blood, toward the virtuous suffering of his death, and toward glorious martyrdom, the crown for which we celebrate him. The master of that place, whose name was Hormizd Guphriz, who was impious, haughty, proud, and boastful, heard a report of his conversion. He sent and had him brought to Mahledgard, a city of the Raziqaye, and there he bound [Mīles] for an entire year,[29] along with two of his disciples, Abursam and Sinay. And with both wounds and blows he punished them twice to make them worship the sun. But they greatly mocked him and condemned his pride and arrogance over them. They were standing firm and magnifying the glory of their God in the true faith.

And at the end of the year, the period of time in which he bound them, there was a great hunt outside on the mountain for this wicked one (i.e., Hormized), and his heart greatly rejoiced at its magnificence. He commanded, and they brought to him the three holy ones in their chains, and when they stood before him, he questioned the blessed Mīles as an insult and said to him: "What are you? Are you a god or a man? And what is your faith? What is your teaching? Show us your truth and make it known so that we might become your disciples. But if you do not want to reveal to us concerning this thing that you possess, then, like one of these animals, I will take your head from you." That blessed one recognized the man's guile and falsehood, and he said to him: "I am a man, and I am not God. I will not reveal my true faith for your false deceit, and I will not pour my pure teaching into your impure ears. But look, I will say one straightforward thing to you: Woe to you! Woe to you, O wicked, lawless one, and to all those who are wicked like you, not

Bema in the East Syriac Church in Light of New Archaeological Evidence," *Hugoye: Journal of Syriac Studies* 5 (2002): 195–211; and Emma Loosley, *The Architecture and Liturgy of the Bema in Fourth-to-Sixth-Century Syrian Churches*, Texts and Studies in Eastern Christianity 1 (Leiden: Brill, 2012).

29. Literally, "season to season."

recognizing God. For in his justice, God will condemn you in the coming age to Gehenna and the darkness that he is preparing. And he will repay your pride with weeping and gnashing of teeth forever because you did not recognize that he gave these good things to you. On this day, you act proudly and enjoy yourselves." This unjust one was sitting upon the throne, and many people were standing before him; when he heard these things, he became very enraged.

He stood up in his anger and unsheathed his saber that was fastened to his side, and he stabbed the holy Mīles in the front of his shoulder and it came out his back. And in his zeal for this unjust one, the brother of this wicked one—whose name was Narsa—also unsheathed his saber and struck him on his side. And he fell before him. And while the exceedingly illustrious one knocked on the gates of Sheol and hastened that he might recline [as] a guest at the banquet of Death, through his beloved death, he prophesied about their terrible death when he said to these two brothers together: "Because you have greatly joined together in wicked brotherhood and bound yourselves in bitter companionship to kill an innocent man and to shed blood freely, look: at this time tomorrow, each one of you will shed your blood by each other's hands in this place. Dogs will lick up your blood, and birds of the sky will eat your flesh. Your mother will be cut off from both of you, and your wives will be widowed from you on the same day." And when he had said these things, the soul of the holy one departed from him. This wicked one gave an order concerning the illustrious Abursam and Sinay, and they were taken up to two high places opposite one another, and he sent many men from his army, and they stoned them there at the same time when the blessed Mīles was killed.

This Guphriz spent the night in that place, and when it became dawn, he came to the wild-animal hunt of no small size, and his heart was exalted and lifted at its magnificence. He disregarded and abolished from his ear the true word. And at the same time that the blessed Mīles was killed, a very tall partition was prepared for those pugnacious brothers; [they were] expert archers and skilled with a lance, experienced with blood and diligent at hunting. Suddenly, a stag broke through the barrier in which the animals were enclosed, and went out swiftly. And both of them, being hasty, rode after it and died swiftly because they killed swiftly. And they trapped it, with one of them on either side. They were equal [to each other] and they both threw arrows so that, both of them across from each other might strike it with skill. And Guphriz's arrow went straight and passed through Narsa's belly; and Narsa's arrow went directly and came out Guphriz's chest. Both archers fell, and they died there in that place in which the blessed Mīles was killed. And there was an astonishing spectacle and trembling noise in that whole place. Animals and birds ate their bodies because Persians are not buried up until the flesh wastes away from the bones, and then the bones are concealed.[30]

During the night, some people from that place stole the corpses of the three martyrs, and they brought them and buried them in a certain village called Malqin. Thus also through their marvelous death, greatness was revealed in them, because captors were always persisting in coming against that place so that they might take it captive and lay waste to it. But whenever they came upon the border of that village, they were restrained, and no harmful thing took place there. And its inhabitants believed that, because of the blessing of the righteous bones that were placed within it, they were not permitted to enter.

The holy ones were crowned on the thirteenth of the lunar [month] of latter Teshri.[31]

---

30. This refers to the ancient Zoroastrian practice of leaving bodies exposed after death. For a brief survey of this practice as it relates to Syriac martyr texts, see Héctor Ricardo Francisco, "Corpse Exposure in the Acts of the Persian Martyrs and Its Literary Models," *Hugoye: Journal of Syriac Studies* 19 (2016): 193–235.

31. That is, November.

4. Jacob of Serugh, *The Fourth Homily on Cain and Abel*

Introduction and translation by Philip Michael Forness

Jacob of Serugh (d. 520/1) left behind one of the largest bodies of writings in the Syriac language. He was born in the middle of the fifth century and trained within an intellectual community in the city of Edessa (modern-day Urfa, Turkey) in the 460s and perhaps 470s. Many works were being translated from Greek into Syriac at this time in Edessa. This had a profound effect on students, like Jacob, whose works engage with both Greek and Syriac traditions. Jacob became a rural bishop, known as a *periodeutes*, by the early sixth century and was already renowned at this time for his literary works. During the last two or three years of his life, he served as the bishop of the city of Batnae of Serugh (modern-day Suruç, Turkey), some forty kilometers west of Edessa and forty kilometers east of the Euphrates River. Although he seems to have been somewhat reticent in his views, Jacob opposed the Christology of the Council of Chalcedon and was involved in ecclesiastical networks that would form the Syriac Orthodox Church later in the sixth century.

Jacob's writings consist of over three hundred sermons or homilies, forty-two letters, and perhaps some other poetic works. A large proportion of his sermons discuss stories from the Old and New Testaments, while others provide theological instruction, commemorate saints, discuss monastic practices, and address various other topics. He composed the majority of his homilies in a strict poetic meter of couplets in which each line has twelve syllables consisting of three four-syllable feet (4 + 4 + 4 / 4 + 4 + 4). Many of the homilies attributed to Narsai and Isaac of Antioch also use this meter. The complex relationships between these authors and their forebears like Aphrahat, Ephrem, and the anonymous poetic tradition are only beginning to be appreciated. The development of the poetic genre stands as one of the crowning achievements of Syriac literary culture in late antiquity.

The homily translated below forms the last of a set of four homilies on the story of Cain and Abel from Genesis 4. Jacob composed them as a set, as he refers at the beginning and end of several of the homilies to what has preceded (see, for example, lines 7–12 below). The first homily in this set narrates the story from its beginning until the murder of Abel (Gen 4:1–8). The second homily covers God's interrogation of Cain about the whereabouts of his brother until his banishment to wander on the earth (4:9–14). The third homily describes God's mercy on Cain by placing a mark on him (4:15) and includes an imaginative account of Cain's return to Adam and Eve's home where Eve mourns for both her sons. The fourth homily offers a resolution to the story through Adam and Eve's third son Seth.

Jacob's homilies on Cain and Abel form one part of a long tradition of interpreting this passage in both the Jewish and the Christian traditions. In Syriac literature from late antiquity, Aphrahat, Ephrem, Isaac of Antioch, Symmachus, and Narsai, as well as the *Cave of Treasures* all comment on this passage. As Johannes Glenthøj's study of this literature demonstrates, Jacob was familiar with a number of these works and engaged with them in the four homilies on Cain and Abel.[1]

The prominent speaking role given to Eve in this homily reflects a feature of many of Jacob's sermons in which women who say little in the biblical text have lengthy speeches in his homilies. This aspect of Jacob's writings is explored in a variety of studies and most recently in a work attributed to—though probably not written by—Jacob in which Eve's mourning is emphasized. Much work remains to be done on this homily as it connects to other exegetical approaches to the story of Cain and Abel and the representation of women and their voices in late antique literature.

The translation is based on Paul Bedjan's Syriac text.[2] Although I follow Bedjan's text, I deviate from his section divisions, which often seemed too restricted. Section titles are added to the text for clarity and do not appear in the Syriac text.

Bibliography

Text and Editions

Bedjan, Paul, ed. *Homiliae selectae Mar-Jacobi Sarugensis*. 5 vols. Paris: Harrassowitz, 1905–10.

---

1. Johannes Bartholdy Glenthøj, *Cain and Abel in Syriac and Greek Writers (4th–6th Centuries)*, CSCO 567, subsidia 95 (Leuven: Peeters, 1997).
2. Paul Bedjan, ed., *Homiliae selectae Mar-Jacobi Sarugensis*, 5 vols. (Paris: Harrassowitz, 1905–10), 5:47–61.

Studies

Brock, Sebastian P. "Jacob of Serugh: A Select Bibliographical Guide." Pages 219–44 in *Jacob of Serugh and His Times: Studies in Sixth-Century Syriac Christianity*. Edited by George Anton Kiraz. Gorgias Eastern Christian Studies 8. Piscataway, NJ: Gorgias, 2010.

———. "A Syriac Life of Abel." *Le Muséon* 87 (1974): 467–92.

———. "Two Syriac Dialogue Poems on Abel and Cain." *Le Muséon* 113 (2000): 333–75. Reprinted in Brock's *Treasure-House of Mysteries: Explorations of the Sacred Text through Poetry in the Syriac Tradition*. Popular Patristics 45. Yonkers, NY: Saint Vladimir's Seminary Press, 2012.

Byron, John. *Cain and Abel in Text and Tradition: Jewish and Christian Interpretations of the First Sibling Rivalry*. Themes in Biblical Narrative 14. Leiden: Brill, 2011.

Glenthøj, Johannes Bartholdy. *Cain and Abel in Syriac and Greek Writers (4th–6th Centuries)*. CSCO 567, subsidia 95. Leuven: Peeters, 1997.

Walsh, Erin Galgay. "Mourning Eve: The Homily on the Women as Attributed to Jacob of Serugh." *Patristica Nordica Annuaria* 33 (2018): 31–59.

TRANSLATION

The Fourth [Homily] on Cain and Abel and on the Consolation of Adam's Household That Came through Seth, Which Was Composed by Mar Jacob

Invocation and introduction

O praiseworthy child who is like his Father as Seth [is like] Adam,
set down on my tongue the beauty of your mystery so that I might
    speak about it!
O Son who through his mystery made Eve rejoice and made her
    mourning pass,
through your power enrich my speech so that I might tell your story!
5   Through the mourning that came to Adam's household I have suffered
    much;

grant, my Lord, that I might speak about their consolation through
        Seth the illustrious one!
For I spoke about that great suffering of Abel
and about the curses with which Cain was cursed by God.
I related to you the sacrifices of Adam's sons,

10   and the story was handed down according to its order in the reading.
Then I spoke about the lamentations of our mother Eve,
and that the mourning of the mother for her beloved ones was strong.
But today I can speak about their consolation
and through what means they let go of their bitter grief.

15   I will first relate which sufferings came upon them,
and then I am going to turn to the consolation that made them joyful.
The first of the sicknesses was their nakedness among the trees,[3]
and the second ulcer was the leaves of reproach with which they were
        clothed.[4]
The third companion was the expulsion from paradise,[5]

20   and another sickness was the murder of Abel, which broke them.[6]
Cain's shaking wove a crown of sufferings for his parents,[7]
and they compounded and all of them became one great mourning.[8]
The various forms of grief called one to another and came upon them,
and the terrors arrived from all sides and broke them.

The only couple on earth is deprived of a child

25   With difficulty they were set free from the nakedness that had driven
        them away,
but when Cain came so that they might delight in him, he murdered his
        brother.
And when on account of the dead one a silent astonishment had
        grasped them,
the living one staggered and by the sign of his trembling he tormented
        them.

3. Adam and Eve become aware that they are naked "among the trees," that is, in the garden
of Eden. See Gen 3:7.
    4. See Gen 3:7.
    5. See Gen 3:24.
    6. See Gen 4:8.
    7. Cain's shaking (Syriac *zaw'ā*) refers to his curse in Gen 4:12, 14, where God says that "he
is going to shake and stagger" in the Syriac translation (*zā'ē' w-nā'ēḏ*).
    8. That is, the various sicknesses, ulcers, and sufferings came together.

The slain one through his blood and the living one through his shaking
were making them suffer.

30 The buried corpse and the body that staggered increased the pain.

The firstborn was trembling, and the sword was drunk with the second
[born].

He was sacrificed and cast down, and his brother was swaying as
though from the wind.

The murderer was beaten down, and the slain one who was buried in
the earth was putrid.

One was being gnawed at by the worm and the other by the shaking.

35 Abel was being torn in pieces, and Cain's body was shaking and
staggering.

One was pierced and cast down, and this other one was standing and
trembling.

The living one was inflicting terror on them by his shaking as though
one who was slain,

and the dead, buried one was wounding them by his sacrifice.

For it was not available [to them] to be consoled about the dead one in
any way

40 nor to be encouraged by the living one.

The destruction of the earth taunted them, and there was no one to
listen.[9]

The place was deprived of inhabitants, and there was no support.

The world was desolate for the two who dwelled in its midst,

and when, look!, they were fruitful so that creation would be filled,
murder came.

45 In the whole world there were only two—Eve and Adam—

and although they were joined together so that the family would multiply, death sprung up.

[There was] one human couple in the expanse of the whole earth,

and although a child was added to them, Abel died.

The ends [of the earth] were empty, and there were no inhabitants
except for them.

50 The earth was broad, and they were left in it without descendants.

The path of the world was extensive and accessible, and its distance
was long,

and two merchants were traveling on it without a retinue.

And when through childbirth a couple of brothers were clinging to
them,

9. Literally, "no listening."

deceit sprung up from one of them and he murdered his brother.

55   The path that had begun to find peace was destroyed through murder,
      and blood cut him off from the pathway of life through Cain's hands.
      In the expansive house of the great world there were only two,
      and when, look!, it began to be inhabited, it was destroyed by blood.
      In the broad district of the world there was one union,

60   and when it had produced a child so that the people multiplied, the
            murderer burst forth.
      A marriage feast had taken place for the earth so that it might find
            peace in Adam,
      and when the wedding banquet thundered because of the childbirth,
            death snatched him away.
      A festival of the world began to inhabit the face of the earth,
      and a robber arose, cast a corpse in its midst, and it was destroyed.

65   A spring of families coursed through the earth so that it might encircle
            the marshes,
      and the enemy came, disturbed it with blood so that he might hinder
            its route.

Eve has no one to comfort her

Eve, the bride, looked at the sons whom she had borne for Adam,
and when, look!, she took delight [in this], one of them arose and
      murdered his brother.
She had no sister to say: "Let your mourning pass!"

70   and no relative so that she might be comforted about her beloved.[10]
      She had no mother and no neighbor to come to her,
      no one close to her and no one advising her to let her suffering go.
      She was weeping, and when she was worn out, she became silent.
      She was faint with sufferings, and there was no companion to raise
            her up.

75   The mother of the nations became drunk on the cup of death,
      and she lay prostrate bitterly with new mourning.
      From the cherished firstfruit that the deceitful Cain had trampled
            down,
      a new taste was mixed with suffering for the household of Adam.
      From the juice that that murderer brought forth first and pressed,

80   he gave them a turbid cup to drink, and they became nauseous from it.

10. In Syriac, all of the people mentioned in lines 69–74 are female.

Adam learns about death

Through the death of Abel, Adam learned what his death was,
and it was through it that he saw that his kind was soil, as it was said.[11]
Through the slain body that rotted on the earth, the concealed voice
      was explained to him,
which had told him: "You shall return to your earth."[12]

85   He saw Abel, the desirable sanctuary that was ruined and cast down,
and through him he grew wise about what the construction of his
      body was.
He saw the composition of the slain body in which death dwelled,
and he comprehended that he also would become soil through death.
Through the palace of the body that had been uprooted, he was able
      to know

90   that the temple of his body was constructed by his maker from dust.
Through the shed blood of the slain body, he was informed
that by grace his nature is rational.
Through the shut mouth that he saw that had become mute, he
      was taught
that the tongue that communicates moves through mercy.

95   Through the eyes of light that diminish before the darkness,
he was enlightened for he saw a luminary by grace.
Through the body that brought forth an odious stench, he understood
that he was also filth but was salted in the soul perceptibly.[13]
Through the death of Abel, he tasted death before [his] departure,

100   and it was in him that he saw the end of his citadel—what would hap-
      pen to him.

Seth as a type of Christ consoles Adam's household

There was no one at that time to console the household of Adam
and no one close by to take care to provide encouragement.
They began a speech of suffering with no audience,
and they raised sounds of groaning on the earth, but no one was
      listening.

105   They were raising up a song of suffering to one another,

---

11. See Gen 3:19.
12. Gen 3:19.
13. There is a wordplay in these lines between "odious" (*sanyā*) and "filth" (*syānā*).

and one received it from the other without anyone in the middle.
In the great world of the whole earth there were only two,
and they started to moan sounds of suffering for themselves.
When they were being persecuted by this great mourning
110 and becoming faint at sadness such as this,
and when suffering was springing up on them from all sides,
so that, look!, they might come to despair through the terrible things
      that had happened—
at that time the mystery of the Son appeared through the noble Seth,
and through his valor he broke down the foundation that suffering had
      constructed.
115 He spoke within the company of sufferings and dispersed them,
and he resisted the mourning and did not endure its companionship.
He struck down grief, and it made way so that he might be reverenced,
and he drove out sadness so that it would leave them.
The young deer had called out at the suffering, the serpent,
120 and the accursed one fled who had bred in them, in the household
      of Adam.
The merciful one provided a great remedy for the great sickness,
and he applied healing medicine to the harsh ulcer.
This passage especially requires simple hearing,
but for comprehension someone who is skilled is needed for the
      audience.
125 If thought, the laborer of the mind, does not listen to me,
my word is concealed cunningly and cannot be heard.
If understanding does not open the door for him to speak,
it is too heavy for hearing and [understanding] does not enter into
      [the hearing].
It is a great mystery, and someone listens to it through comprehension,
130 lest the mind fall short of it when it is spoken.
Become my company and I will travel with you on the path of the
      mystery,
and let us go see the new beauty that happened through him!

Seth is like Adam as God the Son is like God the Father

"Adam begot in his likeness and according to his image,"[14]
and what is this that Moses has carefully written?

---

14. Gen 5:3.

135   If he had not been signifying something that he might reveal to us,
        why was it necessary for him to write about whom Seth was like?
        Look! He recorded the generations from Adam until him,
        and he did not relate this: that someone was like his father.
        The children of Adam were not like their parents,
140   for even if they were alike in certain things, they were only alike.
        And even if it does happen and there is an infant who is like his father,
        he is lesser in something and is not exactly like him.
        As many faces as there are in your gathering, consider and look
        which of them is like another without difference.
145   There is a slight likeness from one person to another,
        but he is not in every way like him, and why is this the case?
        One is the worshiped one. He is like his Father in glorification,
        and a perfect likeness does not exist except for him.
        He is glorified like him,[15] is wondrous in his likeness, is worshiped as he
            also is,
150   is begotten from him, and is like him without difference.
        He is magnificent and is like him, glorified with him, imprinted with
            his Essence:
        no difference, no alteration, no decrease.
        He is like him, he is with him, he is from his womb;
        one is the power, one is the authority, and one is the jurisdiction.
155   "Whoever sees me has seen the Father, the hidden one, openly,"[16]
        for he is his likeness, his power, his wisdom, his valor,
        the likeness of his Father, the arm and strength of his creative power,
        the Son of his right hand, and the great image of his glorification.
        He alone is the one who is like his Father as Seth [is like] Adam,
160   and there is no other child who is equal to his begetter.
        There are some who are like their parents in certain things,
        and familial characteristics proceed with their family to a certain
            extent.
        And as for the one who is much more like his father than the [other]
            children,
        something exists in him that is not completely like [the father].
165   He is either more exalted than him or lesser than him, either in essence
        or in sight, or [his] appearance differs from his.

---

15. Bedjan's edition has a misprint in this line. Rather than "is glorified" (*šbiḥ*), it has "is taken" (*šbiq*), but the manuscript used for Bedjan's edition has *šbiḥ*; see Rome, Vatican Library, Sir. 117, folio 412r.
    16. John 14:9.

It is in Seth alone that the perfect likeness has been seen
so that he might form a type of the only begotten one who is like
    his Father.
For it is written that he was "in his likeness and according to
    his image."[17]
170   It is therefore disclosed that he is like him in every way.
Seth was not distinguished from Adam for whoever looked at him,
but he was wholly like him in truth.
His characteristics were not imprinted upon Cain, even though he was
    the firstborn,
nor his likeness upon the innocent Abel, even though he was the sec-
    ond [born].
175   The mystery preserved the perfect likeness for the third [born]
so that he might form a type of the triune Divinity.
For who was there to console the household of Adam,
if the mystery of the Son of God had not sustained them?
As for the great breach of mourning that came through the new death,
180   the valiant one was able to repair it through his courage.
When the corpse fell on the path of the world, and [the world] was
    destroyed,
a mystery proceeded on [the path] to find peace with the children.
When death entered [and] opened the door of life through the murder,
the likeness of the Son opened [the door and] came out so that the
    earth might be filled.
185   When the foundation of blood was constructed so that no one
    might pass,
the mystery of our Lord broke through it and came out as a valiant one.

Seth consoles Adam's household

In the noble Seth was consolation for the household of Adam,
and at his birth they let go of their earlier grief.
The radiance of the mystery was kindled by his person,
190   and it made those who were darkened because of Abel radiant.
They saw a glorified likeness in him and they wondered at his majesty,
and from that wonder they let go of the mourning onto which they
    were clinging.

17. Gen 5:3.

The likeness of the sun of righteousness rose from him,
and through the consolation of his new light he encouraged them.

195 Eve was looking at him, the likeness of her husband Adam,
and although [Adam] was far away, [it was] as though he were not far
away, for he was in front of her.
She was also consoling Adam through the beauty of his son,
saying to him: "Come! See your image and let your mourning pass!
Come! See yourself and be consoled by yourself, by your likeness!

200 Look at yourself! Behold! Your characteristics! He is entirely you!
Come, O tree, and see your fruit, which is like you!
O exalted eagle, look!, your features upon your fledgling!
Draw near, O valiant one and prince of the earth, father of the nations,
and see your son, whose stock is as exalted as your own!

205 See the one who cultivates the seed of your field! Look! He is like you,
and the sheaf that you gathered is like you in all its beauties!"

Eve's mourning turns to joy

The woman who was mourning for her sons became radiant through
the noble Seth,
and she began singing a song that reveals joy.
She saw the youth who was as valiant and majestic as his begetter,

210 and she called him Seth, a name that reveals consolation.
For this name acquires its explanation from the Hebrews:
"As someone might say: 'I have then been set free from grief.'"[18]
"She named him Seth, [and] she was consoled after Abel."
For this is also its explanation in one of the stories.[19]

215 The one who was grieving saw the beauty of her son and her heart was
relieved,
and she began to relate a speech that proclaims consolation.
She wrote down his name with that appellation that was
encouraging her,

---

18. The interpretation of the name Seth as "consolation" is not self-evident in Hebrew or in Syriac. The work to which Jacob refers in line 214 is unclear. But this explanation was not unique to him, as it is also found in a text entitled the *Death of Adam* preserved in Armenian: Michael Stone, "The Death of Adam: An Armenian Adam Book," *Harvard Theological Review* 59 (1966): 283–91 at 284, 288–89 (see §7).

19. Gen 4:25.

so that when she would relate the name of the youth she would be
    consoled.
Seth became a bridge for his mother that let [her] cross over to joy
220   and a cherished door, for when she entered it she let go of her
    suffering.
She chanted cherished songs to him lovingly,
while she related a story of his brother with sadness.
She sighed for the first [children] with great suffering,
but when, look!, she wept, she saw the last one [and] laughed upon
    meeting him.
225   When the suffering of Abel had provoked her to weep,
love rose up for the noble Seth [for her] to chant.
When the shaking of Cain made her suffer, look!, so that she wept
    for him,
the youth looked at her, she became radiant, [and] she let go of
    lamentation.
When her eyes shed tears for that one who was slain,
230   she looked at Seth, [and] laughter spread on her face.
When she became darkened because of the firstborn who was shaking
    [and] staggering,
the child rushed at her, she laughed with him, [and] there was no
    suffering.
When, look!, she looked at the place of Abel as though out of suffering,
Seth drew near, laid hold of the hems of her garment, [and] she eagerly
    met him.

Eve sings to Seth

235   Her mouth was full of radiant songs for her fruit,
and through the chants she let go of the lamentations for Abel and his
    brother.
She would say to him: "Through you, my son, I am set free from grief,
and through your birth I let go of the suffering for the sons of your
    mother.
My noble son, in you I see Abel your brother.
240   The slain one has come to life, and he is not in Sheol since I gave birth
    to you.
The corpse of your brother has shaken off the dust,
and it seems to me as though he is not slain, for, look!, he is in front
    of me!

God has given me you instead of him so that I might be consoled
    in you,
and I do not grieve because I see you, the light of his mother.
245   I let go of my grief, which Cain your brother brought,
and I am radiant, as though in a light, in you, the light of his mother.
Through your birth, your father Adam will let go of all his sufferings,
for even if he dies, look!, he is still alive in you, the noble one.
You will be a good heir on the earth, which you are going to populate,
250   and in you the root of the just ones will spread to the whole world.
Your brother's family, which has been bereaved, will be enriched
    in you,
and in Abel's place you will be fruitful and multiply all the noble ones.
You will bring forth your wheat, a great heap of people,
and the earth will find peace through you among families and
    generations.
255   You will please the LORD, as your brother Abel pleased [him],
for you will not be slain like him after your sacrifice.
The Most High will be satisfied with your offering that you will offer to
    him,
since envy will not come and enter to sacrifice you as well.
Your sacrifice will be pleasing, and when you have offered it, you will
    not die!
260   You will be like Abel in all the beauties apart from the murder!"
With such [words], look!, Seth's mother chanted to him,
for she let her suffering go, and she who was darkened became radiant
    through him.
And perhaps, my brothers, she was terrified for the youth,
lest Cain suddenly fall upon him.
265   She was prudently guarding him from the murderer,
so that the one who hates those who are cherished might not assail the
    noble one.
The ewe was bleating to the lamb: "My son, do not go far away
lest the wolf, Cain, is lying in wait and expecting you."
Seth was brought up between fear and encouragement,
270   and the good heir came of age to take hold of the earth.
The field of the world had found peace in a new person,
and he began to multiply the blessed family of the household of Seth
    and Enosh.[20]

---

20. Enosh was Seth's child according to Gen 4:26.

Conclusion

Be silent, O tongue, at this point, the end of the story!
Do not then transgress [and] confuse the speech with another speech.
275   The ear has been consoled by listening about Abel.
Turn your voice away from the story that has reached its end!
Look! Other stories on certain matters are summoning you.
Leave this one and proceed to them quickly!
Yes, my Lord, multiply the journey of my word with discoveries,
280   so that I might then make orderly praise rise to you at length!

Ended are the homilies on Cain and Abel that were spoken by blessed
    Mar Jacob.

5. Narsai, *On the Canaanite Woman*

Introduction and translation by Erin Galgay Walsh

Narsai (died ca. 500) composed theologically and exegetically rich verse homilies or mēmrē. As a poet and teacher of exegesis at the School of Edessa and eventually the School of Nisibis, Narsai was an heir to the literary and interpretative traditions set by Ephrem the Syrian (died 373). The translation of Theodore of Mopsuestia's (died 428) writings into Syriac during the first half of the fifth century at the School of Edessa served as a formative influence on Narsai's thought. As a foundational writer for the East Syrian Church (also known as the Assyrian Church of the East), Narsai is frequently studied for his intricate expositions of dyophysite Christology and his role in the doctrinal debates in the wake of the Council of Ephesus.

Mēmrā 32, *On the Canaanite Woman*, provides a sustained treatment of the encounter between the Canaanite woman and Jesus as recounted in the Gospel of Matthew (15:21–28).[1] The poet begins with a lengthy introduction recalling the plots of Satan against humanity and God's response to iniquity in the incarnation. Set within this narrative frame, the plight of the Canaanite woman mirrors the universal, embattled state of humanity. Narsai ushers the Canaanite woman onto the poetic stage, and he focuses our attention on the spiritual acuity of this woman who seeks healing for her daughter. The poetic narrator embellishes the woman's identity by expounding on the significance of her Canaanite background, tying her to the Genesis narratives about Ham and his descendants. This interpretative move not only allows Narsai to characterize her as an enslaved person, but also underscores her extraordinary character as she perseveres in her faith against all odds. Jesus's silence and hesitancy to grant her daughter healing are pedagogical strategies as he proves the woman's faith and reveals the power of her love. Through lengthy imagined speeches and narrative embellishment, the woman emerges as a model of faithful boldness for all

---

1. The narrative found in Matt 15:21–28 parallels the encounter of Jesus with the Syro-Phoenician woman in Mark 7:24–30. Narsai's mēmrā clearly draws on the details of the Matthean text.

Christians to emulate. The rich detail and dramatic casting of this work invite further study of Narsai's poetic style and creativity.[2]

This mēmrā does not appear in printed editions of Narsai's works.[3] Two extant manuscripts contain this mēmrā, including the second-oldest manuscript of Narsai's writings, Diyarbakir MS 70, copied in 1328 near Erbil in modern-day Iraq.[4] The thirty-eight mēmrē contained in this manuscript mirror the liturgical year of Sundays and feast days, and thirty-five of these mēmrē belong to Narsai's poetic corpus.[5] A second manuscript, Vatican Syriac MS 594, was copied in 1918 by a Syrian Orthodox deacon in Mosul for a priest in Diyarbakir, a city in southeastern Turkey. The two manuscripts rarely diverge, suggesting a stable transmission history. The subject matter and style of the mēmrā are consistent with Narsai's other writings, supporting confidence in his authorship.

Bibliography

Studies

Walsh, Erin Galgay. "Holy Boldness: Narsai and Jacob of Serugh Preaching the Canaanite Woman." Pages 85–97 in *Literature, Rhetoric, and Exegesis in Syriac Verse*. Edited by Jeffrey Wickes and Kristian S. Heal. Studia Patristica 77. Leuven: Peeters, 2017.

———. "How the Weak Rib Prevailed! Eve and the Canaanite Woman in the Poetry of Narsai." Pages 199–226 in *Narsai: Rethinking His Work and*

2. Erin Galgay Walsh, "Holy Boldness: Narsai and Jacob of Serugh Preaching the Canaanite Woman," in *Literature, Rhetoric, and Exegesis in Syriac Verse*, ed. Jeffrey Wickes and Kristian S. Heal, Studia Patristica 77 (Leuven: Peeters, 2017), 85–97; Walsh, "How the Weak Rib Prevailed! Eve and the Canaanite Woman in the Poetry of Narsai," in *Narsai: Rethinking His Work and His World*, ed. Aaron M. Butts, Kristian S. Heal, and Robert A. Kitchen (Tübingen: Mohr Siebeck, 2020), 199–226.

3. To identify the manuscripts and printed editions of Narsai's extant works, two important guides are W. F. Macomber, "The Manuscripts of the Metrical Homilies of Narsai," *Orientalia Christiana* 29 (1973): 275–306; and Sebastian P. Brock, "A Guide to Narsai's Homilies," *Hugoye: Journal of Syriac Studies* 12 (2009): 21–40.

4. This manuscript has been digitized by the Hill Museum & Manuscript Library under Chaldean Cathedral (Mardin) 578. Two manuscripts dating to the nineteenth century, identified as Chaldean Patriarchate 70 (M3D) and Chaldean Patriarchate 240 (M5), were housed in Baghdad. Due to the violence and political upheaval of recent years, these manuscripts are not accessible and may be destroyed.

5. Addai Scher, "Notice sur les manuscrits syriaques et arabes conservés à l'archevêché chaldéen de Diarbékir," *Journal Asiatique* 10 (1907): 361–62.

His World. Edited by Aaron M. Butts, Kristian S. Heal, and Robert A. Kitchen. Tübingen: Mohr Siebeck, 2020.

TRANSLATION

Mēmrā of Tuesday: On the Canaanite Woman

Refrain: Blessed is the one who overturned our captivity from the hater by means of one of our race, who triumphed and made us triumph. My brothers!

Proem: the evil one plots against humanity

The hater of humankind made an assault on humanity iniquitously,
and he destroyed the image that had been called by the name of the
    divine Essence.
The killer of humankind became intoxicated with envy toward
    humanity,
and he troubled them with the ugly filth of his bitterness.

5   With an angry zeal the rebel clothed himself against humanity
because mortals were called with the name of the (divine) Essence.
With weapons of beguiling he armed himself in order to destroy them;
with plots he sharpened his blade to shed their blood.
With all shapes he prepared himself for battle,

10   so that he might fulfill the inclination of his bitterness by means of their
    death.
Crafty plots he devised within himself against their lives;
he dug deep and hid snares of death so that he might kill them.
His thoughts wove[6] skillfully a net of iniquity,
so that it might seize and hold the prey of humankind within its womb.[7]

15   On sea and land he extended his thoughts as snares,
and he chased after all the peoples and made them the food for death.

---

6. Vatican Syriac MS 594 (hereafter: V) reads the verb in the singular, with Satan as the subject: "He wove his thoughts into a net of iniquity."

7. V: "within his womb."

Within them he fought with their lives while they were not aware,
and he sent them as spies so that they might chase after their
      companions.
By their own means he waged war with their ranks and subdued them;
20   and with the swords of their thoughts he tore them to pieces.
He threw the quarrel of his rage into their thoughts,
and he incited them to fight one with another.
They destroyed one another as strangers, and they did not understand;
and they tore to pieces the bodies of their limbs as if (they were) not
      people.
25   He taught them (all) sorts of conflict according to his bitterness,
and he instructed them how to attack savagely.
He wrote a deceitful book on the pages of their minds,
that they might read in (it) iniquitously according to his will.
He saw that they were eager to study within his books,
30   and he devoted himself to destroy them with not unseemly things.
He settled among them, and he lived with them and they with him;
and even though they loved him, he hated them and oppressed them.
Not with true love did he enjoy the company of humans,
but (only) that through his company he might trouble the peace that
      was in them.
35   Under the pretext of love he drove them away from the truth,
and with enticements he led them astray with the fallacy of his words.
They became mad and raged—the demons through people and the
      people through demons—
and the world, sea, and dry land, passed by in the likeness of a
      drunkard.

God's response in the incarnation

The creator saw that the evil one disturbed the peace of humanity,
40   and he sent his Hint to return people to the peace of his name.
He sent his Hint through a bodily messenger,
to convey through him the word of peace to humanity.
On the pages of his body he wrote down (the expression of) his loving
      will,
so that bodily beings would see what is hidden through that which is
      revealed.

45   Along with visible limbs he took on his will,
and he approached them to teach them how to return to him.
He composed a (human) body in writing as (one would) a letter,
and the power of his hiddenness signed it and sealed it with his name.
He taught the body to read in itself the mystery of hidden things,

50   and to convey to its companions the interpretation of the mysteries.
As an army commander (the creator) armed and sent him against the
       evil one,
so that by his victory his race might be set free from their debts.
The bodily one came forth (equipped) with the divine will,
and he raised his voice—hidden in that which is revealed—and the
       demons quivered.

55   A new voice the rebels heard, one that cried through a body;
and they shook and were thrown into confusion by the novelty of the
       voice, which was unusual.
The power of the divine Essence roared in creation through the mouth
       of a mortal;
the ranks of the powers of the evil one and of covetous death shook.
(The divine Power) called out the sound of Jesus's name on the earth as
       thunder,

60   and the demons wailed for they were not able to endure the greatness
       of the sound.
With the sound alone he frightened those filled with pride;
and they began to recede from their dwelling places against their will.
Legion, the head of their ranks, heard the sound of (Jesus's) name;
and terror seized him, he wailed and cried bitterly.

65   The news of the name of Jesus went out to all the regions;
and the nations and cities[8] gathered together to listen to his word.
The hidden Hint gathered them together in the harbor of his love,
so that they would come and calm their minds with the peace of his
       name.
They heard that through his word he was persecuting demons and
       healing illnesses;

70   and they came together from everywhere to take medicine for their
       sicknesses.

---

8. V: "citydwellers."

Introducing the Canaanite woman

There came out a woman in whose daughter a demon dwelled[9]
to ask him for a spiritual medicine for the pain from the demon.
Her thoughts along with her limbs prepared themselves to go after
     Jesus,
and her emotions[10] and senses began to aim for the goal of his name.

75   Who taught the daughter of Canaan, the slave of slaves,[11]
to go out and ask for freedom from the son of Abram?
Who revealed to the Canaanite woman, the daughter of Ham, the
     accursed one,
that the son of Shem is able to break the seal (giving her access) to the
     righteous one?
Who revealed to the worshiper of demons, who had been defiled by
     the demons,

80   that at the voice of Jesus demons flee from their dwelling places?
Who wrote for her a new book of the name of the creator,
for a soul that has grown old in the company of demons, haters
     of truth?
Who showed the one who was always heading to the demons' door
to walk on the path of the faith of the one God?

85   The hidden Hint suggested to her in her mind secretly:
"Shun the worship of idols and believe and be saved."
It was he who equipped her with faith just as with a weapon,
to go out and to wage war with the rebel who had captured her
     daughter.
With faith, hope, and love she equipped herself;

90   as with a sword she cut down the evil one with the word of her mouth.
Her mind put on faith as a breastplate,
and she grasped hope as a shield by means of (her) emotions.
At the goal of love her thoughts aimed along with her limbs,
and she ascended to the lofty rank of the name of the triumphant ones.

95   With a hidden weapon she armed herself spiritually,
so she could engage in hidden war with the powers of the evil one.

---

9. Matt 15:22; Mark 7:26. Note how Narsai expands the narrative details and speeches where he alludes to the gospel text.

10. That is, inner movements/stirrings.

11. Here and in the lines that follow Narsai invokes Gen 9:24–27.

She knew that he was hidden, the hater of humankind who was waging
    war against her;
and she prepared spiritual arms to confront his hiddenness.
In hiddenness she forged faith within her mind;
100   and she gained the power to contend with the strong one.

The petition of the Canaanite woman

In faith her limbs geared up in pursuit of her inclination,
and her senses and her emotions raised their voice to beg for mercies.
Mouth and mind alike called out with a humble voice,
and they seized the audacity of invincible faith.
105   As a trumpet the mind called out through the outer senses,
and the mouth expressed the pain of her inner sufferings.
An advocate became (her) mouth for (her) emotions before the Judge,
and the mute ones on behalf of those endowed with speech gave forth
    plaintive sounds.
The accursed one's daughter called out before the son of the righteous
    one resoundingly:
110   "Son of David, have pity and set me free, (in) my enslavement, from
    the captor.[12]
Son of Abram, rich in love, have pity upon the daughter of Canaan,
and save my life from the bondage of slavery to the evil one.
The father of your father cursed my fathers through the mouth of the
    hidden one,
and subjected them to the heavy yoke of the accuser.
115   Noah cursed our father who mocked and derided him impudently,
and he blessed your father who honored and loved wisely.
Just as with a rod the just one chastened the one bold of heart,
and behold the punishment has extended to his offspring up till now.
Enough has our audacity been punished with scourges our father
    endured
120   as we have become servants to the servant who rebelled against the
    maker.
Enough has the iniquitous tyrant subjected the freedom of our souls,
as he mocked and derided the condition of human nature.
And if the offspring of the bold Ham owes the debt of slavery,

12. Matt 15:22; Mark 7:26.

let them be the slaves to the Son of the just Shem rather than to the
    tyrant.

125   Even the just Noah thus explained it in his prophecy:
to Shem will Canaan pay servitude as to a lord.[13]
To you therefore we will repay[14] the debt of love as owed,
for you are from that seed in which the freedom of humanity is
    inscribed.
You are the son of David, the son of Abraham, the son of Shem, and the
    son of Noah,

130   set free your slaves from the strong one and let them be yours.
I have heard about the promise of life that David your father received;
seal his words by deeds as is becoming of you.
For the peace of humanity the divine Hint sent you;
bring into action the coming of your love toward those who are
    divided.

135   I have heard the news about you, which went out on the earth, and the
    rebellious ones feared;
and I went out so as to witness the revealed truth through experience.
By the name of your power I heard that people are chasing out
    demons;
and I came to receive the good news of your name and to bring it to the
    demons.
The tyrannical demon entered and shut himself up in the soul of my
    daughter;

140   he assaulted (her) with ruthlessness in order to rob her life's vitality.
With no mercy he shakes her body and leads astray her soul,
and if your commandment does not reach her, her life will vanish.
Send your Hint swiftly as a messenger,
and let it reprimand the devil before he attempts to shed blood.

145   Give me the mark of the name of your power, I will show it to him,
and behold I am as anxious as a mother whose birth pangs have over-
    powered her.
Write a letter and sign it with the power of your help,
and if he sees it, he will no longer flout your commandment."

13. Cf. Gen 9:26.
14. Or "Let us repay."

Narsai, *On the Canaanite Woman*

The disciples beseech Jesus and his delay

| | With a wailing voice, the daughter of Canaan begged, |
| 150 | and the All Knower, as if he did not hear, put her off.[15] |

With a wailing voice, the daughter of Canaan begged,

150   and the All Knower, as if he did not hear, put her off.[15]

The disciples were astonished at the boldness of her request, at how
  much she asked,

and they approached him and persuaded the healer to send her away
  with the power of his help:

"Give her a medicine of the word of your mouth as you usually do,

and let her go and heal the pain (caused by) the demon who torments
  her daughter."

155   The master answered to his disciples wisely:

"I have only been sent to heal the sons of Jacob.

The sheep who went astray from Israel I have come to seek,[16]

so that they may return and enter the fold of life of the name of the
  creator.

For it is not suitable to give the bread of the free ones

160   to the Canaanites, voracious dogs, who have not been sated with
  iniquity."[17]

The Canaanite woman's response

The daughter of Ham heard that the master of the house called
  her "dog,"

and she grasped the hope that she too would live among the rank of
  the dogs.

The woman who was lost saw the Lord of the flock who visited his
  sheep,

and she hastened to enter the fold of his sweet words.

165   She saw that the dogs also search for food just like the heirs,

and wisely she asked the master of the house for food:

"Yes, it is true and you spoke well, good master;[18]

I am a dog, and I am not worthy of the name of heir.

Yes, yours is the freedom of the free ones,

---

15. Matt 15:23.
16. Matt 15:24.
17. Matt 15:26; Mark 7:27.
18. Matt 15:27; Mark 7:28.

170 yet yours are also the sinners, the peaceful dogs.

Give food to the free ones as they deserve,

and let the dogs live from the crumbs of their tables.

Allow me to live from your aid among the ranks of the dogs,

just as you allow to live the mute creatures along with those who speak.

175 Grant me that I be worthy of the small remainder from your gift,

for there is no one among the created things who does not live from
   the treasure of your love.

Grant me that I receive my vital sustenance along with the silent ones,

and I will live in grace as all the creatures that your Hint sustains."

The victory of the Canaanite woman

O wisdom brought forth by a heart lost in error;

180 and (this heart) has learned and now teaches how to converse wisely.

O knowledge proceeding from a mind mired in sin,

and rather than deceit (this mind) spoke truth before the All Knower.

O mind aged in the service of iniquity,

which has longed to engage with spiritual things not seen by it before.

185 Her modesty and her faith the All Knower regarded with wonder,

and he revealed and uncovered before the eyes of the onlookers the
   truth of her soul.[19]

It is not only now that he saw her and looked upon her with wonder as
   one not knowing,

for her faith had been seen by him well before she spoke.

On her he looked before she fashioned the sound of (her) petition,

190 and he had heard the words of her mouth and of her thoughts.

He knew that the sweet fragrance of his Hint was going to heal the pain
   of her daughter,

and it was clear to him that he was going to persecute the demon with
   the power of his help.

It was not that he tried her by delaying and not listening to her words,

(but) the truth of her love[20] he wanted to reveal to those who did
   not know.

195 He certainly did not reject her or send away from his flock

the sheep that cried out for the love of the Shepherd of all.

19. Lines 185–86 are missing from V.
20. V has "his love."

Not as one unwilling to heal did he turn away and remain silent,
but he (wanted) people to gain boldness when asking for mercy.
By her boldness he taught everyone to be bold in (asking for) his aid,

200 and not to grow weak if one does not receive (aid) quickly.
By his delay he showed favor for the circumcised people
who took pride in being the household of the name of the creator.
He shut the door for the murmuring of the mouth of the bold ones
      (who would argue):
Lo, he abandoned the sons of Abraham and visited the pagans.

205 He considered the hateful seed of their thoughts,
and he uprooted it beforehand, not allowing it to grow and bear fruit.
He knew that if he would answer the daughter of Canaan,
they would argue with him: Why did he have pity on a servant of
      demons?
He also knew that the woman's love was true,

210 and that she would not give up however much he would turn away and
      not answer her.
On this pretext his Hint did not answer swiftly,
so that he would reveal her truth and rebuke the pride of those uncir-
      cumcised in their heart.
The sound of her words was more pleasing to him than any
      other sounds,
and he was expecting her to continue and sing (even) more
      plaintive sounds.

215 By his delay he aroused the honest heart
to play upon the harp of the mouth (and produce) even more sounds of
      its petition.
By her petition he incited the (Jewish) people and taught the peoples
to see the light of faith in the daughter of darkness.
She was from a nation that the demons had deprived of understanding,

220 and as soon as she turned toward him, he gladdened with her light
      those who were in darkness.
As a torch her mouth contained the truth of her soul,
and it surpassed the sphere of the sun in brightness.
Her voice became a herald in the ears of everyone:
Come all who are in need, utter sounds (of petition), and receive aid.

225 The Lord of the house saw that she was committed to live and to
      give life,
and he made her voice into a guide toward reward.

Jesus proclaims his victory

With the sound of his reply he revealed the reward in the hereafter,
(explaining) how he enriches the one who asks without despair.
"O woman, very great is your faith;[21]

230 and the whole world does not stand comparison with the truth of
   your love.
Your mind seized a strong power against the evil one,
and you are not overpowered by the strong one who wages war
   against you.
Wise is your heart and shrewd is your inclination to contend,
and no one knows how to engage in battle more than you.

235 Subtle is your thinking and skilled is your mind to distinguish rightly,
and there is no bird whose wing is as swift as your emotions.
There is no athlete who knows how to embark upon the contest as well
   as you do,
and no archer who aims at the target as well as your endurance does.
Because your love endured and the voice of its entreaty has not
   grown weak,

240 behold, I pay your wage for the toils of your faith.
Because you have been patient and knocked on the door of
   divine mercy,
behold, I am opening the door to your voice: enter and take delight!
Because you counted yourself among the class of dogs, a dumb nature,
behold, I extend a fragment of mercy to your hunger.

245 Because your inclination distinguished wisely and called me 'Lord,'
behold, I ascribe to your lost condition the name of the heirs.
Because you desired and longed ardently to be a lamb in the flock of
   my sheep,
behold, I imprint the seal of my lordship on your mind.
Because you had faith and believed firmly that my aid would be able to
   chase away demons,

250 behold, I am confirming in deeds the truth of your soul.
Behold, I write down the aiding power that is hidden in my words,
and I am sealing it with the hidden Hint, and I am giving (it) to you.
Go and show to the impure demon the seal of my being,
and behold, he will be terrified and will leave his weapon and will
   flee naked.

21. Matt 15:28; Mark 7:29.

255 Go and tell him that Jesus said: Go out from your dwelling place,
and go (and) be pained in the desert far removed from humanity.
Go and inform the overthrower of humanity of his downfall:
behold, torn down is the height of the deceitful building that you built
on earth.
Go and bring the good news to the killer of humanity,
260 for lo, people have come to life through a man whose name is Jesus.
Go and explain to him the power of the meaning of my precious name,
for the name of Jesus is a savior of humankind and an overthrower of
demons.
Go and tell him: behold the king has gone out after his own,
return those whom you held captive and give an account of those who
were lost.
265 Take for yourself the edict that the divine hand signed,
and go and show to the tyrannical servant the annulment of his power.
And yes, true and irrevocable is the power of my words,
behold, the words are followed by the deeds, even while they are
distant.
Behold the demon went out even before seeing the truth in that which
was revealed,
270 and he left his dwelling place as a fugitive before the strong one.
Go and test the truth of my words through experience,
and receive the proof of the great power of my proper authority.
Behold, my will has issued a judicial decision concerning his
wickedness,
and he has begun punishing himself by departing.
275 Behold, he has heard the report that I am threatening his
rebellious nature,
and he cried and howled even before the terrible punishment
reaches him.
Behold, the body that he tortured in his bitterness has come to
rest now,
and the mind that he led astray by his perturbation has been
set straight."

The defeat of the hater of humanity

The king from afar uttered a threat concerning the rebellious one,
280 and the Hint went before the bearer of the writings.

While the messenger was waiting for the king to sign (it),
the deceitful one departed so that his fraud would not be exposed
      openly.
Who taught the evil demon the revealed truth?
While the verdicts were still far away, he declared himself guilty.

285   Who revealed to the all-deceiver that he would be exposed?
He concealed himself from shame before the eyes of everyone.
Who revealed to the cunning wolf, destroyer of humankind:
behold, the son of David has gone out to hunt you down just as his
      father did?
Who showed to the deceitful fox the pathway of the lion?

290   He slipped through the door so as not to be confounded by the power
      of his voice.
The Hint of power upset his heart and weakened his power,
and fear upset him, and he left the cultivated land and came to love the
      desert.
With weeping and lamenting his mouth was filled while he was leaving,
for he saw how harsh the exile was into which he was thrown.

295   In the dwelling place of people he enjoyed himself with his dirty tricks,
and as he saw that he was driven out, he gave up and despaired, for
      there was no consolation.
He saw that the daughter of Ham, a slave, was set free from his slavery,
and he knew that the yoke of his toil was removed from mortals.
In the Canaanite woman he learned and it was revealed to him how
      great his dishonor was,

300   for if the daughter of the cursed one broke his yoke, who would take
      account of him?
Great is the terror that took hold of the evil one in this matter,
and the feeble rib overcame his wiles and trampled his pride
      underfoot.
Great is the wonder that she performed through endurance,
for she engaged in battle with the strong one, and she was not defeated.

305   A great war did the daughter of Ham wage with the rebellious one,
and as arrows did she shoot at him words of faith.
O the strong one who was overpowered by the voice in which he
      took pride
when he heard the sounding voice inside paradise.
O the courageous one who was defeated by the power that he de-
      feated in Eden,

310   and the hands that he bound by the eating of the fruit bound
          him (now).
     With the eating of the fruit he bound Eve who obeyed his word,
     and the fruit returned from inside her limbs and trampled him on
          the earth.
     With the weapon of fruit the guilty one triumphed and made
          Adam guilty,
     and in the son of Adam he was defeated and exposed, for he did
          not triumph.
315   Upon the harp of Eve he played his tunes of deathly bitterness,
     and in the daughter of Eve he heard the tidings of the annulment
          of death.
     In Eden he composed joyful tunes as one victorious,
     and here he lamented in a voice of groans as one condemned.
     With harsh suffering he was groaning, while he heard
320   that everyone was giving blessing to Mary for the fruit that she bore.
     He lamented as for a dead one, the mourning for whom is bitter
     while he was fleeing from the sound of the name of David's son.
     He heard the voice of the woman when she was calling out after Jesus:
     "Son of David, save the daughter of your house from the strong one."
325   Seemly was her voice when she was asking for mercy for her daughter,
     and very hateful it was for Satan, the hater of humanity.
     At the sound of her sighs the crowds on high marveled,[22]
     and the rank of the demons was saddened and was in mourning beyond
          measure.
     As long as she held the name of Jesus on the tip of her tongue,
330   the troubled demon was intensely embittered.
     As long as she prayed with boldness for aid,
     the demon wept and lamented his ruin.

Praise for the Canaanite woman

     O the humble one who gained the power to prevail over demons,
     while those who overpower humans with desires trembled at
          her voice.
335   O the subjected one who was enslaved to false worship;
     she broke herself free from the servitude of the harsh master.

---

22. That is, the angels in heaven.

O the destitute one the dwelling of whose soul the demons had
     destroyed,
while her voice appeased the temple of her daughter that was ruined.
O you, merciful mother, how great is your love
340   that you donned armor against the evil one who had captured your
     daughter!
O you, woman, who through the sacrifice of your faith
pleased the king and reversed your captivity from the captor.
O how much you believed, and how much you loved, and how much
     you endured;
and the strength of your soul did not weaken in its confidence.
345   O nature, how much is the order of its bondage preserved!
For (nature) restored and requited the love that is proper to human
     nature.
Nature goaded the Canaanite woman like a sting,
and she suffered much for the daughter of her womb whom the
     demon harassed.
The crafty serpent pierced her daughter with his deceitful sting,
350   and the poison flew into the soul of her daughter and into her mind.
As her own pain did she regard the pain of the daughter of her limbs,
and she was not comforted until the adversary departed into
     the desert.
With great mourning she sat as with a dead person
as long as the rebellious one raised his voice in the temple of her
     daughter.
355   With weeping and lamentation her mouth was filled at all times
when she heard the disturbed sounds that the demon chanted.
With grievous pain she was beaten by night and by day,
while seeing the twisting of the body and the distress of the soul.[23]
Her mouth was not quiet from bitter wailing
360   until the body of her daughter was quiet, and her limbs were calm.
The flow of tears from her eyes and from her thoughts did not cease
until she saw that the source of the bitterness of the evil one dried up.
She did not take off the armor of lamenting from her mind
until she heard that voice: the demon has gone.
365   She did not think that her daughter was among the living even though
     she was alive
until Jesus's voice raised her as from the grave.

23. That is, of her daughter.

By his voice he raised her from sickness and from the mouth of
    the demon,

and she returned and saw the present life and the eternal life.

The medicine of life he threw in her soul like a seed,

370   and the fruit of faith blossomed within her mind.

She came to life from the death of the demon's destruction, she and her
    daughter,

and she donned the garment of incorruptible faith.

Two benefits did the one (who once was) in error gain through
    her faith:

the deliverance from the demon and belonging to the household of the
    name of the creator.

375   Through the stick with which the demon punished her daughter she
    gained understanding,

and she learned the way to journey on the path toward the hidden one.

Also to the demon a double pain was added:

while he thought that he was (the one) chastising, instead he became
    the one being punished.

In the trap that he set the rebellious one fell unknowingly,

380   and his deceit returned upon his mind as it was written.[24]

He wanted to pacify his own dwelling place and to destroy humans,

and the Hint destroyed his deceitful building and pacified humans.

With the filth of his wrath he wanted to undo the sweetness of peace,

and peace shut out his bitterness from (the world of) mortals.

385   As with wine he intoxicated them with his fury,

and once he experienced spiritual drink, he forgot its must.

As slaves he enslaved the earthly ones,

and one from them rose up and set them free from his slavery.

As contemptible ones he mocked the sons of the earth,

390   and a bodily one raised his voice, and he trembled before him.

He was comfortable and quiet in the dwelling place of humans like
    a king;

and he heard the report of the ruler of people, and he shook and
    was terrified.

Deathly birth pangs seized him at once like a woman giving birth,

when he saw people driving out demons in the name of a man.

---

24. Narsai may intend the narrative of Gen 3 to be understood here.

The demons bemoan their loss

395 "What is this?"—one demon asks his fellow demon—
"for lo, our armies are in panic through the voice of a man.
When was the army of the strong ones overcome by the weak,
as now the earthly ones have persecuted the spiritual ones?
When did those sick in body heal their limbs,
400 as garments of a body are healing the sick bodies?
When did a slave set free the slaves from enslavement,
as now Jesus gives freedom to people?
Perhaps that which is written concerning a human has come to
fulfillment,
namely that he would tread upon the head of our forces when he will
be triumphant.[25]
405 Perhaps it is the time of the completion of the words of Balaam
the priest,
and this is the one whom he called the star of light that will enlighten
humans.[26]
Perhaps true is the saying of the words of that spiritual person,
who announced his conception and called him Lord and the Son of the
most high.[27]
What is happening in this time has never happened before,
410 that the people cry out in the name of a human and the demons shake.
It has never been heard that the dead lived without petition
as this one raises the dead as from sleep."
These things they said, the haters of humanity, one with his neighbor
for they saw a human was bringing the people back from their side.
415 They saw that the deceitful nets of the devices of their troublemaking
were cut to pieces;
the prey escaped that they had hunted from Adam until now.
They saw even a small bird, weak of wing, broke the snare,
and it flew and went beyond the fear of their injuries.
In the Canaanite woman they saw their own downfall,
420 how the weak rib prevailed against the might of the demons!

25. Ps 91:13 (90:13 LXX).
26. Num 24:17.
27. Luke 1:32.

Final exhortation

Come! Feeble race that was defeated by sin, take courage
and don spiritual weapons, join the battle and win!
In your mind hold the shield of faith,
and crown your intellect with the helmet of the salvation of life.
425 Secretly arm your thoughts with wisdom,
and learn how to contend with the spiritual ones.
He is not corporeal, the hater who fights against your lives,
but rather (he is) a spirit who engages in battle with hidden impulses.
Prepare spiritual weapons to confront his concealment,
430 wage war and conquer by means of the endurance of your minds.
Guard us with your living sign so that the evil one will see it and
depart!

6. Simeon of Beth Arsham, *Letter on the Ḥimyarite Martyrs*

Introduction and translation by J. Edward Walters

T hough the *Letter on the Ḥimyarite Martyrs* is written in Syriac, the content of this document shifts the geographic focus from Mesopotamia, the home of Syriac Christianity, to the southwestern corner of the Arabian Peninsula, in what is today Yemen.[1] An opening title attributes this text to Simeon of Beth Arsham, a sixth-century bishop about whom little is known aside from his strong opposition to East Syrian "Nestorian" theology.[2] However, as David Taylor demonstrates, the question of the authorship of this letter, along with other related materials, is difficult to answer with certainty.[3] There are a remarkable number of sources for the events surrounding the persecution of Christians in the area of Najran, a city located on the modern-day border of Yemen and Saudi Arabia, in the early sixth century, and the present document is an integral piece of that constellation of sources. In fact, the letter translated here is one of two Syriac letters that provide details about these events. The first letter was published by I. Guidi in 1881, and the second was discovered and published by I. Shahīd in 1971. While Shahīd strongly advocates for the authentic authorship of Simeon for both letters,[4] others challenge these claims, particularly for the second letter.[5] Furthermore, there is also an expanded narrative of these events in a separate Syriac work known as the

---

1. For a brief overview of the spread of Christianity into the Arabian Peninsula, see Françoise Briquel-Chatonnet, "L'expansion du christianisme en Arabie: l'apport des sources syriaques," *Semitica et Classica* 3 (2010): 177–87.

2. For more on Simeon (or Shem'un), see L. Van Rompay, "Shem'un of Beth Arsham," in *GEDSH*, 376.

3. David G. K. Taylor, "A Stylistic Comparison of the Syriac Ḥimyarite Martyr Texts Attributed to Simeon of Beth Arsham," in *Juifs et chrétiens en Arabie aux Ve et VIe siècles: Regards croisés sour les sources*, ed. J. Beaucamp, F. Briquel-Chatonnet, and C. J. Robin (Paris: Association des amis du Centre d'histoire et civilisation de Byzance, 2010), 143–76.

4. Ifran Shahīd, *The Martyrs of Najrān: New Documents*, Subsidia Hagiographica 49 (Brussels: Société des Bollandistes, 1971).

5. See, for example, Jacques Ryckmans, "A Confrontation of the Main Hagiographic Accounts of the Najrān Persecution," in *Arabian Studies in Honour of Mahmoud Ghul: Symposium at Yarmouk University, December 8–11, 1984*, ed. Moawiyah M. Ibrahim (Wiesbaden: Harrassowitz, 1989), 113–33. Ifran Shahīd responds to Ryckmans in the same volume: "Further Re-

Book of the Ḥimyarites.[6] A shorter version of Simeon's letter is preserved in the *Ecclesiastical History of Pseudo-Zachariah* and the *Zuqnin Chronicle*.[7] Beyond these Syriac sources, other martyrdom accounts related to the same events exist in Greek, Arabic, and Ethiopic. In addition to these literary sources, a number of Old South Arabian inscriptions provide context for the story.[8]

The events of the text are set against a complicated political backdrop: the small kingdom of Ḥimyar, located in the region of modern-day Yemen, was ruled by a Jewish king named Yūsuf Asʾar Yathʾar.[9] While Yūsuf is the first known Jewish king of Ḥimyar, it is clear from numerous inscriptions that the region of Ḥimyar embraced monotheism in the second half of the fourth century.[10] Meanwhile, across the strait known as the Bab al-Mandab, the Christian kingdom of Aksum (Ethiopia) stood as a rival and political threat to Ḥimyar. In the early sixth century, around 523 CE, Yūsuf and his army besieged the city of Najran and began persecuting their Christian community, likely as a provocation toward their Aksumite rivals. If the act was indeed a provocation, then it was successful because the Aksumite king, Kaleb Ella Aṣbeḥa, launched an invasion of southern Arabia, ultimately defeating the Ḥimyarites and installing a Christian king over the region.

---

flections on the Sources for the Martyrs of Najrān" (161–72). Taylor asserts that there is "no common authorship" between any of the Najran materials; "Stylistic Comparison," 172.

6. A. Moberg, *The Book of the Himyarites: Fragments of a Hitherto Unknown Syriac Work* (Lund: Gleerup, 1924).

7. Taylor argues that this short version of the letter, which he calls *Letter C*, may in fact be the "most original form" of Simeon's letter, which was then expanded into *Letter 1*—the document translated here; "Stylistic Comparison," 166.

8. In addition to Taylor's "Stylistic Comparison," see also Luk Van Rompay, "The Martyrs of Najran: Some Remarks on the Nature of the Sources," in *Studia Paulo Naster oblata*, vol. 2: *Orientalia antiqua*, ed. J. Quaegebeur, Orientalia Lovaniensia Analecta, 13 (Leuven: Peeters, 1982), 301–9; and Norbert Nebes, "The Martyrs of Najrān and the End of the Ḥimyar: On the Political History of South Arabia in the Early Sixth Century," in *The Qurʾān in Context: Historical and Literary Investigations into the Qurʾānic Milieu*, ed. Angelika Neuwirth, Nicolai Sinai, and Michael Marx (Leiden: Brill, 2010), 27–59.

9. Also known as Yūsuf Dhu Nuwas; for more information see C. J. Robin, "Joseph, dernier roi de Ḥimyar (de 522 à 525, ou une des années suivantes)," *Jerusalem Studies on Arabic and Islam* 32 (2008): 1–124.

10. The bibliography here is extensive, so I note only a few resources: Iwona Gajda, "Les débuts du monothéisme en Arabie du Sud," *Journal Asiatique* 290 (2002): 611–30; Gajda, "Remarks on Monotheism in Ancient South Arabia," in *Islam and Its Past: Jahiliyya, Late Antiquity, and the Qurʾān*, ed. C. Bakhos and M. Cook (Oxford: Oxford University Press, 2017), 247–56; and Christian Julien Robin, "Le judaïsme de Ḥimyar," *Arabia* 1 (2003): 97–172.

Simeon's letter does refer to the broader geopolitical events, but it focuses on telling the stories of the Najran martyrs. In particular, these events are narrated through a letter written from the king of the Himyarites (the text does not give the name of King Yusūf) to King Mundhir of Ḥirta,[11] located far to the north of Ḥimyar in modern-day Iraq.[12] In this letter, the king of the Ḥimyarites boasts about what they have done to the Christians and urges Mundhir to do the same. Other stories about the martyrs of Najran in Simeon's letter are then relayed by another person who was sent to Najran to report on those events. Thus, Simeon's "letter" is itself a pastiche of sources, which may suggest that it is more of an editorial compilation than a single-author text, likely expanded from a shorter original letter.

Bibliography

Text and Editions

Guidi, I. "La lettera di Simeone vescovo di Bêth-Aršâm sopra I martiri omeriti." *Reale Accademia dei Lincei: Memorie della classe di scienze morali, storiche e filologiche* 3a.7 (1881): 471–515 (Syriac text and Italian translation).

Studies

Beaucamp, J., F. Briquel-Chatonnet, and C. J. Robin, eds. *Juifs et chrétiens en Arabie aux Ve et VIe siècles: Regards croisés sour les sources.* Paris: Association des amis du Centre d'histoire et civilisation de Byzance, 2010.

Bowersock, Glen. W. *The Throne of Adulis.* Oxford: Oxford University Press, 2013.

Nebes, Norbert. "The Martyrs of Najrān and the End of the Ḥimyar: On the Political History of South Arabia in the Early Sixth Century." Pages 27–59 in *The Qur'ān in Context: Historical and Literary Investigations into the Qur'ānic Milieu.* Edited by Angelika Neuwirth, Nicolai Sinai, and Michael Marx. Leiden: Brill, 2010. This is a revision and English translation of an earlier article by the same author: "Die Märtyrer von Nagrān und das Ende der Himyar: Zur politischen Geschichte Südarabiens im frühen sechsten Jahrhundert." *Aethiopica* 11 (2008): 7–40.

11. This is Al-Mundhir (III) ibn al-Nuʿman.

12. The late ancient kingdom of Ḥirta was ruled by the Lakhmids, who played a pivotal role in the Roman-Persian wars, generally as a client state of the Sassanian Empire.

Robin, Christian Julien. "Joseph, dernier roi de Ḥimyar (de 522 à 525, ou une des années suivantes)." *Jerusalem Studies on Arabic and Islam* 32 (2008): 1–124.

Ryckmans, Jacques. "Les rapports de dépendance entre les récits hagiographiques relatifs à la persécution de Himyarites." *Le Muséon* 100 (1987): 297–305.

Shahīd, Ifran. *The Martyrs of Najrān: New Documents*. Subsidia Hagiographica 49. Brussels: Société des Bollandistes, 1971.

Van Rompay, Luk. "The Martyrs of Najran: Some Remarks on the Nature of the Sources." Pages 301–9 in *Studia Paulo Naster oblata*. Vol. 2: *Orientalia antiqua*. Edited by J. Quaegebeur. Orientalia Lovaniensia Analecta 13. Leuven: Peeters, 1982.

TRANSLATION

Letter on the Ḥimyarite Martyrs

From the letter, that is, the story about the Ḥimyarite martyrs, of Simeon, bishop of the Persian Christians, which was sent from Ḥirta of Beth Nuʿman.

Again we will make known to your love, that on the twentieth day of latter Kanun of the year 835 of Alexander,[13] we departed from Ḥirta of Nuʿman with the eminent priest Mar Abraham bar Euphoros, who was sent from Justin,[14] the king of the Romans to Mundhir, king of Ḥirta, so that he might make peace with Rome. We also wrote about [Abraham] in our previous letter, for we and all the believers with us received his grace, because in every way he helps the cause of the believers. He gives permission for those previous things and also the things that we are writing now.

For when we traveled in the desert to the south and to the east, traveling ten days, we came upon King Mundhir across from the mountains that are called the mountains of sand and that in the Arab language of that place are called Ramla.[15] And when we entered Mundhir's camp, the pagan Tayyaye and Maʿdaye[16] met

---

13. That is, January 20, 524 CE.
14. That is, the Roman Emperor Justin I.
15. Or perhaps Ramleh, or Ramallah.
16. These are the names of two Arab tribes.

us and said to us: "What is there for you to do from today and thereafter? Look, your Messiah has been expelled by the Romans, the Persians, the Ḥimyarites, and from every place." And when Mar Abraham the priest, and also we who were with him, had been mocked with these and similar insults by the pagan Tayyaye and Maʿdaye, great distress came upon us, and there was great suffering for all the true believers. For in our vicinity, an envoy came from the king of Ḥimyar[17] to Mundhir, king of Ḥirta, and he brought a letter that was completely full of boasting, in which he made known to [Mundhir] the wicked things he had done to the Christians in Najran, a Ḥimyarite city.

He wrote to him as follows:

The king whom the Ethiopians[18] established in our region has died, and now that the winter has come, the Ethiopians are not able to travel to our region. So, I have taken charge over the whole region of the Ḥimyarites, and before anything else, I planned to do this: I would destroy all the Christians through-out the whole region of the Ḥimyarites, or they would deny the Messiah and become Jews like us. First, [I went after] the Ethiopians who were left in our region, because they were guarding that church that they believed they had built in our region. I was able to stir them up and capture them, and I killed all of them—there were 280 men, monks and laypeople—and I turned their church into our synagogue. Afterward I led my people (120,000 soldiers), and I went to the city of Najran and encamped by it for no small number of days. And when I saw that [Najran] was subdued in the battle, I gave them a word of oath that no harm would come to them if they would hand over the city to me willingly. And in this manner, they were subjugated and they opened the gates of the city.

All of their leaders came out to me, but it seemed to me that it was not right that I should be truthful with the Christians. First, I demanded that they bring to me their gold and their silver and all their possessions; and when they brought [it] to me, I took it from them. I [then] demanded that they show me Pawla, their bishop. They told me that he was dead, but I did not believe them until they showed me his grave. I dug up his bones and burned them with fire, and I also burned their church, along with their priests and everyone I found inside it. Afterward, I demanded that they renounce the Messiah and the cross and that they become Jews like us. But they did not want to. So, I said to them: "Look, now the Romans know that the Messiah was a human; why do you go astray after him? Why [do you think] you are better than the Romans?" And

17. Though he is unnamed here, this is the Jewish king of Ḥimyar, Yusūf Dhu Nuwas.
18. The Syriac text uses the word "Cushites" throughout to refer to the Ethiopian kingdom located just across the Red Sea from Ḥimyar, so I translate it "Ethiopians" for clarity.

we said to them: "We do not demand that you renounce God, the maker of heaven and earth, nor that you worship the sun and the moon and the rest of the luminaries, or any one of the created things; but that you renounce Jesus, who thinks himself God, and that you should say only that he is a human and not God." In many ways we disturbed them, but they did not want to renounce the Messiah, and they did not want to say that he was [only] human. Rather, in their madness they said: "He is God and he is the Son of the merciful one." And they chose to die for him. Their leader spoke vigorously against us, and as he deserved, so he was rewarded, and all their leaders were killed. The rest of them fled and were hidden, and we still have not found them. And we commanded that they be killed wherever they were found, or that they should renounce the Messiah and become Jews with us.

Afterward we brought some of their women and said to them: "Look, you saw with your own eyes how your men blasphemed and said that the Messiah is God and the son of Adonai, and look, they were all killed! But as for you now, spare yourselves and your sons and your daughters; renounce the Messiah and the cross, become Jews like us, and you will live, but if not, you will surely die." They blasphemed even more than their husbands, saying: "The Messiah is God and he is the Son of the merciful one, and it is in him that we believe, and we venerate the cross; we will die because of him. Far be it from us to renounce him or that we should live after our husbands, but with them and like them we will die because of the Messiah." We demanded that they say the Messiah was [only] human and they would live, but they did not want to say [it], and they chose death for themselves because of that deceiver and sorcerer. Those women among them who were called monks, we saw them arguing with those whose husbands had died and they were saying: "It is right that we should be killed first after our husbands"; and they ran and consulted with one another about which of them should die first. And when we heard them arguing, and we saw them consulting one another about which of them should die first, we laughed at their madness because of how they went astray after a man who dared to blaspheme and regarded himself God. We marveled, that even the children they bore, who did not know anything, were being raised in this deception. And when we saw that they were contending with each other in their madness thus, we gave the order, and they were all killed.

One of them, because of her stature, because of her family, and because of her beauty, we were thinking perhaps she might take pity for herself and for her daughter, and she might be persuaded to renounce the Messiah. So we commanded that she not be killed, and thus she entered the city, where she became distressed that she had not died. On the third day we sent [word] to her that if she would renounce the Messiah, she would live, and if she would not renounce [him], she would die. When she heard this word, she ran and came out to the marketplace in the middle of the city, and according to what we had heard about the woman, no one had ever seen her face, and she did not walk in the daytime in the city until that day in which she stood up in the city with her head bared. And according to these things they told me that happened there, she cried out, saying:

My fellow women of Najran, Christians, Jews, and pagans, listen! You know me, that I am a Christian, and you know my family and my tribe, who I am, and whose daughter I am. I have gold and silver, slaves and servants, fields and produce. I do not need anything. And now, my husband was killed because of the Messiah. If I wanted to have a husband, I would not lack a husband. Look, I am saying to you that on this very day, I have forty thousand embossed gold coins sitting in my treasury, aside from my husband's treasury and aside from the gold, silver, jewels, pearls, and decorations that adorn me. There are women among you who have seen them in my house and you know, my companions, that a woman has no days of joy like the days of her wedding feast, and from that point on [there is] grief and groaning. When she gives birth to sons, she gives birth in sickness and wailing; and when she is deprived of sons, there is grief and sadness. And when she buries [her] sons, she buries in mourning and lamentation. But I, from today on, am saved from all of them. In the days of my first wedding feast, I was joyful. And now, my virgin daughters, because they do not have a husband, I have adorned them for the Messiah.

Look at me, my companions, for this is the second time you have seen my face: first at my wedding banquet, and now this is the second. With my face revealed before all of you, I came to my first fiancé; and now with my face revealed, I go to my Lord Messiah, my God, and my daughters, as he came to us. Look at me, my companions; look at me and my daughters, for I am not inferior to you in beauty, and in it I am going to my Lord Messiah, uncorrupted by the apostasy of the Jews. For my beauty will be a witness for me before my Lord, which could not deceive me in the sin of renouncing the Messiah. My gold, my silver, and all the jewels of my adornment, as well as my slaves and attendants, and everything that I have, they will be a testimony for me, that I have not loved them, and I have not renounced the Messiah, my Lord. And now, look, the king sends a message to me, that I should renounce the Messiah and live. But I reply to him that if I renounce the Messiah, I will die, but if I die because of the Messiah, I will live. Far be it from me, my companions, that I should renounce the Messiah, my God, in whom I believe and in whose name I was baptized and I had my daughters baptized. I venerate his cross, and I will die because of him, I and my daughters, just as he died for us. Look, the gold of the earth is abandoned for the earth, and anyone who seeks to have my gold will have [it], and anyone who seeks to have my silver and ornamental jewelry will have it. Look, everything is abandoned, for I am going to receive the Messiah, my Lord instead of it. Blessed are you, my companions, if you hear my words; blessed are you, my companions, if you know the truth, that is: because of him, I and my daughters will die; blessed are you if you love the Messiah. Blessed am I! Blessed am I and my daughters, because of the blessing to which we are going! Therefore, may tranquility and peace come to the people of the Messiah. May the blood of these, my brothers and sisters who were killed because of the Messiah, become a wall for this city if it abides with the Messiah, my Lord. Look, with my face uncovered, I am leaving this city where I lived as a temporary dwelling place, so that I may go with my daughters to another city, and there I will betroth them. Pray for me, my companions, that my Lord Messiah may receive me and forgive me for being alive these three days after the father of my daughters!

We heard the sound of lament from this city to the extent that all of us were disturbed, because we did not know why the women were wailing. And when the men we had sent for came and told us all these things she spoke boldly before the whole city, and that because of her the women were wailing, we wanted to kill them, because they allowed her to deliver this whole speech and deceive the city with her sorcery. Afterward, she came out of the city, with her head uncovered, like a mad woman, with her daughters, and she came and stood before me, with her face uncovered and unashamed, holding her daughters' hands, while they were adorned as if for a wedding feast. She loosened the braids in her hair and wrapped them around her hands, then she straightened her neck, stuck out her throat, and bent her head before me, while crying out: "I am a Christian, and my daughters too, and because of the Messiah we will die. Cut off our heads so that we can go and catch up with our brothers, our sisters, and the father of my daughters."

And after all this insanity, again I contended with her and provoked her to renounce the Messiah and say that he is only a human, but she did not want to say it. And one of her daughters even dared to insult us because she heard us saying to her mother that she should renounce the Messiah. And when I saw that there was no way that she would renounce the Messiah, I commanded, in order to produce terror for all the Christians, and they threw her on the ground.

And we commanded that her daughters be slaughtered and that their blood be poured into her mouth, and afterward that her head be cut off. So, that is what we did to her. Afterward, I commanded that they lift her up from the ground, and I asked her how the blood of her daughters tasted. And she, while in her madness, swore to that deceiver: "Like a pure, spotless offering, so it tasted in my mouth and in my soul." So, we commanded that her head be cut off. I swear to Adonai, the king of Israel, that I was saddened because of her beauty and [the beauty] of her daughters, but I was greatly astounded by her madness, at how she went astray after a sorcerer and deceiver, who dared to blaspheme and regard himself as God, and how she did not spare herself or her daughters.

As for the sons and daughters of those who were killed, it seemed to our chief priests and to us that what is written in the book of the law should be done to them, that "the son should not be punished for the sins of his father."[19] So we commanded that the children be left until they should come to maturity, and then, if they renounce the Messiah and become Jews, they will live. But if they do not, they will also die. Then, we divided them among our nobles.

We have written these things to your kingdom so that you may rejoice. Look, we have not left any Christians, not even one, in this land of ours; you also should do thus for you will cause all the Christians under your authority to fear you, just as also we have done in our domain. Because there are Jews under your authority, in every way be a help to them, and whatever is needed for your kingdom on account of this, send word to us so that we might send [it] to you.

All these things the king of Ḥimyar wrote to Mundhir, king of Ḥirta while they were there in the desert with the eminent priest Mar Abraham bar Euphoros, the same one mentioned above who was sent by Emperor Justin, along with the pure and holy Mar Sergis, bishop of Beth Raṣpa, so that he might make peace between the Persian Tayyaye and the Romans. And when these writings were read before Mundhir of Ḥirta and before many others, there were some things the ambassador of the Ḥimyarites said in mockery, while ridiculing and mocking the Christians and boasting (for those things by which the king of the Ḥimyarites was insulted by the blessed martyrs and by the illustrious Dawma and her daughters, all of these things the king of Ḥimyar did not write in his letter), but that ambassador told these things to the king, and in front of the Jews and pagans, then great distress came to all the Christians, and rejoicing came to the pagans and Jews. And we wrote these things from the letter to Mundhir, and from the words of the ambassador.

After this letter, which was sent from the king of the Ḥimyarites, was read

19. Cf. Deut 24:16.

before Mundhir, king of Ḥirta, about how the Christians who were there were killed, and what persecution and great affliction arose over them because of the name of the Messiah, this King Mundhir was enraged, and in mockery and contempt, he called all the free Christians of his dominion and said to them: "Look here, Christians, for I spoke to you and you did not listen, for I told you to abandon the Messiah but you did not want to. Now, abandon your dedication to the Messiah, for now you have heard what happened to those who did not renounce the Messiah, how the king of Ḥimyar killed and destroyed them, and [how] he burned their church. Look at how the Messiah was driven out by the Ḥimyarites, the Persians, and the Romans, yet you are not persuaded to abandon the Messiah. I am not better than the kings of the Persians and the Romans, who drove out and sent away the Christians, or [better] than the king of the Ḥimyarites, who killed and eradicated the Christians from his land. See how much I am telling you, yet you do not listen to me and you will not abandon the Messiah."

And when King Mundhir said these things before all his nobles,[20] one of the noble Christians, who was stirred up and very zealous, stood up and boldly said to the king: "It is not right for you to say such things, O king. It was not through your madness that we became Christians, for you advised us to abandon the Messiah and to renounce our Christianity. But we are Christians, and our parents and the parents of our parents." Then the king was enraged at him and said to him: "You dare to speak before me?" The faithful, noble one replied and said before the king: "I speak because of the fear of God, and I am not afraid. No one is able to prevent me, because my sword is not shorter than the others. For because I fear God, until death I will stand and fight, and I am not afraid." Then, when King Mundhir saw his courage, how he was not afraid to speak before him, the king was not able to say another thing to him, because of his family and because of his reputation. For he was a great man according to the world, one of the princes of Ḥirta.

And when they came from Ḥirta of Nuʿman, on the second day of the first week of the fast, we learned these things that were not written in the letter to Mundhir. For one of the Ḥimyarite believers came with a certain Christian envoy who was sent to Mundhir from that Christian king whom the Ethiopians installed in the region of Ḥimyar. And while they were in Ḥirta of Nuʿman, it was reported to them that the Christian king who had sent them had died. So, they hired a man from Ḥirta and sent him to Najran so that he could observe and learn the truth and bring a report back to them from Najran. So, this man went and brought the following report:

20. Or "free people."

When [the king] swore an oath to the Najranites and they opened the gates of the city and came out, they received him and handed the city over to him. He spoke falsely in his oaths, and he took their gold and silver, and he burned the bones of the bishop with fire, and he burned the church and the *bnay qyama*, and all the people he found within it. Then they brought all the important people before him—340 men—and he began to threaten the great and illustrious Harith bar Ka'b, who was their leader:

"Why did you want to rebel against me, and rely on that sorcerer and deceiver and think that you would escape from my hand? But now, have pity upon your old age and renounce him, that deceiver, and his cross, and you will live. But if you do not, you will surely die an awful death, you and your companions, and everyone who does not renounce the Messiah and his cross." The old man said to him: "Truly, I am distressed, along with all my Christian companions who are with me in the city, for I spoke to them and they did not listen to me. For I was prepared to come out against you for a fight and to contend with you on behalf of the name of the Messiah, so that either you would kill me or I would kill you. And I was confident in my Lord Messiah, that I would conquer you. But my companions did not allow me to do this. And again, I wanted to lead only my family and my servants and go out against you and contend with you, but the Christians seized the gates of the city, and they did not allow me to go out. And again I told them that they should protect the city and not open the gates for you, and I was confident in my Lord Messiah that the city would not be subdued by you, because it is not lacking in anything. And in this, again my companions did not listen to me. And when you sent them the oath, I counseled them not to believe you. And I told them that you spoke falsely and there is no truth in you. Yet, they were not persuaded to listen to me, and now in my old age you say to me that I should renounce the Messiah my God and become a Jew with you. I might not even live for a single hour, or a single day after I renounce (him), and you ask me to be made a stranger to my Lord Messiah in my old age?

Truly, you have not spoken as a king, nor behaved like a king. For a king who lies is not a king. I have seen many kings, but I have not seen kings who lie. I have authority over myself, and I do not lie in my authority toward the Messiah. Far be it from me that I should deny the Messiah God, for in him I have believed since my childhood, and in his name I was baptized. I venerate his cross, and because of him, I will die. And truly I am blessed, that the Messiah should find me worthy to die for him. Now I know that the Messiah loves me, because I have lived long in this world through the grace of my Lord Messiah, and I have lived well. I have not lacked anything, whether children, grandchildren, or family; my Lord Messiah has multiplied everything for me in this world. And in many battles I have conquered through the power of the Messiah, and in this again I will conquer through the power of the cross. I am also confident that my memory will not cease from this city or from my family. Now I know truly that I will not die forever, knowing and trusting that, as when a vine is pruned and its branches multiply, so also will our people, the Christians, multiply in this city. Do not boast in anything you have done. Look, I am telling you that this city will become great through Christianity, and this church that you burned with fire today will be rebuilt, and it will govern and command kings. And Christianity will rule and extinguish your Judaism, and it will pass through your kingdom and bring an end to your authority."

And when the splendid and illustrious old man said these things, he turned his back and said in a loud voice to the believers who were around him: "Did you hear, my brothers, what I said to this Jew?" And they all cried out: "We heard everything that you said, father!" And again he said to them: "Are these things true or not?" And they all cried out: "They are true and they are in the truth." And again he cried out and said to them: "What do you think? If perchance there is someone among you who is afraid of the sword and will renounce the Messiah, let them be separated from us." And they all cried out: "Far be it from us that we should renounce the Messiah! Take courage, father; take courage and do not be distressed by this, for all of us are like you, and we will die with you on behalf of the Messiah. And there is no one among us who will remain after you in life." And again he cried out and said: "Hear me, all you Christians, pagans, and Jews, if anyone, even my wife, or any of my sons and daughters, or any from my tribe and family, renounces the Messiah, and remains living with this Jew, they are renounced, and they are not from my tribe or my family, and I will have no part or association with them in anything. And everything that I have will go to that church that is going to be built in this city after us. But if my wife, or any of my sons or daughters remains living in any way at all, while not renouncing the Messiah, everything will be theirs, [except for] three properties that the church will choose, they will belong to the church."

Having said these things before all the people, the old man turned toward the king and said to him: "Look, you have heard all these things, so, do not again ask me anything in this matter. Far be it from us that we should renounce the Messiah our God. Look, therefore, there is nothing that prevents us from dying because of the Messiah. The moment of eternal life is here! Renounced is everyone who renounces the Messiah; renounced is everyone who does not confess that the Messiah is God and the Son of God; renounced is everyone who does not confess the cross of God; renounced is everyone who agrees with you and your fellow Jews. Look, we stand before you, do whatever you want to do. Truly I tell you that I used to drink the first cup at a banquet before my companions, and now this cup of death because of the Messiah is mixed for me first. Look, I sign myself and all my companions, as is our custom in the living form of the cross, in the name of the Father, and the Son, and the Holy Spirit." And they all cried out: "Amen and amen." And they signed themselves in the form of the cross, and they all cried out: "Renounced is everyone who renounces the Messiah! Take courage, father, take courage! Look, Abraham, the head of our ancestors, your elder, is expecting you. Renounced is everyone who renounces the Messiah and remains living after you."

When the king saw that there was no way that they would renounce the Messiah, he gave the command that they be brought to the gorge that is called Wadia, and he commanded that their heads be cut off and that their corpses be thrown into the gorge. And when they arrived at the gorge, they all stood together, reached their hands to heaven, and said: "Our God Messiah, come to our aid! Our God Messiah, give us strength! Our God Messiah, receive our souls! Our God Messiah, delight yourself with the blood of your servants, which is poured out on your account! Our God Messiah, make us worthy in your sight! Our God Messiah, we confessed you as you taught us, so confess us before your father, as you have been confessed by us! Our God Messiah, rebuild this church that was burned today by this Jew! Our God Messiah, appoint a bishop for this city, in place of the holy Mar Pawla, for his bones were burned today by this Jew." And they all cried out, giving greetings to one another. And after they greeted one another, the old man stretched out his hand toward them and said and cried out: "May the peace of the Messiah that was given to the bandit on the cross be with us, brothers!" The mighty companions of the old man ran and they were supporting him and bringing him toward the executioners, as if to the head of a banquet table, while they were rejoicing and saying: "Messiah, receive our father and us with him, for we are being killed because of you." The old man knelt on his knees while his companions were holding him, and supporting his hands like Moses on top of the mountain. The executioner struck him and cut off his head, and [the old man's] companions ran and took his blood and smeared it on their faces and on their bodies, as an anointing.[21] Every one of them, wherever they saw a sword drawn, ran, knelt on their knees, and received the sword. And thus they all received the sword. The name of the illustrious victor was Harith bar Ka'b.

21. The Syriac word here, ḥnānā, can mean "pity/mercy" or "favor/grace," but this word also refers to an act of anointing the sick with water and dust that had been mixed with the relics of saints or dirt taken from martyrdom sites. The context here of the men smearing their bodies with the freshly spilled blood of their companion seems to suggest something like the latter connotation. See the entries for this word in Jessie Payne Margoliouth (née Smith), *A Compendious Syriac Dictionary, Founded upon the Thesaurus Syriacus of R. Payne Smith* (Oxford: Clarendon, 1903), 149; and Michael Sokoloff, *A Syriac Lexicon* (Piscataway, NJ: Gorgias, 2009), 472–73.

This also was not written in the letter to Mundhir, but that man who came from Najran said thus:

There was a certain three-year-old child, whose mother came out to be killed and she was holding him [by the hand], and he was running. When [the child] saw the king sitting and clothed in royal garments, he left his mother, and he ran and kissed the king's knees. And the king picked him up and began embracing him and said to him: "What do you desire, to go and die with your mother, or to remain with me?" The child said to him: "Lord, lord, I desire to die with my mother. That is why I came out with my mother, for she was saying to me: 'Come, my son, to go and die because of the Messiah.' But release me, so I can go and catch up with my mother, lest she die and I not see her. For she told me: 'The king of the Jews commanded that everyone who does not renounce the Messiah will die,' but no, lord, I will not renounce the Messiah." The king said to him: "How do you know the Messiah?" The child said to him: "Lord, every day I see him in the church with my mother, and if you come to the church I will show him to you." The king said to him: "Do you love me or your mother?" The child said to him: "Lord, I love my mother more than you." The king said to him: "Do you love me or the Messiah?" The child said to him: "Lord, lord, I love the Messiah more than you and he is better than you." The king said to him: "Why did you come and kiss my knees?" The child said to him: "I thought that you were the Christian king whom I saw in the church, but no, lord, if I had known that you were a Jew, I would not have come to you." The king said to him: "I will give you walnuts, almonds, and figs, and everything you want." The child said to him: "No, I swear to you by the Messiah that I do not eat walnuts of the Jews, nor does my mother eat walnuts of the Jews." The king said to him: "Why?" The child said to him: "Because the walnuts of the Jews are defiled, but release me and let me go to my mother, for she is not yet dead, leaving me alone." The king said to him: "Stay with me, and you will become my son." The child said: "No, [by the] Messiah, I will not stay with you, because your scent is rotten, and the scent of my mother is more pleasing than yours."

The king said to those standing before him: "Look at this wicked root, how he speaks from his childhood. Look how much this deceiver and sorcerer is able to deceive even a child." One of the nobles of the king said to the child: "Come with me; I will take you to the queen, and she will be your mother." The child said to him: "May your face be slapped, lord! For my mother is better for me than the queen, because my mother took me to the church. Release me, so that I may go. Look! My mother has gone and left me alone." And when the child saw that the king would not release him, he bit him on the thigh and said to him: "Release me, you wicked Jew! Let me go to my mother. Release me. Look! My mother will die, and I want to die with her." The king lifted the child and gave him to one of his nobles and said to him: "Watch over him, and when he grows, if he renounces the Messiah, he will live; but if not, he will die." And so, the servant of that man took [the child], wailing and kicking his feet and crying out to his mother, saying: "My lady, my lady! Look, the Jews are carrying me away! Come and get me so I can go with you to the church." When his mother saw him, she shouted toward him and said: "Go, my son. I commit you to the Messiah. My son, do not weep. Look, I will be with you! Go, my son, and stay in the church near the Messiah until I come. My son, look, I will find you. Do not weep, my beloved one; look, the Messiah is there in the church; wait with him for me; wait with him for me, my son. Look I will come after you!" And when she said these things, they cut off her head.

This also was not written in the letter of the king of the Ḥimyarites to King Mundhir, but that man who came from Najran said thus: "The youngest daughter of the blessed Dawma, who was nine years old, when she heard what the king said to her mother, that she should spit on the cross and renounce the Messiah, she filled her mouth with spit, and she spat in the king's face and said to him: 'You are spit upon, because you were not ashamed to tell the queen, my mother, that she should spit on the living cross and renounce the Messiah. You are renounced, and all your fellow Jews, and renounced is everyone who renounces the Messiah and the cross with you. The Messiah knows that my mother is better than your mother, and my family is better than your family, yet you dared to tell my mother that she should renounce the Messiah and spit on the cross. May your mouth be shut, Jew, killer of his lord.'" The daughter of the blessed one said these things to the king, and immediately she was slaughtered, she and her sister, as written above. The name of the victorious beauty is Dawma, daughter of Azmani.

When the writings were read before King Mundhir and many others, there was a great distress for all the Christians, and immediately we wrote copies of them and sent them to you, beloved, while praying that very quickly and without delay and without neglect, these things should be made known to the pure ones, the holy ones, and the bishops fleeing with the Messiah to Egypt. Through them, the chief bishop of Alexandria will know about these things, and they will exhort him to write to the king of the Ethiopians that they should not neglect the matter of the Ḥimyarites, but that they should very quickly help you. May these things also be made known to the cities of the faithful, that is to Antioch, to Tarsus of Cilicia, to Caesarea of Cappadocia, to Edessa, and to the rest of the cities of the faithful, so that they might make a memorial for the holy martyrs who are described above, and so that they might pray for tranquility and peace for the holy churches of the kingdom. They may also inform the bishops of how the Jews destroyed the place of refuge of the churches and the martyrium of the

Romans, and those evil deeds the Jews and their companions did to the Christian people who were in the region of the Ḥimyarites. The bishops of all the cities of the Romans, both the older and the more recent ones, so that they might receive a coin or two, would sell the churches and the martyria to the Jews, and they would destroy them under the cross. Those Jews who were in Tiberias, they sent priests every year and every season, and they would provoke a riot with the Christian people of the Ḥimyarites. But if those bishops are Christians and they would love for Christianity to be established, and [if] they are not associates of the Jews, let them persuade the king and his nobles that the chief priests of Tiberias, and of the rest of the cities, should be taken and locked in prison. We are not saying that wickedness should come to them because of wickedness, but that they should give assurances that they will not send letters or well-known people to the king of the Ḥimyarites, who caused all these wicked deeds that we have written above for the Christian people of the Ḥimyarites. And they should say to them that if they do not do this, we will burn their synagogues, and they will be expelled from under the cross and the Christians will have authority over them. For when the king of the Ḥimyarites hears this, he might take pity on his fellow Jews and cease the persecution of the Christians. But I know that he pursues the gold of the Jews and hides the truth, and the boasting of the Jews and pagans increases. But the love of silver and gold is established in the church, and love is quenched from the shepherds. And because of this, the flocks are taken away from the shepherds, who suffer for their flocks. But we will speak, and they will do what is theirs to do. And this will be seen by the Messiah God, the good shepherd, who handed himself over on behalf of his sheep, and this is the help that he will perform for his flock, purchased with his precious blood. To him be glory and honor and praise and worship, now, and in all times, and forever, amen.

The writer: I found these things, and I also examined and learned from some people who went out and came to that region, who were sent by the king. They said that the Ethiopians had overtaken the Jewish king and bound heavy clay objects around his neck and threw him from a boat into the heart of the sea. And then a Christian king whose name was Alfrana[22] came to rule, and he rebuilt the church and the martyrium for those blessed ones, for it is by their prayers that the weak scribe is protected from all that is wicked. Amen.

End of the story of the Ḥimyarites.

---

22. The client king whom Kaleb installed is known from an inscription as Simyafaʿ Ashwaʿ, and in Greek sources he is called Esimiphaios.

7. The Syriac *Life of Mary of Egypt*

Introduction and translation by Jeanne-Nicole Mellon Saint-Laurent

The *Life of Saint Mary of Egypt*,[1] initially written in Greek, became one of the most popular stories of repentance and love in the corpus of Christian hagiography. Christian tradition commemorates Saint Mary of Egypt as an "Icon of Repentance."[2] The story tells the tale of two saints, Zosimus and Mary, and their journeys to sanctification. Zosimus is an old monk in Palestine whom all monks revere for his righteousness and holiness. The text recounts Zosimus's journey in search of a spiritual guide into the Palestinian desert, where he meets an ascetic woman named Mary. Through their conversation, Zosimus learns more about her story of repentance and how she came to be in the desert.

The story of the friendship and love between these two people, Mary and Zosimus, is one of the most treasured hagiographies from the late ancient world. Mary's narrative circulated in monastic circles in the sixth century. Maria Kouli translated the Greek *Vita* from *Patrologia Graeca* 87.3697–3726.[3] Benedicta Ward translated the Latin text into English in her *Harlots of the Desert* collection of hagiographies.[4] Kouli and Ward mention that versions of this narrative exist in the *Lives of the Monks of Palestine* by Cyril of Skythopolis and *The Spiritual Meadow* by John Moschos.[5] Tradition attributes the most extended version of her *Life* to Sophronios (ca. 560–638), a Chalcedonian patriarch of Jerusalem. In the eighth century, the Latin text of the *Life of Saint Mary of Egypt* was translated by Paul the Deacon from the Greek of Sophronios, and this text can be

---

1. I gratefully acknowledge the help of James Walters and Corey Stephan in editing this translation.

2. Benedicta Ward, *Harlots of the Desert: A Study of Repentance in Early Monastic Sources* (London: Mowbray/Kalamazoo, MI: Cistercian, 1987), 26.

3. Maria Kouli, "Life of St. Mary of Egypt," in *Holy Women of Byzantium: Ten Saints' Lives in English Translation*, ed. A.-M. Talbot (Washington, DC: Dumbarton Oaks, 2006), 65–93. The story exists in twenty-seven Greek manuscripts, but there is still no critical edition of the Greek *Vita* (68).

4. Ward, *Harlots of the Desert*, 26–56.

5. See Festugière André-Jean, *Les Moines d'Orient* (Paris: Cerf, 1963), 3:xviii–xix, 50–51, cited in Ward, *Harlots of the Desert*, 28–29. For John Moschus, see *The Spiritual Meadow*, trans. John Wortley (Kalamazoo, MI: Cistercian, 2008). For further references, see Kouli, "Life of St. Mary of Egypt," 65–66.

found in Patrologia Latina 77.671–90. An English translation of the Ethiopic version of the *Life of Mary of Egypt* was recently published by Jaime Gunderson and John Huehnergard, and this contains further important bibliography on the *Mary of Egypt* hagiographic tradition.[6] Over one hundred manuscripts of this hagiography survive in Greek and Latin,[7] and translations of this *Life* exist in Old English, Italian, Spanish, Portuguese, German, Armenian, Arabic, Ethiopic, and Georgian.[8]

The Syriac translation of the Greek *Life of Mary of Egypt*, translated below, follows the narrative of the Greek *Life* closely, but not verbatim.[9] It is difficult to date this translation with certainty. The Syriac text used for this translation comes from the fifth volume of Paul Bedjan's edition in the *Acta Martyrum et Sanctorum*.[10] Bedjan used Paris MS 234, folio 62–80, a thirteenth-century manuscript that he verified according to BL Add. 14,649 from the ninth century.[11] I follow Bedjan's use of the later MS 234 because I was unable to access BL Add. 14,649.[12] In my translation, I follow Kouli's method of indicating in brackets words or expressions that the text implies.[13] In the footnotes, I refer to Paris MS 234 as "P" and BL Add. 14,646 as "L," following Bedjan's classification.

Bibliography

Text and Editions

Bedjan, Paul. *Acta Martyrum et Sanctorum*, vol. 5. Paris: Harrassowitz, 1895 (Syriac text).

Gunderson, J., and J. Huehnergard. "An Ethiopic Version of the Life of Mary

---

6. J. Gunderson and J. Huehnergard, "An Ethiopic Version of the Life of Mary of Egypt," *Vostok: Afro-Aziatskie Obshchestva: Istoriia i Sovremennost* 3 (2019): 151–69 (online at https://ras.jes.su/vostokoriens/s086919080005252-4-1-en).

7. See Gunderson and Huehnergard, "Ethiopic Version," 151n1.

8. See Gunderson and Huehnergard, "Ethiopic Version," 151.

9. Some places in the Syriac text are difficult to understand. In these places, I find it useful to compare my translation of the Syriac *Life* with the Greek *Life* as well as Kouli's translation.

10. Paul Bedjan, *Acta Martyrum et Sanctorum* (Paris: Harrassowitz, 1895), 5:342–85.

11. Other manuscripts that contain this story are MS Damascus, Syrian Orthodox Patriarchate, codex 12/18 (formerly MS Dayr Al-Za'faran, codex 19), folio 154–157v (twelfth or thirteenth century); MS Sinai, Monastery Sainte-Catherine, Syriac Sp. 46; and MS Dayr Al-Za'faran, codex pap. 116 (Dolabani). See Jeanne-Nicole Mellon Saint-Laurent et al., "Mary of Egypt (text)—ܚܲܝܹ̈ܐ ܕܡܲܪܝܲܡ" in *Bibliotheca Hagiographica Syriaca Electronica* (online at https://syriaca.org/work/357).

12. This translation was produced during the Covid-19 lockdown.

13. Kouli's translation assisted me in identifying biblical references as well.

of Egypt." *Vostok: Afro-Aziatskie Obshchestva: Istoriia i Sovremennost* 3 (2019): 151–69 (English translation of the Ethiopic version).

Kouli, Maria. "Life of St. Mary of Egypt." Pages 65–93 in *Holy Women of Byzantium: Ten Saints' Lives in English Translation*. Edited by A.-M. Talbot. Washington, DC: Dumbarton Oaks Research Library and Collection, 2006 (English translation of the Greek version).

Studies

Ward, Benedicta. *Harlots of the Desert: A Study of Repentance in Early Monastic Sources*. London: Mowbray/Kalamazoo, MI: Cistercian, 1987.

TRANSLATION

The Syriac Life of Mary of Egypt

Again, the story of Mary the Egyptian: she who practiced asceticism in a holy and especially praiseworthy way in the desert near the Jordan [River], and how the great Zosimus found her.[14]

[Omitted: a brief preface by the hagiographer.]

There was a man in the monasteries of Palestine, adorned in good deeds and speech. He had been reared in monastic habits and deeds since the time of infancy.[15] Zosimus was the name of this elder.[16] Let no one think (because the elder has the same name) that I am talking about that Zosimus who was accused once of false doctrine. For this [Zosimus] is one man, and that [Zosimus] is another, and there is a significant difference between them, even if there is one name that they have between them. Indeed, this man Zosimus was orthodox. He was a monk from [his] beginning[s] in one of the monasteries of Palestine, where he had done every type of ascetic practice that is possible. He behaved according

14. L adds a further note: "By the power of our Lord Jesus Christ, we begin to write the story of Mary of Egypt, who had been a whore, who practiced asceticism in the desert near the Jordan."

15. Literally, "swaddling clothes."

16. Throughout the story, the hagiographer translates γέρων as *sābā*. In her excellent translation of the Greek *Life of St. Mary of Egypt*, Kouli translates γέρων as "monk." I follow the more literal rendering "elder" or "old man" in my translation, but it is clear that Zosimus is also a monk.

to the principle of the ascetic way of life. He kept every rule handed over to him by those who had trained him for such a wrestling contest. He was able also to add an abundance to this from himself, as he wanted to subdue the flesh to the spirit. And indeed, he did not fall short of this aim. Because of this, news of the practices of the elder [spread]. Many [monks] came to him from neighboring monasteries (and those from distant places) to be formed in asceticism by his teaching and take up the rule [of his life]. Thus, also this elder became renowned for his type of practice. He never ceased from the study of Scripture, even while he was going to sleep, or rising, or holding with his hands the work of his hands, while partaking of food as was his custom, if indeed it is right to call "food" that which he tasted. For he had one task without ceasing that did not stop: always singing the Psalms and studying Scripture. Thus, many times they said that the elder was worthy of [receiving] a divine vision, as this happened to him through the illumination of God. It is marvelous, unceasing, and even unbelievable. For if the blessed ones who are pure in heart will see God,[17] as indeed our Lord said, it is known that those who purify their flesh and keep watch, always with a vigilant eye of the soul see visions of divine illumination. They receive, in this way, a pledge of the beauty that awaits them.

Zosimus thus said that, so to speak, [from] his mother's bosom he had been placed in the monastery. He accomplished the ascetic course until he was fifty years, as was possible.[18] After that, he became worried, as he said, by certain thoughts, that he had reached perfection in these things and did not need the teaching of another. So, as he said, he thought to himself: "Perhaps there is a monk on the earth who can pass on to me something unknown, or can help me in a kind of asceticism that I do not know or I have not done? Can he be found from among those philosophers practicing [asceticism] in the desert? Or is there a man who goes before me in practice or contemplation?"

While the elder was considering these things in this way, someone was standing before him. He said to him: "O Zosimus, you have contended well and as much as possible for a person. You have beautifully completed the ascetic course. But there is no one among men who is perfect. There is a great contest that has been set, that surpasses the one from before, even if you have not known it. That you might know how many other ways to salvation there are, *flee from your country, from the kinship of your people, and from the house of your Father,*[19] as also Abraham [did], that illustrious patriarch, and go to the monastery that is situated alongside the Jordan River."

17. Matt 5:8.
18. The Greek text says fifty-three years (Patrologia Graeca 87.3700).
19. Gen 12:1.

[Omitted: the story of Zosimus's arrival at the monastery, his reception by the abbot, and his positive first impressions of the monks there. Zosimus also learns of one of the customs of the monastery, which is for the monks to leave the monastery for a few days and spend time in the desert, preparing for the season of Lent.]

In this way, also Zosimus became accustomed to the law of the monastery. He crossed the Jordan, while he took small provisions for the necessities of the body and the tattered garment that clothed him. Indeed, he was following the rule while he was in the desert, and he was occasionally taking provisions according to the necessity of nature. Then he was sleeping while he would recline on the ground a little, getting moderate sleep wherever he was when evening arrived. He would start walking in the trying time of dawn, as he continuously had the strength from his movement without exhaustion. For, as he said, his desire indeed was to be in the desert. He was expecting that perhaps he would find some father dwelling there, who would be able to direct him to that which he desired. For some time, he was completing this [journey] vigorously, as one hastening to some well-known or famous dwelling place. When he had journeyed twenty days on the road, at the sixth hour, he stood [still] for a little while from the journey. And then he turned his gaze to the east, and he completed his usual prayer. He was accustomed to refraining from walking during the journey at ordered times of the day so that he could rest a little from his labor. When he stayed still, he would sing the Psalms, fall[20] on his knees, and he would pray in this way.

While he was singing the Psalms and gazing at the sky in steady contemplation, he saw that to the right of where he had been standing at the sixth hour praying, a shadowy figure like a human body appeared. At first, indeed he was troubled, as he thought that he had seen a demonic illusion, and he was trembling and quivering. But he sealed himself with the sign of the cross and pushed his fear away (and by then his prayer had ended). He turned his eyes, and he saw someone, in truth, who was walking south. The one who had appeared was naked [and had a] black body, blackened from the rays of the sun. And the hair he had on his head was white like wool.[21] But there was so little of it that it did not even reach the neck of the body. When Zosimus saw this, like one who is astonished by delight, he was overjoyed at the glorious wonder. He began to run to the place to which that one that had appeared was hastening. [Zosimus] was rejoicing an inexpressible joy.[22] Not until then had he seen, in all the length of his days [in the desert], the likeness of a human, another living creature, a bird, or the likeness or shade of a terrestrial animal. Therefore, he wanted to know who

20. L reads *rkn* ("bend").
21. Rev 1:14.
22. 1 Pet 1:8.

he was and what sort [of person] this was who had appeared since [Zosimus] was expecting that he might become the eyewitness of great things.

But when that [person] saw Zosimus coming from a distance, he started to run and flee toward the interior of the desert. But Zosimus, as if disregarding his old age, not thinking about the toil of the journey, pushed himself to him, as he hastened to overtake the one who was fleeing from him. Thus, he indeed was pursuing, while the other was pursued. But Zosimus's running was swifter, and little by little, he drew near to the one who was fleeing. But when at last he drew near to be close enough that his voice could be heard, Zosimus began to call out and to utter these [words] with cries and tears: "Why are you fleeing from me, an old man and sinner? O servant of the true God stay with me, [that I might see] who you are, through God, because of whom you have dwelled in this desert. Stay with me, a feeble man who is not worthy. Stay with me, in the hope that you have a reward for your toil. Through God, who never rejects anyone,[23] stay put. Say a prayer and blessing for an old man." When Zosimus said these things in tears, they, running, reached a particular place where some river had impressed itself.[24] (But it does not seem to me that there had been a river there. Yet, this was the place's setting. Still, how would a torrent appear in the ground?)

When he came up to the place discussed above, he who was fleeing went down and then went up to another part. But Zosimus was wearied and not able to run. He stood on the other side of the place that looked like a [dried] river. He added tears upon his tears and groans upon his groans. His weeping was heard in the region. Then the body that was fleeing sent forth a message: "Abba Zosimus, forgive me, for the Lord's sake, since I cannot turn and be seen by you in this way, face to face. For I am a woman, and I am naked, as you see. I am ashamed that my body is not covered. But if you wish to grant this prayer for a sinful woman, untie the ragged garment in which you are clothed, so that with it, I might cover my feminine weakness and turn to you and receive your prayers."

Then astonishment of the mind seized Zosimus, as he said, when he heard that she had called him "Zosimus" by his name; as he was a sharp man and very wise in divine matters, he recognized that she could not have called by name one whom she had never seen or about whom had not heard, unless (clearly) she was illuminated with clairvoyance through heaven.

So, he did what was commanded. When he placed the tattered garment that he had and threw it on her while he stood with his gaze turned backward, she

23. Wis 11:24.

24. As Kouli notes, this riverbed is a sort of wadi, i.e., a river that is dry except in the rainy season; "Life of St. Mary of Egypt," 77n41.

took it, and she tied it, as she was able. Then she covered the parts of her body, the ones that were more fitting to be concealed [compared to] the rest of her. She turned to Zosimus and said to him: "Why have you thought, Father, to come to see a sinful woman? What do you wish to see of me or learn, that you did not hesitate to take up such toil?" He knelt on his knees on the ground, and according to custom asked to receive a blessing, while she also knelt. Both of them were on the ground, while each one was asking his [or her] companion for a blessing. Nothing spoken was heard from them, except [the request for] a blessing. After a duration of much time, the woman said to Zosimus: "Abba Zosimus, it is fitting for you to say a blessing and a prayer, for you are honored with the authority of the priesthood. For many years, you stood at the holy altar, and many times you have administered the divine mysteries." These things laid greater fear upon Zosimus. While the elder was quivering, sweat was flowing profusely, and he groaned. His speech was broken. But then he said to her, with broken and heavy panting: "It is known, O spiritual mother, that you journeyed toward the Lord some time ago, and you have afflicted yourself to the world to a great degree. The spiritual gift that he gave to you manifests itself significantly, that, in this way, he whom you had not ever seen you would call by name and would address as a priest, although you have never seen me. But since grace is not from some renowned office, but is imaged through spiritual habits, you, bless me, for the Lord's sake. Say a prayer for that one who is asking for your perfection."

Then she gave way to the old man's strife, and the woman said: "Blessed be God, who was concerned for the salvation of human souls." Then Zosimus said: "Amen!" And they both stood up from their position of kneeling on their knees. The woman said to the elder: "Why have you come before a sinful woman, O man of God? Why have you wished to see a woman stripped of any virtue? But, indeed, since the grace of the Holy Spirit has directed you so that you might administer the liturgy for me appropriate to this time, tell me, how are the Christian people conducting themselves today? How are the kings? How are the matters of the church being governed?" Zosimus answered her and said with a short word: "My mother, Christ has bestowed a secure peace for all of us through your prayers. But accept the supplication of an old man who is not worthy, and pray to the Lord for the entire world and for me, a sinner, lest the length of time [I have spent] in this desert be fruitless for me." Then she replied to him: "Indeed it is right for you, Father Zosimus, who have the authority of the priesthood, as I said, to pray for me and everyone. This lot has fallen to you. But since we are commanded to act obediently, I will do it readily." When she said these things, she turned to the east. She raised her eyes to heaven, and she stretched out her arms, and she began to pray, whispering. Because of that, Zosimus was not able to understand anything from the things of the prayer. For he was standing, as he said, trembling and gazing at the ground, [and] he was not speaking at all. But he swore, indeed, as he appointed God as a witness, that he saw that she was taking her time in prayer. When he looked out a little from his gaze that was cast down, he saw that she had been lifted from the ground about one cubit,[25] and she was hanging in the air while she prayed. And when Zosimus saw this, he was seized with fear, and he fell upon the ground. As sweat ran down, he was very terrified. He did not dare to say anything. He was speaking to himself repeatedly: "O Lord, have mercy on me." While the elder was cast out on the ground, he was troubled by the thought that indeed she was a spirit. He was supporting himself with prayer when the woman returned and lifted the elder, and she said these things: "What are your troubled thoughts, Father, such that you are offended by me as if I was a spirit, and I would show prayer as a pretense? It is assured, O man, that I am a sinful woman. I have been strengthened[26] by holy baptism. I am not a spirit, but rather earth and ashes.[27] All of me is flesh, and I don't think that there is anything spiritual." Immediately as she said these things, she sealed herself with the sign of the cross between her eyes, indeed on her eyes, lips, and her breast. Then she spoke thus: "May God deliver us from the evil one, O Father Zosimus, and from his ambushes, since his power to take us is great."

[Omitted: Zosimus implores Mary to tell her story.]

When Abba Zosimus had said these and many other things, the woman raised him up and said to him: "I am ashamed, my Father—forgive me—to speak about my shameful deeds. But because you see the nudity of my body, I will uncover to you my deeds, so that you will know how great my shame is and how full of reproach my soul is. For [the reason why] I do not wish to tell you these things of my life is not that I boast, as you think. For what do I have to brag about, [as I was] an instrument of the devil? For I know that when I begin this story, you [will] flee from me, as a person flees from a serpent. Because you will not [be able] to endure[28] to hear this with your ears the disfigured things that I have done, but I will speak them and in no way will I be silent. But I adjure you not to stop praying for me, that there I find mercy on the day of judgment."

While indeed the old man wept uncontrollably, the woman began her story, and she spoke in this way:

My nation is Egypt. While my parents were alive, and I had been living twelve years, I rejected their love. I was in Alexandria, where indeed I first destroyed

25. The length from the elbow to the tip of the middle finger.
26. L adds "however."
27. Gen 18:27.
28. L reads "to bring yourself."

my virginity and where I was found guilty of lustful sexual intercourse. I am ashamed to be thinking about it. It is more discrete to say now briefly what I will speak that you know my lust and love of pleasure. For seventeen years, forgive me, I remained appointed for the people as a tinged woman aflame with licentiousness. For, in truth, it was not for any special gift [that I received], since I did not even receive [anything] when men many times were wishing to give [me something], since I had considered that in this way I could make many men run to me. I was utterly giving myself as a gift of lust. And although you might think that I became rich, I did not receive anything from them. Because of this, I lived by begging, and often I spun cloth. But they did not satisfy the desire that I had, an uncontrollable lust, and I was rolling in mud. This living was considered [life] for me: that I spend [my life] continuously dishonoring nature.

While I lived in this way, one time in summer I saw that a great crowd of men, Libyans and Egyptians, were running toward the sea. I asked a man, then, who happened to meet me, whither indeed were these men running who so hastened? He answered me: "They are all going up to Jerusalem for the exaltation of the holy cross, which, according to custom, takes place in a few days." But then I said to him: "[Would] they take me with them if I wish to join them?" He answered me: "If you have boat fare and money, no one will hold you back." I said to him: "Truly, brother, I do not have the boat fare or money. But I will also go and get up on one of the ships that they have hired, and they will have to nourish me, even if they do not wish. For I have a body, and they will take it in place of boat fare."[29] Then a young man when he heard the shameful nature of my words, he turned away while laughing. When I let go of the distaff that I had been carrying, for indeed I happened to have it, I ran toward the sea. I had seen that [the men] were running in a hurry. I saw some young men standing on the shore of the sea, ten in number or more, vigorous in their bodies and movements, who seemed to me to be sufficient for what I wanted, as it appeared, and they were waiting for the others who were setting sail with them. Others had already gone up on the ship.[30] But then in this way presumptuously, as was my custom, I sprang into their midst. "Take me," I said, "also to where you are going. It is not that I appear to be inexperienced, is it?" Thereupon I spoke other words that were even more disgraceful, and I roused them all to laughter.

29. L differs significantly here from the Paris manuscript: "'I wanted to go with them for this reason—forgive me father—so that I would have customers to satisfy my lust. I said to you, Father Zosimus, not to force me to speak my shameful life. For I shake, as the Lord knows, that I am defiling you and the air through my words.' Then Zosimus, while wetting the ground with his tears, answered her: 'Tell me, my mother, do not cut off the harmony of your beneficial narrative like this.' Then she again took it up and added the following things. The young men...."

30. L reads "ships."

But when these men saw my propensity toward boldness, then they took me and led me up to the ship that was ready for them. And then came those [men] whom they had been expecting, and we set sail from there. How can I speak further, Father,[31] of what happened from here? What tongue could say or what hearing could accept it, for I shudder. Our Lord knows that I pollute the air by my words—[alas,] the things I did on the boat during the journey!

Then Zosimus, while he watered the earth with his tears, answered her: "Tell me for the sake of the Lord, my mother, do not cut short the harmony of the profitable story like this." She then replied: "I will add to my words [that I spoke] previously,"[32] saying:

There was no type of licentiousness, spoken or unspoken, that I was without, as I became a teacher for the miserable men. And now to be sure I am struck with terror that the sea endured my intemperance and that the earth did not open its mouth and lead me alive unto Sheol since I had ensnared souls like this! But as it seems, God was asking for my repentance. He wishes not for the death of a sinner,[33] but instead, he abides in patience and waits for his conversion. Thus, in this way, accordingly, we went to Jerusalem with eagerness. And all the days that I spent before the holy feast, I was engaged in these similar [habits], or, rather, in even worse things. For the young men who were serving me on the sea and the road were not enough for me, but instead, I corrupted many others. Indeed, I brought citizens and foreigners together for this [purpose].

When the holy feast of the exaltation of the salvific cross arrived, I was going around hunting after the souls of young men. Before the break of dawn, I saw all the people rushing to the church. I went running with those who were running. I came thus with them to the courtyard[34] of the church. When the time of the divine exaltation came, I pushed in and was pushed back. I forced myself at the entrance and again was rushing to enter with the crowd. Eventually, miserable and distressed, with much fatigue, I drew near to the door through which one would go within the church, in which was shown the life-giving cross.

As I trod on the threshold of the gate, others were entering without impediment, but some sort of divine power was restraining me, not letting me through the entrance. Again, I was pushed back and again was thrust out, and again I appeared to be alone, standing in the courtyards. I thought that this was

31. L reads "Man."
32. L reads "Things that even the miserable men who did them did not want <to do>, but I compelled them."
33. Ezek 33:11.
34. L reads "courtyards."

happening to me because of feminine weakness, so again I mixed myself in with the others, while I forced myself as I could. I pushed myself again, but I was wearied in vain. Whenever my miserable foot trod upon the threshold, I was pushed back behind it. The church received the others, as it hindered no one else. I alone, miserable woman, it would not accept. Instead, it was as if a great army had been arranged for this, commanded that the entrance be closed before me. Some power prevented me again [from entering], and still, I was standing in the courtyard. Three or four times I endured and did this, then indeed I was humbled. I could not push and be thrust back again. My body had been weakened from the effort.

Thus, when I gave up, I returned and stood in some corner of the gate of the church. Then with difficulty, I perceived the cause that was preventing me from seeing the life-giving cross. For then, the salvific Word touched the spiritual eye of my heart[35] that showed me that it was the detestable nature of my deeds that closed the entrance [of the church] to me. I began then to weep and mourn, and I beat my breast, while I raised groans and laments from the depth of my heart. Then while I cried, I saw the icon of the all-Holy Mother of God, which was standing above the place where I was standing. Firmly I set my gaze on her and spoke to her: "O my Virgin Lady, you who gave birth to God the Word in flesh, I know, indeed I know, that it is not good or right for me, who is polluted in this way, a prodigal in all things, to see your icon, you who are the ever-virgin, pure in body and soul, in whom are pure things and no pollution. For it is right that I, a prodigal, should be despised and hated by you who are pure. But since indeed I have heard that it was on account of this that he became human, God whom you bore, so that he might call sinners to repentance, help me, O Holy Mother, a sinner and alone, who has no one to help her. Command also, my Lady, that entrance to the church might be allowed for me. Do not deprive me of seeing the cross on which God in flesh, whom you bore, was fastened, he who gave his blood for our salvation. Command, my Lady, that also the door might be opened to me to venerate the divine cross, and I give myself, entrusted to you, my Lady, as a worthy guarantor from whose purity he arose. I will not dishonor this flesh again in sin and shameful intercourse. When I see the wood of the cross of your son, I will renounce this world and all its pleasures. Then I will set forth to where you, my guarantor, will help and guide me."

When I spoke these things, I received a certain assurance via the warmth of faith, and I took confidence in [her], a fount of mercy. I moved from the place where I had been standing while I made this supplication. I came in with those

---

35. The Syriac reads ʿaynā d-ruḥā d-lebā, adding d-ruḥā ("spiritual"), which is absent from the Greek. See Ἥψατο γὰρ τῶν ὀφθαλμῶν τῆς καρδίας μου λόγος σωτήριος (Patrologia Graeca 87.3713b).

who were entering, and I mingled into their midst. There was not anything that was pushing me or thrusting me backward. Nor was there anyone holding me back to be near the door through which people were entering the church. Then great wonder and zeal and awe gripped me. All of me was shaking and trembling entirely. Then I came to that door that up to that point had been closed. The force that previously restrained me, now indeed, in the same way, began to make a path for me to enter. Thus, I entered without toil. In this way, I was within the holy of holies. I was deemed worthy for the sight of the life-giving cross. I saw the mysteries of God, as he is the one who is prepared to receive sinners who repent. I threw myself on the ground, and when I venerated the holy ground, I ran and went out and rushed[36] to be in the presence of the one who was [my] guarantor. Thus, I was in the place where the deed of my guarantee was written. And when I kneeled on my knees before the all-holy and ever-virgin Mother of God, I spoke these words: "You, my Lady, who loves all that is good, you have shown through me that you are a lover of humanity. You did not despise the prayer of me, an unworthy woman. I have seen the glory that rightly we prodigals have not seen. Glory be to God, who accepts the repentance of sinners through you. For what more do I, a sinful woman, have to think or say? It is the time, my Lady, for the fulfillment of the guarantee that I pledged. Guide now where you do command, or, rather, be a teacher of salvation to guide me on the way that leads to repentance."

While thus I said these things, I heard someone from afar calling: "If you cross over to the Jordan, you will find peaceful rest." As I listened to this voice, I believed that it was intended for me. While I wept, I cried out and called to the Mother of God and said: "My Lady, my Lady, do not abandon me." When I had said[37] these things, someone saw me going out, and he reached three bronze coins while he said: "Accept these, my mother." I took what was given to me. I bought three loaves of bread with them. I took these as provisions of a blessing. I asked him who had provided the bread: "Where and what is the way, O man, that leads to the Jordan?" Then I learned the gate of the city, which leads one toward this region. I went out then in haste and was heading out on the road while weeping. I went from asking one to another [the way]. I traveled for the rest of the day. It was the third hour of the day, as it seemed to me, when I saw the cross. I went forth, while the sun was setting, toward the west to the Church of John the Baptist, situated near the Jordan.[38] And after I worshiped in the church at first, immediately I descended to the Jordan, and I wetted my face and my hands with this holy water. I partook in the unpolluted and life-giving mysteries

36. L reads "I ran, with people going out and rushing."
37. L reads "asked for."
38. Traditional site of the baptism of Jesus.

in the Church of the Holy Forerunner. And I ate a portion of the loaves, and then
I drank from the waters of the Jordan. I lay on the ground through the night,
and I found a little boat there. I was on the other side. Then I asked my guide to
lead me to the appropriate place. Then I was in this desert, from that time, until
today. I departed afar as I fled, and I settled here, while I wait for my God, who
frees those who return to him from faintheartedness and the storm.[39]

Then Zosimus said to her: "How many years, O my Lady, has it been since
you have been in this desert?" The woman answered him: "It has been forty-
seven years, as I liken it,[40] since I have left the Holy City." Then Zosimus said:
"What did you find or what were you able to have for sustenance, O my Lady?"
She[41] told him: "These two and a half loaves of bread that were dried up and
became like stones. Little by little, I have eaten them, and I have been finishing
them gradually." Zosimus said to her: "Have you easily spent this extent of time
without stress, were you not at all troubled by the sudden change [in life]?" The
holy woman[42] answered: "I tremble to speak about this matter about which
you ask, Father Zosimus. For if it comes to my memory, all these dangers that
I have endured and the thoughts that severely molested me, I fear lest I be laid
low by them again." "My Lady, do not leave out anything," Father Zosimus said,
"whatever you would tell me. For once you have brought this up, it is right for
you, O Mother, to teach all things uninhibitedly."
Then she said to him:

Believe, Father, that for seventeen years, I have dwelled in this desert, I have
wrestled with wild animals, with irrational desires. I attacked them while I took
provision. While I tried to take food, I longed for meat and those fishes in Egypt.
Also, I desired to drink wine, which is beloved to me, for I made use of a lot of
wine while I lived in the world. But there was not even any water there that I
would taste. Severely I have been inflamed [with thirst] and have suffered for
that necessary [element]. Also, an irrational desire of debauched songs entered
me, that was agitating me vigorously and persuading me to sing demonic songs
that I had learned. Immediately while I wept and was beating my breast with
my hands, I reminded myself of the promises that I had made when I went out
to the desert. I became present in my thoughts before the icon of the Mother

39. Ps 55:8 (54:9 LXX).
40. L reads "as it seems."
41. L reads "The woman."
42. L reads "woman." As also the Greek: "Ἔφη δὲ ἡ γυνή" (Patrologia Graeca 87.3716C).

of God, who was my guarantor. I asked and sought from her to chase away the thoughts that were attacking my miserable soul in this way. When I had wept sufficiently and had beaten my breast with all my power, I saw light everywhere that flashed over me. And from then on, I grew strong with a particular strength after the storm had hit me.

How can I tell you, O Father, how my thoughts were stirred toward fornication? Fire from within me, from my miserable heart, was prevailing entirely over me, and it was inflaming all of me entirely. It was inciting desire of intercourse. When suddenly [the desire] placed thoughts like these in me, I threw myself onto the earth, and I watered the ground with my tears. I thought about her who served as my guarantor, and the rule I had transgressed and [how] she was demanding a punishment [for my] transgression. At first, I did not stand up from prostrations on the ground, even if night and day happened to pass, until sweet light shone down on me and chased away the thoughts that molested me. Then, I cast the eyes of my mind unto my guarantor unceasingly, while I asked that she give me help with these dangers that I met in the abyss of this desert. Also, I acquired a helper and an aid of repentance. In this way, I have spent the extent of these seventeen years. I am occupied with great perils, from then indeed till today. My guide stands by me in everything, while she guides me in everything.

Then Zosimus said to her: "Are you not in need of nourishment or clothing?" She answered him:

These loaves of bread, as I told you, were consumed. I was then nourished on roots for seventeen years and on these things of whatever remains that were found in the desert. The clothing that I had when I crossed the Jordan wore out, torn to pieces. Much distress[43] took hold of me, and again I endured great affliction from the flame of summer, while I burned in the heat of the day, and I suffered trembling with the cold in the night. So that many times I was on the ground without breath to speak, and I would remain there motionless. Thus, I wrestled with many various adversities, temptations, and intolerable thoughts, from that point up till today. The power of God in an abundance of ways protected my sinful soul and my weak body,[44] while I understood that the Lord alone saved me from such evil things. While nourishment ran out for me, the hope of my Savior [nourished me]. For I was nourished and covered by the Word of God who has authority over everything. For a human being does not

---

43. Ἀνάγκη / *'ananqi'* ("necessity").
44. See the connection between a sinful soul and a weak body.

live on bread alone;[45] and because they have no covering, they have wrapped themselves around the rock[46] who have taken off the garment of sin.

When Zosimus also heard that she remembered the words of Scripture from Moses, Job, and the book of Psalms, he said to her: "Have you chanced to have read the Psalms or other Scriptures, my lady?" When she heard this, she laughed and said to the elder: "Believe, O man, no other man has been seen by me since I crossed the Jordan, except your face today. Nor has a wild beast or other animal been seen by me since I saw the desert. Indeed, I have never learned Scripture, nor have I heard anyone sing or read [them]. But the Word of God lives indeed and works,[47] and it is the [the Word] that teaches knowledge to humanity. From then to here, this is the end of my story. As I did when I began with this narration, now I make you swear through the incarnation of the Word of God, that you will pray on my behalf to the Lord, I who am a prodigal."

When she had said these things and ended her story there, he hastened to bow down in a blessing, and with tears, he shouted: "Blessed are you God, who has done great, marvelous, glorious, and wondrous things that indeed cannot be numbered.[48] Blessed are you, God, who has shown me, the things you bestow on those who fear you! Truly you do not abandon the ones who seek you, Lord!"[49]

She took hold of the elder. She did not let him lie down entirely in obeisance, but instead said to him: "All the things that you have heard, O man, I make you swear through Christ our God that you do not say this to anyone until God releases me from life. Now it is for you to go in peace and tranquility, and in the coming year you will see me, and you will be seen by me, through the grace by which you are protected. For the sake of the Lord, do that which now I command. During the holy fast of this coming year, do not cross the Jordan as you are accustomed to doing in the monastery." Zosimus marveled that she had narrated the canon of the monastery. Not a thing did he say except: "Glory to you, God who gives great things to those who love you!" She said:

Stay in the monastery, as I said. Beware of going out [of the monastery], even if you should wish. On the evening of the liturgy of the Last Supper, take for me the life-giving body and blood in a holy vessel worthy of such mysteries, and bring [them]. Wait for me on the bank of the Jordan, which is near the areas of

45. Deut 8:3; Matt 4:4.
46. Job 24:8.
47. Heb 4:12.
48. Job 5:9; 9:10.
49. Ps 9:10.

the inhabited [world], so that when you come, I might share in these life-giving mysteries. Since I shared [the Eucharist] in the Church of the Forerunner before I crossed the Jordan, until now I have not been worthy to share in this Eucharist. Now I long for it with an uncontrollable desire. Now I ask you: do not desist from my request, but, rather, from whatever way possible bring me these divine and life-giving mysteries at the time that our Lord made his disciples partakers in the divine Last Supper. Tell these things to Abba Johannis, abbot of the monastery in which you dwell: "Father, take care of yourself and your flock. For certain affairs are happening there that require correction." But I do not wish that you say these things to him now, but when the Lord allows you.

When she had explained these things, she said to the old man: "Pray for me," and she hastened to the deep of the desert again.

[Omitted: Zosimus returns to the monastery and waits a year for his opportunity to see Mary again.]

When the monks came back, and the evening of that liturgy of the Lord's Supper drew near, he did what had been commanded to him. He placed a little of the unpolluted body and the blood of Christ our God in the chalice. Then he also put a few figs and date palms and a few lentils soaked in water in the basket, and he set out in the dead of the evening. He sat by the bank of the Jordan while he waited for the arrival of the holy woman.

When the holy woman delayed, Zosimus did not sleep, but, rather, he gazed unfalteringly at the desert while he waited to see she whom he desired to see. While he sat there, he said from within and to himself: "O indeed, is it that my unworthiness hinders her from coming? Or is it that she came, but she did not find me and has not returned?" While he said those things, he wept. While he wept, he groaned. He raised his eyes to heaven, and he prayed to God and said: "Do not deprive me, O Lord, to see that which I have desired[50] to see. O Lord, may I not go empty handed, while I carry my sins unto reproof." While he prayed these things with tears, another matter fell into his thought. Then indeed he said to himself: "What if she comes? For a ship cannot be found [with which] she would cross the Jordan and be with me, my unworthy self? Woe to my unworthiness! Who has rightly deprived me of this good as this?"

While the elder thought these things, behold! The holy woman arrived. She stood at the edge of the river from where also she was coming. Zosimus stood up, while rejoicing, exulting, worshiping, and glorifying God. But then again, he was struggling with the thought that it would not be possible for her to cross the Jordan. Then he saw her as she made the sign of the cross over the Jordan, for

---

50. L reads "you permitted."

it was a full moon that night, according to what he said, and immediately with the sign [of the cross] she stepped upon the water, and she walked above it and passed over it to him. Indeed, she restrained him who desired to fall on his knees [before her], and she was crying out as she was walking on water: "What are you doing, O Father? For you are a priest, and you carry the divine mysteries!"

Then he assented to what she had said. She crossed over the water and spoke to him: "Bless [me], Father, bless [me]." He answered her while still trembling, for amazement gripped him at the glorious marvel: "Truly the Almighty did not lie who promised that those who have purified themselves make themselves like God, as much as it is possible.[51] Glory to you, Christ our God, who has shown me through your handmaid the measure to which I am far from perfection!"

While he spoke these things, the woman asked that they recite the holy confession of the faith, and indeed also the *Our Father who is in heaven*; and so they began. When this had happened, and the prayer had ended, according to custom, she gave the elder a kiss on his mouth, and then she received the divine mysteries. After she received [them], she lifted her hands to heaven, and she groaned before weeping. In this way, she shouted: "Now, release your handmaiden in peace, Lord, according to your word, since my eyes have seen your salvation!"[52] Thus she spoke to the elder: "Forgive me, Father—and fulfill another desire. Go now to your monastery, while you are protected by divine peace. Come to this streamed in the coming year, where I have conversed with you before. Come no matter what, for the sake of the Lord, and I will be seen again as the Lord wishes." He then answered her: "If only it would be possible that I join you from here that I might always see your precious face! Grant this request of an old man. Take a little of this food that I brought here." Immediately when he said these things, he showed her the basket that he had. She touched the lentils with the tip of her fingers, took three beans from them and brought them to her mouth while she said: "Sufficient is the grace of the spirit that protects the unblemished essence of my soul." When she said these things, again she said to the elder: "Pray for me before the Lord, pray for me. And remember me, your unhappy servant, at all times." While indeed he touched the feet of the holy woman, he asked with tears that she would pray for the church, the empire, and him. He allowed her to go while he was weeping and groaning. For indeed, he did not dare to hang on for a long time to one who cannot be held. Again, she signed over the Jordan, stepped on the water, then she walked. She crossed over it, just as she had before.

Then the elder returned while held with fear and with great joy. He found fault with himself that he had not asked to learn the name of the holy woman.

---

51. The purpose of the ascetic life!
52. Luke 2:29.

But indeed, he was hoping that he would be found worthy of this in the coming year. When the year passed, he went again as usual to the desert, and he rushed to the glorious marvel. When indeed he walked that length of the desert, and he reached certain signs that indicated [his] finding of the place. He was searching right and left as he was going around. He looked every place as a hunter with much experience would hunt in a place for a sweet prey. When indeed he saw nothing anywhere that moved, he began indeed to drench himself with tears. Then he lifted his eyes, prayed, and said: "Show me, O Lord, your inviolate treasure that you have hidden in this desert. I pray, show me that angel incarnate, that one of whom the world is not worthy." When he prayed these things, he walked to the place that was shaped in the form of a riverbed. When he stood at its head, he saw that the holy woman lay dead, there on the side [of the riverbed] where the sun shines forth.[53] In this way, she was forming her hands to signify [prayer] as was proper, as she lay in the manner facing the east. He indeed ran after her, and he washed the feet of that blessed one with his tears. He did not even dare to approach another part of her body.

While then he wept sufficiently, he recited the Psalms, and he completed fittingly at this occasion the prayer over the grave, saying to himself: "Indeed, is it fitting for me to bury the remains of the holy woman? Or indeed would this be pleasing to the holy woman?" When he said this, he saw by her head some writing that was inscribed on the ground, where the following things were written: "Bury, O Father Zosimus, the body of Maria, the poor one, in this place. Return the dust to dust,[54] while you pray for me to the Lord. And pray for me on behalf of the Lord. She died in the month of Nisan,[55] the night of the passion of our Savior, after the reception of the Lord's supper, the divine mystery." While thus the elder read these things that were written, at first he thought to himself: "Who wrote this? For she had said: 'I do not know writing.'" But he rejoiced since he learned the name of the holy woman. For he explained that at once, after she had shared in the divine mysteries by the Jordan, immediately in that place where she had been, she died. Zosimus had traveled this path twenty days with fatigue; Maria had run it in an instant and immediately departed to God. As he glorified God and drenched her body with tears, he said: "It is time, poor Zosimus, that you complete that which was commanded. But how will you do this, O miserable one, since there is nothing for digging at hand?" When he said this, he saw upon the hill a small piece of wood that lay there. He took it, and he began to dig. Indeed, since the earth was dry, in no way did the [earth] give way

---

53. That is, the east.
54. Eccl 3:20.
55. L reads "Pharmouthi according to the Egyptian, April according to the Romans."

to the elder, who was stumbling. As sweat ran down [his face], he was fatigued, and he was not able to finish anything.

[Omitted: Zosimus buries Mary's body with the help of a lion.]

When the man again came to his monastery, he told all these things to the monks. He hid nothing [from them] about all the things that he had heard or the things he had seen. He told them everything, little by little, from the beginning, so that all would be amazed at the great things of God and, with fear and trembling, would celebrate the death of the holy woman. And indeed, John the abbot found men in the monastery who required correction so that the word of this holy woman not be in vain or without purpose. Also, Zosimus died in the monastery when he was approximately one hundred years old.

[Omitted: a short conclusion by the hagiographer.]

The deeds of Mary of Egypt have been completed, who is from Atridon, who in a holy way, practiced asceticism in the desert near the Jordan River.

8. Timothy I, *Letter 47*

Introduction and translation by Aaron Michael Butts

Timothy I was an influential catholicos of the Church of the East for more than forty years (780–823).[1] Around sixty letters of his survive, and these provide fascinating insights into how the catholicos led the Church of the East during a pivotal time at the beginning of the ʿAbbāsid Caliphate (750–1258). The present letter deals with two principal topics. The first is Timothy's efforts to produce three copies of the Syriac translation of the Septuagint column of Origen's Hexapla. This Syriac translation, known in modern scholarship as the Syro-Hexapla, was produced by the Syriac Orthodox translator Paul of Tella in 616–17. In addition to being the first mention of the (Syro-)Hexapla in East Syriac sources, this section of the letter provides a rare—and captivating—glimpse of scribal culture and manuscript copying. The second topic of the letter is the discovery of Hebrew manuscripts in the region of Jericho. This incredible story anticipates the discovery of the Dead Sea Scrolls by more than a millennium. In addition, it might explain the existence of the so-called Apocryphal Psalms in the Syriac tradition.[2] The Syriac Apocryphal Psalms are a group of five poetic compositions, numbered 151–55, that are first attested in a Syriac manuscript datable to the twelfth century.[3] Two of these psalms (154 and 155) are also found in the Qumran Psalms Scroll (11QPsª). This letter might be the proverbial silver bullet to explain how noncanonical Hebrew Psalms could be transmitted into Syriac after the original translation of the canonical Peshiṭta many centuries earlier. Together, both parts of this letter shed light on biblical studies in the Church of the East at the beginning of the ʿAbbāsid period and especially Timothy's activities in this area.[4] Beyond these two main topics, the letter is filled with many

1. In general, see V. Berti, *Vita e studi di Timoteo I patriarca cristiano di Baghdad* (Paris: Association pour l'avancement des études iraniennes, 2009).

2. See A. M. Butts, "Psalms 151–155: Syriac," in *Textual History of the Bible*, vol. 2, ed. F. Feder and M. Henze (Leiden: Brill, 2020), where further details and references can be found.

3. Note that Ps 151, which is found also in the Septuagint, has a broader circulation in Syriac than the other four.

4. See R. B. ter Haar Romeny, "Biblical Studies in the Church of the East: The Case of Catholicos Timothy I," *Studia Patristica* 38 (2001): 503–10.

other intriguing details. These range from referring to Caliph al-Rashīd (786–809) as the "victorious king," as is common in Syriac sources of the time,[5] to Timothy's mention of the appointment of bishops for the Church of the East, not only in the Middle East but spreading eastward into Central and East Asia, with Turkestan and Tibet expressly mentioned. Toward the end of the letter, Timothy returns to where he began, by discussing manuscripts, asking the recipient of the letter to send some manuscripts, search for others, and make copies of yet others.

Bibliography

Text and Editions

Braun, O. "Ein Brief des Katholikos Timotheos I über biblische Studien des 9. Jahrhunderts." *Oriens Christianus* 1 (1901): 299–313.

Heimgartner, M. *Die Briefe 42-58 des ostsyrischen Patriarchen Timotheos I*, pp. 79-87 (Syriac) and 63-72 (German). CSCO 644–45. Leuven: Peeters, 2012.

Studies

Brock, Sebastian P. "Timothy I." In *A Brief Outline of Syriac Literature*, 240–45. 2nd ed. Kottayam, India: Saint Ephrem Ecumenical Research Institute, 2009) (English translation, to which the present one is very much indebted).

---

5. Timothy is perhaps best known for his *Letter 59*, which takes the form of a dialogue with Caliph al-Mahdī (775–85). The text is edited with a German translation in M. Heimgartner, *Timotheos I, Ostsyrischer Patriarch: Disputation mit dem Kalifen Al-Mahdi*, CSCO 631–32 (Leuven: Peeters, 2011); an English translation (with a facsimile edition of a Syriac manuscript) is available in A. Mingana, *Timothy's Apology for Christianity*, Woodbrooke Studies 2 (Cambridge: Heffer, 1928), 1–162.

Letter 47

To the revered of God, Bishop Mar Sergius, metropolitan of Elam.[6] The sinner Timothy bows to your reverence and asks for your prayer.

We have read the letters of your reverence that were sent to us about the Hexapla,[7] and we now know everything that you have written in them. We hereby give thanks to God for your health and for the good direction of your leadership, and we as sinners ask God's mercy that your affairs come to a beneficial and glorious conclusion.

Concerning the book of the Hexapla, about which your reverence has written, we have already written and informed you last year that a Hexapla, copied on sheets in the Nisibene format, was sent to us in the care of our brother Gabriel,[8] syncellus of the victorious king.[9] We hired six scribes and two people to dictate, who dictated to the scribes according to the text of the exemplar. We copied all the Old Testament, together with Chronicles, Ezra, Susanna, Esther, and Judith, in three copies.[10] One was for us, and two were for the praiseworthy Gabriel, one of which was for Gabriel and the other for Beth Lapaṭ.[11] For, this is what Gabriel had written and instructed.

The manuscripts have now been copied with great work and with care, as well as with great torment, expense, and labor in six months more or less. Indeed, there is nothing more difficult to copy or to read than this, since the items in the margins are so numerous—I mean (the readings) of Aquila, Theodotion, Symmachus, and others, which take up almost as much space as the text of the

6. Sergius was a fellow student of Timothy at the School of Mar Abraham bar Dashandad in Bashosh, and he ultimately succeeded Pethion as head of the school. Sometime between 792 and 799, he was consecrated metropolitan of Elam, also known as Beth Huzaye or Khuzistan. A majority of Timothy's letters are addressed to this Sergius.

7. He means, of course, the Syriac translation, known in modern scholarship as the Syro-Hexapla, of the Septuagint column of Origen's Hexapla.

8. This is Gabriel bar Bokhtisho' (died 827/828); see A. M. Butts in *GEDSH*, 169–70.

9. This is a common Syriac expression at the time for "caliph," here referring to al-Rashīd (786–809).

10. This sentence is interesting for thinking about the biblical canon at this time in the Church of the East, as well as in Syriac Christianity more broadly; for a recent study, see L. Van Rompay, "The Syriac Canon," in *Textual History of the Bible*, vol. 2, ed. F. Feder and M. Henze (Leiden: Brill, 2020).

11. Also known as Gondeshapur, the chief city of Elam (for which, see n. 6 above).

Septuagint in the body of the manuscript.[12] The signs above these readings are numerous and differ from one another. How many of them there are no one can even say! What's more, we happened to have had evil, greedy, provincial scribes: eight men for six months or less. The manuscripts were copied, as far as possible, by the method of correction, given that they were copied by dictation. So, they were gone over a second time and read. Due to the great work and correction, my eyes have been destroyed and more or less have gone dark. You can tell the weakness of our sight from these uneven lines that we are writing.[13]

Even the exemplar from which we copied had problems, and the Greek words in it had mostly been copied in reverse. The knowledge of Greek of the person who copied this exemplar is not any better than our own, except that he did not realize the reversal of the characters of writing, whereas we are at least aware of that.[14] In addition, he was unaware of the interchange and changing of characters, with a *chi* instead of *kappa*, *zeta* instead of *chi*, and all sorts of others. We, however, know how these things are.

At the end of each book, the following was written: "This was written, collated, and copied from an exemplar of Eusebius Pamphilus and Origen."

This is the way that the Hexapla was copied. It has endless differences from what we possess.[15] It seems to me that the one who translated this exemplar in our hands worked from the versions of Theodotion, Aquila, and Symmachus, since it has more similarity with them than with the Septuagint.

I had thought that a Hexapla had already been sent to your reverence. When you wrote, immediately we wrote to the excellent Gabriel that he should fulfill his promise to you. But, if he does not want to send you a copy, let him write to us, for we will copy it again and send it to you. That is all on that.

We have learned from some Jews, worthy to be believed, who now recently became disciples of Christianity, that ten years ago some books were found near Jericho in a dwelling in a mountain. They said that the dog of an Arab man who was hunting went into a cleft after some game and did not come out. Its owner went after it and found a chamber in the mountain, in which there were many

---

12. The Syro-Hexapla, like the Septuagint column of the Hexapla, had numerous text-critical signs indicating variants among the various Greek versions as well as the Hebrew text.

13. An obvious allusion to Paul's autographic claim in Gal 6:11 (see also 1 Cor 16:21 and 2 Thess 3:17).

14. This seems to be tongue in cheek, since Timothy had at least some knowledge of Greek; see, for instance, his comments on collaborating on Syriac and Arabic translations of Aristotle's *Topics* in his *Letter 43* and *Letter 48*. Edited with German translation in M. Heimgartner, *Die Briefe 42–58 des ostsyrischen Patriarchen Timotheos I*, CSCO 644–45 (Leuven: Peeters, 2012); English translation with helpful commentary in Sebastian P. Brock, "Two Letters of the Patriarch Timothy from the Late Eighth Century on Translations from Greek," *Arabic Sciences and Philosophy* 9 (1999): 233–46.

15. That is, the Syriac Peshiṭta version.

books. That hunter went to Jerusalem and relayed this to the Jews. Many of them came, and they found books of the Old Testament as well as others in Hebrew script. Since the one who told me about this knows the script and is literate, I asked him about certain verses that are adduced in our New Testament as coming from the Old, but there is no mention at all of them in the Old Testament, neither among us Christians nor among those Jews. He told me that there is, and they are found in those books that had been discovered there.

When I heard this from that disciple, I asked him also for others as well, and I found the same exact story without change. I wrote about this to the excellent Gabriel as well as to Shubḥalmaran, metropolitan of Damascus, so that they might look into these books and see if there is in any place in the prophets the seal: "He will be called Nazarene,"[16] or "What no eye has seen, nor ear heard,"[17] or "Cursed is everyone who hangs on wood,"[18] or "He turned back the boundary of Israel, according to the word that the Lord spoke through Jonah the prophet from Gad Ḥfar,"[19] or others like them, which were adduced in the New or Old Testaments but are not at all in what we possess.[20] I further implored them that, if these verses were found in those books, they certainly had to translate them. In addition, in (the psalm that begins:) "Have mercy on me, O God, according to your grace,"[21] it is written: "Sprinkle upon me the hyssop of the blood of your cross and clean me."[22] This phrase is not found in the Septuagint, not in any of the other versions, and not in the Hebrew. That Hebrew man told me: "We found a psalter among those books that has more than two hundred psalms." I have written concerning these matters to them.

I think that these books were perhaps placed by the prophet Jeremiah, Baruch, or someone else among those who heard the word of God and trembled at it. For, when the prophets learned through divine revelation of the captivity, plunder, and burning that would come upon the people because of their sin, as those who were truly convinced that not one of the words of God would fall to the earth, they hid those books in the mountains and caves, and they buried them so that they would not burn in fire and not be plundered by captors. Those who hid them, after a span of seventy years or less, died. When the people returned from Babylon, no one remained from those who had placed the books. Therefore, Ezra and others were compelled to investigate, and they discovered what the Hebrews possessed.

16. Matt 2:23.

17. 1 Cor 2:9.

18. Gal 3:13.

19. 2 Kings 14:25.

20. This formulation as well as the last quotation of 2 Kgs 14:25 differs from the first formulation in now including references of the Old Testament to another passage in the Old Testament.

21. Ps 51:1.

22. Ps 51:7.

The Bible among the Hebrews consists of three volumes: one that after some time the seventy translators translated for King Ptolemy, who is worthy of a wreath of accolades; another that others translated after some time; and yet another that is kept among them.

If these verses are found in the previously mentioned books, it is obvious that they are more trustworthy than those among the Hebrews and those among us. Although I have written, I have not received any answer from them about this, and I do not have anyone capable whom I could send. This matter has become like a burning fire in my heart, and it inflames my bones.

Pray for me! My body is very weak, my hands are entirely unable to write, and my eyes are weak. These are the signs and harbingers of death. Pray for me that I am not condemned at the judgment of our Lord.

The Spirit has recently anointed a metropolitan for Turkestan, and we are also preparing to anoint a different one for Tibet. We have sent another to Shiharzur and another to Radan, since Nestorius of Radan has passed away. Another we are preparing for Ray, since Theodoros has passed away; another for Gurgan; another for Balad—namely Cyriacus of Beth 'Abe; another for Dasen, since Jacob has sunk into the pit in which there is no resurrection; and another for Beth Nuhadra, since it has no bishop. Therefore, beseech with us the lord of the harvest to send out workers for his harvest.

Shubḥalisho' of Beth Daylamaye has fastened the crown of martyrdom. We have sent to his location ten monks from Beth 'Abe. Pray for me, revered of God, my Lord.

Send to me the *Apology of Eusebius of Caesarea for Origen*, for I will read it and send it back. Search for the *Homilies on the Soul* by the great patriarch Mar Aba, for there are three of them, and we have only one.[23] Copy and send to us the homilies of Rabban Mar Narsai that we do not have.[24] For, the revered of memory Ephrem wrote to us that there are many there that are not here. Write to the tyrant of Persia and inform him that every metropolitan who is appointed by a bishop and his coordainers is subject to the canon of the church of God, to the synod of the 318,[25] and to the canons of Mar Aba.[26]

---

23. Though no work of his on the soul survives, this is likely Aba I (died 552); on whom, see L. Van Rompay in *GEDSH*, 1.

24. That is, the foundational East Syriac poet Narsai (died ca. 500); see A. M. Butts, "Narsai's Life and Work," in *Narsai: Rethinking His Work and His World*, ed. Aaron M. Butts, Kristian S. Heal, and Robert A. Kitchen, Studies and Texts in Antiquity and Christianity 121 (Tübingen: Mohr Siebeck, 2020), 1–8.

25. That is, the Council of Nicaea.

26. The same Aba I as found in n. 23, of whom a number of canons indeed survive.

9. Theodore bar Koni, *Scholion, Mēmrā 10*

Introduction and translation by Aaron Michael Butts

Theodore bar Koni taught at the exegetical School of Kashkar in south-ern Mesopotamia at the beginning of the 'Abbāsid period (750–1258). He is best known for his *Scholion*, completed in 792/793, which is a manual of the theology of the Church of the East.[1] In its present form, the *Scholion* is composed of eleven mēmrē. The first nine are organized according to the biblical text: mēmrē 1–5 treat the Old Testament, whereas 6–9 treat the New Testament. These mēmrē are not structured as a running com-mentary, but rather are in the form of questions and answers, a genre employed by other Syriac exegetes. In addition to questions of a strictly exegetical nature, Bar Koni often discusses various philosophical and theological concepts within these first nine mēmrē. The *Scholion*'s tenth mēmrā, which is of interest here, is an apology for Christianity against Is-lam.[2] The question-and-answer format of the previous mēmrē is replaced in this mēmrā by a dialogue between a teacher, who speaks on behalf of Christians, and a student, who speaks on behalf of Muslims, or as stated in the text *ḥanpē* ("pagans"), which seems to be a wordplay with Arabic *al-ḥanīf* ("a true believer, muslim"). The tenth mēmrā is an important source for understanding Muslim-Christian relations in the early 'Abbāsid period.[3] The eleventh and final mēmrā of the *Scholion* is a description of what Bar Koni calls "all the heresies before and after Christ." These include Zoroastrianism, Mandeism, Manicheism, various types of Gnosticism, as well as the "heresies" of the Quqites, Orphites, and the Bardaisan-ites, to name only a few. One of the sources of the eleventh mēmrā is the *Anakephalaiōsis*, an abridgement of the *Panarion* of Epiphanius of Salamis (died 403).

1. See Sidney H. Griffith "Theodore bar Kônî's Scholion: A Nestorian Summa contra Gen-tiles from the First Abbasid Century," in *East of Byzantium: Syria and Armenia in the Formative Period (Dumbarton Oaks Symposium, 1980)*, ed. Nina G. Garsoïan, Thomas F. Mathews, and Robert W. Thomson (Washington, DC: Dumbarton Oaks, 1982), 53–72.

2. See Sidney H. Griffith, "Chapter Ten of the Scholion: Theodore bar Kônî's Apology for Christianity," *Orientalia Christiana Periodica* 47 (1981): 158–88.

3. In general, see Michael P. Penn, *Envisioning Islam: Syriac Christians and the Early Muslim World*, Divinations: Rereading Late Ancient Religion (Philadelphia: University of Pennsylvania Press, 2015).

Bibliography

Text and Editions

Brade, L. *Untersuchungen zum Scholienbuch des Theodoros bar Konai*. Göttinger Orientforschungen: Syriaca 8. Wiesbaden: Harrassowitz, 1975 (Syriac and German translation of Urmia recension of Pauline Epistles).

Hespel, R. *Théodore bar Koni: Livre des scolies (recension d'Urmiah)*. CSCO 447–48. Leuven: Peeters, 1983 (Syriac and French translation of additions in Urmia recension).

Hespel, R., and R. Draguet. *Théodore bar Koni: Livre des scolies (recension de Séert)*. CSCO 431–32. Leuven: Peeters, 1981 (French translation of Siirt recension).

Scher, A. *Theodorus bar Kōnī: Liber Scholiorum*. CSCO 55, 69. Leuven: Peeters, 1910–12 (Syriac of Siirt recension).

TRANSLATION

Scholion, Mēmrā 10

An admonition and refutation, which has been written in simple language, and a disputation in question-and-answer form against those who, though they profess to have received the Old Testament, and they confess the coming of our Lord, are actually far from both of these, and they are demanding from us an apology for our faith not from all our books but from those that they also confess.

May your uprightness, O brother John, know that the thoughts that you considered to be obscure in the Holy Scriptures, I have sufficiently gathered and set in the nine mēmrē before this one, (both) as it appeared to that one who strengthens the weak and as anyone is able to know from the book and the discussion in it, [for we have not left outside of our path][4] one obscure interpretation that we have not set in this book. This we have taken pains to do, as I have said many times, first, for the benefit of myself; second, for the easing of your desire, because you have demanded this from us; and, third, so that we might articulate those interpretations of the holy books before the lesser knowledge

4. Not found in all manuscripts.

of those who have recently approached the contemplation of the reading of the commentaries of the blessed interpreter.[5] Although the matter was laborious, we have forced ourselves to do it, because the benefit of others[6] was more honorable in our eyes than the easing of ourselves, not so that we might boast in this, because theoretical speculation does not belong to us; ours is this: That we labor in collecting.

Now, it seemed to me that I should join this mēmrā to the book whose title was placed above, because I thought that the benefit from it was not small and especially that it seems that its goal is other than a dispute against heresy. Although it is an admonition against pagans[7] and a confirmation of the faith, we have set it as questions, as has been our custom throughout all the book: on behalf of pagans is the student, and on behalf of Christians the teacher. It is now time for us to approach this, as the prayers of the saints accompany us.

Teacher: Do you believe in one God or many?

Student: One.

Teacher: Is he from before creation or at creation?

Student: From before creation.

Teacher: How do you demonstrate that he is one, that he is from before everything, and that he is creator?

Student: From thought, from facts, and from the witness of the blessed Moses.

Teacher: Explain.

Student: *From thoughts*: every rational being is moved [to confess that he has a cause and how] this cause is embedded in the progress of his nature. It is believed *from facts*:[8] through the opposing changes that are in creation, which while numerous and diverse appear[9] to be one thing, and their antagonism, even though it seems to be in opposition, is gathered to one thing. Another thing, which is greater than all these, the blessed Moses taught; he said: "In the beginning, God created the heavens and the earth."[10] Clearly, he proclaims God's role as creator.

Teacher: Do you confess that Moses is not from the race of the Hebrews?

Student: Truly (he is).

Teacher: Answer, then, relatedly, why were the people of the Hebrews chosen in their entirety?

5. That is, Theodore of Mopsuestia (died 428).
6. Other manuscripts read "of those who are lacking."
7. See introduction to translation.
8. Though the word is different from that used above.
9. Some manuscripts read "appear to adapt."
10. Gen 1:1.

Student: This is known to everyone: on account of Abraham's righteousness, all his race was honored.

Teacher: This is not what I asked you, why did God not choose others, that you might answer me, on account of his righteousness Abraham was chosen. But, it is on account of what was he chosen? If you say on account of righteousness, Noah and Shem were also righteous.

Student: I know that it was on account of his excellence that he was chosen, according to God's witness about him.

Teacher: On account of his righteousness, Abraham was chosen. This is clear, but another cause is sought. For, if you say only on account of his righteousness, you curse God, you place him under human passions, and you deny his blessings to the saints in the expulsion of their offspring who are from the divine household. If these things are true, you must demonstrate another cause.

Student: If this is not it, then that other cause is that, because Moses was prepared to give the law, it was necessary for God to set them apart and choose them.

Teacher: This is not the exact cause because it seems that however much they were holding the law, it was not correcting them, and it was also unable to benefit the entire world. Whatever thus appeared to be weak was not showing care for those who received it. But, I ask you what is the cause of its corollary: Was the law for the choosing? Or the choosing for the law?

Student: The law was for the choosing.

Teacher: If the law was the cause of the choosing, it is known that God did not choose them without knowing the conduct of its recipients. But, knowing well, he made a beginning with the righteousness of Abraham in order to create an incentive for excellence. Again, concerning the law, it is necessary to ask: What is the full cause of its giving?

Student: As far as I know, it was given on account of two causes. First, in order to bind the people to the fear of God. For, thus, he is known by the sacrifices that they bring to him, though he is not in need. Second, to teach the pagan people, who worship creatures, that the one who is worshiped among the house of Israel is truly God and, as far as possible, to make others part of his household.

Teacher: These two things that you have said seem to carry the shadow of truth, though they lack substance.

Student: How then?

Teacher: We see that it is not the people who benefitted in some way from his laws, for in every place God appealed and called out against them that they had worshiped creatures, and due to this he led them into various captivities, as is even the case now. Also, they did not benefit no matter how much the threats of judgment frightened the ones who had received it. If these things are thus, it is necessary for another cause to be proclaimed.

Student: I do not know another cause. You, if you are so convinced, say.

Teacher: I say this, that the choosing of Abraham, and the giving of the law, and the revelations to the prophets, and the care for the people, and any other matters that are unnecessary for us to narrate are on account of nothing other than the revelation of our Lord, Jesus Christ, from them.

Student: Demonstrate.

Teacher: From the fact that after he appeared, there has not again been care or zeal as before, and this is even though they now seem to keep the law more than in previous times.

Student: I agree with what you have said, because it is true that this is the case.

Teacher: If it seems from testing the facts that the goal of the economy of God in the Old Testament is entirely congruent with the economy in the New Testament, then we should leave from here and show how those new things—concerning which you are divided—agree with the old ones. First, we will ask: how much of what is written in the two Testaments is true or not?

Student: I agree with everything in the Old Testament, because I know that there is neither addition nor subtraction there, according to the speech of that one who has transmitted this teaching to us. However, I do not agree with everything in the New Testament, because there are many things that have been corrupted. When they were not there, others introduced them for error and mixed them up.

Teacher: What are the things in the New Testament with which you do not agree?

Student: I believe that Christ was born from a virgin woman, that he was sent from the one who gave the law, that he was resurrected and judged, and that he is now in heaven. But, I am unable to believe that I should call him "Son of God," as you blaspheme, that God has a Son who was born from him, and that he is of the same nature.

Teacher: It seems that this is what is keeping you from our confession, for we confess that God has a Son who was born from him and that he is of the same nature, perfect in everything like him.

Student: Indeed, maintaining that it is possible for a simple and formless nature to beget prevents me from believing, although I also do not agree with baptism, the sacraments, and the crucifixion.

Teacher: The mode of your disagreement with us, then, is not singular, but you deny the entire economy. For, it is through these things that the difference with the Old Testament is known. Whoever does not confess and keep these things also does not know Christ. But, I ask you, do you now receive completely all the words of the Old Testament? Or, some of them, yes, but others, no.

Student: Even if I confirm that all these have been given by God, there are many that were useful only in their particular time. But, now, they are void, and I do not keep them.

Teacher: Which are the ones that you keep? And which not?

Student: The Sabbath, the sacrifices, the observance of days, the distinction between foods, I do not keep, because they have been abrogated. But, the confession in one God, worship to the west, and the education to the coming of Christ, since it is impossible for them to be abrogated, I keep, because if they were abrogated then also all the law would be abrogated, and God, its giver, would necessarily be made a liar.

Teacher: If the one who gave them is the same, what is the cause that these are abrogated, but those are valid?

Student: I think that these were abrogated because they were not useful for the knowledge of all common humanity, but only the weak knowledge of the Jews was affirmed by them, as I have said, for it went astray differently here and there. Because of this, they were given along with the granting of a law, which was given to them separately. For the rest, they were not any benefit. But, knowledge of God, nearness to him, laws that impede odious things, and the teaching about Christ are useful to the Jews as well as to all people. Therefore, it is impossible that they be void.

Teacher: Those things that are void, how are they void?

Student: God rendered them void by Christ.

Teacher: What is the cause?

Student: That thus it seemed right to him to benefit us through those matters of Christ.

Teacher: So, you show Christ to be contrary to the Old Testament?

Student: God forbid that this be the case! As if Moses on the one hand said: "Do not kill!," and Christ on the other hand said: "Kill!"

Teacher: Do you confess only Moses or all the prophets?

Student: I believe all the words of the prophets, as those who have been sent by a single one.

Teacher: In the matters of Christ, do you confess only Christ or also his disciples?

Student: I told you above that I confess Christ and his teaching. But, you do not properly possess that teaching. Rather, you have many traditions that are not true, by which you basically blaspheme against God.

Teacher: We will explain later how we teach the truth that we know without mixing falsehood with our confession, but now let us proceed to the following question: Since you have confessed that you agree with the law, we will show you the truth of our teaching with which you disagree. Not only is it not foreign to the law, but our teaching's mystery has been traced and depicted in it. Because we confess both Christ and the law, we will see who truly holds Christ according to the teaching of the law. First, I ask you, where is it actually possible to show whether or not Christ has come?

Student: I am able to show from three places that the coming of Christ has already happened.

Teacher: What are these?

Student: One is the cessation of the law, the second is the great demonstration of his gospel, and the third is from the witness of that one who has transmitted this teaching to us.

Teacher: Do you agree with all the words spoken in the law about Christ? And that they have been fulfilled by his coming?

Student: It is clear that, if I have at one time confessed his coming, then I must necessarily also confess that the prophecies about him have been fulfilled, lest I fall into the disbelief of the Jews.

Teacher: It is necessary then for you to say the words spoken in the law about Christ so that truth is better known than falsehood.

Student: I do not know the law precisely.

Teacher: If you do not know, will you agree with what I say?

Student: If you do not corrupt the witnesses that have been rightly said, I will accept them.

Teacher: It is impossible for the words that have been spoken about Christ in the Old Testament to be changed. If it happened and someone strayed from their goal, then likewise he would also corrupt their truth. From there, also his teaching would be lying. If it happens that you disagree, I will bring a Jew, an enemy of our truth, that he might bear witness about the matters that I will say. But, I ask that you have a vigilant mind. I will be a Jew, and you the judge.

Student: Tell me these things then.

Teacher: First, let Jacob, the father of the tribes, come, and from him we can hear what is expounded upon about Christ in the form of the blessings to Judah, from whom his birth would be received: "The rod shall not depart from Judah, nor the scepter from his feet, until the one who has the kingdom comes, and he is the expectation of the peoples."[11] About his suffering: "His eyes are redder than wine, and his teeth are whiter than

11. Gen 49:10.

milk."[12] "He whitens his garment in milk, and in the blood of grapes his covering."[13] About his entry into Jerusalem, riding a donkey: "Let him bind his donkey to a grapevine and the colt of his ass to a vine shoot."[14]

After this Moses proclaimed him, saying: "May the Lord raise up a prophet for you from your brothers like me."[15] "May it happen that every soul that does not listen to that prophet, may it be destroyed from its people."[16] About these things our Lord himself bore witness: "Moses has written about me."[17]

After this one, David, the king and prophet, proclaimed about his divinity by saying: "Your throne, God, is forever and ever."[18] About his humanity: "The Lord said to my Lord: 'Sit at my right hand.'"[19] About his suffering: "The kings of the earth and the rulers arose and took counsel together about the Lord and about his Christ."[20] About his entrance into Jerusalem with the praise of crowds: "From the mouth of young children and infants, you have established praise."[21]

After David, Isaiah: "Behold, a virgin will conceive and give birth to a son, and his name shall be called Emmanuel."[22]

Zechariah the prophet proclaimed: "He will ride on a donkey and on the foal of an ass."[23]

Daniel in Babylon: "Christ shall come and be killed, and the city of holiness shall be destroyed by his death."[24] He also numbered the days with precision.

These and others more numerous than these that bear witness to his coming are in the Old Testament. Do you believe them? Or not? It is impossible for someone to come to Christ unless he has first been instructed and been confirmed in these. For, even if there are many who believe in Christ, such as the Manicheans, the Marcionites, the Dostheans, and the rest of the heretics, they are liars, and their confession is not true, because

12. Gen 49:12.
13. Gen 49:11.
14. Gen 49:11.
15. Deut 18:15.
16. Compare Lev 23:30.
17. John 5:46.
18. Ps 45:6.
19. Ps 110:1.
20. Ps 8:2.
21. Ps 2:2.
22. Isa 7:14.
23. Zech 9:9.
24. Dan 9:26.

it was not built on the foundation of the prophets and apostles. If someone presses them with precision, then immediately the deception of their
denial of Christ is revealed, in that an opposite God has been exalted in
the vain apparitions that they devise, and they accuse all that is visible.

Student: You have rightly said that these words that you have narrated are the door
and entrance to confessing Christ. I am unable to say that I do not agree
with them because everyone who does not agree with these disturbs the
entire economy of God from the beginning until now and is found to be
a denier of Christ. These have rightly been confessed up until now, and
there is no disagreement about them, because we are unable to resist the
Scripture. But, see that even if it is from there that we confess Christ, the
practice of other things that you have added, which are not written in the
law, is impious, and it is necessary to defend these as well, if it is possible.

Teacher: Which are those things that are foreign to you?

Student: Baptism, the Eucharist, the veneration of the cross, the fact that you call
him the Son of God, and how you worship him as God, along with other
things like these that are full of audacity, so as to abandon the worship of
God and worship instead made things—this approaches the work of paganism.

Teacher: As I see it, had you believed in the true Christ, you would have accepted
also the witnesses about him that we have narrated above as well as also
those things by which we can be called Christians, but because you scorn
these things you deny the holy sacraments by which Christianity is established, and you make God stand against his own nature. So that the truth
of our confession might be better known, we will demonstrate from here
with the help of God. We will begin first with the mystery of baptism, and
we will make a defense of it. For, the entrance to Christianity is along this
path. Then we will proceed to the other matters. First, we ask what is the
cause that you do not confess baptism. For, your lie about baptism extends
to the one who gave it.

On baptism

Student: I do not accept baptism because, first, it is not written specifically in the
Torah; second, the one who has transmitted this teaching to us did not
teach us about it; third, as I see it, it is not useful for the teaching of the
fear of God.

Teacher: If it is because it is not specified in the Torah that you refuse it, why do you
not also refuse to eat animals that are unclean according to the law? For,

anyone who eats them is sentenced to death.[25] If you say it was abrogated by Christ, it is necessary for you also to show in which place it is written. If this was abrogated by Christ when it was not commanded in the law to be abrogated, like the Sabbath and the sacrifices, and you accept these, then you should also accept baptism, because our Lord has transmitted it.

Student: Have you said that Christ was baptized?

Teacher: Completely.

Student: Baptism, then, is also sought for fulfillment. How do you call him "God" and the "Son of God"?

Teacher: It is not in that he is God and the Son of God that he was baptized, but in that he is Christ. But, tell me: do you say that Abraham was circumcised?

Student: Truly.

Teacher: What did circumcision benefit the one to whose righteousness God bore witness before circumcision? If Abraham was circumcised, and it was not on account of himself that he was circumcised, but that through it he might tread a path for his seed to the household that is with God, why do you deny for Christ the baptism that he has transmitted, through which those who believe in the treasure of true children are inscribed? But, I ask you, do you receive the teaching of Christ or not?

Student: I accept the teaching about Christ.

Teacher: I did not say "about Christ" but "of Christ." Whoever accepts the teaching about Christ but scorns the teaching of Christ clearly denies Christ.

Student: I also do not scorn the teaching of Christ. God forbid! But, I said that baptism is without use after the teaching about Christ.

Teacher: This is the entry door to being inscribed in the household of Christ. If not, tell me what is the cause that, though God was able to draw the Jews to himself only through word, this was not enough for him, but (he drew them to himself) by the stamp of circumcision?

Student: I say that circumcision was only given to be a sign of the covenant between God and those who received it, and to be a separation between foreigners and the household.

Teacher: Was it possible for someone to be called a Jew without it?

Student: No.

Teacher: Why?

Student: Because in this way God wanted there to be an entrance by it into his household.

---

25. Though the Torah, especially Leviticus and Deuteronomy, contain lengthy discussions of unclean animals, death is never prescribed as the penalty for breaking food laws.

Teacher:	Whoever does not bear this mark on his flesh, even if he loves the law myriad times over, was he added to the household of Abraham?
Student:	No.
Teacher:	Accept also this baptism of Christ: just as someone is unable to be called a Jew apart from circumcision, so too someone is unable to be called a Christian apart from baptism.
Student:	What is necessary about baptism?
Teacher:	What is necessary about circumcision? Was God unable to have a people without it? Rather, just as there he determined that through it they would join his commandments, so also here he established baptism. But, tell me, by what else are we being inscribed for Christ and distinguished from pagans? For, now there are many who wear the name of Christ but are far from Christianity.
Student:	Then, as you have said, everyone who is baptized in water is a Christian, and so rightly Marcionites and Dostheans say: "We are Christians," for just like you they are baptized in water.
Teacher:	It is not that everyone who is baptized and who baptizes is a Christian. If not, then consider everyone who is circumcised in whichever way a Jew.
Student:	No.
Teacher:	Why?
Student:	Because circumcision in and of itself is insufficient to bring to the fear of God, for there are those who are circumcised because of illnesses and others because of tradition, and they are not Jews.
Teacher:	Is anyone who keeps the law and does not receive circumcision permitted to enter the house of the Lord?
Student:	No.
Teacher:	So also it is with baptism, without which it is impossible for someone to be a Christian. Everyone who is baptized and does not fulfill the laws of Christians is falsely called a Christian. If you doubt this, give me a Jew who is not circumcised or that everyone who is circumcised is a Jew.
Student:	Are you baptized in Christ or like Christ? If you say "in Christ," then you will not be made part of God's household.
Teacher:	We are baptized "like Christ," because he also was baptized, as well as "in Christ," because he is also God. For, the name Christ clearly shows that he is human in one way, but God in another, because there are many who have been called messiahs,[26] but it did not remain with them, because they were anointed in temporal oil. This one, however, (was anointed) in

26. The word translated "Christ" throughout this passage is the same as that for "Messiah," or even more literally "the anointed one."

the Holy Spirit, as the blessed David teaches: "Because of this, God, your God, has anointed you with an oil of joy more than your companions."[27] Therefore, we are baptized in God clothed with Christ.

Student: It seems that you have confirmed what they say about you that you worship a human. For, this is shown by the fact that you have said: "We are baptized in Christ."

Teacher: I do not think that you have understood what we are saying that "we are baptized in God clothed with Christ." We say that Christ from the beginning of when he is received is not distinct from God, the Word, who received him later. It is clear that we are baptized not in a created nature.

Student: I say that baptism is not necessary. For it does not provide any benefit for the fear of God. Thus, that one who has transmitted to us this teaching taught us.

Teacher: Did that one who transmitted this teaching to you receive it from God to say this? Or from his own conscience? If from his own mind, we will not abandon the teaching of the Scriptures and follow human thoughts. If you say from God, where was this God who taught this who has been unknown for six hundred years or more since Christ appeared, for all who have confessed this mark have become disciples to him? If you say that baptism was and is outside of his will, how did he make it grow from small to big when it was fighting against him? How did he strengthen it by frequent miracles, which he was doing through the hands of its proclaimers? For, it is clear that Christianity has been victorious through weak and despised ones. It seems from the facts that without sword and without shield it was able to subdue kings and their rulers. How did these things happen through baptism if it is at war with God?

That you have said that water does not add anything to the fear of God, you are also unable to show that the cut of circumcision adds anything to the fear of God. Although we put on power through the sanctity of baptism from that power who created the natures, we do not say that the nature of water adds something, but it serves as mediation: God sanctifies us through the mediation of the priest and sets us apart that we might be in his household. Just like the royal seal on workers, so also believers are marked with it. When it is kept without sins, it is able to work every sign through the hands of the ones who have received it. The saints, who keeping it well through their works drive out demons and heal every illness, bear witness to the fact that this is the case.

Student: Is baptism in and of itself, without good conduct, able to complete some-

27. Ps 45:7.

one in the fear of God. If it is possible, what provisions do you make for good conduct? Do evil things! For baptism will easily make you righteous. If this is wicked and if good conduct is necessarily required, is it not useless? Do we not rightly say that it is not required?

Teacher: It is the principle point[28] of fear of God and then good conduct is next after it. Just as it is impossible for the limbs to stand without a head, so also it is impossible for good conduct to be completed without it. If not, then show me a headless body! Or a roof without foundations! Or Judaism without circumcision! Or food without drink! Or seed without rain! Or child without father! For, in baptism we are gathered from error, and we are inscribed as members of God's house. Only then do we adapt our conduct according to the goal of our calling. Just as someone is unable to be born in this life without first having been conceived, so also everyone who after the coming of Christ until now is not born from baptism does not have life in themselves.

Student: But, see that it is not written in the law that Christ will come to give baptism. For this reason, it is difficult for me to believe it.

Teacher: Even if it is not written, its goal is inscribed, just as we have said above, in circumcision and in the crossing of the (Red) Sea. Even if not, you are unable to show precisely that Christ was resurrected and judged and that they were written in the Old Testament. We do not consider their giver to be a liar since they have not been written, because the main point of all this is that our Lord Christ who has transmitted baptism to us is believed, and whoever does not accept baptism denies Christ.

Student: I accept that these matters of baptism possess a likeness in the Old Testament in every way, but the Eucharist that you give and that you call it the body of Christ, who is able to endure such a blasphemy?

[The text continues with sections on the Eucharist, on the will and person (i.e., Christology), on the veneration of the cross and of Christ, on the entrance of our Lord into Jerusalem (i.e., the celebration of Palm Sunday), and on the Son.]

28. Literally, "head."

2

ARMENIAN

Introduction and Bibliography by Jesse S. Arlen

A rmenian Christianity took root among a people who lived at the cross-roads of the Eurasian empires and cultures of both West (Roman, Byzantine, Ottoman Turkish) and East (Iranian [Parthian, Sassanian, Safavid], Arab, Russian). Ever open to interchange with others in various realms (liturgy, theology, etc.), for two millennia Armenian Christianity has maintained a unique and creative witness to the revelation of God in Christ.

Christianity first arrived in Armenia through Syriac missionaries via Edessa. Subsequent Armenian tradition even claimed Abgar the Black, king of Osroene, as an Armenian king (still remembered today in every divine liturgy) and ex-tended the apostleship of Addai (Thaddeus) from Edessa into Armenia, thus granting the Armenian Church apostolic claims.[1] Certain words unique to the new religion were borrowed from Syriac in this early phase, such as k'ahanay for "priest." A second, slightly later stream came from the West, whose traditions are preserved in the *History of Armenia* by Agat'angeghos. It tells the story of female virgin monastics from Rome martyred in Armenia—Gayianē, Hṙip'simē, and their companions—and the activity of Grigor the Illuminator, of Parthian noble stock but raised in Caesarea (Cappadocia), through whom King Trdat of Armenia and his royal court were converted in the early fourth century around the same time as Constantine (see text 3 below).

While the court's approval led to the promulgation of the new faith in Ar-menia, the Good Religion (Zoroastrianism) remained popular. In fact, com-munities of Zoroastrian Armenians survived into the twentieth century, and vestiges of pre-Christian beliefs and practices are still present in many of the traditions and rituals of the Armenian Church today.[2] Most of the major feasts

---

1. Valentina Calzolari, "Réécriture des textes apocryphes en arménien: l'exemple de la légende de l'apostolat de Thaddée en Arménie," *Apocrypha* 8 (1997): 97–110.

2. James R. Russell, *Zoroastrianism in Armenia*, Harvard Iranian Studies 5 (Cambridge:

and festivals of the liturgical year incorporated pre-Christian practices (such as transfiguration and *Vardavar*), while animal sacrifice (*matagh*) became a sanctioned ritual.[3] Patterns of societal organization that Armenia shared with Iran also influenced church structure. For example, the position of bishop and catholicos (supreme patriarch), in addition to parish priest, were hereditary or dynastic offices throughout many periods of history.

The royal court's adoption of Christianity as state religion of Armenia should be understood against the backdrop of the wider political events of the age. In 224 the Sassanians overthrew the Parthian rulers of Iran, and since a junior branch of the Parthian Arsacids (Arshakuni) were ruling in Armenia, Armenia inclined toward support of the Roman Empire in its wars against the Sassanians. The adoption of Christianity thus strengthened a political alliance between the Arsacid King Trdat and Constantine. After years of shifting borders that divided the Armenian realm into separate spheres under Roman and Sassanian control, in 387 a more lasting partition was arranged at the Treaty of Ekegheats' between Theodosius I and Shapur III, by which the Sassanians secured approximately four-fifths of Armenia.[4]

The mission of Mashtots' and Sahak to create an alphabet for the Armenian language at the turn of the fifth century, in addition to serving their evangelistic agenda, helped to provide a unifying force for the divided Armenian realm. This became all the more important after the last Arshakuni monarch was deposed at the request of the highly independent Armenian *nakharark'* ("nobles" or "hereditary lords") and replaced with a Persian *marzpan* (military governor).[5] Division among the factious *nakharark'* came to the fore in the second half of the fifth century. Led by the Mamikonean family, certain *nakharark'* rose up in resistance to the policy of Sassanian Emperor Yazdegerd II to impose Zurvanism (Zoroastrianism) throughout Armenia, while other *nakharark'* fought on the Sassanian side. The climax of this struggle, the Battle of Avarayr in 451, was immortalized by the historians Eghishē and Ghazar, and a tradition of military martyrdom in defense of the faith arose in the wake of memorializing the fallen Christian war-

---

Harvard University Press, 1987); Russell, *Armenian and Iranian Studies*, Harvard Armenian Texts and Studies 9 (Cambridge: Harvard University Press, 2004).

3. Russell, *Armenian and Iranian Studies*, 469–75; Fred C. Conybeare, "The Survival of Animal Sacrifices inside the Christian Church," *American Journal of Theology* 7 (1903): 62–90.

4. Nina G. Garsoïan, "Aršakuni Dynasty," in *The Armenian People from Ancient to Modern Times*, ed. Richard Hovannisian (New York: Saint Martin's, 1997), 1:63–94.

5. Nina G. Garsoïan, "Naxarar," in *Encyclopaedia Iranica* (online at https://iranicaonline .org/articles/naxarar); Garsoïan, "The Marzapanate," in *The Armenian People from Ancient to Modern Times*, ed. Richard Hovannisian (New York: Saint Martin's, 1997), 1:95–115; Nicolas Adontz, *Armenia in the Period of Justinian: The Political Conditions Based on the Naxarar System*, trans. Nina G. Garsoïan (Lisbon: Calouste Gulbenkian Foundation, 1970).

riors.[6] In the latter half of the fifth century, Armenia secured religious autonomy from the Sassanian Empire, and Christianity became increasingly dominant.

With the creation of the alphabet came a prolific translation project beginning with the Scriptures and biblical commentaries and extending to other theological, conciliar, homiletic, hagiographic, catechetical, and liturgical texts from Syriac and Greek. Works by Irenaeus, John Chrysostom, Eusebius, Basil of Caesarea, Gregory of Nazianzus, Gregory of Nyssa, Cyril of Jerusalem, Cyril of Alexandria, the writings of the desert fathers and monastics, Evagrius, Aphrahat, Ephrem the Syrian, and others were translated.[7] Armenians also began composing original works in a variety of genres, the works of Koriwn (text 1) and Eznik (text 2) being two of the earliest examples.

Armenian attests a prominent historiographical tradition, with original histories composed in every period from the fifth century onward. Some of the most important historians from the early period include Agat'angeghos, the *Epic Histories* (*Buzandaran Patmut'iwnk'* or P'awstos Buzand), Eghishē, Ghazar of P'arpi, and at least a stratum of that attributed to Movsēs of Khoren.[8] The histories of all these early writers have been translated into English with scholarly studies. Many later histories, however, remain less studied. In line with the alphabet's invention as a tool for the evangelizing Christian religion, the vast majority of literary works composed in Armenian issued from a religious milieu (including the histories), produced and transmitted in monastic settings. Much of this literature has been published, but comparatively little has been translated, and much remains to be explored.

Later periods of translation rendered into Armenian a corpus of Greek works of philosophy, logic, grammar, rhetoric, mathematics, and the natural sciences, most of which were produced in an Armenian style that faithfully maintained Greek word order and syntax and is known as the Hellenizing or Hellenophile School (*Yunaban dprots'*) of translations.[9] Some of the prominent translations

---

6. S. Peter Cowe, "Ełišē's 'Armenian War' as a Metaphor for the Spiritual Life," in *From Byzantium to Iran: Armenian Studies in Honour of Nina Garsoïan*, ed. Jean-Pierre Mahé and Robert W. Thomson (Atlanta: Scholars Press, 1997), 341–59.

7. Levon Ter Petrossian, *Ancient Armenian Translations* (New York: Saint Vartan, 1997).

8. Robert W. Thomson, "The Major Works of Armenian Historiography," in *Armenian Philology in the Modern Era: From Manuscript to Digital Text*, ed. Valentina Calzolari and Michael E. Stone, Handbook of Oriental Studies 8: Uralic and Central Asian Studies, vol. 23/1–7 (Leiden: Brill, 2014), 303–20.

9. Gohar Muradyan, *Grecisms in Ancient Armenian*, Hebrew University of Armenian Studies 13 (Leuven: Peeters, 2012); and Abraham Terian, "The Hellenizing School: Its Time, Place, and Scope of Activities Reconsidered," in *East of Byzantium: Syria and Armenia in the Formative Period (Dumbarton Oaks Symposium, 1980)*, ed. Nina G. Garsoïan, Thomas F. Mathews, and Robert W. Thomson (Washington, DC: Dumbarton Oaks, 1982), 175–86.

include the *Ars Grammatica* of Dionysus Thrax, a handbook of rhetoric (*Girkʿ pitoyitsʿ*) of Aphthonius, works of Philo, Porphyry, Aristotle, and Dawitʿ Anyaghtʿ (David the Invincible), among many others.[10] This provided the basis for an educational system in Armenian. Many original Armenian commentaries on these works were then produced to facilitate their use in a school setting. Other important theological works, often related to the christological controversies that tore apart the Eastern Christian world, were also translated at this time, notably Timothy Aelurus of Alexandria's *Refutation of Chalcedon*, as well as other works of a more mystical nature, such as the Pseudo-Dionysian corpus. Some Greek and Syriac works translated into Armenian—including Irenaeus's *On the Apostolic Preaching*, Eusebius's *Chronicon*, and some of Ephrem's *madrāše*—were lost in their original languages and survive only in Armenian.

From the fourth to early seventh centuries, the Armenian Church enjoyed a certain primacy over the other Christian churches of the Caucasus, the Georgian (Iberian) and Caucasian Albanian. Evangelization of these two realms was linked with Armenia and according to Koriwn (text 1), Mashtotsʿ created alphabets for both the Georgian and Caucasian Albanian languages to serve—as in the Armenian case—as an evangelistic tool and medium of Christian literature. In the early seventh century, the Georgian Church accepted Chalcedonian Christology, breaking ranks with the Armenians and Caucasian Albanians. This further exacerbated relations between the imperial Byzantine and the largely anti-Chalcedonian Armenian Church, leading to formal division at this time, although some Armenian communities aligned with imperial orthodoxy and were eventually absorbed into it.[11] Over the centuries, while the Byzantine Church pursued the dissection of Christ's nature in ever more recondite ways and sought to impose the new definitions of later councils on the churches of the Christian East, Armenian theologians countered by defending their position according to the understanding of the pre-Chalcedonian councils and Greek fathers. Unable to argue against the theology of their own fathers, unrelenting Byzantine polemicists instead focused on incidental differences of liturgical practice.[12]

10. Francesca Gazzano, Lara Pagani, and Giusto Traina, *Greek Texts and Armenian Traditions: An Interdisciplinary Approach*, Trends in Classics Supplement 39 (Berlin: de Gruyter, 2016).

11. Nina G. Garsoïan, *L'Église arméniennes et le grand schism d'Orient*, CSCO 574, subsidia 100 (Leuven: Peeters, 1998); Gérard Garitte, *La narratio de rebus armeniae: Édition critique et commentaire*, CSCO 132, subsidia 4 (Leuven: Peeters, 1952); and Nikoloz Alexsidze, *The Narrative of the Caucasian Schism: Memory and Forgetting in Medieval Caucasia*, CSCO 666, subsidia 137 (Leuven: Peeters, 2018).

12. Abraham Terian, "Miaphysites, Armenian," in *The Oxford Dictionary of Late Antiquity*, ed. Oliver Nicholson (Oxford: Oxford University Press, 2018), 2:1017.

The rise of Islam and expansion of the caliphate in the seventh century changed the landscape of the Near East. The Armenian realm came under Arab dominion in 661, with Georgia, Armenia, and Caucasian Albania administered as a single province (*Armīniya*) by an Arab governor (*emīr*). As the centralized power of the caliphate waned over time, the local caliphal governors gained increasing power, as did the *nakharark'*.[13] In the ninth and tenth centuries, some managed to secure autonomous kingdoms within the larger structure of the caliphate. These include the Bagratuni, Artsruni, and Siwni, whose rulers sponsored public works projects, including the building of palatial churches and monastic complexes, and commissioned manuscripts and other artistic religious works to showcase their wealth and power and express their piety. These monastic institutions became the spiritual and intellectual centers of the Armenian realm, the loci of knowledge production and transmission. The fourth and fifth authors featured here issue from a renowned monastery founded in the Artsruni realm in this period, Narek.

In the second half of the tenth century, the Byzantine Empire began expanding into eastern Anatolia, annexing territory and seizing the Bagratuni capital of Ani by the mid-eleventh century. Shortly thereafter, the Seljuk Turks arrived from the east and drove back the Byzantines from their newly won lands. This upheaval led to the first major dispersion of Armenians, as many fled their homeland northwest to the northern Black Sea coast and Transylvania and southwest to Cilicia, establishing communities there with churches and monasteries. In the latter, a medieval Armenian kingdom arose that became an important player during the Crusades.[14] It also fostered a period of architectural, artistic, and literary flourishing and interchange with other peoples that led to many new original compositions and translations from Greek, Latin, Syriac, and Arabic, as well as a hopeful period of ecumenical relations between Armenian church leaders with their Latin and Byzantine counterparts.[15] In these dialogues, the sixth author

13. J. Laurent and M. Canard, *L'Arménie entre Byzance et l'Islam depuis la conquête arabe jusqu'en 886*, Armenian Library of the Calouste Gulbenkian Foundation (Lisbon: Bertrand, 1980); Aram Ter-Ghewondyan, *The Arab Emirates in Bagratid Armenia*, trans. Nina G. Garsoïan (Lisbon: Calouste Gulbenkian Foundation, 1976); and Alison Vacca, *Non-Muslim Provinces under Early Islam: Islamic Rule and Iranian Legitimacy in Armenia and Caucasian Albania* (Cambridge: Cambridge University Press, 2017).

14. Gérard Dédéyan, *Les Arméniens entre Grecs, Musulmans, et Croisés: Étude sure les pouvoirs arméniens dans le Proche-Orient méditerranéen (1068–1150)*, 2 vols. (Lisbon: Calouste Gulbenkian Foundation, 2003); and Claude Mutafian, *L'Arménie du Levant (XIe–XIVe siècle)* (Paris: Les Belles Lettres, 2012).

15. Sirarpie der Nersessian, *Miniature Painting in the Armenian Kingdom of Cilicia from the Twelfth to the Fourteenth Century*, Dumbarton Oaks Studies 31 (Washington, DC: Dumbarton Oaks, 1993); Isabelle Augé and Gérard Dédéyan, eds., *L'Église arménienne entre Grecs et Latins*

presented here played a significant role. Law, medicine, poetry, historiography, liturgy, and hagiography are some of the many genres that were cultivated in the Cilician period between the eleventh and fourteenth centuries.

While thanks to material and literary evidence the presence of Armenian Christians in Jerusalem is traceable to the fourth century, it is during the Cilician period that the Armenian patriarchate there gained official status in 1311 (though a patriarch had been functioning as early as the seventh century). It along with the monastic Brotherhood of Saint James (which traces its own history back to the mid-fifth century) are the two major Armenian institutions of the Holy City to survive to the present day.[16] The importance of Jerusalem to the Armenian Church can be seen in many ways, including the influence of Hagiopolite liturgical practices on Armenian liturgical forms and a continuous history of pilgrimage there from the fourth century onward.[17] A small community of Armenians resided in Jerusalem as early as the fifth century, and the importance of Armenians to Jerusalem's long and complex history is perhaps best manifested by their ownership to this day of approximately one-sixth of the Old City (the Armenian Quarter).

The deposition of the last Armenian king of Cilicia in 1375 marked a transformation in Armenian society, as the hereditary *nakharar* structure dissolved and Armenians no longer enjoyed autonomy in any portion of their native homeland. The diaspora expanded as merchants began to travel across land and sea to peddle their wares. Two further mass movements of Armenians from their homeland of eastern Anatolia increased the dispersion. First, the Celali uprisings of the late sixteenth and early seventeenth centuries led to what has been called the "Great Flight" of Armenians westward to settle in and near the capital of the Ottoman Empire. This led to increasing prominence in the newly founded Armenian patriarchate of Constantinople and the rise of a wealthy business class (*amira*), who sponsored cultural production, as the Ottoman capital emerged as the center of culture, language, and religious life among Armenians living in the Ottoman Empire. Second, in the context of the many battles along the borders of the Ottoman and Safavid Empires, in 1604 Shah 'Abbas I deported thousands of Armenians from their homeland in Julfa to his capital at Isfahan to a suburb that

---

fin due XIe–milieu du XVe siècle (Paris: Geuthner, 2009); and Isabelle Augé, *Églises en dialogue: Arméniens et Byzantins dans la seconde moitié du XIIe siècle*, CSCO 633, subsidia 124 (Leuven: Peeters, 2011).

16. Michael E. Stone, Roberta R. Ervine, and Nira Stone, eds., *The Armenians in Jerusalem and the Holy Land*, Hebrew University Armenian Studies 4 (Leuven: Peeters, 2002).

17. Charles A. Renoux, *Le codex arménien Jérusalem 121*, Patrologia Orientalis 35.1, 36.2 (Turnhout: Brepols, 1969, 1971); and Renoux, *Le Lectionnaire de Jérusalem en Arménie: Le Čašocʿ*, Patrologia Orientalis 44.4, 48.2, 49.5 (Turnhout: Brepols, 1989, 1999, 2004).

came to be known as "New Julfa." From there, their global network—and thus also small Armenian diaspora settlements—expanded into scores of port cities across the Eurasian landmass, including those in the West such as Amsterdam, Venice, and Marseille and Eastern ones such as Calcutta, Madras, and Jakarta as they made use of the new maritime passages of the early modern period.[18] Due to their active merchant class, Armenians accessed the new technology of the printing press at a very early date: the first Armenian book was printed in 1512. Thanks to the *amiraner* of Constantinople/Istanbul and the merchants of New Julfa, Armenians were able to make widespread use of this new technology to sponsor the printing of books in scores of cities over the next several centuries, including those issuing from the Catholic Armenian intellectual religious order of Mkhit'arists in Venice and Vienna, founded in the eighteenth century.[19]

The rise of Enlightenment-inspired nationalism in the eighteenth and nineteenth centuries led to a quest for independence that stretched into the twentieth. However, as the Ottoman Empire was remade into the Turkish nation-state, one of its first acts was to order the deportation and slaughter of its Christian population of Armenians, Greeks, and Assyrians.[20] As a result of this genocide, survivors flocked to the West, increasing the population of earlier communities and forming new ones, particularly in Europe and the Western hemisphere. The small portion of historic Armenia that was formerly under the Russian Empire declared a short-lived republic then became part of the Soviet Union, becoming an independent republic again after the Soviet Union disbanded. Today, more Armenians live outside their ancestral homeland than within it, and Armenians and their churches can be found in hundreds of cities throughout six continents, in addition to the sliver of their historic homeland that is the contemporary Republic of Armenia.

In addition to producing a massive library of original literature from the fifth century onward, Armenian Christian culture includes great works of artistic and architectural beauty, that although they fall outside the scope of this short introduction, have received the interest and attention of art and material historians and

18. Sebouh D. Aslanian, *From the Indian Ocean to the Mediterranean: The Global Trade Networks of Armenian Merchants from New Julfa* (Berkeley: University of California Press, 2011).

19. Sebouh D. Aslanian, *Early Modernity and Mobility: Port Cities and Printers across the Armenian Diaspora, 1512–1800* (New Haven: Yale University Press, forthcoming).

20. Bedross Der Matossian, *Shattered Dreams of Revolution: From Liberty to Violence in the Late Ottoman Empire* (Stanford: Stanford University Press, 2014); Ronald Grigor Suny, *"They Can Live in the Desert But Nowhere Else": A History of the Armenian Genocide* (Princeton: Princeton University Press, 2015); and Donald Bloxham, *The Great Game of Genocide: Imperialism, Nationalism, and the Destruction of the Ottoman Armenians* (Oxford: Oxford University Press, 2005).

museums alike.[21] As is true for the other Christian traditions of the East, much of this culture's material and literary culture remains to be explored as well as integrated within the history of the more well-known Western traditions. The texts presented here are meant to whet the appetite of the reader and give a taste of the riches of the Armenian corpus, which has greatly rewarded all who have taken the time to learn *Grabar* (Old Armenian) and immerse themselves in its literature.

Bibliography

Adontz, Nicolas. *Armenia in the Period of Justinian: The Political Conditions Based on the Naxarar System*. Translated and revised by Nina G. Garsoïan. Lisbon: Calouste Gulbenkian Foundation, 1970.

Alexsidze, Nikoloz. *The Narrative of the Caucasian Schism: Memory and Forgetting in Medieval Caucasia*. CSCO 666, subsidia 137. Leuven: Peeters, 2018.

Aslanian, Sebouh D. *Early Modernity and Mobility: Port Cities and Printers across the Armenian Diaspora, 1512–1800*. New Haven: Yale University Press. Forthcoming.

———. *From the Indian Ocean to the Mediterranean: The Global Trade Networks of Armenian Merchants from New Julfa*. Berkeley: University of California Press, 2011.

Augé, Isabelle. *Églises en dialogue: Arméniens et Byzantins dans la seconde moitié du XIIe siècle*. CSCO 633, subsidia 124. Leuven: Peeters, 2011.

Augé, Isabelle, and Gérard Dédéyan, eds. *L'Église arménienne entre Grecs et Latins fin due XIe milieu du XVe siècle*. Paris: Geuthner, 2009.

Bloxham, Donald. *The Great Game of Genocide: Imperialism, Nationalism, and the Destruction of the Ottoman Armenians*. Oxford: Oxford University Press, 2005.

Calzolari, Valentina. "Réécriture des textes apocryphes en arménien: L'exemple de la légende de l'apostolat de Thaddée en Arménie." *Apocrypha* 8 (1997): 97–110.

Calzolari, Valentina, and Michael E. Stone, eds. *Armenian Philology in the Modern Era: From Manuscript to Digital Text*. Handbook of Oriental Studies 8: Uralic and Central Asian Studies. Vol. 23/1–7. Leiden: Brill, 2014.

Conybeare, Fred C. "The Survival of Animal Sacrifices inside the Christian Church." *American Journal of Theology* 7 (1903): 62–90.

---

21. Christina Maranci, *The Art of Armenia: An Introduction* (Oxford: Oxford University Press, 2018); Sirarpie der Nersessian, *Armenian Art* (New York: Thames & Hudson, 1978); Jean-Michel Thierry and Patrick Donabédian, *Armenian Art* (New York: Abrams, 1989); Helen C. Evans, ed., *Armenia: Art, Religion, and Trade in the Middle Ages* (New York: Metropolitan Museum of Art, 2018); Thomas F. Mathews and Roger S. Wieck, eds., *Treasures in Heaven: Armenian Illuminated Manuscripts* (New York: Piermont Morgan Library, 1994); Thomas F. Mathews and Roger S. Wieck, eds., *Treasures in Heaven: Armenian Art, Religion, and Society* (New York: Piermont Morgan Library, 1998); and Theo Maarten van Lint and Robin Meyer, eds., *Armenia: Treasurers from an Enduring Culture* (Oxford: Bodleian Library, 2015).

Cowe, S. Peter. "Armenian." In *The Oxford Handbook of the Literatures of the Roman Empire.* Edited by Daniel L. Selden and Phiroze Vasunia. Oxford: Oxford Handbooks Online, 2021. https://doi.org/10.1093/oxfordhb/9780199699445.013.3.

———. "The Bible in Armenian." Pages 143–61 in *New Cambridge History of the Bible 600–1450,* vol. 2. Edited by A. E. Matter and R. Marsden. Cambridge: Cambridge University Press, 2012.

———. "Elišē's 'Armenian War' as a Metaphor for the Spiritual Life." Pages 341–59 in *From Byzantium to Iran: Armenian Studies in Honour of Nina Garsoïan.* Edited by Jean-Pierre Mahé and Robert W. Thomson. Atlanta: Scholars Press, 1997.

Dadoyan, Seta B. *The Armenians in the Medieval Islamic World: Paradigms of Interaction, Seventh to Fourteenth Centuries.* 3 vols. New Brunswick: Transaction Publishers, 2011–14.

Dédéyan, Gérard. *Les Arméniens entre Grecs, Musulmans, et Croisés: Étude sure les pouvoirs arméniens dans le Proche-Orient méditerranéen (1068–1150).* 2 vols. Lisbon: Calouste Gulbenkian Foundation, 2003.

Dédéyan, Gérard, ed. *Histoire du peuple arménien.* 2nd ed. Toulouse: Privat, 2007.

Der Matossian, Bedross. *Shattered Dreams of Revolution: From Liberty to Violence in the Late Ottoman Empire.* Stanford: Stanford University Press, 2014.

der Nersessian, Sirarpie. *Armenian Art.* New York: Thames & Hudson, 1978.

———. *Miniature Painting in the Armenian Kingdom of Cilicia from the Twelfth to the Fourteenth Century.* Dumbarton Oaks Studies 31. Washington, DC: Dumbarton Oaks, 1993.

digilib. Digital Library of Armenian Literature. American University of Armenia (online at http://www.digilib.am).

Dorfmann-Lazarev, Igor. *Arméniens et Byzantins à l'époque de Photius: Deux débats théologiques après le Triomphe de l'Orthodoxie.* CSCO 584, subsidia 106. Leuven: Peeters, 2004.

———. *Christ in Armenian Tradition: Doctrine, Apocrypha, Art (Sixth–Tenth Centuries).* Monograph issue, *Journal of Eastern Christian Studies* 68, nos. 3–4 (2016): 217–402.

———. "Studies of Armenian Christian Tradition in the Twentieth Century." *Annual of Medieval Studies at Central European University* 18 (2012): 137–52.

Dum-Tragut, Jasmine, and Dietmar W. Winkler, eds. *Monastic Life in the Armenian Church: Glorious Past—Ecumenical Reconsideration.* Orientalia-Patristica-Oecumenica 14. Berlin: LIT, 2018.

Evans, Helen C., ed. *Armenia: Art, Religion, and Trade in the Middle Ages.* New York: Metropolitan Museum of Art, 2018.

Garitte, Gérard. *La narratio de rebus armeniae: Édition critique et commentaire.* CSCO 132, subsidia 4. Leuven: Peeters, 1952.

Garsoïan, Nina. *Armenia between Byzantium and the Sasanians.* Collected Studies 218. London: Variorum, 1985.

————. *Church and Culture in Early Medieval Armenia*. Variorum Collected Studies 648. Brookfield, VT: Ashgate, 1999.

————. *L'Église arménienne et le grand schisme d'Orient*. CSCO 574, subsidia 100. Leuven: Peeters, 1999.

————. *Interregnum: Introduction to a Study on the Formation of Armenian Identity (ca. 600–750)*. CSCO 640, subsidia 127. Leuven: Peeters, 2012.

————. "Introduction to the Problem of Early Armenian Monasticism." *Revue des études arméniennes* 30 (2005–7): 177–236.

————. "Naxarar." In *Encyclopaedia Iranica* (online at https://iranicaonline.org/articles/naxarar).

————. *The Paulician Heresy: A Study of the Origin and Development of Paulicianism in Armenia and the Eastern Provinces of the Byzantine Empire*. Columbia University Publications in Near and Middle East Studies A.6. Paris: Mouton & Co., 1967.

————. *Studies on the Formation of Christian Armenia*. Variorum Collected Studies 959. Aldershot: Ashgate, 2010.

Hacikyan, Agop J., ed. *The Heritage of Armenian Literature*. Vol. 1, *From the Oral Tradition to the Golden Age*. Vol. 2, *From the Sixth to the Eighteenth Century*. Vol. 3, *From the Eighteenth Century to Modern Times*. Detroit: Wayne State University Press, 2000.

Hewsen, Robert H. *Armenia: A Historical Atlas*. Chicago: Chicago University Press, 2001.

Hovannisian, Richard, ed. *The Armenian People from Ancient to Modern Times*. Vol. 1, *The Dynastic Periods: From Antiquity to the Fourteenth Century*. Vol. 2, *Foreign Dominion to Statehood: The Fifteenth Century to the Twentieth Century*. New York: Saint Martin's, 1997.

Laurent, J., and M. Canard. *L'Arménie entre Byzance et l'Islam depuis la conquête arabe jusqu'en 886*. Armenian Library of the Calouste Gulbenkian Foundation. Lisbon: Bertrand, 1980.

Mahé, Annie, and Jean-Pierre Mahé. *Histoire de l'Arménie des origines à nos jours*. Paris: Perrin, 2012.

Mahé, Jean-Pierre. "L'église arménienne de 611 à 1066." Pages 457–547 in *Histoire du christianisme des origines à nos jours*, vol. 4: *Evêques, moines et empereurs (610–1054)*. Edited by Gilbert Dagron, Pierre Riché, and André Vauchez. Paris: Desclée, 1993.

Maranci, Christina. *The Art of Armenia: An Introduction*. Oxford: Oxford University Press, 2018.

Mathews, Thomas F., and Roger S. Wieck, eds. *Treasures in Heaven: Armenian Art, Religion, and Society*. New York: Piermont Morgan Library, 1998.

————. *Treasures in Heaven: Armenian Illuminated Manuscripts*. New York: Piermont Morgan Library, 1994.

MH = Matenagirk' Hayots' (*Armenian Classical Authors*). Vols. 1–15: Antelias, Lebanon, 2003–2010; vols. 16–21: Erevan, Armenia, 2012– (some volumes online at https://matenadaran.am).

Muradyan, Gohar. *Grecisms in Ancient Armenian.* Hebrew University of Armenian Studies 13. Leuven: Peeters, 2012.

Mutafian, Claude. *L'Arménie du Levant (XIe–XIVe siècle).* Paris: Les Belles Lettres, 2012.

Nersessian, Vrej. "The Armenian Tradition." Pages 41–57 in *The Orthodox Christian World.* Edited by Augustine Casiday. New York: Routledge, 2012.

———. *The Tondrakian Movement: Religious Movements in the Armenian Church from the Fourth to the Tenth Centuries.* Allison Park, PA: Pickwick, 1988.

Ōrmanean, Maghak'ia. *The Church of Armenia: Her History, Doctrine, Rule, Discipline, Liturgy, Literature, and Existing Condition.* 6th ed. Translated by G. Marcar Gregory. Burbank, CA: Western Diocese of the Armenian Church of North America (original Armenian edition published in 1911 in Constantinople/Istanbul; there exist many editions, translations, and reprints).

———. *A Dictionary of the Armenian Church.* Translated by Bedros Norehad. New York: Saint Vartan, 1984.

Papazian, Michael. *Light from Light: An Introduction to the History and Theology of the Armenian Church.* New York: SIS, 2006.

Pogossian, Zaroui. "Female Asceticism in Early Medieval Armenia." *Le Muséon* 125 (2012): 169–213.

———. "Women at the Beginning of Christianity in Armenia." *Orientalia Christiana Periodica* 69 (2003): 355–80.

Renoux, Charles A. *Le codex arménien Jérusalem 121.* Patrologia Orientalis 35.1, 36.2. Turnhout: Brepols, 1969, 1971.

———. *Le Lectionnaire de Jérusalem en Arménie: Le Čašoc'.* Patrologia Orientalis 44.4, 48.2, 49.5. Turnhout: Brepols, 1989, 1999, 2004.

Russell, James R. *Armenian and Iranian Studies.* Harvard Armenian Texts and Studies 9. Cambridge: Harvard University Press, 2004.

———. *Zoroastrianism in Armenia.* Harvard Iranian Studies 5. Cambridge: Harvard University Press, 1987.

Stone, Michael E., Dickran Kouymjian, and Henning Lehmann. *Album of Armenian Paleography.* Aarhus: Aarhus University Press, 2002.

Stone, Michael E., Roberta R. Ervine, and Nira Stone, eds. *The Armenians in Jerusalem and the Holy Land.* Hebrew University Armenian Studies 4. Leuven: Peeters, 2002.

Suny, Ronald Grigor. *"They Can Live in the Desert But Nowhere Else": A History of the Armenian Genocide.* Princeton: Princeton University Press, 2015.

Tchekhanovets, Yana. *The Caucasian Archaeology of the Holy Land: Armenian, Geor-*

gian and Albanian Communities between the Fourth and Eleventh Centuries CE. Leiden: Brill, 2018.

Ter-Ghewondyan, Aram. *The Arab Emirates in Bagratid Armenia.* Translated by Nina G. Garsoïan. Lisbon: Calouste Gulbenkian Foundation, 1976.

Terian, Abraham. "The Hellenizing School: Its Time, Place, and Scope of Activities Reconsidered." Pages 175–86 in *East of Byzantium: Syria and Armenia in the Formative Period (Dumbarton Oaks Symposium, 1980).* Edited by Nina G. Garsoïan, Thomas F. Mathews, and Robert W. Thomson. Washington, DC: Dumbarton Oaks, 1982.

———. "Miaphysites, Armenian." Page 1017 in *The Oxford Dictionary of Late Antiquity,* Vol. 2. Edited by Oliver Nicholson. Oxford University Press, 2018.

Ter Petrossian, Levon. *Ancient Armenian Translations.* New York: Saint Vartan, 1997.

Thierry, Jean-Michel, and Patrick Donabédian. *Armenian Art.* New York: Abrams, 1989.

Thomson, Robert W. *A Bibliography of Classical Armenian Literature to 1500 AD.* Corpus Christianorum. Turnhout: Brepols, 1995.

———. *Studies in Armenian Literature and Christianity.* Variorum Collected Studies 451. Brookfield, VT: Ashgate, 1994.

———. "Supplement to *A Bibliography of Classical Armenian Literature to 1500 AD*: Publications 1993–2005." *Le Muséon* 120 (2007): 163–223.

Toumanoff, Cyril. *Studies in Christian Caucasian History.* Washington, DC: Georgetown University Press, 1963.

Vacca, Alison. *Non-Muslim Provinces under early Islam: Islamic Rule and Iranian Legitimacy in Armenia and Caucasian Albania.* Cambridge: Cambridge University Press, 2017.

van Lint, Theo Maarten, and Robin Meyer, eds. *Armenia: Treasurers from an Enduring Culture.* Oxford: Bodleian Library, 2015.

Young, Robin Darling. "Armenian." Pages 75–85 in *A Companion to Late Antique Literature.* Edited by Scott McGill and Edward J. Watts. New York: Wiley, 2018.

Zakarian, David. "The 'Epic' Representation of Armenian Women of the Fourth Century." *Revue des études arméniennes* 35 (2013): 1–28.

———. *Women, Too, Were Blessed: The Portrayal of Women in Early Christian Armenian Texts.* Armenian Texts and Studies 4. Leiden: Brill, 2021.

1. Koriwn, *The Life of Mashtots'*

Introduction and translation by Jesse S. Arlen

Koriwn (ca. 390–ca. 447) was a disciple of Mashtots' (died ca. 440),[1] inventor of the Armenian alphabet. After the alphabet's invention, Koriwn was sent by his master to Constantinople along with a few other disciples to join Eznik and Yovsēp' in studying Greek and collecting and translating theological texts. Like the other disciples of Mashtots', Koriwn conducted more translations than original compositions, and his literary style bears influence from his immersion in Greek literature. His *Life of Mashtots'* (*Vark' Mashtots'i*)—or, as he refers to it in the opening of his text, the *Memorial to the Armenian Alphabet and Mashtots'*—is one of the earliest original compositions in Armenian.

The *Life* is a hagiographic encomium to Mashtots', focusing on his invention of the alphabet and evangelistic work. The earliest account of the alphabet's invention to survive from antiquity, it is not the only one. Ghazar of P'arpi's *History of Armenia*, which treats the fifth-century resistance of the Armenian Christian *nakharark'* to the Zurvanite (Zoroastrian) Sassanian Empire and the Armenian *nakharark'* loyal to them, also narrates the invention of the alphabet, and although citing Koriwn as a source, bears some differences with the latter's version. Ghazar lays greater emphasis on the role of Catholicos Sahak in the alphabet's invention and goes out of his way to disparage the role of Syriac and elevate the model of Greek, motivated in part by his pro-Roman/Greek and anti-Persian/Syriac Mamikonean patrons as well as his own biases in light of the events contemporary to his writing.

The third version belongs to the *patmahayr* (father of history) Movsēs of Khoren (ca. fifth/eighth century), an elusive figure awash with scholarly controversy, whose *History of Armenia*—from the creation of the world up to the fifth century—likewise contains an account of the alphabet's creation. This version is the one that, along with Movsēs's *History* as a whole, became hallowed by subsequent Armenian tradition. Elaborating in midrashic fashion upon Koriwn's comparison between Mashtots' and Moses

---

1. While the earliest sources refer to him as Mashtots', some later sources use Mesrop. He is known today as Mesrop Mashtots'. See James R. Russell, *Armenian and Iranian Studies*, Harvard Armenian Texts and Studies 9 (Cambridge: Harvard University Press, 2004), 597–608.

and his description of the "state"—induced by the ascetic and intellectual labors of *Mashtots'*—that facilitated the "birth" of the letters, Movsēs relates that the state was neither "a dream in sleep, nor a vision while awake, but in the depths of his heart there appeared to the eyes of his soul a right hand writing on rock,"[2] like the revelation of the Ten Commandments to Moses. And just as Jews revere that revelation, the man through whom it came, and the script(ures) that expressed it, ever since the invention/ gift of their own script and through it the transmission of the Scriptures, liturgy, and writings of the fathers, Armenian Christians have venerated their alphabet and its creators as sacred media of divine revelation, memorialized in the liturgical calendar's Feast of the Holy Translators.

Bibliography

Text and Editions

Koriwn. The *Life of Mashtots*. Translated by Bedros Norehad. New York: Armenian General Benevolent Union, 1964. Reprinted in Krikor H. Maksoudian, *Koriwn, Vark' Mashtots'i: A Photoreproduction of the 1941 Yerevan Edition with a Modern Translation and Concordance, and with a New Introduction*. Delmar, NY: Caravan, 1985. Reprinted on pages 152–81 in *The Heritage of Armenian Literature*. Vol. 1, *From the Oral Tradition to the Golden Age*. Edited by Agop J. Hacikyan. Detroit: Wayne State University Press, 2000.

Mahé, Jean-Pierre. "La *Vie de Maštoc'*, traduction annotée." *Revue des études arméniennes* 30 (2005–7): 59–97.

MH 1.227–72 (Armenian text of long and short versions).

Winkler, Gabriele. *Koriwns Biographie des Mesrop Maštoc', Übersetzung und Kommentar*. Orientalia Christiana Analecta 245. Rome: Pontificio Istituto Orientale, 1994.

Studies

Mathews, Edward G., Jr. "Early Armenian and Syrian Contact: Reflections on Koriwn's *Life of Maštoc'*." *Saint Nersess Theological Review* 7 (2002): 5–19.

———. "The *Life of Maštoc'* as an Encomium: A Reassessment." *Revue des études arméniennes* 24 (1993): 5–26.

2. Moses Khorenats'i, *History of the Armenians*, trans. Robert W. Thomson, rev. ed. (Ann Arbor, MI: Caravan, 2006), 315.

Orengo, Alessandro. "L'invenzione dell'alfabeto armeno: Fatti e problemi." *Rhesis: International Journal of Linguistics, Philology, and Literature: Linguistics and Philology* 7 (2016): 9–27.

Russell, James R. "On the Origins and Invention of the Armenian Script." *Le Muséon* 107 (1994): 317–33.

Terian, Abraham. "Koriwn's *Life of Mashtots'* as an Encomium." *Journal of the Society for Armenian Studies* 3 (1987): 1–14.

TRANSLATION

The Life of Mashtots' (MH 1.229, 234–41)

I was considering composing a monograph as a memorial to the God-given alphabet of the Ashkenazi[3] nation and the Armenian realm, when and in what year it was bestowed, through what sort of man such a newly given divine grace appeared, and also about that man's enlightening teaching and angelic religious life of virtue. And while my mind was turning all this over and while I was working alone and worrying over remembering the details, a commission came to me from an honorable man called Yovsēp',[4] a disciple of that man mentioned above, and along with it the encouragement of other fellow disciples of our teaching. Taking into account my particular position as a disciple, although I was the least and it was a task beyond my ability, I was nevertheless engaged by the unequivocal command and eagerly began right away to write in a book what had been proposed. I beseeched them to collectively labor together with me in prayer and in committing ourselves to divine grace, so that we might sail more freely and straightly over the expansive waves of the sea of teaching.

And now, let us begin by way of a preface to examine whether or not it is too audacious to signify in writing the life of perfect men.

[Omitted: a lengthy discussion follows. Encouraged by both the Bible's own recording of the lives of exemplary people as well as that of early Christian hagiographers, he concludes that it is permissible to write the life of a holy man.]

The man I indicated in the preamble and was so eager to tell about was named Mashtots', from the village of Hats'eakk' in the province of Tarōn, the son of a

---

3. The connection between "Ashkenazi" and Armenian derives from Jer 51:27.
4. Catholicos from 437 to 452.

blessed man called Vardan. In the years of his youth he was trained in Greek literary arts, then he arrived at the court of the Arsacid kings in Greater Armenia and was appointed to the royal chancellery, where he became a minister to the commands given by the ruler, when a certain Aṙawan was chief minister in the realm of Armenia. Mashtots' was informed and erudite in civil institutions and earned the devotion of his soldiers through his military expertise. Even then he devoted himself with eagerness to reading the divine Scriptures, by which he was soon enlightened. He dove into and plunged the depths of all the particulars of the God-given commandments, and having adorned himself with all preparation, he served in the ministry of the princes.

And after that he converted himself to the service of God, the lover of humankind, in accordance with the measure of the gospel. He stripped himself of the desire to bear authority and took up the cross of boasting, going out after the crucified one, who gives life to all.[5] And being persuaded by the commandments, he joined the cross-bearing troop of Christ, and immediately entered into eremitic ascesis. In accordance with the gospel, he bore many and all kinds of bodily torments in all manners. He subjected himself to all spiritual disciplines: solitude, mountain-living, hunger and thirst, vegetarianism, lightless confinement, wearing haircloth, and stretching out on the floor for a bed. Often, he would forego the easy rest of night and the necessity of sleep, in the twinkling of an eye passing the night in standing sleeplessness. He did all this for several years. And he found some others and attached them to himself to become his disciples in this evangelical way of life that had become familiar to him. Thus, having endured by the strength of his will all temptations that arrived upon him, he became radiant, intimate with and pleasing to God and humans.[6]

Then the blessed one took his faithful companions with him and went down to the disorderly and irremediable regions of Goght'n.[7] And there came forth to meet him the prince of Goght'n, a man who feared and loved God, whose name was Shabit'. He proved himself a hospitable and guest-honoring host, serving them in a pious manner worthy of the disciples of the faith of Christ. Meanwhile, the blessed one applied himself right away to the evangelical task, taking into his hands the entire district with the loyal assistance of the prince. He took all captive from the traditions of their fathers and led them from satanic demon-worshiping service into obedience to Christ.

And when he was sowing the word of life among them and instructing them all in the worship of God, very great signs appeared among them, manifest even to the

5. Matt 16:24.
6. Luke 2:52.
7. A wine-producing region known for the long persistence there of pagan practices, songs, and traditions.

inhabitants of the district: demons took flight in different forms and likenesses, escaping into the region of Media. With even more concern, he reflected about how to comfort all his compatriots in this way. He increased his prayers with perpetual moaning, imploring God with arms outstretched and ceaseless tears, meditating upon the word of the apostle and saying fervently: "I have sorrow and undiminished pains in my heart on account of my brothers and kinsfolk."[8] Surrounded and entrapped thus with sorrowful concerns, he plunged deeply into various designs about how he might find a way out of the situation.

After lingering for many days in the same state, he then arose and arrived at the residence of the holy catholicos of Greater Armenia, who was known by the name of Sahak,[9] whom he found well disposed and preoccupied with the same anxiety. And coming together with united purpose, they rose early to offer up great prayers and powerful requests to God that all souls would attain the salvation brought by Christ. And they did this for many days. Then as a gift from the all-bountiful God [the idea] came upon them to assemble together in council the blessed ones united in concern for the realm, in order to arrive at the invention of letters for the Armenian nation. After occupying themselves with many attempts and tests and patiently enduring many labors, they then informed the king of Armenia, whose name was Vramshapuh,[10] about their preliminary research.

The king told them about a certain Syriac man, a bishop of the nobility called Daniel, who had unexpectedly invented alphabetic letters for the Armenian language. After he had told them about the invention of Daniel, they urged the king to diligently pursue whatever was necessary for acquiring them. So he sent someone named Vahrich with decrees to a priest named Habēl, who was a relative of Daniel, the Syriac bishop. When Habēl heard this, he hastened to the residence of Daniel and first was himself instructed by Daniel in the letters and then he received them from him and sent them to the king in the land of Armenia. They reached him in the fifth year of his reign. After he had received the characters from Habēl, the king together with the holy ones Sahak and Mashtots were delighted. However, after realizing that the letters were not sufficient to wholly express the syllables and articulations of the Armenian language—especially since these letters were culled and resuscitated from the literatures of other peoples—they then returned once again to their same concern, and for some time sought a way out of the predicament.

To this end, in the fifth year[11] of Vramshapuh, king of Armenia, the blessed Mashtots took a class of youth by order of the king and with the agreement of Saint Sahak, and after taking leave of one another with a holy kiss, he rushed off,

8. Rom 9:2–3.
9. Catholicos from 387 to 438.
10. King of Armenia from 401 to 413.
11. That is, 405 CE.

traveled, and arrived in the region of Aram, to two cities of Syria, one of which was called Edessa and the other Amida. He presented himself to the holy bishops, one of whom was named Ṙabbula[12] and the other Acacius, who went out to meet them along with the clergy and princes of the cities. After showing much honor to the newly arrived, they received them with solicitude in accordance with the rank of those who bear the name of Christ. Meanwhile, the vardapet[13] who loved his disciples divided those he brought with him into two groups and arranged for some to study Syriac literary arts in the city of Edessa and assembled the others in the city of Samosata to study Greek literary arts there.

Then along with his companions, he resumed his usual fasts, prayers, sleepless nights, and tearful implorations, his severe lifestyle, his concerns and groans for his realm, remembering what was said by the prophet: "Whenever you groan, then you will be saved."[14] Thus he patiently endured many labors in order to invent a means of help for the good of his nation. And to him the state was granted by the God of all graces: in the manner of a father to give birth to a new and wondrous offspring, letters for the Armenian language, by his holy right hand. And then he immediately composed, engraved, and named them, arranging them in syllables, articulations, and sonorous signs.

Then, taking leave of the holy bishop, he went down together with his helpers to the city of Samosata, where he was lavished with the greatest honors by the bishop and church there. And in that same city he found a certain copyist of Greek literature, Rufinus by name, and together with him fashioned and brought to completion all the particular features of the letters—the fine and heavy strokes, the short and the long, the single and the doubled.

Then they turned to translation along with two men who were their disciples, the first of whom was called Yovhan from the district of Ekegheats' and the second Yovsēp' from the house of Paghin. They began to translate the Scriptures, commencing with the Proverbs of Solomon, who in the very beginning recommends becoming a knower of wisdom: "To know wisdom and instruction, to understand wise speech."[15] This book was written by the hand of that copyist while teaching the youth to be copyists of the same writing.

Then he received epistles from the bishop of the city and, taking leave of them, he brought all his companions to the bishop of Syria. He presented the God-given letters to those who had formerly received him there, at which the holy bishops and all the churches lifted up many praises to the glory of God, no

12. Bishop of Edessa (seated 411/412–35). Given the date in question, Mashtots' likely met with Ṙabbula's predecessor, Paqida (seated 398–409).

13. An ordained teacher, an office unique to the Armenian Church. See Robert W. Thomson, "Vardapet in the Early Armenian Church," Le Muséon 75 (1962): 367–82.

14. Isa 30:15.

15. Prov 1:2.

less than for the consolation of the disciples. Afterward he took leave of them and taking all his companions and the epistles bearing good news along with the gifts given by grace,[16] he set out on his journey by the grace of God. He passed the nights in inns with good fortune and with spirit-filled joy arrived in the realm of Armenia, in the region of the district of Ayrarat, at the outskirts of the New City,[17] in the sixth year of Vramshapuh, king of Armenia.

The great Moses did not rejoice so greatly in his descent from Mount Sinai— not to say that he was more [happy], but much less. For that man who had seen God descended from the mountain holding in his hands the commandments received from and written by God. But because of the people who wrought a deed worthy of vengeance, who had turned their back on the things of the Lord and fallen to the earth, who, treacherous to the Lord, fell prostrate before idols smelted by their own hands, the heart of that one bearing the commandments was pierced and broken. For you see the sorrow of the one carrying the tablets made manifest in his breaking them to pieces. But our blessed one, on behalf of whom the present discourse is composed, did not face the same deeds that were done back then. Rather, he himself along with his companions were filled with spiritual consolation, and since they were sure of the enthusiasm of those about to receive the gift and were expecting their joy, they shared the good news at every step of their journey. Let no one consider us too audacious for what was just said, thinking: "How could someone compare and equate such a humble man with the great Moses, with the one who spoke with God, the wonder-worker?"—which we might be blamed for. Yet in faith we could say even more. For neither overtly nor in secret should one despise what comes from God. Because the grace of the one all-powerful God is dispensed to all nations born of the earth.

And now, when the one worthy of memorial came close to the royal city, word was brought to the king and bishop. Taking along with them the assembly of nobles, the troop of dynasts, they went out of the city to meet the blessed one at the bank of the river Řah.[18] Having exchanged with one another the longed-for greeting, they turned into the city with shouts of exultation, spiritual songs, and sublime blessings, passing the days in festive joy.

Then the blessed caretakers took with them the sudden discovery of the object of their search and requested of the king young children with whom they might try out the letters. And after many of them had become acquainted with them, the king gave a command to carry out instruction with them everywhere. Through this the blessed one attained the beautiful station of vardapet and for two years organized and conducted his teaching with these same letters. And in

16. That is, the Armenian letters.
17. That is, Vagharshapat, where the cathedral of Ējmiatsin is located.
18. That is, the Araxes River.

this way, they plunged into all the particulars of the ordinances of the law, until they were entirely liberated from their natural character.

Then they undertook the divine work of cultivating the evangelical craft: translating, copying, and teaching. They contemplated in particular the sublimity of the commandments spoken by the Lord, which came to the blessed Moses, concerning all things that came into being, the sublimity of the divine ordinances that were passed down and inscribed in books to be preserved for the generations to come. There were orders like this to the other prophets also: "Take a new, large scroll and write on it with the pen of a scribe."[19] And elsewhere: "Write your vision on a tablet, and set it in a book."[20] And David indicates even more clearly that the God-given laws are destined for all nations when he says: "Let this be written for another nation";[21] and: "The Lord will recount for the peoples in books."[22] It is this that Christ, the Savior of all, came and fulfilled with the commandment given by grace: "Go out into all the nations";[23] and: "This gospel will be proclaimed throughout the entire universe."[24] It is that which our very own blessed fathers were bold to do, spreading their cultivation with hopeful eagerness out in the open and bearing fruit, in accordance with the gospel.

In that time, our blessed and dear Armenian realm became marvelous beyond measure. For all of a sudden Moses, the teacher of the law, in the company of the prophets, and the foremost Paul along with the whole assembly of the apostles, together with the gospel of Christ, which gives life to the cosmos, came together all at once through the hands of the two companions and were found to be Armenophone and speaking Armenian.

Thereafter heartfelt joy and a sight to delight the eye met the onlooker. For a land that was foreign even to the rumors of those regions in which all the wonders worked by God were accomplished, all at once and right away became informed about all things that happened. Not only what had transpired in the time of the pious, but also that of the primordial ages and those yet to come, the beginning and the consummation, and all the traditions given by God.

[Omitted: the rest of the Life narrates the evangelizing work of Mashtots', Sahak, and their disciples throughout Armenia, Georgia, and Caucasian Albania—for whose peoples, according to Koriwn, Mashtots' also invented alphabets—and also their translations and original compositions, the founding of monastic circles, and the other religious work they engaged in until their deaths.]

19. Isa 8:1.
20. Isa 30:8; Hab 2:2.
21. Ps 102:18 (101:19 LXX).
22. Ps 87:6 (86:6 LXX).
23. Matt 28:19.
24. Matt 24:14.

2. Eznik of Koghb, *Refutation of the Sects* (or, *On God*)

Introduction and translation by Jesse S. Arlen

Eznik (ca. 380–ca. 455) was a disciple of Mashtots'. After the invention of the alphabet, Mashtots' sent him along with another disciple named Yovsēp'—who later became catholicos (seated 437–52) and commissioned Koriwn's *Life of Mashtots'*—to Edessa and then to Constantinople to study and gather texts to translate from Syriac and Greek into Armenian. Eznik was in the Byzantine capital in 431 during the Council of Ephesus, and different portions of a letter of his to Mashtots' concerning that council are preserved in the seventh-century florilegium of theological and christological patristic and conciliar writings compiled by Catholicos Komitas I (ca. 560–628, seated 615–28), known as the *Seal of Faith* (*Knik' hawatoy*), as well as another important collection of theological documents known as the *Book of Letters* (*Girk' T'ght'ots'*).

Upon his return to Ashtishat, then see of the Armenian Church, Eznik presented to church leaders the canons of the Councils of Ephesus and Nicaea. He then worked with Catholicos Sahak Part'ew (ca. 340–438, seated 387–428) on modifying the existing translations of the Bible to match a Greek edition brought with him from Constantinople, and engaged in many other works of translation, including biblical commentaries. He is most known for a theological treatise called either *Refutation of the Sects* (*Eghts aghandots'*) or *De Deo* (*On God*). These titles reveal the twin aspects of Eznik's project: to refute the teaching of the various religions, sects, and philosophies in competition with the nascent Armenian Church and to present orthodox instruction concerning the Deity and the nature of reality.

After a lengthy opening against gnostic and dualistic views concerning the origin of evil, the *Refutation* is divided into four parts. Each is directed against a different group or belief system: (1) heathens (i.e., pre-Christian Armenian religious beliefs); (2) Persians (i.e., Zurvanism, the version of Zoroastrianism that enjoyed royal sanction under the Sassanian Persian Empire); (3) Greeks (i.e., ancient Greek philosophers and their schools, notably Pythagoreans, Platonists, Stoics, and Epicureans); and (4) Marcionite teaching, which for centuries enjoyed a significant following in Persian and Armenian spheres. The selection below is drawn from part one of the *Refutation* in which Eznik engages with imaginary interlocutors holding to pre-Christian Armenian folk beliefs.[1]

Bibliography

Text and Editions

Eznik Kołbacʻi. *De Deo*. Edited and translated by Louis Mariès and Charles Mercier. Patrologia Orientalis 28. Paris: Firmin Didot, 1959.

Eznik of Kołb. *On God*. Translated by Monica J. Blanchard and Robin Darling Young. Eastern Christian Texts in Translation 2. Leuven: Peeters, 1998.

MH 1.429–513 (Armenian text of *Refutation of the Sects* and *Letter to Mashtotsʻ*).

Studies

Russell, James R. "Eznik of Kołb." Vol. 9.2/pp. 129–30 in *Encyclopaedia Iranica* (online at https://iranicaonline.org/articles/eznik-of-kolb).

TRANSLATION

Refutation of the Sects (or, *On God*) *(MH 1.457–59)*

All this was said to demonstrate that whatever appears is bodily and whatever does not appear is bodiless. And among bodily beings there are those that are thick bodied and those that are thin bodied, as the apostle says: "Bodies of heavenly beings are of one kind and bodies of earthly beings of another."[2] By "earthly beings" he means humans, animals, birds, and crawling creatures; and by "heavenly beings" he means sun, moon, and stars. He is talking about them and not angels, for from there he continues the same thought and says: "There is one glory of the sun and another glory of the moon."[3] In short, whatever is touched or

---

1. See Eznik of Kołb, *On God*, trans. Monica J. Blanchard and Robin Darling Young, Eastern Christian Texts in Translation 2 (Leuven: Peeters, 1998), 90–94.
2. 1 Cor 15:40.
3. 1 Cor 15:41.

observed by the senses or affects them is bodily, while whatever does not affect the senses is bodiless. The element of light is fine, but since it is observed by the eye, it is bodily. The element of air is fine, but since it affects the body with cold it is bodily. The element of fire is fine, but since it affects the body with heat, it is bodily. The same goes for the element of water, which is finer than some, but thicker than light things.

And now, since angels and demons are bodiless, it follows that there exist no offspring among them. But they say: "For *hambaruk*ʻ[4] there are offspring and they die." First, let us see whether any rational creatures other than angels, demons, and humans actually exist and then let us come to examine whether some of the demons are bodily and others bodiless.

That there is no rational creature outside of these three classes—angels, demons, and humans—is manifest from all the God-given Scriptures and from the nature of creatures. But even though certain names are mentioned even by the Scriptures—*yushkaparikkʻ* or *hambarukʻ* or *parikkʻ*—they are spoken according to the fantasies of human minds and not according to nature.[5] For demons have a way of showing themselves in many forms, and then humans give them names according to their forms. Whenever towns and villages are ruined and demons begin to dwell there, revealing themselves in various deceptive shapes, people give them names according to their false shapes, calling one *yushkaparik*, another *parik*, and another *hambaru*.[6] In the same way, the Scriptures, in accordance with human fantasies and in order to signify the intensity of the country's ruin, come to say that *yushkaparikkʻ*—which in the Greek language it calls *ishatsʻulkʻ*[7]—dwell in ruins. Now, will they try to demonstrate that *ishatsʻulkʻ* are to be found in Babylon? Thus, it is evident that *yushkaparikkʻ* and *ishatsʻulkʻ* are just names without persons, and the Scriptures use them according to the

---

4. The *hambaru*, along with the *parik* and *yushkaparik* mentioned a few lines later, were female spirits or fairies of Iranian/Armenian folk belief. See Russell, *Zoroastrianism in Armenia*, 449; Mardiros H. Ananikian, "Armenian," in *The Mythology of All Races*, ed. John Arnott MacCullough (Boston: Marshall Jones, 1925), 7:91–92; and Hrach K. Martirosyan, *Etymological Dictionary of the Armenian Inherited Lexicon*, Leiden Indo-European Etymological Series 8 (Leiden: Brill, 2009), 790–91.

5. *Yushkaparikkʻ* are mentioned in the Armenian Bible at Isa 13:21 where the Septuagint has σειρῆνες (*seirēnes*, "sirens") and at Isa 34:11, 14 where the Septuagint has ὀνοκένταυροι (*onokentauroi*, "donkey-centaurs"). *Hambarukʻ* are mentioned in the Armenian Bible at Job 30:29; Isa 13:21; and 43:20 where the Septuagint has σειρῆνες (*seirēnes*, "sirens").

6. In the biblical passages referred to in the previous note, the beings in question are all mentioned in association with the wilderness or ruined cities.

7. Literally, "donkey-bulls" for ὀνοκένταυροι (*onokentauroi*, "donkey-centaurs"). See Ananikian, "Armenian," 91–92.

custom of human fantasies, just as they named them in order to signify the ruin of Babylon. . . .[8] [*lacuna*]

. . . like the *ishats'ul*, which they say came from a cow, and a certain *pay*[9] from a human, and the *aralēz*[10] from a dog. It is not that they are certain persons, but rather come from the made-up tales and idle prattle of minds led astray by demons, for an invisible being does not arise from a bodily one, just as a bodily one does not arise from an invisible being. Never has a *pay* arisen from a human *so as to have a creaturely visage,*[11] nor has the *ishats'ul* arisen from cows so as to dwell in sea pools. Because it is not possible for a bodily being to live in water, just as it is not possible for an aquatic creature to live on dry land. No being has arisen from a dog so as to live according to some invisible powers such that when some fall wounded in battle, it comes beside them, licks their wounds, and restores them to health. Rather, these are all myths and old wives' tales and come especially from error caused by demons.

But they argue yet further and insist upon their statements. One says: "In our village an *ishats'ul* worked on a cow and we all constantly hear its bellowing." And another says: "I saw a *pay* with my own eyes." Perhaps one might even claim to have seen an *aralēz*. But if in former times the *aralēz* would lick the wounded and restore them to health, then why do they not lick the wounded and restore them to health now? Are there not the same battles and do the wounded not fall in the same way as before? But they say: "In that time there were heroes."

And concerning the gods let us demand of them: "Were the gods in fact bodily or bodiless?" If they were bodily it is evident that they were formerly humans, and then after the shades of humans received worship, they called them "gods." So then, if they were bodiless, it would not have been possible for those bodiless beings to copulate with bodily women. For if there were any way to do that, Satan would never stop having little satans born of women. But whoever is bodiless is also without seed, because seed is proper to bodily beings and not to bodiless beings, and to be born of a woman without seed was only ever possible for one, who is the creator of bodily nature. And since he willed it, he was capable of being born of a virgin without copulation. Therefore, none of the pagan sages,

---

8. See Isa 13:19–22.

9. The *pay* is a spirit of Iranian/Armenian folk belief, perhaps the male counterpart of a *parik* (fairy). See Ananikian, "Armenian," 91–92.

10. The *aralēz*, also spelled *yaralēz* or *aṙlēz*, was a mythological dog that, as Eznik explains below, would lick the wounds of a hero fallen in battle—as in the legend of Ara and Shamiram—in order to restore him to health. See Russell, *Zoroastrianism in Armenia*, 344, 416–19; and Ananikian, "Armenian," 90.

11. The italicized portion of text is corrupt and the reconstruction conjectural.

having looked at the impotence of each of the gods, dared to say that someone was born of a woman without copulation.

And as there exist no births among demons, likewise there is no death. While only the Deity is by nature immortal, who is eternal and did not receive from anyone a beginning of coming into being, he without jealousy bestowed immortality as a gift upon the primordial and rational beings. I am speaking of angels and demons and also of human souls from which humans come into being, because they are of two natures: bodily and bodiless. And truly they arise by birth, multiply through copulation, and die in their bodies—but not in their souls—on account of transgressing the command. But angels and demons do not increase through birth nor diminish through death, but just as they were established, so also they persist in the same number without increase or decrease.[12]

12. Luke 20:34–36.

3. *The Teaching of Saint Grigor*

Introduction and translation by Jesse S. Arlen

The Teaching of Saint Grigor is a lengthy catechetical instruction embedded as a long sermon within the *History of Armenia* of Agat'angeghos, an anonymous author whose name in Greek means "messenger of good (tidings)." The larger *History* chronicles the conversion of King Trdat and the Armenian realm to Christianity at the beginning of the fourth century. A popular work across the Christian world, different versions survive in Arabic, Ge'ez, Greek, Latin, and Syriac.

The *History* purports to be an eyewitness account commissioned by King Trdat to chronicle fourth-century events. Weaving together different traditions, the narrative begins with the murder of the Arsacid King Khosrov of Armenia by Grigor's father Anak, a Parthian noble who carried out the deed in service of the Sassanian King Ardashir. Both Grigor and Khosrov's son Trdat were then raised in the Roman Empire, the former as a Christian in Caesarea in Cappadocia. Through the intervention of Emperor Diocletian, Trdat is established on the Armenian throne and Grigor enters into his service without revealing his background. Grigor's Christian identity is discovered when he refuses to engage in the worship of Anahit—goddess associated with fertility, waters, wisdom, and victory—and is imprisoned in the deep pit (*khor virap*) at Artashat.

The next episode relates the escape of a group of thirty-five female monastics led by their abbess Gayianē from Roman territory, sparked by Diocletian's attempt to forcefully marry one of the virgins named Hṙip'simē. King Trdat, whom Diocletian requested to find and return the virgins to him, is overcome by Hṙip'simē's beauty and seeks to possess her for himself, but he is overpowered by her in a wrestling match. The virgin monastics are then martyred, and Trdat is subsequently transformed into a wild boar as divine punishment for his crime. After fifteen years in the pit, Grigor is brought out and heals the king, who along with his royal entourage accepts Christianity. It is at this point that the *Teaching* is inserted, taking the form of Grigor's instruction on biblical salvation history and Christian doctrine to Trdat before his baptism.

The rest of the *History* treats Grigor's consecration as bishop in Caesarea, the baptism of Trdat, the court and nobles, and thousands of Armenians—for which reason Grigor is dubbed "the Illuminator"—his overthrow and destruction of pagan temples, consecration of martyria and churches, evangelization of Armenia, and finally the participation of his son and successor Aristakēs at the Council of Nicaea.[1]

The *Teaching* is a key source for understanding the theology of the early Armenian Church. Its impact on subsequent Armenian theology is profound. Beginning with creation, it comments upon the entire scriptural corpus as well as the acts and missions of the early apostles, including those to Armenia. It contains theological reflection and instruction on a diverse array of topics. The section translated below concerns the baptism of Christ and gives a sense of the author's style of theological instruction. While exploring the different implications of Christ's baptism, he circles back on several recurring themes, connecting them with previous moments in creation and salvation history, as he comments on the biblical narrative and celebrates the mystery of salvation.[2]

Bibliography

Text and Editions

Agatʻangeghos. *The Lives of Saint Gregory: The Armenian, Greek, Arabic, and Syriac Versions of the History Attributed to Agathangelos.* Translated with introduction and commentary by Robert W. Thomson. Ann Arbor, MI: Caravan Books, 2010.

MH 2.1289–1735 (Armenian text of *Agat'angeghos*, with the *Teaching* on 2.1425–1646).

Thomson, Robert W. *Agathangelos: History of the Armenians*. Albany: State University of New York Press, 1976.

———. *The Teaching of Saint Gregory*. Rev. ed. AVANT: Treasures of the Armenian Christian Tradition 1. New Rochelle, NY: Saint Nersess Armenian Seminary, 2001.

Studies

Thomson, Robert W. "Agathengelos." Vol. 1.6/pp. 607–8 in *Encyclopaedia Iranica* (online at https://www.iranicaonline.org/articles/agathengelos).

---

1. For a historiographical study of these events, see Robert Thomson's translations and commentaries listed in the bibliography.

2. See Robert W. Thomson, *The Teaching of Saint Gregory*, rev. ed., AVANT: Treasures of the Armenian Christian Tradition 1 (New Rochelle, NY: Saint Nersess Armenian Seminary, 2001), 120–25.

The Teaching of Saint Grigor (MH 2.1490–96)

For thirty years he was quiet and did not reveal himself,[3] increasing in physical stature according to the natural growth of the body.[4] Then, he submitted to baptism.[5] First, he sent forth John the forerunner,[6] the greatest of the prophets,[7] to prepare a way for him and to make straight the paths for his revelation.[8] John consented to give the baptism of repentance—not the baptism that is the divine seal of illumination for unending life but rather the holy baptism of repentance. As in the age of Moses, when God desired to appear to them, he commanded them to wash and purify themselves[9] in order to be worthy to become seers of God's visible glory; in the same manner, John came and washed the people with repentance,[10] so that whenever the Son of God appeared, they would be well prepared to draw near and in a worthy manner give heed to his teaching, to make a way in their hearts so as to be able to receive the Lord of all in gentle and humble lodgings.

Then, he came and was himself baptized by John.[11] He set about to write an eternal covenant, sealing it with his own blood, in order to give life to all through illuminating and life-giving baptism. He commanded all humans born of earth, all fleshly creatures, to imitate this Godlike image of salvation. Now, when he came to the seal-giver John to be baptized, John was seized with awe and refused, saying: "I should be baptized by you."[12] Hearing this, he answered, commanding him to boldly baptize him, saying: "Allow this now, for it is necessary to be like this so that we fulfill all righteousness."[13]

And what is that righteousness, if not what Zechariah, the father of the same John, cried out by the Holy Spirit, saying: "He remembered the oath that he

---

3. Luke 3:23.
4. Luke 2:52.
5. Matt 3:13–17 and parallels.
6. Matt 3 and parallels.
7. Matt 11:11; Luke 7:28.
8. Matt 3:3 and parallels; Isa 40:3.
9. Exod 19:10–11.
10. Matt 3:11 and parallels.
11. Matt 3:13 and parallels.
12. Matt 3:14.
13. Matt 3:15.

swore to Abraham our father, to give us salvation without fear of our enemies, from the hands of all who hate us; to worship him in holiness and righteousness."[14] About this the singer also says: "He remembered his covenant with Abraham and his oath with Isaac, and for Jacob he established his commandment and for Israel his oath unto ages."[15] Through the faith of the fathers, he blessed the whole earth, blessed and fulfilled the promises, and for the same reason he himself descended into the waters, and all at once constituted water to be purifying and renewing.

And since he made the first earth emerge from water by command, and, nourished by water, all plants, reptiles, wild beasts, animals, and birds emanated from the earth through the verdure of the waters; in that same way, he made verdant the womb of the generative waters of baptism. Through water he purified and renewed the oldness of this worn-out, earthly matter, which had been worn down by sin, had become old and stripped of the Spirit's grace. Therefore, he opened once again the invisible Spirit's womb through visible water, adorning anew the newly born and newly feathered for generation in the font, clothing them all in luminous robes so that they might once more be born anew.

Because even in the beginning at the time of creation, the Spirit of the Deity was circling above the waters.[16] And from there he fashioned the form of creatures and commanded their coming into being and establishment. He also commanded the firmament of heaven to be established[17]—the habitation of fiery angels—which appears to us as watery. In the same way that he came to fulfill the covenant he made with the fathers, he himself descended into the waters and purified the lower waters of this earth, which humans had polluted through sin. So, by treading on the waters with his own feet, he purified them and made them become purifying.

And as formerly the Spirit was circling above the waters, in the same way she will dwell in water and receive all who are born through it. Now, the waters joined together above are the habitation of angels. But he made these waters below to be as those waters above. Because he himself descended into the waters so that all would be renewed by the Spirit through the waters and become as angels, and that unto the age the same Spirit through the waters would present all for adoption.[18] Because he opened the gates of the waters below so that the upper gates of the heavens would be opened, in order that he might elevate all to adoption in glory.

14. Luke 1:73–74.
15. Ps 105:9–10 (104:9–10 LXX).
16. Gen 1:2.
17. Gen 1:8.
18. Rom 8:15, 23.

For the true Son of God humbled himself and descended into the waters of baptism in order to fulfill the promises to the fathers and the gospel. Before that, he had taken upon himself circumcision[19] in order to bestow grace and distribute good things to both parties, so that by being circumcised he would fulfill the basis of the promises and extend invitations to those worthy of the feast, the inheritance of adoption. And in baptism he gives life to all the baptized by having himself been baptized. He made baptism honorable by himself descending into baptism.

And it was there that he was first perceived and recognized to be the true Son of God, through the proclamation of his Father and the same one's Spirit descending upon him.[20] For truly there he was perceived and made known in the fulfillment of the Father's prophecy: "Behold, my child will understand; he will be lifted up and exalted and glorified exceedingly."[21] For thirty years he moved about silently and unseen among them, and then he came to baptism and in baptism was made known to all. John testified, saying: "This is the one, about whom I was saying: 'He who comes after me was before me.' For he was actually first. For from his fullness we all have received grace."[22] And the Spirit descended upon him in the likeness of a dove.[23]

Yet why actually should the Holy Spirit of God appear in the likeness of a dove? In order to teach to those who saw that there is no other way to approach the Son of God except in innocence and righteousness and purity, so that they would take that form from the likeness of the dove and bear it in themselves. Because he is the searcher of hearts[24] and knower of hidden things and revealer of all secrets. For he knows everything and is able to fulfill everything he says, and nothing is impossible for him. As Gabriel said to the holy virgin: "Nothing will be impossible for God,"[25] who exposes the hidden intentions of humans' hearts and reproaches them, "who separately created each of their hearts, who understands all their works,"[26] of those who would approach him.

For this reason, the Spirit descended in the form of a dove: to teach those who saw to draw near to the Son of God with purity of mind, to receive the good gifts of the Spirit, and to become pleasing to the Father. For this reason, the Son of God came and fulfilled the covenant to the fathers, being called by them "son." For this reason, the Son of God came to be baptized: to establish the baptism of all who would be baptized—for there he handed down this tradition, revealing

19. Luke 2:21.
20. Matt 3:16–17 and parallels.
21. Isa 52:13.
22. John 1:15–16.
23. Matt 3:16 and parallels.
24. Ps 44:21 (43:22 LXX).
25. Luke 1:37.
26. Ps 33:15 (32:15 LXX).

salvation for all; and to be understood and known, so that from then on he might disclose and reveal to the world his life-giving teaching of truth.

As the prophet says, speaking in the voice of the Lord's Son: "Approach me and hear this: from the beginning I did not speak anything in secret or in a dark place of the earth; for when he was, I was there. And now, the Lord, the Lord has sent me and his Spirit."[27] Do you see the unity of being? "When he was, I was there," he says, making manifest the consubstantial hypostasis[28] of the Trinity, coworkers in establishing and united in renewing. Then when the heavens opened the Father cried out: "This is my beloved Son,"[29] and the Spirit descended in the likeness of a dove, so that the consubstantial mystery of the hypostasis would become manifest in the coming of the Son.

And what is that which was said: "From the beginning I spoke," if not the prophecies of the holy prophets, which he himself in them spoke concerning himself. And through the consubstantial mystery with the Father and Spirit, he came and appeared here, at the end of times. "Who from the beginning was the Word, and the Word was with God, and the Word was God. That one was from the beginning with God. Everything came into being through him, and without him there came into being nothing that has come into being. Through him was life, and that life was light for humans. And the light was shining in darkness there, and darkness did not overcome it. There came a man sent from God, whose name was John. This one came to bear witness, to testify concerning the light, so that all would believe through him."[30]

Now, fulfilling and completing everything, the light of the Son of God passed into our midst to illuminate every human that comes into the world,[31] that light which darkness was not able to confront or overcome. By this light the world came into being, yet it did not recognize him.[32] Now, for this reason, he came: in order for them to perceive his light, and become sons of God.[33] He came to confirm the law and the prophets,[34] to surpass the models, and establish the truth.[35]

---

27. Isa 48:16.
28. *Zawrut'iwn* (literally, "power") is one of the most common terms used by the author to denote "hypostasis" (ὑπόστασις).
29. Matt 3:17 and parallels.
30. John 1:1–7.
31. John 1:9.
32. John 1:10–11.
33. John 1:12.
34. Matt 5:17.
35. John 1:17.

4. Anania of Narek, *On This Transitory World*

Introduction and translation by Jesse S. Arlen

Anania (ca. 910–ca. 990) was one of the central figures of tenth-century Armenia, a vardapet whose significance is only in recent years being appreciated. He was the first abbot of Narek monastery, located near the southern shores of Lake Van near the capital of the Artsruni kingdom of Vaspurakan. Narek was one of a number of endowed cenobitic monastic complexes founded or refounded in the tenth century that became centers of spiritual, liturgical, and intellectual life. It was particularly known for its mystical spirituality, excellent singers, and vibrant liturgy.

Anania authored a number of important works. Contemporary authors mention his *Refutation of the T'ondrakians*, written against an antihierarchical and anti-church-establishment movement popular in Armenia toward whom Narek monastery and its monks were accused of being sympathetic. Unfortunately, only a fragment of this text survives today. He also composed a treatise against Byzantine dyophysite Christology, called *The Root of Faith*, and a sublime encomium *On the Holy Universal Church*, which finds its context in the midst of these internal and external ecclesiological divisions and controversies that racked his age. Another text treats numerology.

His *Book of Instruction* is comprised of six treatises written at the request of the future Catholicos Khach'ik I Arsharuni (seated 972–92), probably for regulating life among monks living together in the newly established cenobitic complexes. One instruction is addressed to priests, while others treat topics such as caution regarding thoughts, humility, patience, and peace-making. Three other instructions survive, one concerning compunction and tears, the teaching and literary style of which had an impact upon Grigor and his *Book of Lamentation*.

The one translated here, entitled *On This Transitory World*, is significant in light of the economic flourishing of the autonomous kingdoms of Armenia in this period. Making use of the Solomonic wisdom books, Anania warns against being taken in by the illusions of worldly success and prosperity. In the latter half of the work, the poetic prose turns into rhythmic poetry, foreshadowing the work of his disciple Grigor.

Bibliography

Text and Editions

MH 10.310–657 (complete works in Armenian).

Studies

Cowe, S. Peter. "The Renewal of the Debate between Royal and Monastic Ideology under Gagik I of Vaspurakan as a Factor of Commercial and Economic Revival." Pages 242–58 in *Armenia between Byzantium and the Orient: Celebrating the Memory of Karen Yuzbashian (1927–2009)*. Edited by Bernard Outtier, Cornelia B. Horn, et al. Texts and Studies in Eastern Christianity 16. Leiden: Brill, 2020.

———

TRANSLATION

On This Transitory World (MH *10.348–55*)

Moreover, you asked this: "How can a person separate their mind from earthly things and despise this life, which is passing away, and only desire God and his kingdom?"[1] Anania.[2]

So then if you desire to overcome the world[3] and not be ensnared in the illusions of this present life, then take counsel with yourself in your mind and prove with wisdom how human life is empty and transitory, and all that is present is passing away and will vanish like a dream.

It is like this: perhaps you enter an elegantly painted palace and enjoy the sight, yet when you go out from there, it has already passed away, as much for you as for one who did not see it, and you desire to see it again. For humans are

---

1. On the biblical background to this question, see 1 John 2:15–17 and also 1 Cor 7:31. The request to write on this topic came from Bishop Khach'ik, who commissioned the work.

2. Anania's name here functions like a signature.

3. 1 John 5:4–5 and John 16:33.

deprived of this life not only when they die, but even while living. The glory of one day gives way to another, and that of one moment in a moment.

For if you summon singers and hear a cheerful sound, when your ears are cut off from the sound, it has passed away, as much for you as for one who did not hear it, and you desire to hear it again. For this reason, Solomon says: "The eye is not satisfied by seeing, nor the ear by hearing."[4]

As in a dream you see yourself as a king in glory and opulence, yet whenever you wake up you have nothing with you except only what you remember: "I saw this in a dream." So also, even if from dawn to dusk you eat and drink and are ministered to by many, yet when evening comes it has passed away and, on the morrow, appears as another dream, and again you are hungry and in want. For this reason, Solomon also says: "All the toil of humans is for their mouth, yet it is not satisfied."[5]

As a person sets out in the morning and goes along a road and sees vineyards, gardens, and flowers, and various lovely things, and after traveling arrives at an inn, and when evening comes, he has nothing with him except only what he remembers: "I saw this along the road." So also for you, even if from dawn to dusk you enjoy all earthly pleasures, yet when evening comes, they have passed away, and you desire to enjoy them again. For this reason, the prophet says: "As people eat and drink in a dream, yet when they awake, [they realize] their hope was in vain. Like this also is all human glory."[6]

As a person's clothing grows old and worn out, loses its color, and becomes useless, so also is a person's body. Little by little it wastes away and grows old. Our hair ages and becomes white, beauty fades, eyesight deteriorates, our mental faculties dim, and the body loses its strength. And if our time is prolonged, it only grows more decrepit, for the body is the tomb of the soul and is called "a living dead thing."[7] And so, there is nothing stable among visible things.[8]

And if someone has a friend, that also is disrupted, for either the friend dies, or moves away, or grows distant, or, for whatever reason, turns love to hate.

And if someone desires to sin and performs a sinful act fulfilling their will, they are not satisfied, because that instantly passes away, and they become empty again. As Solomon says: "Sometimes a man goes mad for a woman, and some-

---

4. Eccl 1:8.
5. Eccl 6:7.
6. See Isa 29:8; 40:6–8; Wis 3:11.
7. This echoes the ancient Greek pun σῶμα σῆμα (sōma sēma, "[the] body [is a] tomb"), associated with the Pythagoreans as well as Orphic doctrine. See Plato, *Cratylus* 400c and *Gorgias* 493a.
8. This echoes a saying of the ancient author Heraclitus reported by Plato in *Cratylus* 402a (πάντα χωρεῖ καὶ οὐδὲν μένει, "all things give way, and nothing remains") in addition to the teaching of Ecclesiastes.

times he hates her. The wages of sin—listen!—is that one is punished by God and reproached by people."[9]

Now, wisely consider this so that you are not deceived by this life. When you have occasion to sit down to eat, drink, and enjoy yourself, recall to mind that as soon as we rise up and give thanks, look—this joy too passes away.

And when you see people gloriously adorned, recall to mind that—look—they [will] die and turn to dust. As the prophet says: "All humans are grass, and all human glory like the flower of grass."[10]

And when you see spring, radiant and delightful, think about how soon this spring passes and winter comes. When you see a morning, bright and joyous, recall to mind that soon morning passes and night comes.

And when people praise and glorify you, do not become proud and happy, because that too diminishes from day to day and falls into oblivion. There is nothing stable among visible things. For this reason, the apostle says: "Hope that is visible is not hope,"[11] because it is subject to change.

And sadness is mixed with all earthly joys. As the sea never lacks waves, so also humans never lack sadness. For if someone has no wife or children, he is sad that he is without memorial and without heir. If he obtains a wife and children, he becomes even sadder, for his worries multiply and he is unable [to manage them], his disposition becomes unstable and brings sorrow. If one grows old, one loses one's strength, is despised by family, children, and servants, and becomes sorrowful as a result.

If one is poor, one is afflicted by torments and hardships. If one is rich, one is afflicted by many doubts and worries over possessions. For this reason, the misery of the rich is greater than that of the poor, because the rich desire to surpass all and be more famous than all others and are unable to achieve that. While the poor do not strive for that but seek only after a very small shelter and with all ease find their daily food. But it is impossible for the one who desires greatness to be satisfied. For this reason, the apostle says: "Those who desire to be rich fall into all manner of senseless and harmful temptations."[12] Whereas the one who entirely renounces earthly things is comforted and finds rest.

Now, meditate on all this and keep it firmly in mind so you are able to overcome the world:

> Humans also can quickly be changed,
> for although they rise up as the heavens,

---

9. While reminiscent of proverbial wisdom teaching, this does not appear to be an exact reference to any saying from the Solomonic corpus.

10. Isa 40:6.

11. Rom 8:24.

12. 1 Tim 6:9.

they are reduced to dust like the earth.
They spread out as a cloud,
and dissipate like a raindrop.
They bloom radiant as a flower,
and wither away like grass.
They flare up as a flame,
and fade away like smoke.
They whirl about as a storm,
and fall apart like a spiderweb.
They erupt like a furnace,
and are extinguished as flickering embers.
They surge like the sea,
and sink to the depths like sand.
They stand stately as a tree,
and fall away like a leaf.

Now they think themselves stable as a mountain,
and then they vanish like a shadow.
Now they roar like a lion,
and then they become weak as a gnat.
Now they blow in your face like a furious wind,
then they evaporate into the air as mist.
Now they rise like a flood,
and then they are driven off by the wind like brushwood.

Today happy and tomorrow sad,
in the morning healthy and at evening in pain,
today glorious and tomorrow contemptible,
today rich and tomorrow poor,
today terrifying and tomorrow terrified,
today in greatness and tomorrow in the grave,
today in treasure and tomorrow in the tomb.

One moment they conquer and the next they are defeated,
today enviable and tomorrow lamentable,
in the morning a friend and at evening an enemy,
today they gather and tomorrow they scatter.

Now in unity and then divided,
today in prosperity and tomorrow in flight,

now loyal and then duplicitous,
today powerful and tomorrow powerless,
now ministered to by many servants and then in servitude to others,
today satisfied and tomorrow in want,
now rejoicing and then panic-stricken,
today master and tomorrow servant,
now sovereign and then under sovereignty,
today in peace and tomorrow in tumult,
now famous and then forgotten,
today laughing and tomorrow weeping,
now in plenty and then in deprivation,
today without worry and tomorrow worry-stricken,
today they pursue and tomorrow they are pursued,
now loved and then hated,
today close and tomorrow distant,
now usurpers and then usurped by other usurpers.

In the morning they hear good news and rejoice,
at evening they go into mourning and lament.
Now they seize the possessions of the poor and fill their home with
        treasures,
then they are betrayed into the hands of usurpers and deprived of all.

They build elegant constructions with much expenditure,
then they die and leave behind a ruin.
People pass by them and say:
"Where could its builders and those who enjoyed them now be?"

And there is nothing stable in this life,
but everything is changeable like a shadow;
and like a candle snuffed out by the slightest thing,
so also a human's life is suddenly removed from our midst.
The time of youth lasts only a few days,
then white hairs begin to come—harbingers of death,
and the body, wasting away, loses its strength.

So then, do good works now, while time is at hand, because night is coming
when no one can work.[13] As the apostle says: "The day of the Lord arrives like

13. John 9:4; Gal 6:10.

a thief in the night."[14] As the prophet says: "All humans are grass and all human glory like the flower of grass."[15] And Solomon says: "Vanity of vanities, everything is vanity. Everything is empty. . . . Everything came from dust and returns to dust."[16] And a human's life passes away like the wisps of clouds,[17] and declines like a single day. And the Lord himself says: "What benefit is it to people if they gain the whole world and lose their own soul?"[18] And the apostle says: "What is visible here is for a time, but what is invisible there is eternal."[19]

So when earthly magnificence seduces your mind, meditate on all this and seek help from God, and through the grace of Christ you will overcome the world, to the glory of the Father and the Son and the Holy Spirit, unto ages of ages.

---

14. 1 Thess 5:2.
15. Isa 40:6.
16. Eccl 1:2; 3:20.
17. Wis 2:4.
18. Matt 16:26 and parallels.
19. 2 Cor 4:18.

5. Grigor of Narek, *Book of Lamentation, Discourse 1, Discourse 88*

Introduction and translation by Jesse S. Arlen

G rigor (ca. 945–1003) spent nearly his entire life within the walls of Narek monastery. At a tender age his mother died and soon after his father, Khosrov (ca. 900–ca. 960),[1] was appointed bishop of Andzewats'ik'.
Khosrov then entrusted his two younger sons—Yovhannēs and Grigor—
into the care of the monastery led by Anania, his wife's cousin. Thanks to
Anania, Grigor received a superior monastic education. His many literary
works bear the imprint of his intellectual and spiritual setting.

He authored a mystical *Commentary on the Song of Songs* at the request of Prince Gurgēn Artsruni (coreigned as king of Vaspurakan with
his brothers, 977–1003), a commentary on Job 38–39, as well as compiling
a commentary on the Lord's Prayer. He wrote a number of festal works
for liturgical celebrations. Extant are five encomia, eleven litanies, and
thirty hymnic odes, the latter striking for their poetic and mystical genius.
A few instructional prose works survive as well as a letter concerning
the T'ondrakians that preserves the major points of Anania's lost *Refutation of the T'ondrakians*. He also composed a moving eulogy at the death
of Anania.

In the latter years of Grigor's life, he composed the ninety-five poetic
prayer discourses that comprise the *Book of Lamentation*, medieval Armenian literature's pearl of great price. Known popularly as the *Narek*, it
has been read, prayed, loved, and cherished, as well as used for all manner
of mystical, healing, and protective ends by every subsequent generation
of Armenians down to the present day. Leaving aside biblical books, the
Book of Lamentation is the most copied and published of Armenian texts.
In recent years, it has been translated into numerous languages, thus fulfilling the vision Grigor had for it. For although it was begun at the request of
monks and hermits to be used in their solitary prayer, his vision expanded,
and his ambitious creative project came to include in its audience "every
nation of rational beings planted on the earth."[2]

---

1. Khosrov was an important figure and author, most known for his mystical liturgical
commentaries. See Xosrov Anjewac'i, *Commentary on the Divine Liturgy*, trans. S. Peter Cowe,
Armenian Church Classics (New York: Saint Vartan, 1991).

2. *Discourse 3B*. It is worth mentioning that in early 2015—during a mass to commemorate

The secondary literature on Grigor and his book is vast, and his major works are translated into English. The translation below of the preface and two discourses from the *Book of Lamentation* give a sense of the ambitious intentions Grigor had for his book.

Bibliography

Text and Editions

Gregory of Narek. *The Blessing of Blessings: Gregory of Narek's Commentary on the Song of Songs*. Translation, introduction, and notes by Roberta R. Ervine. Cistercian Studies 215. Kalamazoo, MI: Cistercian, 2007.

———. *Le livre de prières*. Introduction, translation, and notes by Isaac Kéchichian. Preface by Jean Mécérian. Sources Chrétiennes 78. Paris: Cerf, 1961.

———. *Tragédie; Matean ołbergut'ean; Le Livre de Lamentation*. Introduction, translation, and notes by Annie Mahé and Jean-Pierre Mahé. CSCO 584, subsidia 106. Leuven: Peeters, 2000.

Grigor Narekatsi. *Speaking with God from the Depths of the Heart: The Armenian Prayer Book of St. Gregory of Narek*. Translated by Thomas Samuelian. Yerevan: Vem, 2002.

MH 10.1015–1110; *MH* 12 (complete works in Armenian).

Terian, Abraham. *The Festal Works of St. Gregory of Narek: Annotated Translation of the Odes, Litanies, and Encomia*. Collegeville, MN: Liturgical Press, 2016.

Studies

Beledian, Krikor. "L'espace et le temps dans l'oeuvre de Grégoire de Narek." Pages 11–37 in *Sagesses de L'orient ancien et chrétien: La voie de vie et la conduite spirituelle chez les peuples et dans le litteratures de l'orient chretien, Conférences I. R. O. C. 1991–92*. Edited by René Lebrun. Sciences théologiques et religieuses 2. Paris: Beauchesne, 1993.

Cowe, S. Peter. "The Impact of Time and Place on Grigor Narekac'i's Theology, Spirituality, and Poetics." *Le Muséon* 108 (1995): 85–102.

Mahé, Jean-Pierre, Paul Rouhana, and Boghos Levon Zekiyan, eds. *Saint*

---

the martyrs of the Armenian Genocide—Pope Francis inaugurated Grigor of Narek into the small class of Doctors of the Universal Church, thus bestowing the highest honor and authority that the Roman Church could grant to a theologian and recognizing the universal relevance of Grigor and his book.

Grégoire de Narek et la liturgie de l'Église: Colloque international organisé par le Patriarcat Arménien Catholique à l'Université Saint-Esprit de Kaslik (USEK), Liban. Actes publiés: *Revue Théologique de Kaslik* 3–4. Kaslik: Faculté Pontificale de Théologie, 2009–10.

Mahé, Jean-Pierre, and Boghos Levon Zekiyan, eds. *Saint Grégoire de Narek: Théologien et Mystique; Colloque International tenu à l'Institut Pontifical Oriental.* Orientalia Christiana Analecta 275. Roma: Pontificio Istituto Orientale, 2006.

Papazian, Michael. *The Doctor of Mercy: The Sacred Treasures of St. Gregory of Narek.* Collegeville, MN: Liturgical Press, 2019.

Terian, Abraham. "Gregory of Narek." Pages 278–92 in *The Wiley-Blackwell Companion to Patristics.* Edited by Ken Parry. Oxford: Wiley-Blackwell, 2015.

TRANSLATION

Book of Lamentation (MH 12.49–54, 535–38)

Compositions

of beneficial discourses full of grief,
of remorse,
of instructions profitable to the soul,
of reproaches against the self,
of life-giving guides to repentance,
of voluntary acceptances,
of revelations of things invisible,
of confessions of sins;

showings of secrets,
unveilings of things covered,
expositions of things hidden;

powerful salves for incurable wounds,
efficacious remedies for unseen ills,
solutions of many parts for perilous pangs,
for the needs of all natures;

occasions for tears,
prompts for prayer;

at the request of the father monks and the many hermits,
a book of lamentation,
composed by Grigor, a monk of Narek monastery.

Discourse 1

Out of the depths of the heart speech with God[3]

A

A voice of sighs, of groaning, of laments, a cry of my heart,
I offer up to you, O seer of secrets.

Placing it over the fire of my burning, sorrowful self,
I present the oblation of my quivering mind's desires,
sent up to you through the censer of my will, billowing with
      savory smoke.

Smell the odor, and look upon it, O compassionate one,
more favorably than a whole burnt sacrifice,
offered up with heaping smoke.
Receive this composition of discourses in little parts
to you for pleasure and not for anger.

May it rise up out of the depths of my mystery-bearing chamber
      of sensations,[4]
to arrive swiftly before you,
a voluntary gift of me,
a rational sacrifice,
burnt by the power of grease that is the fat in me.

3. Each discourse begins with this superscript.
4. That is, his heart.

And when I plead my case with you, mixed with supplication,
     O mighty one,
may it not appear loathsome to you,
like impious Jacob's elevated hands,
according to the complaint of Isaiah,[5]
or as the injustice of Babylon,
which the parable of the seventy-second psalm indicates;[6]
but rather, may it be acceptable to your will,
like the fragrant, pleasing incense of the tabernacle at Shiloh,[7]
which David set up and restored
as a resting place for the ark of the covenant,
returning it from captivity,[8]
a parable for my lost soul,
found again.

B

But your dreadful voice in retributive judgement
resounding forcefully in the valley of vengeance,[9]
gives birth to twin forces in me, rising up to combat,
portending subsequent movements of opposing commotions
revealed in my soul;
tumults of mobs
smashing into one another, sword against armor,
troops of thoughts, evil ones against good ones,
taking me captive unto death,
according to the ancient event,
before the arrival to me of grace,
which Paul, the chosen one among the ranks of the apostles,
making comparison between Moses and the salvation of Christ,
demonstrated to be victorious.[10]

---

5. Isa 1:11–17 at 1:15.
6. Ps 73:7–8 (72:7–8 LXX).
7. Shiloh was the original location of the tabernacle. See Josh 18:1; 1 Sam (1 Kgdms LXX) 1:3.
8. 2 Sam (2 Kgdms LXX) 6.
9. Joel 3:14.
10. That is, demonstrated grace, the salvation of Christ, to be victorious. See, for example, Acts 13:38–39; Rom 3:19–28; 5:12–21; 8:2–3; Gal 3:10–14.

"The day of the Lord is near,"[11] as Scripture says,
in the narrow valley of the field of Jehoshaphat[12]
and the ravine of Kidron.[13]
Those small tribunals of justice at their appointed time,
in the temporary life of this age,
prefigure for me what is to come.
And since the kingdom of God become flesh
has drawn even more near to me,
I am found blameworthy of many more and far graver wrongs
        compounded,
which will reproach me and narrate the truth [about me] in
        great detail.

It will be worse for me
than when his hand was raised up in those former times
to strike against the Edomites and Philistines
and other barbarous nations.
Because their sentence was measured in years,
while the punishment for my debts
has limit without termination.

"Dread, pit, and snare"[14] inescapable
according to the prophet and parable teller,
with great anxiety have arrived at my gate,
depicting there my everlasting shame.

It is yours only to work wonders,
[to transform] medicinal fruits into remedies of life
for the all-wavering doubts of my endangered soul, O atoner of all,
praised in ineffable glory of limitless height,
unto ages of ages,
Amen.

---

11. Isa 13:6; Ezek 30:3; Joel 1:15; 2:1; 3:14; Obad 15; Zeph 1:7, 14.
12. Joel 3:2.
13. 1 Kgs (3 Kgdms LXX) 15:13; 2 Chr 29:16; 30:14.
14. Isa 24:17; Jer 48:43.

Discourse 88

A renewed addition of redoubled groaning to the same entreaty in a discourse of supplications by the same watcher.[15]

Out of the depths of the heart speech with God

A

And now, with shattering of my spirit, with abandonment of my mind,
with brokenness of my heart,
I pour forth water of my will and drops of tears,
remembering that of the prophet Samuel at Mizpah,[16]
which he took and poured from a bowl before you, O seer of all,
an example for the people
to cast themselves down with confession,
and in submission at your life-giving feet.

B

And now, receive this verbal tapestry of miserable groans;
smell this gift of discourse, a bloodless sacrifice, O king of heaven;
bless and purify the text of this book of lamentation,
and after it is written, seal it for an eternal monument
with the services of those pleasing to you.

May it stand before you perpetually,
and be remembered in your ears continually.

May it be pronounced by the lips of your chosen ones,
and spoken by the mouths of your angels.

May it be unrolled in the presence of your throne,
and offered in your holy court.

---

15. Following the first one, nearly all of the subsequent discourses begin with this line.
16. 1 Sam (1 Kgdms LXX) 7:1–6 at 7:6.

May it be incensed in the temple of your name,
and exude fragrance at the altar of your glory.

May it be kept in your treasury,
and stored among your possessions.

May it be recounted in the ears of the nations,
and proclaimed in the hearing of the peoples.

May it be engraved on the doors of the mind,
and imprinted on the threshold of the senses.

As when alive, may it narrate my own,
when confessing iniquities;
and although I will meet my end, being mortal,
yet by the continuation of the discourse of this book
may I be written alive.

May it remain incorruptible in your will, O Lord.
May it always be elevated over me, who am worthy of punishment,
as a continuous judge, impartial reprover,
shameless reproacher, unsparing censurer,
implacable denouncer, savage ridiculer,
heartless betrayer, undeliverable torturer,
unbribable executioner, merciless revealer,
audacious publisher, complainer heard throughout the world;
and with the resounding blasts of a great trumpet,
without silence or ceasing,
may it confess my debts.

C

May this book, with my voice, as me, in my place, cry out,
may it disclose things covered, proclaim secrets,
howl what was done, resound forgotten things,
reveal the invisible, pronounce the pretexts,
proclaim of the depths, tell of sins,
strip bare things unseen, show the forms of things hidden.

Through it may snares be perceived, stumbling blocks discovered,
may unspeakable things be reproved, the remnants of evils wrung out,
and may your life of grace and mercy reign, O Christ,
in my bones dried up in the treasure chest,
through which, at the time of resuscitation,
at the entrance of the first light of spring,
on the glorious day of restoration,
by your dew my soul will have grown,
by this immortal salvation;
and sending forth shoots of intelligible goods
rising up, never more to dry out,
I will become green again and flower anew,
according to the hope-providing Scripture breathed by you.[17]

And to you, the only Savior, to your Spirit, and the Father, sharing in
      Essence,
to your united lordship and your ineffable Trinity,
with mystic praise, glory and bowing down,
unto ages,
Amen.

---

17. Isa 26:19; Ezek 37.

6. Nersēs Shnorhali, *Hymn for the Sunrise Hour, Instructional Preface to a Prayer of Nersēs, Prayer of Nersēs*

Introduction and translation by Jesse S. Arlen

Catholicos Nersēs IV of Hromkla (1102–73, seated 1166–73) is called "Shnorhali," literally, "grace filled" or "graceful," both because of his creative gifts in theological and poetic composition and because of his gentle, amiable character and ecumenical spirit, manifested in his epistolary exchanges with Byzantine Orthodox and Roman Catholic hierarchs over the question of church unity. Along with his nephew Grigor Tghay (ca. 1133–93, ruled 1173–93) and his grandnephew Nersēs of Lambron (1153–98), he stands out as one of the great churchmen, theologians, and writers of Cilician Armenia.

Nersēs was born in the fortress of Tsovk', a descendant of the junior branch of the Pahlawuni, who traced their ancestry to Grigor the Illuminator. He received a monastic education and was trained for theological writing and church leadership. An avid reader and spiritual heir of Grigor of Narek, his mystical bent is evident in the many hymns (*sharakank'*), odes (*tałk'*), and litanies (*gandzk'*) he composed that now fill the liturgical services of the Armenian Church. He wrote hundreds of riddles and proverbs to provide engaging and accessible spiritual instruction to a popular audience. He is also the author of lengthy poetic works on historical topics, most famous of which are *Jesus the Son* (*Yisus Ordi*), a lament for the fall of Edessa (*Oghb Edesioy*), and a history of Armenia (*Vipasanut'iwn*). Important letters survive as well as instructional works and commentaries, among other prose writings.

There is a pronounced focus on light and the sun in the hymn translated below, which was composed for the Sunrise Hour (*arewagali zham*), one of the services of the Liturgy of the Hours (*Zhamagirk'*). It finds its context in his wider effort to bring into the Apostolic Church the "Children of the Sun" (*arewortik'*), native Zoroastrian Armenians who worshiped light and the sun.[1] Despite Shnorhali's efforts, some were never converted

---

1. A letter he wrote about this is translated in James R. Russell, "Children of the Sun," in Russell's *Zoroastrianism in Armenia*, Harvard Iranian Studies 5 (Cambridge: Harvard University Press, 1987), 515–39.

to Christianity and remained in certain mountainous regions of Armenia into the twentieth century.

Also translated is a prayer he composed for the common Christians of his day to memorize and pray, known popularly by its opening words, *Hawatov Khostovanim* ("With Faith I Confess"). It now forms part of the Hour of Rest (*hangstean zham*). His introduction to the prayer describes his reason for writing it and includes comparisons with Muslim prayer practices.

Bibliography

Text and Editions

MH 21 (vol. 1 of complete works in Armenian).

Studies

Findikyan, Michael Daniel. "On the Origins and Early Evolution of the Armenian Office of Sunrise." Pages 283–314 in *Crossroads of Cultures: Studies in Liturgy and Patristics in Honor of Gabriele Winkler*. Edited by Hans-Jürgen Feulner, Elena Velkovska, and Robert F. Taft. Orientalia Christiana Analecta 260. Rome: Pontificio istituto orientale, 2000.

[Keshishian], Aram I, Catholicos of the Holy See of Cilicia. *St. Nerses the Gracious and Church Unity: Armeno-Greek Church Relations (1165–1173)*. Antelias, Lebanon: Armenian Catholicosate of Cilicia, 2010.

Russell, James R. "Children of the Sun." Pages 515–39 in Russell's *Zoroastrianism in Armenia*. Harvard Iranian Studies 5. Cambridge: Harvard University Press, 1987.

———. "The Credal Poem Hawatov Xostovanim ('I Confess in Faith') of St. Nersēs the Graceful." Pages 999–1029 in Russell's *Armenian and Iranian Studies*. Harvard Armenian Texts and Studies 9. Cambridge: Harvard University Press, 2004.

———. "A Credo for the Children of the Sun." *Journal of the Society for Armenian Studies* 4 (1988–89): 157–60.

Zekiyan, Boghos Levon. "Nersès IV Šnorhali." Pages 134–50 in vol. 11 of *Dictionnaire de spiritualité: ascétique et mystique, doctrine et histoire*. 24 volumes. Paris: Beauchesne, 1935–95.

TRANSLATION

Hymn for the Sunrise Hour (MH 21.1183)

Light, creator of light, primal light,
dwelling in unapproachable light, heavenly Father,
blessed by the choirs of beings composed of light.

Refrain: At the rising of the light of this morning
make your intelligible light rise in our souls.

Light rising from light, righteous sun,
ineffable birth of the Father, Son,
before the sun, your name exalted with the Father.

Light emanating from the Father, source of goodness,
Holy Spirit of God,
the children of the church along with angels praise you.

Light, triune and one, indivisible holy Trinity,
we earthborn creatures along with the heavenly ones always
      praise you.

Instructional Preface to the Prayer That Was Made by Lord Nersēs, the Brother of Grigor, Overseer [i.e., Catholicos] of Armenia (MH 21.1204–6)

A prayer for common Christians—old and young, men and women—that all should learn and teach one another: priests their people, fathers their sons, mothers their daughters, and friends their friends. They should pray with it five times a day with twelve kneelings in the morning hour, at mealtime, at midday, in the evening, and at rest. But if someone is negligent or too lazy to perform five prayers, let that one pray four times, or three, or two, or even one time a day, so that at least that one might be recognized to be a Christian, and might recognize oneself to be a creature of God and bow down before him. And if any are too indolent to learn all the words of the prayer—although they learn even many devilish ones with eagerness[2]—let them

---

2. Perhaps a reference to popular, contemporary songs.

learn half of it or even less. For even if they learn just three stanzas and were to pray them with three kneelings at the hour of prayer, it would be received before God.

And if any Christians neglect learning and praying this, let them be reproved by the erroneous sect of Muḥammad, who even in battles do not forgo the prayers that he taught them, let alone at a peaceful hour. Whereas our people when outside the place of prayer do not even remember the name of God, since they do not care about the order of prayer as do the worshipers of God[3] but love empty talk more than prayer. And even when some do come to priests to pray, they either stand with mouth closed or engage in dialogue with one another, for they neither know the words of the prayers nor listen attentively to the psalms and services of the priests.

For this reason, we composed this prayer in simple and clear language, so as to be easily grasped by the common folk. It is brief in words with twenty-four stanzas in accordance with the hours of day and night and in accordance with the letters of the holy prophets. It is powerful in meaning, since it contains in itself much more than the like of our usual requests to God. And we gave it to our people to study so that every Christian would memorize it, so that wherever one might happen to be at the hour of prayer, one might speak with God through it—whether at church or at home, whether in the field or some workplace or on the road. And they who learn and pray it sincerely—with fervent heart and tears—all the requests that are written in it will be fulfilled for them in life and after death. Whereas those who despise it and do not learn it, they themselves will see the harm that comes about to them.

We have outlined the reason for making this prayer, so that they will no longer object that "because we don't know the words of prayers—for that reason we don't pray." But let such people be informed that Satan endeavors to block no other good work of ours so much as prayer, because he knows that through our prayers he is driven off from us and God comes to dwell in us.

Now let us ask God, the doer of good, to open the eyes of your minds so that all of you will eagerly learn it and pray it with faith and be heard by God. And while praying, remember in Christ Grigorios,[4] the catholicos of Armenia, and the same one's brother, Lord Nersēs, the author of this prayer. And those of you who copy this prayer in a book, write also this instructional discourse. And those who copy this will be written in the book of eternal life. And those who learn and pray it will receive mercy from Christ. And those who teach it to their friend will have a reward from God. And those who copy it, let them not add a letter or word more or less or otherwise to this original copy, but may all copies be alike, wherever they copy it. And those unexperienced in letters, let them give it to be copied by those who know how to do it rightly, so that it may be done correctly.

3. A reference to the Liturgy of the Hours performed in monasteries.
4. Grigor III Pahlawuni (seated 1113–66).

Prayer of Nersēs (MH 21.1207–14)

The words of the prayer composed by Nersēs the Sage
for common Christian people
directed to the holy Trinity and one deity
to Father and Son and Holy Spirit. Amen.

1   With faith I confess and bow down to you,
     Father, Son and Holy Spirit,
     uncreated and immortal nature,
     creator of angels and humans and all that comes into being.
     Have mercy upon all your creatures and upon me, a great sinner.

2   With faith I confess and bow down to you,
     indivisible light, united holy Trinity and one deity,
     creator of light and dispeller of darkness;
     dispel from my soul the darkness of sin and ignorance
     and illumine my mind at this hour,
     to pray to you according to your pleasure,
     and to receive from you my requests.
     And have mercy upon all your creatures and upon me, a great sinner.

3   Heavenly Father, true God,
     who sent your beloved Son in search of the lost sheep.[5]
     I have sinned against heaven and before you.
     Receive me as the prodigal son[6]
     and clothe me with the primordial garment,
     which I stripped off of myself through sin.[7]
     And have mercy upon all your creatures and upon me, a great sinner.

4   Son of God, true God,

---

5. Matt 18:12–14; Luke 15:3–7.
6. Luke 15:11–32.
7. The primordial garment and clothing metaphors are part of the epic theological expression of fall and redemption in Syriac, from where it entered Armenian theological discourse. See Sebastian P. Brock, "Clothing Metaphors as a Means of Theological Expression in Syriac Tradition," in *Typus, Symbol, Allegorie bei den östlichen Vätern und ihren Parallelen im Mittelalter*, ed. M. Schmidt, Eichstätter Beiträge 4 (Regensburg: Pustet, 1982), 11–40; and James R. Russell, "The Epic of the Pearl," *Revue des études arméniennes* 28 (2001–2): 29–100.

who humbled yourself from the bosom of the Father[8]
and took a body from the holy Virgin Mary
for our salvation;
you were crucified and buried and you rose from the dead,
and you ascended to the Father in heaven.
I have sinned against heaven and before you.
Remember me like the robber,
when you come in your kingdom.[9]
And have mercy upon all your creatures and upon me, a great sinner.

5   Spirit of God, true God,
who descended in the Jordan[10] and in the holy upper room[11]
and illumined me through baptism in the holy font;
I have sinned against heaven and before you.
Purify me anew with your divine fire,
as the apostles with fiery tongues.[12]
And have mercy upon all your creatures and upon me, a great sinner.

6   Uncreated and sinless nature,
I have sinned against you in my mind, in my spirit, and in my body;
do not remember my previous sins,
for the sake of your holy name.
And have mercy upon all your creatures and upon me, a great sinner.

7   Seer of all,
I have sinned by thought, by word, and by deed;
expunge the manuscript of my transgressions,
and write my name in the book of life.
And have mercy upon all your creatures and upon me, a great sinner.

8   Searcher of secrets,
I have sinned against you willingly and unwillingly,
knowingly and unknowingly;
grant forgiveness to me, a sinner.
For from my birth in the font until today,
I have sinned before your divinity,

8. Phil 2:6–8.
9. Luke 23:32–43 at 23:42–43.
10. Matt 3:13–17 and parallels.
11. Acts 1:13 and Acts 2.
12. Acts 2:3.

with my senses and with my body parts.
And have mercy upon all your creatures and upon me, a great sinner.

9   All-caring Lord,
       place holy reverence of you as guardian before my eyes,
       no more to look indecently,
       and before my ears,
       no more to listen eagerly to evil speech,
       and before my mouth,
       no more to tell lies,
       and before my heart,
       no longer to devise evil,
       and before my hands,
       no more to work injustice,
       and before my feet,
       no longer to walk in the ways of iniquity;
       but direct their movements
       to be always virtuous in accordance with your commandments.
       And have mercy upon all your creatures and upon me, a great sinner.

10   Living fire, Christ,
       inflame my being
       with the fire of your love, which you cast to earth,[13]
       to burn up the vices of my soul
       and purify the conscience of my mind,
       to clean away the sins of my body
       and kindle the light of your knowledge in my heart.
       And have mercy upon all your creatures and upon me, a great sinner.

11   Wisdom of the Father, Jesus,
       give me the wisdom to think, speak, and do good
       before you in every moment;
       and save me from wicked thoughts, words, and deeds.
       And have mercy upon all your creatures and upon me, a great sinner.

12   Willer of good, Lord, fulfiller of wills,
       do not let me walk according to my individual will,
       but guide me to be always a lover of your goodwill.
       And have mercy upon all your creatures and upon me, a great sinner.

13. Luke 12:49.

13   Heavenly king,
      grant me your kingdom,
      which you promised to those who love you,[14]
      and strengthen my heart to hate my sins,
      love you alone,
      and do your commands.
      And have mercy upon all your creatures and upon me, a great sinner.

14   Caretaker of creatures,
      protect by the sign of your cross
      my soul and body
      from the deceptions of adversarial demons,
      from temptations to sin,
      from unjust men,
      and from all perils to soul and body.
      And have mercy upon all your creatures and upon me, a great sinner.

15   Guardian of all,
      may your right hand be a shield above me
      day and night,
      while sitting at home and while traveling on a journey,
      in sleep and at rising,
      so that I may never be shaken.
      And have mercy upon all your creatures and upon me, a great sinner.

16   My God,
      who open your hand
      and fill all creatures with your sweetness,
      to you I commit my being;
      take care of and provide for the needs of my soul and body
      from this time forth unto the end of the age.
      And have mercy upon all your creatures and upon me, a great sinner.

17   Converter of the wayward,
      convert me from evil habits to good habits,
      and nail into my soul the dreadful day of death,
      the fear of Gehenna,
      and love for the kingdom,
      that I may repent of my sins

14. John 14–16.

and work righteousness.
And have mercy upon all your creatures and upon me, a great sinner.

18   Fountain of goodness,
make tears of repentance flow from my heart
like the prostitute,[15]
so that I may wash away my individual sins
before I depart this world.
And have mercy upon all your creatures and upon me, a great sinner.

19   Bestower of mercies,
grant that I may come to you
with orthodox faith,
with good deeds,
and in communion with your holy body and blood.
And have mercy upon all your creatures and upon me, a great sinner.

20   Lord, doer of good,
commit me to a good angel
to give up my soul gently,
and to pass undisturbed through the evil spirits of wickedness
that are below heaven.
And have mercy upon all your creatures and upon me, a great sinner.

21   True light,
make my soul worthy
to see the light of your glory
at the day of calling,
and to repose in the hope of good
in the lodgings of the just
until the day of your great coming.
And have mercy upon all your creatures and upon me, a great sinner.

22   Just judge,
when you come in the glory of the Father
to judge the living and the dead,[16]
do not enter into judgement against your servant,
but save me from the fire of the age,

15. Luke 7:36–50 at 7:38.
16. Matt 16:27; 1 Pet 4:5.

and allow me to hear
the blissful calling of the just into your heavenly kingdom.
And have mercy upon all your creatures and upon me, a great sinner.

23   All-merciful Lord,
have mercy upon all those who trust in you,
my own and strangers,
those I know and those unknown to me,
the living and the dead;
grant also forgiveness of transgressions
to my enemies and those who hate me,
and turn them from the malice
they bear toward me,
so that they may be worthy of your mercy.
And have mercy upon all your creatures and upon me, a great sinner.

24   Glorious Lord,
receive the petitions of your servant
and fulfill my requests for good
through the intercession of the Holy Mother of God,
John the forerunner,
Saint Stephen the protomartyr,
your holy apostles and prophets,
martyrs,
vardapets,
holy patriarchs,
holy ascetics,
virgins,
and all your holy ones, heavenly and earthly.

Glory, honor, and worship to you,
indivisible holy Trinity,
unto ages. Amen.

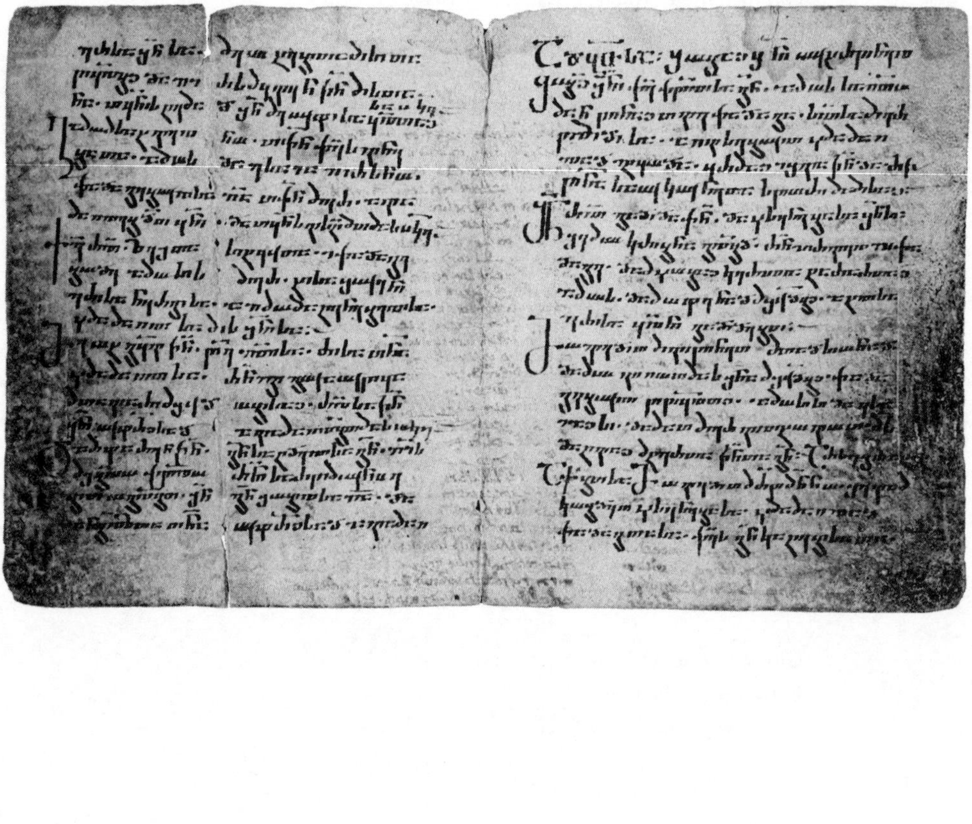

3

GEORGIAN

Introduction and Bibliography by Jeff W. Childers

S
ituated between the Black Sea and the Caspian Sea amid the Greater and Lesser Caucasus Mountain Ranges, ancient Georgia faced difficult geography. The terrain and climate could be harsh, especially in the mountainous regions, but the lands were also perched precariously at the crossroads between the warring Roman and Persian Empires until the seventh century, and between the Byzantine Empire and the Arab caliphate for centuries thereafter. Georgia was bordered to the southwest by lands generally controlled by the Romans/ Byzantines, to the east by Azerbaijan, and to the south by Armenia, which, like Georgia, was contested territory in the struggle between the colossal superpowers on either side.[1] The north provided access to various invaders, especially along the eastern seacoast, including the Huns, a threat that figures in the *Martyrdom of Saint Shushanik* translated here. The Greeks called the land Iberia, a name that occurs often in sources from all periods. The designation "Georgia" has roots in Persian and Arab names for the country and its people.

Under immense political pressures, by late antiquity Georgia was split into a number of feudal regions. As the plights of Shushanik and Habo will illustrate,[2] the rulers of these regions rarely enjoyed much independence, often having to act as the agents of outside powers. The principal regions included Tao-Klarjet'i to the southwest, Abkhazia to the northwest, Kakhet'i-Heret'I to the east, and the large region of Kart'li in the middle, with its major centers at Tbilisi (Georgian Tp'ilisi) and Mtskhet'a. Kart'li was the principal region of central Georgia and became the focus of the unification of Georgia, begun by David III Kouropalates of Tao who invaded Kart'li at the end of the tenth century and was largely

1. For an overview of the history of Georgia during the period covered in this book, see D. Rayfield, *Edge of Empires: A History of Georgia* (London: Reaktion, 2012), 11–131.

2. On the significance of the hagiographic sources for understanding the political history of the nation, see S. H. Rapp Jr., *The Sasanian World through Georgian Eyes: Caucasia and the Iranian Commonwealth in Late Antique Georgian Literature* (Farnham: Ashgate, 2014), 1–165.

completed by his foster son Bagrat III, who was king of Abkhazia from 978 and crowned king of Georgia in 1008. In the translations here, the term Kart'li is translated "Georgia"; the Georgians refer to themselves as *kart'velians*. During the ninth and tenth centuries, Christianity in Georgia played a pivotal role in helping the people acquire a sense of unity, integrating national identity, language, and religion.[3] Under David IV the Builder (1089–1125) and Queen Tamar the Great (1184–1213) a united Georgia flourished, prior to the Mongol invasions of the mid-thirteenth century.

Apart from legends of early apostolic preaching, archeological evidence from burials in Urbnisi and the ancient capital of Mtskhet'a suggests that Christianity may have been brought to Georgia as early as the third century, perhaps by Jewish immigrants.[4] The traditional national legend points to the foreign slave woman Nino, who is credited with converting the Georgian King Mirian III of Kart'li and his family to Christianity in the fourth century.[5] The historicity of the Nino tale is debatable, but it is clear that Christianity did make major inroads into Georgia in the fourth century. By the fifth century Christianity was the dominant faith, progressively supplanting Zoroastrianism and other local religious practices.

It is most likely that the Georgian alphabet was created as part of a Christian mission initiative during the early fifth century, to pave the way for translating the Bible and the liturgy into Georgian. Armenian legends associating the alphabet's invention with Mesrob/Mashtots', who devised the Armenian script in the early fifth century, are tendentious. Similarities to the Greek alphabet suggest that it may have been the basic model for the Georgian instead.[6] However, the early Georgian Church and its literary traditions were decisively influenced by the Armenian Church and, alongside the Armenian, by Syriac Christian traditions. The first translations of portions of Christian Scripture into Georgian date from the fifth century, possibly originating from the southwestern border region of Tao-Klarjet'i, an area of early widespread and sustained Christian activity. The most primitive literary strata of Georgian theological literature, including the

---

3. See K. Lerner, "Georgia, Christian History of," in *The Blackwell Dictionary of Eastern Christianity*, ed. Ken Parry et al. (Oxford: Blackwell, 1999), 212–13.

4. See C. Haas, "Mountain Constantines: The Christianization of Aksum and Iberia," *Journal of Late Antiquity* 1 (2008): 101–26. A brief but helpful summary of the history of Christianity and the Georgian Church may be found in S. H. Rapp Jr., "Georgian Christianity," in *The Blackwell Companion to Eastern Christianity*, ed. Ken Parry (Oxford: Blackwell, 2007), 137–55.

5. English translation in D. M. Lang, *Lives and Legends of the Georgian Saints*, rev. ed. (Crestwood, NY: Saint Vladimir's Seminary Press, 1976), 13–39.

6. See D. Rayfield, *The Literature of Georgia: A History* (Oxford: Oxford University Press, 1995), 1–26.

Bible, display the influence of Syriac roots, mediated mainly through Armenian channels, as evidenced by the impact of Armenian literature and numerous Syro-Armenianisms in Georgian translations and transliteration.[7] The geographical proximity of Syriac and Armenian Christian communities ensured that those churches would greatly impact early Georgian Christian literature, theology, religious practices, and ecclesial politics. However, the Georgians also felt much direct Greek influence, possibly due to the number of Greek settlements along the coast of the Black Sea, or perhaps even due to the early and strong Georgian presence in Palestine. From the fifth century, Georgian monks were very active in Palestine, and key monastic centers such as that at Mar Saba were the scene of vibrant Georgian literary activities.[8] Georgian literary production occurred in multiple locations from an early time, within and beyond the confines of Georgia. Alongside original Georgian literature, translations were made from Greek, Syriac, and Armenian sources; in some instances, the originals have not survived and the Georgian versions represent our best—or even only—access to otherwise lost texts.

The Georgian ecclesial hierarchy was subject to the patriarch of Antioch until the late fifth century, when the church asserted independence under its own catholicos. Although many within the Georgian Church were christologically dyophysite, at the Synod of Dvin in Armenia (506), representatives of the Georgian Church joined the Armenians in rejecting the Chalcedonian formula of 451 and asserting a miaphysite stance, emphasizing the unity of Christ against the perceived "Nestorian" duality of Chalcedon.[9] The Syrian Orthodox and the Armenian churches remain miaphysite to this day, along with the Coptic Church and other Eastern communions. However, due partly to Greek theological, ecclesial, and political influence, by the early seventh century the Georgian Church came to reject miaphysitism and affirm Chalcedon. This resulted in the Armenian condemnation of the Georgian Church at the third Synod of Dvin (609). It also meant that the Georgian Church and nation affiliated even more closely with the Greek Orthodox Church and the Byzantine Empire,[10] eventually coming to view the traces of Syriac and Armenian influences at its roots with some suspicion. During the Byzantine revivals of the tenth and eleventh centuries, Georgian

7. See Rayfield, *Literature of Georgia*, 19–20, 22–25; and M. van Esbroeck and I. Ramelli, "Georgian Language and Literature," in *Encyclopedia of Ancient Christianity*, ed. A. di Berardino, T. C. Oden, et al. (Downers Grove, IL: IVP Academic, 2014), 2:122.

8. See P. M. Tarchnišvili and J. Assfalg, *Geschichte der kirchlichen georgischen Literatur*, Studi e testi 185 (Vatican City: Biblioteca Apostolica Vaticana, 1955), 24–39.

9. M. F. Castelfranchi, "Georgia," in *Encyclopedia of Ancient Christianity*, ed. A. di Berardino, T. C. Oden, et al. (Downers Grove, IL: IVP Academic, 2014), 2:119–20.

10. Rapp, "Georgian Christianity," 142–46.

Christian scholarship engaged in major projects to revise its early versions of the Bible and other literature to reconcile it more exactly with the Greek.[11] Translators also undertook the task of rendering many Greek theological and secular works into Georgian for the first time. The impact of these intellectual endeavors was especially prominent in the work of the Georgian Athonites, who not only dramatically transformed Georgian literature but also played a decisive role in the transition of Mount Athos from an assemblage of hermitages to a major Orthodox monastic center.[12]

The translations here represent key aspects of the Georgian Christian tradition. The early heritage includes many tales of the heroic exploits of mighty saints and martyrs.[13] The challenges and persecutions they faced reflect the political tensions besetting Georgia for much of its late antique and medieval history, tensions often expressed in religious terms. It is telling that many of the early heroines and heroes of Georgian Christianity, like the Armenian Princess Shushanik and the Arab perfumer Habo from Baghdad, are foreigners. Their narratives bear witness to Georgia's constant awareness of its crossroads status as a buffer between greater world powers, while also declaring vindication when celebrated foreigners are seen to adhere faithfully to the Christian faith of Georgia, despite enormous pressures. Excerpts from the lives of the most important of the early Georgian Athonites are translated here. Their lives chronicle the establishment of the Iviron Monastery on Mount Athos, detailing much of the transformative Christian scholarship that occurred there. Established on Athos at a pivotal time, the Iviron Monastery and its founders left an indelible impact on the Eastern Orthodox spiritual tradition. The *Life of Porphyry of Gaza* represents a type of early Georgian translation literature, outside the Bible. Its source text is lost, and its account of the Christianization of a major late antique city features prominently in discussions about the historicity of the events.

The system of transliteration of Georgian names and words in the translations is intended to aid reading rather than achieving precise philological consistency. Transliterations of Georgian works in the bibliography are more precise. The bibliographies favor works in English, though the reader will find that those works often point to materials in other languages.

11. See J. W. Childers, "The Bible in the Languages of the East: Georgian," in *New Cambridge History of the Bible*, vol. 2: *From c. 600 to c. 1450*, ed. R. Marsden and E. A. Matter (Cambridge: Cambridge University Press, 2012), 174–77.

12. See T. Grdzelidze, *Georgian Monks on Athos: Two Eleventh-Century Lives of the Hegoumenoi of Iviron* (London: Bennett & Bloom, 2009), 11–50.

13. See Rayfield, *Literature of Georgia*, 40–49.

Bibliography

Blake, R. P. "Georgian Theological Literature." *Journal of Theological Studies* 26 (1924): 50–64.

Castelfranchi, M. F. "Georgia." Vol. 2/pp. 118–22 in *Encyclopedia of Ancient Christianity*. Edited by A. di Berardino, T. C. Oden, et al. Downers Grove, IL: IVP Academic, 2014.

Childers, J. W. "The Bible in the Languages of the East: Georgian." Pages 162–78 in *New Cambridge History of the Bible*, vol. 2: *From c. 600 to c. 1450*. Edited by R. Marsden and E. A. Matter. Cambridge: Cambridge University Press, 2012.

———. "The Georgian New Testament." Pages 293–327 in *The Text of the New Testament: Essays on the Status Quaestionis*. Edited by B. Ehrman and M. Holmes. 2nd ed. New Testament Tools, Studies, and Documents 42. Leiden: Brill, 2012.

Esbroeck, M. van, and I. Ramelli. "Georgian Language and Literature." Vol. 2/pp. 122–23 in *Encyclopedia of Ancient Christianity*. Edited by A. di Berardino, T. C. Oden, et al. Downers Grove, IL: IVP Academic, 2014.

Haas, C. "Mountain Constantines: The Christianization of Aksum and Iberia." *Journal of Late Antiquity* 1 (2008): 101–26.

Kekeliże, K. *Żveli kʿartʿuli literaturis istoria* (*History of Old Georgian Literature*). Vol. 1. Tbilisi: Mecʿniereba, 1960 (in Georgian; see also P. M. Tarchnišvili and J. Assfalg below).

Kiladze, N. "Georgia, Christian Thought in." Pages 214–18 in *The Blackwell Dictionary of Eastern Christianity*. Edited by Ken Parry et al. Oxford: Blackwell, 1999.

Lang, D. M. *Lives and Legends of the Georgian Saints*. Rev. ed. Crestwood, NY: Saint Vladimir's Seminary Press, 1976.

Lerner, K. "Georgia, Christian History of." Pages 210–14 in *The Blackwell Dictionary of Eastern Christianity*. Edited by Ken Parry et al. Oxford: Blackwell, 1999.

Martin-Hisard, B. "Georgian Hagiography." Vol. 1/pp. 285–98 in *The Ashgate Research Companion to Byzantine Hagiography*. Edited by S. Efthymiadis. Farnham: Routledge, 2011.

Outtier, B. "Langues et littérature géorgienne." Pages 261–96 in *Christianismes orientaux: Introduction à l'étude des langues et littératures*. Edited by M. Albert et al. Paris: Cerf, 1993.

Rapp, S. H., Jr. "Georgian Christianity." Pages 137–55 in *The Blackwell Companion to Eastern Christianity*. Edited by Ken Parry. Oxford: Blackwell, 2007.

———. *The Sasanian World through Georgian Eyes: Caucasia and the Iranian Commonwealth in Late Antique Georgian Literature*. Farnham: Ashgate, 2014.

Rapp, S. H., Jr., and P. Crego. *Languages and Cultures of Eastern Christianity: Georgian*. Worlds of Eastern Christianity (300–1500) 5. Oxford: Routledge, 2012.

Rayfield, D. *Edge of Empires: A History of Georgia*. London: Reaktion, 2012.

————. *The Literature of Georgia: A History*. Oxford: Oxford University Press, 1995.

Tarchnišvili, P. M., and J. Assfalg. *Geschichte der kirchlichen georgischen Literatur*. Studi e testi 185. Vatican City: Biblioteca Apostolica Vaticana, 1955 (adaptation and translation of K. Kekeliże's 1941 edition).

Thomson, R. W. "The Origins of Caucasian Civilization: the Christian Component." Pages 25–43 in *Transcaucasia, Nationalism, and Social Change: Essays in the History of Armenia, Azerbaijan, and Georgia*. Edited by R. G. Suny. Rev. ed. Ann Arbor: University of Michigan Press, 1996.

Tuite, K. "Early Georgian." Pages 145–65 in *The Ancient Languages of Asia Minor*. Edited by R. D. Woodard. Cambridge: Cambridge University Press, 2008.

1. Jacob Cʻurtaveli, *Martyrdom of Saint Shushanik*

Introduction and translation by Jeff W. Childers

Widely recognized as the oldest piece of surviving Georgian literature, the *Martyrdom of Saint Shushanik* tells the tale of an Armenian princess married to the Georgian Governor Varskʻen who abandons
his Christian faith to embrace the Zoroastrianism of his Sassanian masters. Shushanik, whom the Georgian text calls "queen," remains a faithful
Christian, but at great personal cost. Her husband pressures her violently
to convert, without success. Her recalcitrance is an embarrassment for
Varskʻen, making Shushanik a political liability. The story personalizes the
great religious and political conflicts that shook these border regions in
the fifth century, when relationships between the Roman and Sassanian
Empires could be extremely tense and violent.

The drama takes place in the marchlands between Armenia and Georgia, and Shushanik came quickly to be revered as a mighty heroine in the
Christian churches of both nations. Multiple versions of her martyrdom
were composed in Georgian and Armenian. The Georgian text translated
here bears the marks of being the account composed closest to the events.
It purports to be the work of Shushanik's priest and confessor, Jacob Cʻur-
taveli, and is usually dated to the time shortly after her death and before
the death of Varskʻen (i.e., 475–84). The text gives some indication of having been slightly revised after the schism between the Georgian and Armenian churches in 607, but otherwise appears to have been little altered
from its ostensibly late-fifth-century composition.

The translation below excerpts most of the text, with a few omissions for
the sake of length. Months and days are given according to the earliest manuscripts; some calendrical differences occur in the sources due to variations
in the traditions regarding the commemoration of the martyr's death.

Bibliography

Text and Editions

Abulaże, I., et al., eds. *Żveli kʻartʻuli agiograpʻiuli literaturis żeglebi* (Old Georgian Monuments of Hagiographical Literature). Vol. 1: *V–X Centuries*,
pp. 11–29. Tbilisi: Mecʻniereba, 1963–64 (in Georgian).

Studies

Birdsall, J. N. "Gospel Allusions in the Georgian Martyrdom of St. Šušanik."
Pages 185–96 in *Collected Papers in Greek and Georgian Textual Criticism.* Edited by J. N. Birdsall. Texts and Studies 3.3. Piscataway, NJ: Gorgias, 2006.

Peeters, P. "Sainte Sousanik martyre en Arméno-Géorgie (†13 Décembre 482–484)." *Analecta Bollandiana* 53 (1935): 5–48, 245–307.

Rapp, S. H., Jr. *The Sasanian World through Georgian Eyes: Caucasia and the Iranian Commonwealth in Late Antique Georgian Literature,* pp. 33–103. Farnham: Ashgate, 2014.

Tarchnišvili, P. M., and J. Assfalg, *Geschichte der kirchlichen georgischen Literatur,* pp. 83–87. Studi e testi 185. Vatican City: Biblioteca Apostolica Vaticana, 1955.

<hr />

TRANSLATION

Martyrdom of Saint Shushanik

October 17: Martyrdom of the holy Queen Shushanik

Now I will fully and reliably relate to you the account of the departure of the blessed Saint Shushanik.

(1) It was in the eighth year of the reign of the king of Persia[1] that Varsk'en the Pitiakhsh,[2] son of Arshushay, traveled to the royal court.[3] Varsk'en had previously been a Christian, born of a Christian father and mother. His wife was the daughter of Vardan,[4] the Armenians' commander-in-chief. She is the one about

1. That is, 466, the eighth regnal year of *Shahan shah* Peroz I, ruler of the Sassanian Empire 459–84.
2. Pitiakhsh (Iranian *bidakhsh*) is a title designating the toparch, or governor, under Sassanian rule. Varsk'en was charged with defending the marchlands between Georgia and Armenia. He was killed by the Georgian King Vakhtang I Gorgasali in 484.
3. At the Sassanian capital city Ctesiphon.
4. Vardan Mamikonian (died 451), the eminent Armenian military commander who led a revolt against the Sassanians, helping to win religious independence for Armenian Christians; revered as saint and martyr of the Armenian Church.

whom I am writing you. She was named Vardi,[5] after her father, but was affectionately called Shushanik.[6] As I have said, she had been a God-fearing woman from her childhood. Because of her husband's wickedness, she prayed constantly in her heart and entreated everyone to pray for him, so that God would convert him from his foolish ways and he would come back to his senses about Christ.

As for Varsk'en—who can adequately speak about this wretched and thrice-pitiable lost man, who betrayed precious faith in Christ? Or who would not weep for this man, who saw no persecution, no terror, no sword, nor prison for the sake of Christ?

For when Varsk'en appeared before the Persian king, it was not to receive some honor but to offer himself utterly to the king by denying the true God and worshiping the fire.[7] So he cut himself off fully from Christ. Yet this wretched man tried to win favor with the Persian king by asking him for a wife, saying: "I will also convert my current legitimate wife and children to your religion." (He made this promise, without taking Shushanik into account.) Then the king was glad, instructing Varsk'en to marry his own daughter.

(2) Then the Pitiakhsh took his leave of the Persian king. As he approached the borders of Georgia, the land of Heret'i,[8] he decided to have his nobles, his sons, and his attendants informed that they should meet him, so that he could enter the country among them, thereby appearing loyal. So he sent one of his servants by means of courier horse, who came to a village they call C'urtav.

Once the servant arrived, he went in to appear before our Queen Shushanik, enquiring after her well-being. But the blessed Shushanik spoke to him like a prophetess, saying: "If he is alive in spirit, you and he are both alive. If you are both dead in spirit, then let this greeting of yours return back to you."[9] The man dared not answer her. But Saint Shushanik asked him insistently, invoking oaths, so the man told her the truth, declaring: "Varsk'en has denied the true God."

When the blessed Shushanik heard this, she fell on the ground, striking her head on the floor and speaking with bitter tears: "The wretched Varsk'en has become pitiable indeed, for he has abandoned the true God, professing the religion of the fire-worshipers and joining the godless!" Then she got up, left her palace, and went into the church, filled with the fear of God. She took three sons and one daughter with her, bringing them before the altar and praying: "Lord God, they

5. Varden means "Rose."

6. A Georgian form of Susanna, the heroine of apocryphal additions to Daniel. Also the name of one of Jesus's disciples (Luke 8:3).

7. Zoroastrianism, the state religion of Persia, was known for its fire shrines and rituals involving fire.

8. A region of eastern Georgia, under Sassanian control.

9. See Matt 10:13.

are your gifts; preserve them, pure from the holy baptismal font, by the mercy of the Holy Spirit, to be one flock of the one shepherd, our Lord Jesus Christ."

When the evening service was finished, she found a little house near the church. Filled with sadness, she went into it, leaning against a corner and weeping with bitter tears.

(3) Now the bishop who was attached to the Pitiakhsh's household, whose name was Apots, was not there, because he had gone to the house of a certain holy man to ask him about some matter. And I too, Queen Shushanik's confessor,[10] was with the bishop. Suddenly a deacon came to us from home and reported all this to us, regarding the Pitiakhsh's arrival and the queen's actions. Being overcome with grief we wept profusely, distressed by our manifest sins.

I got up early and went to the village where the blessed Shushanik was. When I saw her in distress, I wept with her too, saying to the blessed Shushanik: "You are about to enter into a great struggle, queen. Attend carefully to your faith in Christ, so that the enemy will not find a place to feed within you, like a cancer." Saint Shushanik replied to me: "Priest, indeed I am prepared for a great struggle." I told her: "So you are! Be strong, patient, and courageous." Then she said to me: "This affliction belongs to me alone." But I responded: "Your affliction is our affliction, and your joy is our joy—ours not just because you have been our queen, but because you have regarded us as your children."

Then I spoke to the blessed one secretly: "If it pleases you, report to me the account of your labor, that I may know it and write it down." She replied to me: "Why do you ask me this?" I responded: "Do you stand firm?" She said to me: "May it never happen that I should take any part in the sinful deeds of Varsk'en!" "He has a cruel mind," I responded. "He will subject you to great torment and violence." Then she said to me: "Death at his hands is better for me than uniting with him to the destruction of my soul. For I have heard what Paul the apostle said: 'The brother or sister is not bound; let them leave.'"[11] I replied: "This is true."

(4) While we were talking, a certain Persian arrived and came into the presence of the blessed holy Shushanik, and said in a mournful voice: "How has such a peaceful household become so pitiful, turning joy to grief?" But he had come as part of a plot by Varsk'en and said this in a guileful way, wanting to entrap the blessed one. The holy woman recognized his deceptive intention and became even more firmly resolved.

Three days later, Varsk'en the Pitiakhsh arrived. The Persian spoke to him secretly and said: "I perceive that your wife has left you. But I tell you: say nothing harsh to her, for it is the way of women to be moody."

10. That is, Jacob C'urtaveli.

11. See 1 Cor 7:15, where the apostle Paul allows for the dissolution of a marriage between a Christian believer and an unbeliever.

The next day, when the Pitiakhsh got up he summoned us priests and we went to him. He greeted us cheerfully, telling us: "Do not shun or spurn me." We responded: "You have condemned yourself and condemned us as well!" Then he began to speak, saying: "How could my wife do such a thing against me? Now go and tell her: 'You have toppled my image[12] and put ashes on my bed, deserting your place and going elsewhere!'"

Saint Shushanik replied: "I have neither erected nor toppled your image. Your father erected shrines for the martyrs and built churches, but you have ruined your father's deeds and torn down his good works. Your father brought saints into his home but you have brought devils into yours. He confessed and believed in the God of heaven and earth, but you have rejected the true God and worshiped the fire. Just as you have renounced your maker, so I have poured contempt upon you. Even if you subject me to great torment, I will not share in your actions." We reported all this to the Pitiakhsh, who roared with rage.

(5) Then the Pitiakhsh sent his brother Jojik and Jojik's wife, his sister-in-law, along with the bishop attached to his household, instructing them to say the following: "Get up and come back to your place! Do not cling to this intent of yours, or I will drag you back by force!"

So they came and went in before the queen, speaking great encouragement to her. Then Saint Shushanik told them: "Wise people, you speak well, but do not believe that I was just his wife. I thought I would convert him to my faith and he would confess the true God. And now you try to compel me to do this. May this never be! And you, Jojik, are no longer my brother-in-law, nor I your sister-in-law, nor is your wife my sister, for you are on Varskʻen's side and participate in his deeds." Jojik said to her: "I am sure that he will send his servants and they will drag you away by force." But Saint Shushanik replied: "If he binds me and drags me away, I am happy to have such a verdict from him."

When they heard this from her, they all wept. Jojik got up tearfully and went outside. But Saint Shushanik said to the bishop: "How can you encourage me to do this, since he has denied God?" Jojik exhorted her: "You are our sister. Do not destroy this noble house." Saint Shushanik responded: "I know that I am your sister and we were brought up together, but I cannot do this. He has become guilty of murder, and you all share in his guilt."

When they continued to pressure her greatly, the blessed Saint Shushanik got up to go. Taking her copy of the Gospels with her, she said tearfully: "Lord God, you know that I am earnestly willing to meet my death."

She said this and then went away with them, taking her Gospel with her as well as the holy books of the martyrs. When she entered the palace, she did not go to reside in her chamber but in a little cubicle. Then Saint Shushanik raised

---

12. That is, dishonored his person.

her hands to heaven, saying: "Lord God, none of the priests have been found to be merciful, nor has a single such person appeared among these people, but they have all handed me over for death to Varsk'en, the enemy of God!"

(6) Two days later that wolf came into the palace and told his servants: "Today I and Jojik and his wife will dine together. Let no one else come in." When evening arrived they called Jojik's wife and decided to bring Saint Shushanik to dine with them. When it was time for dinner, Jojik and his wife went in to Saint Shushanik and tried to get her to come eat with them, for she had spent those days without eating. They were very insistent, compelling her to come with them into the palace. But she ate nothing. Jojik's wife brought her some wine in a glass, urging her to drink a little. Saint Shushanik responded angrily: "When has it ever been the case that men and women dined together?" She flung out her hand and knocked the cup back into her face, and the wine spilled.

Then Varsk'en began to hurl wicked curses, kicking her with his foot. He picked up a fire poker and smashed her head, burying it in her head and damaging one of her eyes. He hit her face mercilessly with his fist, dragging her back and forth by her hair, roaring like a cruel beast and shouting like a madman. Then his brother Jojik got up to help her and they struggled, until he struck Varsk'en. Tearing the veil off her head, Jojik barely pulled her out of his hands, like taking a lamb away from a wolf. Saint Shushanik lay on the ground as though dead. Varsk'en cursed her family and called her the desolator of his household. He ordered her to be bound with chains put on her feet.

After his rage had calmed a little, the Persian came to him and fervently implored him to release Saint Shushanik from her chains. After much pleading, he ordered her released and taken to a cell and guarded closely, with a single servant, and no one else allowed to come in and see her, neither man nor woman.

(7) When it was daybreak, he inquired of her servant: "How are her injuries?" He replied: "She cannot be healed." Then he himself went in to look at her and was surprised at the severity of her swelling. He commanded the servant: "Let absolutely no one come in and see her." He himself went out hunting.

But I got up and went to speak to the guard: "Just let me come in by myself and I will see to her wounds." But he replied: "No, because he may find out and kill me." I said to him: "Wretch, were you not raised by her? Even if he kills you for her sake, what of it?" Then he let me in secretly. When I went in, I saw her face busted open and swollen and raised my voice and wept. But Saint Shushanik said to me: "Do not weep for me, because this night has been for me the beginning of joy." I said to Saint Shushanik: "Let me wash the blood from your face and the ashes that have fallen into your eyes. I will apply ointment and medicine, so that perhaps you may heal." "Do not say that, priest," Saint Shushanik told me. "For this blood is the cleanser of my sins."

But I persuaded her to take a little of the food that had been sent by Bishop Samoel and John, who were secretly taking care of her and helping her. Saint Shushanik said to me: "Priest, I cannot taste anything, for my jaws and several of my teeth are broken." Then I brought a little wine and bread and dipped it in, and she tasted a little.

I was in a hurry to get out, when Saint Shushanik asked me: "Priest, should I send this jewelry to him, before he comes looking for it? It is no longer useful to me in this life." I answered: "Do not be in a hurry about it. Let it remain with you."

While we were talking together, a boy came in and said: "Is Jacob here?" I said: "What do you want?" He replied: "The Pitiakhsh is calling for you." I was surprised, wondering: "Why is he calling for me at this hour?" I hurried and went. He said to me: "Priest, do you know that I am leaving to fight the Huns?[13] I will not leave my jewelry with her since she is not my wife. Someone else will be found to wear it. Go and bring all of it to me." I went and reported this to Saint Shushanik. She was very glad and thanked God and sent me with all of it and I brought it to the Pitiakhsh. He received it from me, inspected it, and found it all complete. Then he said again: "Someone else will be found to adorn herself with this."

(8) When the Great Fast[14] had come, the blessed Shushanik came and found a small cell near the church and lived there. There was a little window in the cell and she shut it, staying there in the darkness, keeping vigil, praying and weeping. One of the retainers of the Pitiakhsh said to him: "During the Fast, say nothing to her."

When it was Monday of Easter week, the Pitiakhsh returned from fighting the Huns. The devil burrowed into his heart, and he got up and went to the church and said to Bishop Apots: "Give me back my wife! Why are you keeping her from me?" Then he started cursing and violently blaspheming God. But a priest said to him: "Lord, why are you acting this way and speaking such evil, cursing the bishop and speaking angrily against Saint Shushanik?" He hit the priest on the back with his staff, so that he dared not speak any more.

So Saint Shushanik was dragged through the mud and over the thorns from the church to the palace, like they were dragging a corpse. In many places thorns covered the ground. He pressed the thorns with his own feet, so that Shushanik's clothes and flesh were painfully shredded by them. This is how they brought her to the palace. He ordered her bound and beaten, mocking her and saying: "Look,

13. The Huns were threatening to invade Sassanian territory from the north by means of Derbent (Darband).
14. That is, Lent.

your church is of no use to you, nor your Christian supporters, nor their Lord."
They beat her with a stick some three hundred times, without any complaints
or groans coming out of her mouth. Then Saint Shushanik said to the wicked
Varsk'en: "Wretched man, you have had no pity on yourself, apostasizing from
God. How will you have pity on me?"

When he saw how much blood was flowing from her tender flesh, he ordered a chain put around her neck and instructed a chamberlain to take Saint
Shushanik away to the fortress and put her into a dark prison to die.

(9) A certain deacon from the bishop's staff stood near Saint Shushanik when
she was being led from the palace. He wanted to tell her: "Stand firm!" But the
Pitiakhsh glared at him and he was able to say only about this much: "Sta . . . !"
Then he fell silent and hurriedly ran away.

Then Saint Shushanik was led barefoot, with her hair unkempt, like a peasant.
No one dared to cover her head, because the Pitiakhsh was following her on
horseback, abusing her with severe insults.

A large crowd of women and men walked along with the saint, a countless
multitude following behind her, their voices raised in weeping as they tore their
cheeks and shed profuse tears of pity for Saint Shushanik. But Saint Shushanik
looked back at the people and said: "Do not weep, my brothers, my sisters, my
children, but remember me in prayer. I now take my leave of you, for you will
never see me come out of the fortress alive." When the Pitiakhsh saw the crowd,
and the weeping of the men and women, old and young, he chased them down
with his horse and made them all run away. When they reached the fortress
bridge, the Pitiakhsh said to Saint Shushanik: "This will be the last walking you
do, for you will never come out alive, until four bearers carry you out."

After they entered the fortress, they found a certain small house on the north
side, tiny and dark, and there they locked up the saint. They left the chain that
had been put around her neck, and the wicked Varsk'en sealed it with his seal.
But Saint Shushanik said: "I am happy about this, that I will be tortured here,
and there I will rest." The Pitiakhsh said to her: "Yes, yes—rest!"

Then he posted guards on her, instructing them to kill her with hunger. Then
he told them this: "I tell you, if any man or woman should enter here, look out for
yourselves, your wives, your children, and your homes—I will not be responsible
for what I shall do to you!"

(10) Then he left the fortress. On the third Sunday he summoned one of the
guards, asking him: "Is that miserable woman still alive?" He told him: "Lord,
she appears closer to death than to life, for she will probably die from hunger
alone, since she will take no nourishment." The Pitiakhsh answered: "Do not
worry about it; leave her alone, let her die."

But I spoke to the guard, pleading earnestly with him and promising to give him a vessel, until he eventually let me go in, telling me: "Once night falls, go in alone." When the guard brought me in, I saw the lamb of Christ, beautiful as a bride, adorned with chains, and my heart would not let me hold back my loud weeping. But Saint Shushanik said to me: "You are not weeping about this good thing, are you?" The guard said to me: "If I had known this would happen, I would not have let you in." Then I began speaking to fortify her, as much as God gave me the ability to speak. Then I took my leave of her and ran hastily back to my house.

Then the Pitiakhsh went away to Chor.[15] His brother Jojik was not on hand when all this was done to Saint Shushanik. When Jojik arrived, he set out after the Pitiakhsh, reaching him on the borders of Heret'i, where he pleaded earnestly with him to order that she be released from her chains. Under such pressure, he ordered her release, but just from the chain. When Jojik came, he removed the chain from her neck. But Saint Shushanik was not released from shackles until the very end.

For she stayed in the fortress six years, blooming with divine rituals: fasting, constantly in vigils, standing in continual prayer, tirelessly reading the holy books. She shone forth, beautifying the whole fortress with her spiritual lyre.

(11) From then on her works became known throughout all Georgia. Men and women used to come and offer their vows, and whatever they needed was given to them through the holy prayer of the blessed Shushanik, to whom God, the lover of humanity, would grant requests: a child to the childless, healing to the sick, and sight to blind eyes.

There was a certain Persian woman, a mage,[16] who had the disease of leprosy. She came to Saint Shushanik, who instructed the woman to abandon her Mazdeism[17] and become Christian. The woman quickly agreed. She explained to the woman: "Go to Jerusalem and you will be cleansed of your leprosy." She received this eagerly, setting out on the road in the name of our God Jesus Christ, and she was healed of her disease. After she returned, she went back there joyfully to thank Saint Shushanik, then she went away to her own house, whole and happy.

(12) In place of the work of silk embroidery, Saint Shushanik very eagerly took to hand the Psalter. After a few days she learned the 150 Psalms, by which she offered day and night a pleasing hymn to the heavenly king, along with tears.

They reported to the blessed Shushanik: "Your children have converted to Mazdeism." Then she threw herself down before God, wailing loudly and beating

---

15. Fortress at Derbent (Darband) on the shore of the Caspian Sea.
16. That is, belonging to a line of Zoroastrian priests.
17. That is, Zoroastrianism.

her head against the ground, groaning: "I thank you, Lord my God, for they did not belong to me but were gifts from you! As you will, your will be done, Lord. Protect me from the deeds of the enemy."

I went and saw Saint Shushanik, who was spent and weak from her weeping. Since the holy bishop had sent food and I urged her to eat, she ate a little, and we thanked God. Before that time, her children used to come and see their mother. But after they had turned away and denied God, they no longer dared to see her, and she hated even hearing their names.

(13) Then the Pitiakhsh sent messengers and said: "Either do my bidding and come to the palace, or if you will not come home, I will send you to Chor or to the Persian court by donkey. But Saint Shushanik replied: "Wretched and stupid man. Whether you send me to the Persian court or to Chor, who knows whether I will meet some good and avoid this evil?" The Pitiakhsh considered these words that she had spoken: "Who knows whether I will meet some good?," thinking: "Perhaps one of the nobles will marry her." From then on he sent no one to her. But Saint Shushanik was talking about vicious torments and trials, that it might be pleasing to God.

The Pitiakhsh chose her own foster brother to bring her to the palace. When he said to her: "Listen to me and come back to the palace and do not let your house remain desolate," Saint Shushanik replied: "Tell that godless man: 'You slew me and said to me: "You will not leave the fortress on your feet alive." But now, if you can raise the dead, first raise your mother, who is buried at Urdi. For if you cannot raise her, neither will you be able to bring me out unless you drag me by force.'" When they repeated the message to the Pitiakhsh, he said: "Indeed I said that."

The next day, a certain man came in and spoke to Saint Shushanik, saying: "Your response to him was well spoken, because by means of that stratagem he was trying to trick you, as he had in mind some evil for you." Saint Shushanik said to him: "You do not think God was sleeping,[18] who prepares the words for a person's mouth, do you? For the Lord himself says: 'I will give you an answer.'"[19]

(14) When she had finished her sixth year in prison, she became sick with disease on account of great fatigue from her mighty labors—something I had predicted, as I had told her: "Do not overdo it, for you are putting a heavy burden on your flesh. It will not endure it, and then you will not be able to do some good work, while keeping such harsh fasts, constant vigils, and exerting yourself daily in chanting psalms and hymns." Yet by no means did she give her body any rest, so that she became exhausted like ashes.

18. See Ps 121:4.
19. Luke 12:12.

In those six years, during the Great Fasts of the fifty days of Easter, she would not sit down, day or night, nor sleep nor take any food—except on the solitary day of the Lord's Day she would partake of the flesh and blood of Christ our God. And she would take just a little vegetable stew—very little—but she would not eat any bread until the end of the festival.

[Omitted: further details of Shushanik's ascetic rigors.]

(15) When the seventh year began, the holy and thrice-blessed Shushanik acquired sores in her flesh on account of her ceaseless labors. Her feet swelled and pustules appeared all over her body. The sores were large and had worms in them. She took one of the worms out and showed it to me in her hand, thanking God. She said: "Priest, do not be upset by this sight, for there the worm is greater and does not die."[20] When I saw the worm, I became very distressed and cried loudly. She replied sharply: "Priest, why are you sad? Rather than being eaten by immortal worms, it is better to be consumed here in this life by mortal ones!"

[Omitted: Jojik and his family, notable ecclesial leaders, and many people of noble and common status visit Shushanik in prison to pay their final respects.]

(18) Then the day of her calling arrived.[21] So she summoned the bishop attached to her house, Apots, and thanked him for his compassion, like that of a father and foster parent. She called for me, poor sinner that I am, and committed to us the relics of her bones, ordering us to bury them in that place where they had first dragged her out. She said: "Though I deserve no more than an eleventh-hour worker in the vineyard,[22] may all of you be blessed forever and ever."

She thanked God, saying: "Blessed is the Lord my God, for I have attained the privilege to lie down on him peacefully and sleep."[23] Then she committed her spirit to the Lord who mercifully receives all.

(19) Then the blessed and conscientious Bishop John took a sacred cloth to wrap her holy and honorable remains. We took up her body that was severely damaged and worm eaten, washed off the earthly worms and discharge, and dressed it in linen wrappings. Then the two bishops, John and Apots, were like a strong team of oxen bearing heavenly treasure. Amid many spiritual psalms and with lit candles and aromatic incense, we took up her honorable bones and brought her out to the holy church. Then we deposited the holy praiseworthy and honored relics of Saint Shushanik in the prepared place. That night, like angels we stayed awake and spent the whole night glorifying God on the lyre of David—the all-powerful God and his Son our Lord Jesus Christ, who is able do

---

20. See Mark 9:48.
21. The year would be 475, according to the internal clues of the account.
22. See Matt 20:6–16.
23. See Ps 4:8.

all things for all, giving life to both men and women and granting the power of his own victory to everyone who seeks him with singleness of heart.

(20) Saint Shushanik's suffering started on Wednesday, January 8. Her second beating happened on Monday of Easter week, with further torment on May 19. Her death occurred on October 17, during the festival of the blessed saints and martyrs Cosmas and Damian,[24] on a Thursday. We instituted a commemoration of Saint Shushanik for the purpose of glorifying and praising God, the Father, Son, and Holy Spirit, who deserves glory forever and ever. Amen.

24. Venerated as martyrs slain during the Roman Emperor Diocletian's persecution, ca. 287.

2. John Sabanisże, *Martyrdom of Habo, the Perfumer from Baghdad*

Introduction and translation by Jeff W. Childers

Composed by the Georgian eyewitness John Sabanisże (son of Saban) at the end of the eighth century, the following gives an account of a young perfumer from Baghdad, an Arab Muslim, who converts to Christianity. The young man Habo (also known as Abo) becomes attached to the provincial Georgian governor or regent, Nersēs, when the latter was imprisoned in Baghdad due to his repeated insubordination to the Arab rulers. When Nersēs is released and travels to Apkhazeti (Abkhazia) to distance himself from the Arab threat, his companion Habo is struck by the unfettered Christian piety he observes in this land far from Arab Muslim interference, and he eventually converts to Christianity.

The risks associated with a Muslim's conversion to Christianity are highlighted throughout the story. Habo is portrayed as a man learned in Muslim texts and traditions who becomes even more radically devoted to Christian learning and piety upon his conversion. The tale points to the sorts of pressures that Georgian Christians faced after the Saracen conquests, when their lands were under caliphate control. Recounting the story of an Arab convert to Christianity was meant to reinforce the faith of beleaguered Christians in the buffer provinces of Georgia, caught between the center of Arab power and the Christian Byzantine Empire. Habo's heroic death in Tbilisi and the signs attending his martyrdom underscore for the reader not only the saint's piety, but also the significance of Tbilisi as a city of stalwart faith. The site at the Metekhi cliff on the Mtkvari River is revered as the place where the saint's bones were hurled into the flood.

The narrative is accompanied in the manuscripts by the correspondence between John and the Georgian Catholicos Samoel. The translation below excerpts most of the narrative account, with selected omissions for the sake of length. The letters, an eschatological prologue, and a concluding eulogy in rhyming prose have also been omitted.

Bibliography

Text and Editions

Abulaże, I., et al., eds. *Żveli k'art'uli agiograp'iuli literaturis żeglebi* (Old Georgian Monuments of Hagiographical Literature). Vol. 1, *V–X Centuries*, pp. 46–81. Tbilisi: Mec'niereba, 1963–64 (in Georgian).

Studies

Shurgaia, G. "Ioane Sabanisdze." Pages 334–37 in *Christian-Muslim Relations: A Bibliographical History*. Vol. 1, (*600–900*). Edited by D. Thomas and B. Roggema. Leiden: Brill, 2009.

———. *La spiritualità georgiana: Martirio di Abo, santo e beato martire di Cristo di Ioane Sabanisdze*. La spiritualitá Cristiana orientale 3. Rome: Studium, 2003.

Tarchnišvili, P. M., and J. Assfalg, *Geschichte der kirchlichen georgischen Literatur*, pp. 94–95, 411–12. Studi e testi 185. Vatican City: Biblioteca Apostolica Vaticana, 1955.

TRANSLATION

Martyrdom of Habo, the Perfumer from Baghdad

January 7: Martyrdom of the holy and blessed witness of Christ Habo, who was martyred in Georgia, in the city of Tbilisi,[1] at the hands of the Saracens; related by John, son of Saban, by the order of Samoel, who through Christ was the catholicos of Georgia.[2]

[Omitted: the account begins with copies of the correspondence between John and Samoel. Chapter 1 supplies an eschatologically charged description of the hardships that Georgians experience under Muslim rule.]

1. Georgian Tp'ilisi.
2. The catholicos is head of the self-governing Georgian Orthodox Church. Samoel's catholicosate was near the end of the eighth century.

John Sabanisże, *Martyrdom of Habo, the Perfumer from Baghdad*

2. *The holy martyr Habo's arrival in Georgia and his baptism*

This happened at a time when the ruling prince of Georgia, whose name was Nersēs,[3] son of the ruling prince Adarnase, the Kuropalates,[4] was summoned to the land of Babylon by its ruler at that time, the Saracen Commander of the Faithful[5] Abdullah,[6] who was in the great city of Baghdad that he had built. Due to the accusations of evil men, Nersēs, ruling prince of our land of Georgia, was put into prison, where he was kept for three years, until by God's order Abdullah the Commander of the Faithful died, and his son Mahdi[7] succeeded him. But the beneficent God persuaded Mahdi, Commander of the Faithful, to release Nersēs, taking him out of his bitter prison and releasing him to be ruling prince here again, in his own country.

Now, O lover of Christ, I wish to tell you about this holy and blessed martyr Habo, what sort of man he was and how he came here. He was a descendant of Abraham, of the children of Ishmael, and the race of the Saracens. He came neither from foreign stock nor was he the son of a concubine, but he was of pure Arab blood on both his father's and his mother's sides. His father, his mother, his brothers, and his sisters lived there in the city of Baghdad in Babylon. He was a young man of about eighteen, or at least seventeen years old. He wanted to come here with the ruling prince Nersēs, so he attached himself to Nersēs as a servant. The skilled Habo was good at mixing fragrant ointments, as well as being learned in the writings of the Saracens, the children of Ishmael, the sons of Abraham, the offspring of Hagar.

Habo did not decide on his own to come to our country. Just as the Lord said to the blessed Abraham in the land of the Chaldeans: "Depart from your country and your nation and your father's house and come to the land I will show you,"[8] this son of Abraham did not think of it himself but was compelled by God. He left his father and mother, his brothers and sisters, his kin, possessions, and lands, and just as the Lord says to do in the holy Gospel, he traveled here with Nersēs

---

3. Nersēs, the "ruling prince," was provincial governor or regent of eastern Georgia, ca. 760–72, 775–79/80; as governor, he resisted Arab control and was held captive punitively in Baghdad for a period.

4. Adarnase III, a prince of the Nersianid Dynasty in eastern Georgia, ca. 748–60; *kuropalates* was a Byzantine court title used for rulers in the Caucasus; its use here attests to the enduring legacy of Byzantine tradition in Georgia even under caliphate rule.

5. *Amira mumnisa*, from the Arabic title *amir al-mu'minin* ("commander of the faithful"), a traditional title used of some eminent Arab military commanders, including caliphs.

6. Al-Mansur (also known as Abu Ja'far 'Abdallah; 754–75).

7. Al-Mahdi (774/775–85).

8. Gen 12:1.

for the sake of the love of Christ.[9] When he got to Georgia he stayed with Nersēs the ruling prince. Because of his virtue, he came to be loved by all the people, and he went on to learn how to write and converse freely in Georgian. Then he began reading and learning the holy books of the Old and New Testaments, for the Lord enabled him to understand. He used to come to the holy church, listening constantly to the holy Gospels and the readings from the Prophets and the Apostles. He would ask questions and get information from many theological experts, some of whom, by raising opposing arguments, actually became sources of learning for him. This is how Habo came to be perfectly knowledgeable in all the doctrines that the holy church has from Christ.

Then Habo rejected the religion of Muhammed and abandoned the rites and the worship of his native land. He loved Christ with all his heart, choosing this word: "They reported to me the thought of the unbelievers but it was not the same as your law."[10] Yet he could not openly reveal himself as a Christian. He fasted and prayed to Christ in secret, looking for a safe place where he might receive the baptism of Christ, since he was afraid of the Saracens who held and occupied our land.

At that time the Saracen authorities became very angry with Nersēs again so he fled, for the Saracen army aggressively fought against him. Yet the Lord kept him out of their hands and he passed through the gateway of Ossetia, which they call Dar-i-Alan.[11] When he fled, he had about three hundred of his men with him, including Habo, the blessed servant of Christ.

Then, when the blessed Habo saw that he was far away from the terror and violence of the Saracens, he was in a hurry to join Christ and was baptized in the name of the Father, the Son, and the Holy Spirit, by the hands of the honorable priests. For by the grace of the Holy Spirit, there are many towns and villages in that northern territory that remain in the Christian faith untroubled. From then on, full of the grace of Christ, the blessed Habo committed himself to fasting and prayer unhindered.

After some time, Nersēs asked the king of the north to let him leave for Ab-khazia,[12] having already sent his mother, his wife, his children, his possessions, and all his household on ahead, because that country was safe from Saracen tyranny. [*Omitted: The king allows Nersēs and his company to leave.*] The blessed Habo was praying and fasting throughout the time of the journey, constantly singing psalms. When they got to the land of Abkhazia, the prince of that land

9. See Matt 19:29.
10. See Ps 119:85.
11. "Gate of the Alans" (in Persian), a river gorge enabling passage through the mountains to the north.
12. A region on the east coast of the Black Sea, largely under Byzantine influence.

welcomed Nersēs and all the people accompanying him. When Nersēs saw his mother the queen, his wife, and his children, everyone joyfully thanked God that they had been reunited safe and sound.

[Omitted: the prince and ecclesial leaders of Abkhazia bless Habo, who rejoices to be in regions dominated by the Christian faith, adjoining territories under the sway of "the great city of Constantinople."]

When the blessed Habo saw the surpassing love for God that most of the people in the region had, and their constancy in prayer, he was filled with a godly zeal, recalling the word of the holy apostle: "It is always good to imitate good."[13] So in the winter season, on the seventeenth of January, the commemoration of our holy father Antony, Habo undertook severe labor. Living in the city as if he were in the desert, he fought back against our enemy, the devil. Through silence and fasting he weakened his own youthful flesh, so that he would be able to "extinguish all the flaming arrows of the devil."[14] He remembered how our Savior, after his holy baptism, had gone out into the desert and defeated the deceiving tempter, the devil, through prayer and fasting. So the blessed Habo uttered not a single word among people, conversing only with God alone through his prayers. In this manner he spent three months, persistent in prayer and in silence. Throughout these holy days of the Great Fast,[15] for seven weeks he would take the Holy Mystery, the body and blood of Christ, on the Lord's Day and on Saturday, and would also take small amounts of food then. He did this until he reached the holy day, the great feast of Easter, the resurrection of Christ our God. Then he stopped his severe fasting and loosened his tongue from its muteness to glorify God.

[Omitted: the caliph's appointment of Nersēs's nephew Stephen as prince of Georgia prompts Nersēs to seek permission from the caliph to return to his homeland. Once granted, he and his company make preparation to travel to Georgia.]

As they were leaving the land of Abkhazia, the prince of Abkhazia summoned the blessed Habo and said to him: "Do not leave this land, for the land of Georgia is under the control of the Saracens, and you are Saracen by birth. They will not tolerate you being among them as a Christian. I fear for you, that they may cause you to revert from the Christian faith, whether willingly or not, so that you destroy all the hard work of your devotion." But the blessed Habo told him: "Since Christ has accepted me, rescuing me from the darkness of my original ignorance and making me worthy of the light of his baptism,[16] I will never reject

13. Gal 4:18.
14. Eph 6:16.
15. That is, Lent.
16. In Georgian, "to receive light" is an idiom meaning "to be baptized."

his name. Even if they give me gigantic piles of gold and silver, or interrogate me with torture and beating, they cannot remove me from the love of my Lord. So now—do not try to hold me back, O servant of God. For what advantage is there in my being here, where there is no fear, nor the possibility of dying for Christ? I beg you to let me go, that my Christianity may become plainly known to those who hate Christ, for I have heard from the holy Gospel what our Savior said: 'No one lights a candle and puts it under a basket, but they set it on a lampstand so that it may give light to all. In the same way, let your light shine in the presence of people.'[17] So why should I hide this true light, with which Christ has enlightened me? I will never hide from the fear of death, for I have learned from the holy apostle that 'the cowardly cannot inherit the kingdom of God.'[18] Therefore I am not afraid to die, for I seek the kingdom of Christ." Thus he persuaded the prince to let him leave.

So Habo went with Nersēs to the land of Georgia and entered the city of Tbilisi, where he went around openly as a Christian. When the Saracens who had known him before saw that he was a Christian, some of them cursed him and others insulted him, some tried to intimidate him and others mistreated him, while still others tried to convert him with gentle words. But he held fast to Christ, untroubled by any of them. For three years he went around openly as a Christian throughout the city and all the surrounding villages, but "no one put their hands on him to do evil, for his time had not yet come."[19] Instead, lovers of Christ who knew his piety before God took care of him by providing him with food and clothing.

3. *Martyrdom of Saint Habo*

You who love Christ and love the martyrs, receive from me this blessed account of that holy martyr and laborer for Christ, who by his strength and glory was crowned through Christ!

In the reign of our Lord Jesus Christ, in the year 786[20] after the passion, death, and resurrection, when Constantine, son of Leo, ruled over the Chris-

---

17. Matt 5:15–16.
18. See 1 Cor 6:9.
19. John 7:30.
20. The manuscripts have a variety of discrepant dates in this paragraph, revealing scribal confusion about the numbers, but synchronizing the rulers listed shows that the date was 786. Constantine VI (son of Leo IV) was emperor 780–97; Musa al-Hadi was caliph 785–86; Stephen III was Nersēs's nephew and provincial governor of Georgia 779/780–86; and Samoel VII was catholicos in the 780s.

tians in the great city of Constantinople; and Musa, son of Mahdi, Commander of the Faithful, ruled among the Saracens, during the catholicosate of Samoel in Georgia; while Stephen, son of Gurgen, was ruling prince, in the year 6389 of creation, on Friday, January sixth, Epiphany, we observe the martyrdom of this holy blessed witness and virtuous master Habo in the city of Tbilisi. Now this is how it happened.

A short time before this, they seized the blessed martyr of Christ and brought him before the magistrate, the emir of the city of Tbilisi, and they imprisoned him due to his belief in Christ. After some time, Stephen the ruling prince of Georgia interceded on his behalf and brought him out of prison and let him go. After just a few days, the holy martyr's accusers were enraged, being filled with spite against the Christians. They concocted together a plot against the saint, going in before the magistrate, for another emir had assumed leadership in the city of Tbilisi. They said to him: "There is a certain young man in this city who was originally Saracen, having been raised in and living according to the religion that our Prophet Muḥammad gave us. Now he has abandoned our religion and calls himself a Christian; he goes fearlessly throughout the city, teaching many of our people how to become Christians. You should order his arrest and have him tortured and beaten until he confesses the religion of our Prophet Muhammed. Otherwise, put him to death, so that his words will not make many imitators of him."

When some Christians heard what they were accusing him of, they went quickly to report to the blessed Habo: "Now look! They are searching for you so they can imprison you to torture and beat you." They tried to convince him to retreat and hide, but he told them: "I am prepared not only for torture for the cause of Christ but even death." So he went out, cheerfully and openly going through the quarters of the city. Then the judge's servants came and seized Habo and brought him into the prison.

The magistrate asked him: "What is this I hear about you, that you are Saracen by birth and homeland but have rejected your ancestral religion and have become deceived among the Christians? Now get ready to pray according to the religion in which your parents reared you." But the blessed Habo, being strengthened by Christ and filled with a spirit of faith, said to the emir, the magistrate: "You are right to say that I was originally Saracen, born to it by my father and my mother. I was trained in Muḥammad's religion and used to live in it, so long as I remained in ignorance. But then God showed me favor, choosing me from among my brothers and kin and saving me through Jesus Christ, the Son of God and my God. He instructed me in a better way, so I left my former religion as something woven together through the artifice of men, a cunning belief born of clever fables. Now I follow the true faith of the holy Trinity—Father, Son, and Holy Spirit—given through Christ. In this faith I have been baptized and in this faith I now worship, for this is the true God. Now I am a Christian, without any doubt."

The magistrate said to him: "Give up this stupid notion! If you have followed the Christians because of your material need, I will now give you greater gifts and honor." The blessed Habo replied to him: "You may keep your gold and silver to yourself, for your own destruction. I seek no honor from people, for I possess a gift through Christ, a crown of life imperishable and everlasting honor in heaven."

Then the magistrate ordered him bound hand and foot with an iron chain and he was thrown into prison this way. But the blessed man rejoiced, thanking the Lord and saying: "I am grateful to you, my Lord and Savior God, Jesus Christ, for making me worthy of being interrogated and imprisoned for the sake of your holy name!" This happened on the twenty-seventh of December, on Tuesday, on the commemoration of Christ's disciple, the protodeacon, protomartyr, and prince of all martyrs, Saint Stephen. It was fitting and proper for it to happen so that the prince of all martyrs, along with all the rest of the martyrs, would aid him, with the result that this latter martyr of Christ would not be hindered from being counted along with their heroism.

So the blessed Habo stayed in prison, fasting, praying, and singing psalms constantly, day and night, with no rest. He also did charitable work, for he sold everything he had to provide for the hungry and needy prisoners who were with him. But the false teachers and his accusers kept coming in to him. Some of them were trying to flatter him by saying: "Son, do not betray yourself, do not barter away your young life for Christianity or cut yourself off from your brothers and family and make us all sad." Others tried to frighten him, saying: "What use will your Christ be to you? Who is going to save you from our hands? For fire and torment is already being prepared for you, if you do not return to us." The blessed one did not listen to them, but kept praying and continued to sing psalms silently in his mind. After they spoke for a long while, he told them: "Say nothing to me, for I, like a deaf person, have not heard anything, and I have become like a mute person who says nothing. I have become like a deaf person with whom there is no point talking, for I hope in the Lord: 'Get away from me, evildoers, and I will seek the commands of my God.'"[21] Since they were unable to shake the righteous man, they went away humiliated.

The blessed Habo stayed in prison nine days. All day he fasted, and at night he kept vigil until morning. But on the ninth day he said to all the Christian prisoners and the others who were with him: "Tomorrow is my departure from

21. Ps 119:115.

the flesh, when I go to join my Lord and God Jesus Christ." For the Lord had revealed this to his martyr. Then he took off his clothes and gave them to be sold, so that they could buy candles and incense to light for him. He provided these to all the churches of the city, to burn for him. He also sent requests around to all the priests, asking them to pray for him, so that he would not be turned from his faith in Christ but instead be made worthy of the labors of the martyrs of Christ. He spent the night of the holy festival in vigil, holding up two large candles and standing in the middle of the prison. He remained standing on his feet until morning, without sitting down, until he had finished chanting the Psalms and the candles had burned out in his hands, that were bound to his neck with iron chains. As he stood without moving, he said: "I will lift up my eyes to the Lord; he is always before me, for he is at my right hand, so that I shall not be moved," and the words that follow.[22]

When the tenth day dawned, it was the day of the festival of the Savior's baptism, the sixth of January. It was a Friday. The blessed Habo said:

This is a great day for me, for I see the twofold victory of my Lord Jesus Christ. On this festival day he went down to the Jordan River, stripped for baptism, and destroyed the heads of the sea monster hidden in the watery depths by divine power. It is also mine today to strip off the fear within this flesh of mine, the garment that clothes my soul, and go down into the middle of the city as though into the deep sea and be baptized in my own blood with fire and spirit, just as John the forerunner preached.[23] And I will go down once again into the waters to be baptized a second time, for today the Holy Spirit is going around over all the waters, by which the faithful ones of Christ are baptized as in the Jordan River. By stripping off my body, I will mock and trample underfoot the tricky devices that my crafty enemy plotted for me in this city. And it was also on a Friday like this that my Lord Jesus Christ, with his hands stretched out on a cross of his own will, dishonored and exposed in every corner of the land the enemy of the whole world. Now grant me also the opportunity to wage war against the enemy of the Christians, making him an object of laughter and mockery for all the Christians by shedding my blood for the sake of Christ. He supposed that through the fear of death he could separate me from the love of my Lord Jesus Christ,[24] but I will ridicule his plot and conquer him with the help of Christ, repaying the twofold debt that I owe my Lord.

---

22. Ps 16:8 (= 15:8 in the Georgian Bible).
23. See Matt 3:11; Mark 10:38.
24. See Rom 8:39.

Then he asked for water and washed his face and anointed his head with oil, saying: "Once I was a perfumer, skilled at preparing aromatic ointments. But this anointing today is for my burial.[25] From now on I will no longer be anointed with the transitory oil of my sojourn here. Instead, as Solomon the Wise taught me in the Song of Songs: 'I ran in the aroma of your fine ointments,'[26] O Christ, who filled with the imperishable perfume of your faith and love. You know, Lord, that I have loved you more than myself."

After he had said this, he went into the holy church, and they offered him the holy sacrament, the body and blood of Christ. It was the third hour of the great festival day, and when he had taken the true and life-giving sacrament, he said: "I thank you, my Lord and God, Jesus Christ, who has given me your life-giving flesh as food for my journey and your honored blood for my joy and my strength. Now I know you have not left me, but stand beside me and are with me. From now on I will take no more of that other food[27] from which I get hungry again, nor that other drink from which I get thirsty again. This is enough for me, sufficient for eternal life. Now, though I walk among the shadows of death, I will not fear evil, for you my Lord are with me."[28]

As soon as he finished saying these things, the magistrate's servants arrived, and he said goodbye to all the Christian prisoners, telling them: "Remember me in prayer, for you will see me no longer in this transient world." They brought him out with his hands and feet bound with chains. He was led through the city, and the Christians and his friends were weeping for him, but the holy Habo said to them: "Do not cry for me but be glad, for I am going to my Lord. Send me on my way with prayer, and may the Lord's peace protect you." But he went along like someone who had turned a corpse into a walker; that was how he saw his own body. And by his own spirit he was made to walk along, by reciting this passage of Psalm 119: "Blessed are the blameless in the way, who walk in the law of the Lord."[29] After chanting this verse he would repeat what that blessed robber said: "Remember me, Lord, when you come with your kingdom."[30]

This is how he came to the judgment court of the emir, his judge. When he arrived, he boldly made the sign of the cross at the gate and he crossed himself as well. They brought him before the magistrate, who asked him: "What is this, young man? What thoughts have you got in your head?" Filled with the Holy Spirit, the saint replied: "I have given thought, and I am a Christian!" The magistrate said:

25. See Matt 26:12.
26. See Song 1:3.
27. See Matt 26:29.
28. See Ps 23:4.
29. Ps 119:1 (= 118:1 in the Georgian Bible).
30. Luke 23:42.

"You have not abandoned this idiocy and foolishness of yours?" The blessed Habo responded to him: "Though I used to live in ignorance and foolishness, nevertheless I later became worthy of Christ." The magistrate asked: "Do you not realize that you are making these words of yours into a death sentence?" Habo replied: "If I die, I have faith that I will live with Christ. Why do you prolong this? Do what it is that you want to do to me! For I am like that wall on which you are leaning—I do not hear your empty words, for my mind is with Christ in heaven." The magistrate said to him: "What is this sweetness that you possess from your Christ, so that you show yourself no pity, even when it comes to your own death?" The holy Habo answered him: "If you wish to know his sweetness, then believe in Christ and be baptized in him, and then you will become worthy to experience his sweetness."

At that the emir became angry and ordered him taken outside and beheaded. The servants led him from the judgment court to the palace courtyard and removed the iron bonds from his hands and feet. But the blessed one himself suddenly tore off the robe he was wearing. Stripped naked, he made the sign of the cross over his face and body, saying: "I thank you and bless you, holy Trinity, for you have made me worthy to attain to the struggles of your holy martyrs!" After saying this, he folded his arms in the shape of a cross behind his back, and with a cheerful face and confident spirit he called out to Christ and bent his neck to the sword. They struck him three times with the sword, thinking that the fear of death would separate him from Christ. But the holy martyr received the sword in resolute silence, until he committed his soul to the Lord.

[Omitted: those who had accused Habo get permission from the magistrate to take Habo's body into custody, fearing that the Christians will honor and gain benefit from the martyr's remains.]

Then they went and picked up his honorable body from the ground and put it into a reinforced box along with his clothing. They dug up from the ground the blood that the righteous one had shed, leaving absolutely nothing on the ground, and put it into a jar. Then they put the holy one on a cart, just like those mighty Holy Forty,[31] for the place where they cut off the holy martyr's head was by the doors of the holy church dedicated to the Holy Forty, so it was appropriate that he be made like the heroic Holy Forty martyrs. After they brought that holy man's sacred body outside the city, to a location called the Place of Lamentation (for the cemetery of the people of the city was there), they removed him from the cart and put him on the ground. Then they took firewood, straw, and oil, piling it on top of the saint's body and setting fire to it, until they had burned up the

---

31. A reference to the forty martyrs of Sebaste, a group of Roman soldiers martyred under the Roman Emperor Licinius in 320. The traditional account became well known, and many churches in the East were dedicated to them.

flesh of the holy martyr. This happened at a place to the east of the city fortress that they call The Dungeon, at the edge of a cliff on the bank of the large river that runs to the east of the city, named Mtkvari.[32] They let none of the Christians come there until they had finished burning that holy martyr's flesh. As for the holy martyr's bones, they could not burn them up, so they folded them up inside a sheepskin, and after tying them up tightly, they took them and dropped them into the great river, below the city bridge on which the honored Cross of the Bridge had been erected. The water of the river became the winding sheet for those holy bones, and the watery depths became a tomb for the holy martyr, so that no one could casually come to them. The enemies of Christ acted in this way, and so the blessed man fought the good fight.[33]

Then a great many of the city's Christians set out, casting off any fear of the despotic rulers, going out to the place where they had burned the corpse of the holy martyr. Elderly people were hurrying along with their walking sticks, the lame were hopping like deer, youths were running, the children raced each other, and the women were like those brilliant holy women who carried perfumes and ran to bring ointments to the holy tomb of Christ our God.[34] These really became like those women, because they wept as they ran, carrying candles and incense in their hands. They were all coming with joy and thankfulness to Christ. They gathered up even the dirt from that place, bringing many people who were afflicted with illnesses, and they were healed that very day. But Almighty God showed his power even more greatly, honoring his martyr and revealing a marvelous sign, so that everyone would know that he was a martyr of Christ.

When the day was turning to evening and it was the first hour of the night, the Lord sent down a fiery star over that place, like a lamp of flame, which stood for a long time over the place where they had burned the blessed martyr of Christ. It stood high in the sky until the third hour of the night, or even longer, giving out a shining flash totally unlike earthly fire, resembling a frightening flash of lightning, which all the townspeople saw, even the magistrate—everyone, including the Christian inhabitants, all the Saracens, and any visitors from elsewhere. For a long time they saw it with their very eyes, until it put even the tyrants to shame. Some of the servants of the magistrate, the emir, went to inspect the place, because they suspected that the Christians were burning a light there. But as they neared the location they saw the star going up higher in the sky, and they could not approach the place because they were gripped by the fear of God.

32. The Mtkvari River, also known as the Kura.
33. See 2 Tim 4:7.
34. See Mark 16:1; Luke 24:1.

On the second night, the waters produced an ever more wondrous light. Some who were amazed by this heavenly fire appearing above the earth and below the sky wanted to hide these marvels, but no waters could control them, nor could the fierce swells of the waves extinguish them. At the place where they had dropped the God-honored bones of the blessed martyr into the depths, below the bridge, lights shone in the form of a pillar, like lightning. It stood shining for a long time, brightly illuminating the river on both sides, lighting up the cliff, the bank, and the bridge, from top to bottom. The whole crowd saw it, so that everyone believed he was truly a martyr of Jesus Christ, the Son of God. This happened so that everyone, whether believers or unbelievers would realize that. For the word of the Lord is true that says: "If anyone serves me, my Father in heaven will honor him."[35] If he demonstrated such honor to Habo's perishable flesh, how much more will we see him crowned imperishably among the angels with glory and honor at the resurrection of the righteous? And those people will be ashamed by their witless lunacy, who have denied Christ, striking and persecuting and destroying his saints, whom the Lord will receive in heaven.

But now, beloved, from now on we should receive those blessed first martyrs all the more readily, so that because of what we have seen of this new martyr we may believe in the first ones too, speaking the word of the blessed David: "Honorable before the Lord is the death of his holy ones."[36] To him glory is due, now and always, and forever and ever. Amen.

[Omitted: chapter 4 is a eulogy of Habo.]

35. John 12:26.
36. Ps 116:15.

3. George the Athonite, *The Lives of John the Iberian and Euthymios the Athonite*, and George the Minor, *The Life of George the Athonite*

Introduction and translation by Jeff W. Childers

E arly Georgian Christian leaders were known for their asceticism and scholarship, influenced especially by early Syriac and Armenian traditions. By the early seventh century, the Byzantine heritage was playing a much larger role in shaping not only the theology of the Georgian Church but the contours of its spirituality as well. The convergence of these influences combined with the redoubtable Caucasian spirit to produce a strikingly robust ascetic spirituality. Georgian monks became renowned for their diligence, leadership, and scholarship, occupying key roles in prominent monastic centers that lay far from their homeland—in Palestine and around Antioch, in Constantinople and the wilderness of Sinai, and in the distant spiritual center of Orthodox monasticism, the peninsular Mount Athos in Greece. The translations below narrate three generations of ascetic leadership at the Iviron (Georgian) Monastery on Mount Athos during the tenth–eleventh centuries.

The tenth–eleventh centuries were momentous for the Byzantine Empire and society, including the Byzantine Church. The empire enjoyed expansion yet was repeatedly beset by threats from within and without. The church experienced revivals in art and architecture, liturgy, education, and the production of ecclesial literature. Monastic revivals were at the center of many of these developments. Mount Athos had attracted a number of solitary monks, hermits, and anchorites, practicing a mainly individualized form of asceticism. At the end of the tenth century, and largely due to the influence of the celebrated Athanasios (died ca. 1003), a more communal form of monasticism was encouraged and took root at Athos. John the Iberian and his son Euthymios were instrumental in these foundational developments, and the Iviron Monastery came to play a leading role at Athos for many years. Sanctioned and supported by emperors and revered for its discipline, Iviron was a center of rich scholarship, grounded in the indefatigable intellectual endeavors of Euthymios and George.

These texts are meant to inform members of the community about the backgrounds and accomplishments of their heroic forebears. They hold up models of devotion, leadership, and scholarship for aspiring disciples to imitate. They also supply information about the legacies of these spiritual masters, in terms of the communities they helped establish and the literary inheritance they passed down. It would be difficult to overestimate the collective impact of Euthymios and George on Georgian ecclesial literature. Although the Georgian culture already had a sizable corpus of original and translation works, many more works remained to be composed or translated. Some of the older materials were seen to be rather old-fashioned linguistically—or even defective, due to their deviation from accepted Greek norms or because of the traces of Armenian (and Syrian) influences still evident within them, arousing suspicion about their orthodoxy. Even the Georgian Bible was seen to require attention. Euthymios translated Revelation into Georgian for the first time (as in some other Eastern traditions, it never functioned as canon). As for George's careful revisions and retranslations of Scripture—these were rapidly received as the standard authorized text of the Georgian Church.

The translations are taken from two *Lives*: the first is that of John and Euthymios, a work composed by George the Athonite; the second is from the *Life of George*, composed by his own disciple, George the Minor (Giorgi M'cire). The originals are long texts. John, Euthymios, and George were embroiled in Byzantine politics and engaged in theological controversies over such things as Greek and Roman eucharistic practices, one of the monumental debates of the day. George defended the independence of the Georgian Church against the patriarch of Antioch's claims. Most of these lengthy portions are omitted in the translations that follow. The translations select key portions of the accounts in order to illustrate the character of these monastic leaders and to highlight their contributions to Georgian sacred literature, scholarship, and enduring Byzantine ascetic institutions.

Bibliography

Text and Editions

Abulaże, I., et al., eds. *Żveli k'art'uli agiograp'iuli literaturis żeglebi* (Old Georgian Monuments of Hagiographical Literature). Vol. 2, *XI–XV Centuries*, pp. 38–127. Tbilisi: Mec'niereba, 1967 (in Georgian).

Studies

Gothóni, R., and G. Speake, eds. *The Monastic Magnet: Roads to and from Mount Athos*. Bern: Lang, 2008.

Grdzelidze, T. *Georgian Monks on Athos: Two Eleventh-Century Lives of the He-goumenoi of Iviron*. London: Bennett & Bloom, 2009.

Hussey, J. M., and A. Louth. *The Orthodox Church in the Byzantine Empire*. Oxford History of the Christian Church. Oxford: Oxford University Press, 2010.

Khintibidze, E. *Georgian-Byzantine Literary Contacts*. Translated by A. Tchan-turia. Amsterdam: Hakkert, 1996.

Kiladze, N. "Georgia, Christian Thought in." Pages 214–18 in *The Blackwell Dictionary of Eastern Christianity*. Edited by Ken Parry et al. Oxford: Blackwell, 1999.

Tarchnišvili, P. M., and J. Assfalg, *Geschichte der kirchlichen georgischen Liter-atur*, pp. 35–37, 126–74. Studi e testi 185. Vatican City: Biblioteca Apos-tolica Vaticana, 1955.

TRANSLATION

The Lives of John the Iberian and Euthymios the Athonite by George the Athonite

The lives of our blessed fathers John and Euthymios, and an account of their worthy acts, as described by the poor Hieromonk George[1]

(1)
[Omitted: the text begins with a doxology and a brief list of the heroes the work celebrates.]

Due to the passing of time all things are forgotten, yet all things are known and visible to God. He knows the beginning and end of each person, so that those who have attained virtuous lives shine always before him. They do not need our commemoration. Yet in his wise providence, God has made it so that the beautiful and divine subjects of the world's creation, the Lord's commands and regulations, along with the praiseworthy lives and actions of those worthy and blessed ser-vants of his that he has benevolently chosen to reveal in every generation for the sake of helping humanity, are written down in books. This is so that the divine and

---

1. Euthymios's successor was also known as George the Hagiorite (1009–65), George the Athonite, or Giorgi Mt'acmideli ("George of the Holy Mountain"). George composed this work sometime after 1040.

excellent deeds of which we read may compel us to praise the Lord, desiring him and being enlightened by his commands so that we will be eager to fulfill them. By remembering the great servants of God who were from among us, we become zealous to imitate the divine manners of those who, like talking icons, are set forth as models of his virtues, teaching wisdom and robust courage to those who wish to attain eternal life. This has been made known in books from the beginning of the world until the present time, as well as in the lives of glorified saints. Those who have labored to write about their lives and their deeds are remembered fondly within the church, considered worthy of prayer and blessing.

Since the aforementioned blessed fathers of the church were in no way inferior to those first saints who shone forth, but were themselves adorned with all the virtues and fulfilled the divine commands, their lives should not be forgotten. Furthermore, since my spiritual fathers instructed me to undertake this work, I beg your worthinesses, pious fathers, not to fault me for doing so.

[Omitted: the author claims as his sources reliable persons with direct knowledge of the blessed fathers, along with the testimony of their enduring literary and architectural works and the communities they established.]

Our blessed father John was truly worthy and loved by God, one who chose to live humbly like Abraham, in exile as a stranger. He submitted himself obediently to the spiritual fathers, and like them God glorified him and made him famous because of his virtues—and especially through giving him a cherished son, the blessed Euthymios, whose very name points to the excellence of his virtues. Euthymios appeared as the jewel of our nation, an emulator of the holy apostles, who enriched the Georgian language and land. Through the testimonies of the books he translated, we see that our church was enriched by the knowledge of illuminating wisdom. The fruits of his work gladden all who are near and far, for like a resounding golden trumpet, the sweetness of his translations reaches not only the land of Georgia but that of Greece as well, since he translated Balavariani and Abū Qurrah[2] and a number of other books from Georgian into Greek.

[Omitted: the author expresses his hope that his account of the blessed fathers' exploits will rekindle the passion of those who have become lazy in their devotion.]

(2) Let us come back to our former subject. Our blessed father John was Georgian by birth, descended from parents and family who were famous and distinguished among David Kouropalates's nobles.[3] He was strong and courageous; physically he was tall and robust, mentally he was wise and intelligent, full of the fear of God and all sorts of good works. David Kouropalates, blessed be his name,

2. The Georgian epic *Balavariani* records the tale of Barlaam and Josaphat, as it is known in the West. Theodore Abū Qurrah was a ninth-century Christian author who wrote in Arabic.

3. David III Kouropalates was a Georgian prince who ruled 966–1000/1001. He set the stage for a unified Georgia and became a strong patron of Christian culture. *Kouropalates* is a high Byzantine court title.

loved John and treated him as family. Yet because of the passionate love of Christ burning hot in his heart, John hated all the glory of this world, considering it refuse: money and riches, wife and children, and relatives. He gave it all up, leaving everything of this world behind. He left behind even his own self, in keeping with the Lord's words,[4] taking up a cross and going away secretly to enter the Lavra[5] of the Church of the Four.[6] At that time Father Moses and Father Gelasios were at the Lavra of the Church of the Four. John made himself known to them and got from them secretly their blessing for the monastic way of life, and for a while he stayed there in complete obedience, amazing everyone by his conduct.

Once his deeds made him famous, he received the blessing of the blessed fathers and made for the land of Greece, trying to escape human glory. Thus he arrived at Mount Olympos[7] and stayed for a while in a monastery, diligently tending mules and humbly completing other menial jobs.

At that time the Greek emperor gave the Upper Lands to David Kouropalates, demanding some of the children of noble families as hostages in exchange. John's brother-in-law handed over John's son, Euthymios,[8] along with the others. When John heard about this, he went to the imperial city and, whether he had wished to or not, made himself known. Because the emperors knew Father John's father-in-law Abuharbi, they welcomed him with love and graciousness. And so by divine providence and by imperial decree, he brought his own son back with him to Olympos.

After some time, because his fame had spread so that both Greeks and Georgians esteemed him highly, this bothered him, so he fled again to a foreign place. With his son and some disciples he went to the Holy Mountain, to the Lavra of the great Athanasios,[9] and took up residence there.[10] He remained there, without revealing himself, obediently doing everything with humility and peace, working in the kitchen for two years or more.

(3) At that time the great T'ornike became a monk back in his own land.[11] He

---

4. See Matt 16:24.

5. A *lavra* (also *laura*) is a type of monastic complex common in the East, having scattered cells for hermits, centered around a church.

6. Built by David Kouropalates in the tenth century, the Church of the Four was dedicated to the Father, the Son, the Holy Spirit, and Holy Wisdom.

7. The Mount Olympos in Bithynia.

8. Euthymios would have been ten–twelve years old.

9. Athanasios (died ca. 1003) was largely responsible for instituting a communal form of monasticism at Mount Athos in the last part of the tenth century. Previously Athos had been the refuge of solitary monks, hermits, and anchorites.

10. John arrived sometime between 963 and 969.

11. That is, in Georgia, specifically Tao. Like John the Iberian, T'ornike was from a noble Georgian family. He distinguished himself as a general under David III Kouropalates before he was tonsured as a monk (around 970). Though he sought the reclusiveness of asceticism after his

had heard that John was on Olympos, and since he loved John very dearly, he organized for the journey and went up to Olympos, but he could not find him there. He quietly investigated the matter and heard that John had gone up to the Holy Mountain. Without informing the emperors, he secretly went to the Holy Mountain and received the blessing of monasticism from the hands of John.

As we have said, T'ornike went up to the Holy Mountain and arrived at the Lavra of the great Athanasios. Since it was useless to hide his identity, he revealed himself and they embraced him with spiritual affection, and there was great rejoicing in the monastery that day, because the great Athanasios was not ignorant of T'ornike's exploits, high nobility, and bravery. Therefore, from then on they held him in high esteem, for although T'ornike himself did not wish this, God reveals and glorifies those who are worthy of him.

After a while it became known that they were on the Holy Mountain and the number of Georgians there grew. When our blessed fathers saw this, in their great wisdom they decided: "It is not right for us to stay in the monastery, for others will join us and we cannot send them back." And so, by the decision of Father Athanasios, at a lovely, uninhabited spot one mile away they built the Church of Saint John the Evangelist, along with cells, and they stayed there for many years as angels of God.

[Omitted: despite his reluctance, the noble T'ornike is pressed back into military service in order to aid David III Kouropalates in quelling a rebellion. After a victorious campaign, he receives honors and treasure, returning to the Lavra with great distinction.]

(7) After some time, our fathers came to a decision, saying: "We cannot stay here, for we are men of great reputation and more Georgians will be joining us." So they decided to build a separate monastery.[12] By the grace of God they found a lovely place in the middle of the Holy Mountain, and through much sweat and work they built a monastery and churches dedicated to the Holy Mother of God and to Saint John the Baptist. Using their own funds, they also bought many places, monasteries, and hermitages around the main monastery, all the way up to the sea—places that were attractive, desirable, and very suitable to stay in for spiritual monks.

[Omitted: T'ornike returns from the east with treasure and with numerous Georgians and Greeks seeking to live as monks on Athos, along with privileges from the emperors, all of which facilitate the establishment of the monastery.]

---

fighting, coming to Athos around 973, his fame followed him. In 978 he was pressed back into service by the Byzantine emperors to collaborate with David in putting down a revolt. Hence his reputation as a "soldier-monk." But the honors he received—as well as the significant treasure—provided the imperial support and resources necessary to found Iviron, and so T'ornike (whose tonsured name was John) is considered the *ktetor*, or official founder, of the Iviron Monastery.

12. The Iviron monastery, i.e., monastery of the Iberians (Georgians), granted by imperial decree in 979/980.

(8) These dear and honorable fathers of ours donated great wealth and many precious things to the Great Lavra and to all the monasteries on the Holy Mountain, which at that time were poor and not so well inhabited. They entrusted many valuables and possessions to the center of the complex, where the whole mountain would gather, distributing wealth collectively and to individuals.

[Omitted: there follows a description of the monastery's donations and charitable acts toward all the monasteries of the mountain. After T'ornike dies, John and Euthymios travel to Spain to escape from conflicts in the community and to investigate rumors that people related to the Georgians are to be found in Spain. At the insistence of the Byzantine emperors, the blessed fathers appear before them in Constantinople and return to the mountain.]

(10) After a short while John was afflicted with the disease of gout, so that he spent many years lying prostrate on his bed, suffering in great pain. Yet he continually praised God, as happy for this severe disease as for any large treasure or gift of imperial honor.

Seeing what a great disability he had, John asked Father Euthymios to assume the care of the monastery. But Euthymios respectfully sought to make his father excuse him from this, for the problems of the world were bothersome to him and he did not wish to become involved in its troubles. Yet it was impossible for him to disobey an aged father suffering with illness, so whether he wanted to or not, he assented, and until his father's death, he obediently managed the affairs of the monastery as a steward by his father's command, doing nothing apart from his father's decision.

[Omitted: John's friends, the celebrated monk John Grdzelisdze and former Bishop Arsenios, come to Athos.]

(12) After this, our beloved Father John, having suffered with the aforementioned illness, departed and went to God, enriched with an abundance of virtues and having accomplished the will of God.

Aware of his impending departure, Father John gave to Euthymios all the power and authority to institute for the monastery any ordinances or rules he wanted.

[Omitted: John provides for the ongoing leadership of the monastery, under Euthymios and their kinsman George. John emphasizes the benevolent and providential support of the emperors. He blesses the brothers, exhorting them to hospitality and charity.]

After he had spoken many words and left a written note, he blessed Euthymios with a heavenly blessing, offering up in his hands his own holy soul to God. Then he departed, lying back peacefully on his bed, on the fourteenth of June.[13] He now intercedes for the life of our souls.

13. John died ca. 1002.

[Omitted: Euthymios builds a church atop his father's grave. Miracles are reported in connection with John's burial place.]

(13) Now let us come back to our former subject. As we mentioned above, Father John brought his son Euthymios from the imperial city. First he educated him in Georgian, after which he instructed him fully in Greek. The grace of God was on Euthymios from childhood, and he received from God a capacity to interpret the Scriptures and was filled with the grace of the Holy Spirit, as it was disclosed to his father, the blessed John, through the revelation of the Holy Mother of God. For during his youth, while still a child, Euthymios became very sick and was close to death. The blessed John reported: "I lost hope for his life, for I thought his soul was about to depart, since he had no speech left remaining in him nor any voice. Very upset, I went to the Church of the Holy Mother of God and fell down before the icon of the Holy Queen, begging through fervent tears the undefiled and perpetual virgin Mother of God to help and relieve him. I summoned a priest to come quickly so that he might commune with the body and blood of the Lord. And while I was flustered, I went to see what was happening, opening the door of the cell where I had left him lying. At once I smelled a wonderful aroma, for the Holy Mother of God was looking after him. By her grace he was sitting upright on his bed, completely healed and unharmed."

"When I had recovered my senses, I asked him: 'What happened, son?' He answered me: 'A glorious queen rose up in front of me and spoke to me in the Georgian language: "What is it? What is wrong with you, Euthymios?" I told her: "I am dying, queen." As soon as I said this, she came near and took my hand, saying: "Nothing is wrong with you. Get up, do not be afraid, and speak Georgian fluently!" And now look—I am no longer the least bit sick, as you see!'" The blessed John went on to say: "Until then, he could speak Georgian only with difficulty, and I was very sad because of this. But since then, as though from a spring, speech that is far more pure than that of any Georgian has been flowing from him unceasingly. And when I saw this, I fell down before the Holy Mother of God and thanked her, our hope, praising and glorifying God. Amen."

Father John told Euthymios: "My son, the land of Georgia is in great need of books and lacks many texts. I see what God has granted you. Now strive to multiply your gift from God." Euthymios, who was obedient in everything, followed his father's instruction at once and began translation. Everyone was astonished, such translations, apart from the first ones, had never been done in our language, nor will the like ever be made, I believe.

Many of these books were sent to David Kouropalates. When he saw them, being a faithful man, he was very glad and glorified God, saying: "Thanks be to God, who in our day has revealed a new Chrysostom!"[14] He sent letter after letter, instructing Euthymios to continue translating and sending the texts. The beloved one kept translating tirelessly, not allowing himself any rest but day and night kept diligently at the sweet honey of the divine books, through which our language and church were sweetened. He translated so many divine books that it is scarcely possible to number them, of which we will mention only a few, so that the faithful of Christ may learn about the rest of them from the books themselves. For he translated not only at Olympos and on the Holy Mountain, but if we count each and every text, he also translated in the imperial city and on the road and in every other such place.

Euthymios translated, as we have said:

Commentary on the Gospel of John
Teachings of Our Father Saint Basil, and his Commentary on the Psalms
Book of Saint Climacus
Book of Saint Makarios
Teachings of Maximus
Book of Saint Isaac, in which are the selected teachings of other fathers
Book of Saint Dorotheos
Martyrdom and Miracles of the Martyr Saint Demetrios the Great
Life and Martyrdom of Saint Stephen the Younger
Life and Martyrdom of Saint Clement the Pope of Rome
Martyrdom of Saint Clement of Ancyra
Life of Saint Basil the Great of Caesarea
Martyrdom of Saint Acepsimas
Life of Saint Gregory the Theologian and his homilies
Life of Saint Bagrat
Martyrdom of Saint Mina and Saint Hermogene
Homilies of Saint Gregory of Nyssa: the Enkomion on his brother Basil the
    Great, On Virginity, the Interpretation of the "Our Father," On Holy Fast-
    ing, the Commentary on the Life of Saint Moses the Prophet, On the
    Ascetic Life, which one of the brothers asked him to do
Vision of the Apocalypse of John, and the Commentary of Andreas of Crete
    on the vision
Homily on the Two Natures of Christ by Saint John Damascus, and another
    on the Birth of the Holy Mother of God
Life of Athanasios the Great
Martyrdom of the Three Youths, Alphaeus, Philadelphus, and Cyrenus
Life of Saint Onuphrius the Grazer

14. Literally, "Goldenmouth," so called after the most celebrated Christian preacher in the East, John Chrysostom ("Goldenmouth").

Life of Saint Mary of Egypt
Teachings of Saint Zosimos
Teachings on Faith by the father Saint Ephrem
The Short *Synaxarion*[15] for the Year
Journeys and Preaching of Saint John the Evangelist
Commentaries on the Epistles to the Galatians, the Thessalonians, and the
    Romans
Complete Hymns from the Triodion[16] and hymns for many saints
Martyrdom of the Martyr Saint Procopios
Commentary on the Gospel of Saint Matthew
Journeys and Preaching of Saint Andrew the Apostle
Greek Blessing for the Schema and Blessing for a Monk
Canon Law of Saint John the Faster and the Sixth Council
Acts of the True Faith
Prayers of Saint Martyrios
Martyrdom of Saint Febronia
Martyrdom of Saint Anthimus and Saint Vlassios and Thousands of Others
Martyrdom of Saint Theodore Stratilates and Theodore of Perge and Saint
    Eustratios and Saint Eustathios and His Children
Teachings of Saint Cassian
Book of Dialogues
Miracles of the Holy Archangels
Life of Saint Nicholas
Book by Gregory the Theologian
Eight Reflections by Maximus
Basil's Homily on the Sevenfold Vengeance of Cain
Greek Nightly Prayer
Greek Prayers and Canons of the Fathers
Life of Saint Antony the Great

Our pious father translated all these and very many more books, and by doing
so he multiplied the talent entrusted to him. The larger part of the aforementioned books were translated while his father John was still alive and in charge
of all the concerns and supervisory matters of the monastery. As I mentioned
previously, the blessed John lay sick for many years and Euthymios served his
illness day and night. He remained in leadership for fourteen years, tending three
hundred souls and governing the Great Lavra. Most of the supervisory matters

15. Abbreviated anthology of lessons for liturgical reading according to the church year,
featuring brief lives of the saints.
16. Liturgical book for use in the weeks leading to Easter.

of the Holy Mountain were handled by the blessed one, while he himself also fulfilled the severe rigors of the monastic rule. Even with all these things he did not forsake the beneficial work of translation, allowing himself no rest, but suffering in all sorts of ways, even as he remained vigilant throughout the night. For he was translating most of the books at night by candlelight, due to his excessive busyness and all the administrative concerns of which we have spoken.

[Omitted: various episodes illustrate Euthymios's piety and great knowledge. A detailed description of his habits and ascetic rigors establish the rules and regulations of the monastery for the monks who abide there.]

(22) Our holy Father Euthymios was calm in demeanor, pure and humble in mind, enlightened and holy in spirit, strong in body, well composed in divine affairs and activities as well as in stature. He would affirm nothing nor even speak without the testimony of Scripture. In church he stood upright, for he would stand without a staff or leaning against the wall, his arms crossed close to himself as though he were a stout pillar. He kept his face and eyes aimed toward the ground. But who is able to speak of his activities in his cell, of which only God is aware, since he carried everything out in secret? He wore a coarse-clothed cloak, and over the cloak a heavy chain. Any virtue one might seek could be found in him, perfected, excellent, and beautiful. He preserved his sanctity and virginity unspoiled and without blemish, like an angel of God living in heaven. But the most surpassing of his virtues and crown of all was his translation of books for the enlightenment of our people.

[Omitted: Euthymios's administrative duties impede his translation projects.]

(23)

[Omitted: disorder occurs in the Great Lavra, prompting the emperor to summon Euthymios to Constantinople to explain the situation.]

As I said, our pious Father Euthymios went up to the imperial city. When the emperor found out about his arrival, he met him with great honor and asked him about the business of the Lavra. A great deal of time passed before a certain disputatious matter concerning the Lavra was fully resolved. The Feast of Saint John the Theologian arrived, and according to his custom, Euthymios celebrated it with great glory, caring for many poor people and cheering the monks who were with him, serving them himself and giving them goods in plenty. After this, he broke his fast and took a little break from work. When he got up, he recalled an icon of Saint John the Evangelist that he commissioned an iconographer to embellish. So he instructed his disciple to go and tell the man how he should decorate it. Then he said: "I am concerned that you will not be able to explain what we need, my son. Help me onto a mount and I will go myself instead."

Now the mule was newly purchased and defective, but they did not yet know about its unfitness and poor quality. After traveling for a while, Euthymios encountered a poor man asking for charity and our holy father stopped to give him some alms. The poor man stood up to receive the alms, all covered in rags. But when the unfit animal saw him, it suddenly panicked and began to bolt, hurtling this way and that, severely injuring our holy and beloved father. When he fell, a large crowd gathered around him, because everyone knew him, and they started crying and mourning. Then they carried him to the monastery where he was staying.

When Emperor Constantine heard about it, he was very distressed and sent one of his attendants to inquire after him. Likewise many citizens, nobles, princes, and courtiers who believed in him and loved him all came, bowing down to kiss him tearfully before leaving. Concerning the Georgians, what more can be said? For they stayed continually near his angelic body, lamenting their orphanhood with great mourning.

And so amid prayers and with the grace of God our thrice-beloved and pious Father Euthymios departed, leaving us in tremendous sorrow because we were bereft of our sweet and dear father. But he departed to the unshadowed light of God, with all the saints who have pleased God since the beginning, and now he intercedes for the life of our souls before the holy Trinity. His honorable relics were brought up to the monastery and buried in the crypt of the Church of Saint John the Baptist. And those who approach with faith receive an overflowing measure of healing grace because of his boldness before God.

Our thrice-beloved Father Euthymios died on Monday, the thirteenth of May, in the eleventh indiction,[17] the year 6536 from the origin of the world, to glorify the Father, the Son, and the Holy Spirit, to whom be glory and honor now and always and forever and ever. Amen.

[Omitted: the author presents a brief account of the monastery under the leadership of John's and Euthymios's kinsman George, who was head of the monastery until he was exiled for his involvement in a plot against Emperor Romanos[18] (i.e., 1019–29).]

(26) In the name of the Father and the Son and the Holy Spirit, and by the intercession of the Holy Mother of God, I, Father George, during the time of my leadership of the monastery,[19] translated the relics of Saint Euthymios from the Church of the Baptist to the great Church of the Mother of God while I was head of the monastery.

Holy and pious Father Euthymios, have mercy on us your servants, strangers and poor, living as aliens. Help us so that we may be forgiven on the day of judgment for our countless sins and protect our lives from the devil's snares and from human deceptions.

---

17. That is, 1028. Euthymios was in his early 70s.
18. Romanos III Argyros (1028–34).
19. George the Athonite was leader of the Iviron Monastery 1044–56.

The Life and Acts of Our Holy and Blessed Father George the Athonite
by George the Minor[20]

(1)

[Omitted: the text begins with a brief prologue.]

The mercy of God has not failed to produce worthy persons from time to time for the purpose of comforting our weak and lame nation, so that by seeing and hearing about their virtues we will be motivated to imitate their worthiness. By doing so we rejuvenate the discerning power of our souls, like young eagles,[21] and we renew it, like the moon, so that we may walk through the dark night of this life as happily as though it were daytime, chasing all those darkness-loving things out of our souls. Thus, having become successful in the virtuous life, we shall readily expect the coming and brilliant last day to arise like the morning dawn.

[Omitted: the author extols the subject of his work. Whereas God's providence supplied the Georgian people with its brilliant luminary Euthymios, the life of George is testimony to God's ongoing and abundant generosity to the nation.]

Our holy father, the great Euthymios departed from the world, as we have already said. Sometime later, the kindness of God and the grace of our father revealed this great worker of divine grace, the holy Father George, the subject of the following report, as we describe and tell about him so that later generations will learn and understand. Just as that blessed one described the life of the great Euthymios as the type and icon of virtue for the generations that followed, by God's mercy we shall not be idle but we shall describe the whole type of George's life, from his birth to his death. May God be with us, the one whom he loved and who loved him, and the prayers of that holy father, who compelled me to undertake this work[22] in order to glorify God, to whom be glory, now and always and forever and ever. Amen.

(2) Our holy Father George was Georgian by family. Yet although in the mystery of the divine liturgy only one homeland is honored, which is paradise, the dwelling place of our first father, and one city, which is the heavenly Jerusalem, built of living stones whose maker and architect is God, and one heritage, which

---

20. George the Minor (Giorgi M'cire) was one of the disciple of George the Athonite; composing this life not long after his master's death in 1065, he himself died sometime after 1083.

21. See Isa 40:31.

22. That is, George the Recluse, of Mount Mirabilis near Antioch, who was a spiritual father to George the Athonite.

is the divine likeness—let no one think that we have nothing honorable to report about the homeland and holy family of our father or that we shall steal away what is true on the basis of disreputable facts. For this blessed man was from a Georgian family, as we have said, his ancestors being from the God-serving and God-protected land called Samtskhe. He himself was born in the region of T'rialet'i, as the following facts will show you.

[Omitted: the author provides details regarding George's parents and siblings. His mother Mary receives a vision foretelling George's birth. As in Greek his name means "farmer," George's service to God is destined to fill the storehouse of the faithful with wheat.]

(3) But let us come back to the beginning. After some time the gift that had been promised them by God was born to George's parents.[23] He grew both physically and spiritually, nourished by the grace of the Holy Spirit. He was filled with the fear and love of God from childhood, as it is written: "Day and night the law of the Lord was his desire and he meditates on his law day and night."[24] This is why he became like a tree planted by the flowing stream of divinely inspired writings, and in his time he produced lovely fruit worthy of the heavenly treasuries.[25]

When he turned seven, his parents fulfilled their promise and brought him to the aforementioned monastery of Tadzrisi, where his sister was, and devoted him to God, thanking God who had provided such good fruit. Although from childhood he was left without his parents' care, he was like a fine shoot that shows signs of being productive from early on, as David says: "The righteous will flourish like a date-palm and grow like a cedar of Lebanon. They are planted in the house of God and flourish in the courts of the house of our God."[26] Thus he grew up in the monastery like a beautiful sapling. He was taught the holy writings by his own sister, a worthy woman, showing signs beforehand of the yield of fruit that he would produce. Those who saw him were amazed at the sharpness and agility of his mind and that he would flourish and bring forth fruit so quickly. As it is written about Moses: "From a tender age he was beautiful before God."[27] When he had stayed in the monastery for three years and was ten years old physically, mentally he seemed gray-haired and venerable to those who saw and heard him.

[Omitted: episodes from George's childhood illustrate God's care for him. His

---

23. In 1009. George's mother Mary had received a vision in which she was promised her son, George.

24. Ps 1:2.

25. See Ps 1:3.

26. Ps 92:12–13.

27. Acts 7:20.

intellectual abilities and diligence are such that his learning rapidly surpasses that of his peers.]

(5) I know that many of you wish to hear how he acquired Greek instruction, or who it was that collected for us such a great treasure as his. It was Peris, son of Jojiki, the son-in-law of the sister of Bagrat's[28] son Basil. Why have I mentioned Basil's sister? Because the saint used to say: "This worthy woman was no less in her service to God than her brother, the blessed Basil." This Peris and his wife made the good decision to locate a godly man who would be a fine teacher of their souls, acting as a check on disorder and always remaining very close to them. For this purpose the two of them investigated the matter and confirmed that they could find no one more intelligent than George the Scribe. After much pleading and begging, they convinced George the Scribe to move in with them, entrusting to him every aspect of their spiritual and physical lives. He brought along with him his blessed nephew, the young George,[29] because he was very useful to him as a canonarch[30] who could recite by heart, and with reading books and serving him in other ways, for George the Scribe was old.

When the good couple saw the child, they were very happy. The godly woman accepted him as her own child. They stayed for a long while, in a good and God-pleasing way of life. But then Emperor Basil[31] became angry with Peris and beheaded him, for they accused him of treason.[32] Thus by royal command they took this worthy woman along with her household away to Constantinople, where they stayed for twelve years.[33]

During their stay there, through the efforts of the uncle of this astonishing child—and even more, I should say, through the efforts of that godly woman—they handed the young George over for instruction to the philosophers and rhetoricians, men who were adorned with both sorts of lives, for they were not seculars but God-fearing monks, acclaimed by all. So by his twelfth year George demonstrated the utmost acuity and diligence, excelling due to the sharpness of his intellect and the mental capacity he had acquired over a long period. Due to his sharp mind, he surpassed the quick witted and diligent, outdoing them in every way, to the point that the Greek youths were very amazed at such acuity and sharpness of mind. They envied his diligence and were inspired to imitate him as much as possible.

---

28. Bagrat III (died 1014) ruled Abkhazia from 978 and Georgia from 1008, unifying large portions of the kingdom of Georgia. Little is known of Bagrat's son Basil of Khakhuli, except that he was reputed to be a learned and pious monk.

29. That is, George of Athos.

30. A lead cantor or reader in the Eastern liturgical tradition.

31. Basil II (976–1025).

32. Peris was executed in 1022 for taking part in a revolt.

33. 1022–34.

When he had stayed at school for twelve years, he had accepted the good seeds of learning in the furrows of his soul like a field, which in time would yield produce, filling the soul of the famished and enriching the church of God. Then that godly woman, by imperial order, was sent from that suburban house to Tvartstapi, and she brought the young George and his uncle along with her. Then they learned that George's mother had died and that his father was near death so he was taken to be with George (the Scribe) in Tvartstapi, so they could be together. But the young George went away with his uncle Saba to Khakhuli.[34]

(6) When George turned twenty-five years old, he bowed his neck to the sweet yoke of monasticism. Although he had been like a monk since childhood, he had just not taken the monastic vows. Because the great Hilarion,[35] his spiritual guide and instructor in the labors of monasticism, was about to leave the flesh, George received the monastic vows from his hands. Hilarion had been his first guide and for him the cause of all good things.

[Omitted: George expresses the desire to live as a solitary. He sets out for Jerusalem, evading those who would impede him from these rash actions by disguising himself as a traveling beggar. When he arrives at the Black Mountain near Antioch, he becomes the disciple of George the Recluse. After three years of direction, he continues to visit the holy sites of Jerusalem. George the Recluse sees in him God's chosen instrument by which to complete the work that Euthymios began, translating sacred texts into Georgian.]

(8) George was sent by George the Recluse to the Holy Mountain,[36] like a faithful disciple and loyal child, with a gift like that of his holiness, he was sent to our holy Father Euthymios, so that from the source of the spring of wisdom that gushed forth to irrigate our nation the man of God would take his fill of the streams of comprehension so that the firmament of our churches would be thoroughly saturated. As the prophet Isaiah says: "The law will go out of Zion, and the word of God will judge from Jerusalem."[37]

Although we have had the Scriptures and the true and right faith from the beginning, yet our land is far from the land of the Greeks. And the evil Armenians, perverse and wicked,[38] were sown among us like unholy seeds, so that we were severely harmed. For our nation was pure and innocent, but they, whether for

---

34. Khakhuli was a prominent Georgian monastery founded by David Kouropalates in Tao, a district in the southwestern part of Georgia. The monastery was an important literary and educational center.

35. Hilarion of Tuala at Khakhuli.

36. The year was 1040.

37. Isa 2:3.

38. The echoes of Armenian influence in early Georgian was seen as suspect due to Armenian's heretical miaphysite Christology.

the sake of order or because they were tempting us to stumble, made it so that whatever writings we had were translated from theirs.

For these reasons, the mercifulness of God looked after our nation and raised up for us a new Chrysostom, our holy Father Euthymios. Like a thirteenth apostle he completely cleansed our country from these aforementioned tares[39] through his many translations of the Holy Scriptures, as we said at the beginning of our account, along with the rules and canons of the church that confirm our faith. All these writings he left for us, flowing from the Holy Mountain and God-built Lavra as though from the river of Eden, spreading on the shore of our country and nation like living streams.

As we have already mentioned, because of the premature death of our father Euthymios, our books were left unfinished, and so once again the benevolence of God gave us a gift—Joshua after Moses, Eleazar after Aaron, Elisha after Elijah, and Timothy after Paul. Like them, George completed the will of his teacher, so that the blessed father finished whatever Euthymios had left incomplete.

[Omitted: George comes to Athos and spends seven years in extreme self-discipline, doing menial tasks.]

(10) Let us come back to our former subject. While this holy man was at the Great Lavra, in the sort of life and ascetic practice we mentioned above, his spiritual father the monk George the Recluse became aware that our father had neither accepted the honor of the priesthood nor begun to translate the books. This was very troubling to him, so he sent from the Black Mountain[40] his disciple, a worthy and good man by the name of John, to bring him a message, chastising him for not fulfilling his wishes. The blessed George was doing this not out of rebelliousness against his father, but because he regarded himself as utterly worthless, for he remembered the word of the Lord: "Whoever exalts himself will be humbled."[41]

[Omitted: George reluctantly accepts the priesthood and becomes an honored leader. His work leading clergy impedes his undertaking the translation projects for which he has been gifted.]

After a short while, he recalled the punishment associated with hiding his talent,[42] and he became even more afraid due to his disobedience of his teacher. Therefore, like a wise architect, he first laid a good foundation when he started building the church of God, translating the *Synaxarion*[43] first of all, for this is the

---

39. See Matt 13:24–30.

40. Monastic center near Antioch.

41. Matt 23:12.

42. See Matt 13:44.

43. Anthology of lessons for liturgical reading according to the church year, featuring brief lives of the saints.

foundation of the church, without which it is impossible to guide the church. For if any church does not have a *Synaxarion*, even if it has all sorts of other books, it is eating honey without experiencing its sweetness. The *Synaxarion* is, as we have said, the church's first jewel. Although the *Synaxarion* had been translated by the holy Father Euthymios, he composed a very short version of it, since he was occupied with translating other books. We have also heard this, that if his holy days had been extended, he would have translated the whole thing.

After the *Synaxarion*, the holy Father George translated the Gospel Readings Collection for the Year, the Paul Readings Collection for the Year, the Prophets for the Year, and the Great Blessings. He translated Genesis, which is the life of Abraham. He finished the hymns for the month of September, which Father Euthymios had begun by translating the first hymn. He translated again the great Paul in his entirety, along with the Catholic Epistles of the apostles. He translated these eight books at the Holy Mountain out of his own means, all while he was engaged in the service of the church, for he had been appointed deacon, as we mentioned.

After this, since he had been tested in many ways and was always found to be holy and blameless, like gold tested in many furnaces, all the brothers with united will and resolve led him to the high ladder of the office of head of the monastery, placing him on the throne of our holy Father Euthymios,[44] thereby putting the candle on the lampstand according to the words of the Gospel,[45] to enlighten the whole community of brothers. Thus humility exalts those who obtain it, glorifying them here but even more in heaven.

[Omitted: the text describes George's monumental and taxing duties as head of the monastery, along with his many accomplishments in that role. On visits to Constantinople, he meets Emperor Constantine Monomachos and the Georgian King Bagrat. Bagrat's mother Mary learns ascetic piety under George's instruction. Several episodes show how George comes to earn the respect of Bagrat and his family.][46]

(15) He was distinguished by living such a radiant life and by administering the flocks entrusted to him. For sometimes he was in the imperial city in the presence of pious emperors for the sake of necessary and appropriate matters and at other times he was at the monastery, administering monastic affairs and directing and ordering the lives of the brothers. Then, by the providence coming from God, he reflected and determined that his God-given talent of translating the divinely inspired books was not multiplying. So he took his leave from the

---

44. George was head of the monastery 1044–56.
45. See Matt 5:15.
46. Constantine IX Monomachos (1042–55); Bagrat IV, king of Georgia 1027–72.

leadership of the monastery, asking forgiveness of all the brothers. He left the monastery, without taking anything with him, not even money. As for the books he had translated as deacon or as leader of the monastery, he left all of them to the church: the *Great Synaxarion*, the Gospel Readings Collection, the Paul Readings Collection, the Blessings, the Studite,[47] and so many other books.

So he left the monastery empty-handed himself, except that some God-loving people gave him food, because he fled the monastery two times. This was the last one. The reason for his first flight was to avoid monastic leadership, since he wanted to keep to himself in quietness, so he fled the disturbances and turbulence of communal life. This is why he fled in secret, but when he got to the Black Mountain, his own director George chastised him greatly for leaving his rational flock, reminding him of what the Savior said to the apostle Peter: "If you love me, shepherd my sheep."[48] For this reason, by order of his own director he returned to the Holy Mountain and was compelled by all the brothers to undertake the business of monastic leadership again. He remained in this previously described administration for some time, then made his second departure in order to translate the holy books. He entered the imperial city in order to obtain his freedom from the emperor.[49] The emperor was irritated, but eventually was persuaded and did not oppose George's request. George also had the help of Mary the mother of Bagrat, for she was also there, as we said before. George collected bread for three persons at the Saint Symeon monastery and so arrived at the Black Mountain, carrying imperial letters. They welcomed him gladly, showing him great love and building him up in every way possible.

[Omitted: George ventures to Jerusalem to deliver charitable gifts on behalf of Mary, mother of Bagrat, who is dissuaded from going herself due to the hazards of the journey.]

(16) Let us come back to our former subject. After he had finished giving consolation and comfort to the poor, the holy Father George set out again for the Black Mountain and, by God's will, arrived in peace and gave encouragement to the pious Queen Mary, who after a short time went away to her own royal land to be with her son King Bagrat. This holy monk, now freed from all the disruptions and preoccupations, and free from every concern, began to translate the holy books as the Holy Spirit enabled him.[50] For you know this: that no other such translator has appeared in our language apart from our holy Father Euthymios, nor, I think, will one appear. George translated most of the books at night, so

---

47. Probably the *Studite Typikon*, an influential manual stipulating the structures of daily worship developed at the Studion Monastery in Constantinople.

48. John 21:17.

49. The year was 1056.

50. This episode of George's translation work on the Black Mountain occurred 1056–59.

that he could keep translating while also completing his daily worship without hindrance. He never allowed himself any rest, but day and night was occupied with the sweet honey of the holy books, by which he has sweetened our language and adorned the holy churches. By his golden books he has enriched us abundantly and immeasurably, for he was like a craftsman producing gold, just as it is written about alchemists, who by their manifold wisdom bring forth gold from the depths of the earth, expose its brilliance in a furnace and through fire. In the same way, by the fire of the Holy Spirit, the mind of our holy father became a furnace melting this verbal gold, purifying the gold by separating it from the lead and clay. For any books that were completely untranslated and foreign to our language, he brought them up out of the ignorance of the depths into the light, exposing their brilliance. Others that had been translated before, yet were still not well refined, or over time had become tarnished by ignorant and stupid users, as we have described, through the furnace of his own holy intellect he brought them out and purified them. Still other books had been translated by our holy Father Euthymios, yet due to his lack of time remained incomplete and partly composed, George expanded and finished. There were others that he compared to the Greek, correcting any defects and polishing poor style or inaccuracies, as he had done with the Gospels and Paul.

I should mention the titles of some of the books that the blessed one translated, thereby letting them disclose this holy man's labors to the believers in Christ, since he translated not only on the Holy Mountain and the Black Mountain, but if we were to enumerate them all, also in the imperial city, on the way to Sulumbria, in Antioch, at Saint Symeon, at Kalipos, and other such places. Some of the books were copied two or three times; it is hard to imagine one man copying in his lifetime so many books that had already been translated, much less that anyone could compose full translations of the books as this amazing man did, in such a sublime and divinely brilliant way. He translated, as I have mentioned,

> *Great Synaxarion*, the foundation of the churches
> Gospel Readings Collection for the Year
> The complete Paul, the Acts of the Apostles, and the Catholic Epistles of the apostles
> Paul Readings Collection for the Year
> Prophets for the Year
> Twelve volumes of the Menaion,[51] in full and with divine brilliance
> The festal Stichera[52] for the year, which are written with the months

---

51. Liturgical book in the Byzantine tradition, with fixed annual cycle of services, organized by the months of the church year.

52. A *sticheron* is a particular genre of hymn used in the Eastern liturgical tradition.

The daily Stichera, the Idiomela without the Hirmi,[53] as they are in Greek, as
   well as the same Stichera placed under the Hirmi

Along with these he wrote many other fine things, including:

The Lenten Stichera
Great Octoechos,[54] the jewel of the church, filled with many other good
   things
Great Lenten Triodion
Easter hymns,[55] also filled with a variety of good things
Books of the Catecheses of Theodore the Studite—the readings for Great
   Lent
Commentary on Genesis composed by Chrysostom
Book of the Sixth Council
Epistles of Saint Cyril, and other holy fathers on the condemnation of the
   heretic Nestorius
A book of Gregory of Nyssa, the beauty and praise of which is beyond any
   description
Book on the Six Days composed by Saint Basil
Book of the Epistles of Saint Ignatius the pious
Book of Psalms—the Daviti, the jewel and crown of all books

For the ambitious reader who loves the father—or rather I should say, loves
God—and wants to be able to learn about the contents of each book, he will
find at the end of this volume a numbered list and explanation of each book
along with a divinely appealing and brilliant colophon, that the holy monk John[56]
Patrikios (formerly Petrik) wrote down when he copied these holy books for
himself. With much labor and great care, he described these holy books, including every song and hymn in detail.

Our pious Father George translated all these and many other books besides,
thereby multiplying the talent entrusted to him.

*[Omitted: the rest of the account narrates George's exploits and travels in the
latter part of his life, until his death in 1065.]*

---

53. An *idiomelon* is a *sticheron* with its own distinctive melody. A *hirmos* is the opening
stanza in a hymn, setting the rhythm and melody of the hymn.
   54. Liturgical anthology of hymns arranged in eight parts (*octo*) according to the eight
musical tones used in Byzantine hymnody.
   55. Liturgical book for use in the weeks after Easter.
   56. Most manuscripts have "John," though one has "Peter." The latter may be correct, as
Peter is mentioned several times in the text, the only person distinguished by the title *patrikios*.

4. Mark the Deacon, *The Life of Porphyry of Gaza*

Introduction and translation by Jeff W. Childers

G eorgian sacred literature includes a large body of translation literature, especially from Greek, Syriac, and Armenian sources. In a number of instances, the translations preserve texts for which the originals
have not survived.

The Georgian *Life of Saint Porphyry of Gaza* was translated from a
Syriac original that no longer exists. We have a Greek version of the life,
but major differences between it and the Georgian/Syriac version have
sparked heated scholarly debate as to which of the two is closer to the original composition. Some maintain that the Georgian version represents the
earliest known form of the story, partly because it derives from a Semitic
(Syriac) original, and the language of the common people of Gaza was a
Semitic dialect (called "Syriac" in the text). Other features of the Georgian
invite scholars to assess it as the earlier form of the story.

Historians are particularly interested in the tale because it provides one
of the few surviving detailed accounts of a highly significant late antique
occurrence: the imperially backed destruction of eminent non-Christian
shrines in major cities of the empire, marking decisive transitions in religion, culture, and political power. It also illustrates the rise of a new
form of civic power in Christian empire, the monk-bishop. However,
great debate exists as to whether the account of Porphyry and his Christianization of Gaza, including the destruction of the celebrated Marneion
and the building of a grand new church, are authentic historical events.
Some see the text as a later work of pious fiction, with little grounding in
historical fact. Archeological work in Gaza promises to shed some light
on the subject.

The story is told from the vantage point of an eyewitness and Porphyry's disciple, the deacon Mark, with the key events happening between
about 392 and 420. The lengthy text has been greatly abbreviated, with
excerpts selected to highlight aspects of the story that may have led many
believers in different communities to find the story of Gaza's conversion
to Christianity edifying.

Bibliography

Text and Editions

Gelat'i manuscript, K'ut'aisi 1, folios 192v–225v.

Peeters, P. "La vie géorgienne de Saint Porphyre de Gaza." *Analecta Bollandiana* 59 (1941): 65–216.

Studies

Childers, J. W. "The Life of Porphyry: Clarifying the Relationship of the Greek and Georgian Versions through the Study of New Testament Citations." Pages 154–78 in *Transmission and Reception: New Testament Text-Critical and Exegetical Studies*. Edited by J. W. Childers and D. C. Parker. Texts and Studies 3.4. Piscataway, NJ: Gorgias, 2006.

Hill, G. F. Marcus Diaconus: *The Life of Porphyry, Bishop of Gaza*. Oxford: Clarendon, 1913.

Lampadaridi, A. *La conversion de Gaza au christianisme: Le Vie de S. Porphyre par Marc le Diacre (BHG 1570)*. Subsidia hagiographica 95. Brussels: Societé des Bollandistes, 2016.

Mussies, G. "Marnas God of Gaza." *Aufstieg und Niedergang der römischen Welt* 18 (1990): 2412–57.

Rapp, C. "Mark the Deacon, *Life of St. Porphyry of Gaza*." Pages 53–75 in *Medieval Hagiography: An Anthology*. Edited by Thomas Head. Garland Reference Library of the Humanities 1942. New York: Garland, 2000.

Rubin, Z. "Porphyrius of Gaza and the Conflict between Christianity and Paganism in Southern Palestine." Pages 31–66 in *Sharing the Sacred: Religious Contacts and Conflicts in the Holy Land, First–Fifteenth Centuries CE*. Edited by A. Kofsky and G. G. Stroumsa. Jerusalem: Izhak ben Zvi, 1998.

Trombley, Frank R. *Hellenic Religion and Christianization, c. 370–529*. Vol. 1/ pp. 188–204. 2nd ed. Religions in the Graeco-Roman World 115. Leiden: Brill, 1995.

van Dam, R. "From Paganism to Christianity at Late Antique Gaza." *Viator* 16 (1985): 1–20.

The Life of Porphyry of Gaza

Life of Saint Porphyry, Bishop of Gaza, which Mark the Deacon composed in Gaza, a city of Palestine

[Omitted: in a preamble much shorter than that of the Greek, the author laments his inadequacy to tell the story of the great Porphyry, eulogizing the saint by emphasizing his endurance under persecution and his achievement in rescuing Gaza from the error of idolatry.]

(4) Gaza is a large city of Palestine on the borders of Egypt, in which live a countless multitude of people. Its inhabitants and the great populations outside its boundaries were caught deeply in the grip of the error of idol worship. At that time, Saint Porphyry became worthy to receive the honor of the high priesthood over the city.

As for his ancestral home, originally he was from the city of Thessalonica, being the very rich son of nobles of that city. Through God the desire came upon him to become a monk, so he immediately left his parents and glory. Spurning honor and despising his kinsmen and his vast possessions, he fell in love with monasticism. He left Thessalonica and went to Egypt, subsequently entering Scete[1] to become a monk. After a few days he became worthy to receive his earnest desire: the habit of monasticism.

He stayed there with the holy fathers for five years, exerting himself mightily and remaining fervent in monastic endeavor. From the fathers he learned the acquisition of all virtues and to endure trials for God' sake. Afterward he was stirred by divine impulse to go over to the Holy City Jerusalem in order to venerate the life-giving cross of our deliverer and the place of his resurrection, so he left and came to worship at the holy venerable sites. From there he went down to the Jordan to dwell in a certain cave, where he lived for a period of five years in great exertion and diligence.

[Omitted: Porphyry becomes ill and feeble due to his prolonged fasting and vigils.]

(5) In those days I came from my own country of Asia[2] in order to pray in Jerusalem. I stayed there a long time, and every day I used to come to the holy

---

1. A monastic community of loosely confederated cells and hermitages in the Scetis Valley region of Egypt.

2. That is, the eastern Roman province of Asia.

sites and pray, working with my hands to support myself since I was a writer of books. I would see Saint Porphyry every day, praying ardently at the holy sites. I was astounded at the zealous fervor he achieved through unceasing daily exercises, despite his bodily infirmity.

One day I met him on the steps going up to Holy Kat'olike.[3] I saw the saint ascending but due to his physical infirmity he was not strong enough to ascend the steps on his own, so I took hold of him from behind to help his ascent. But the saint responded to me indignantly, saying: "Let me go up, brother! I do not consider myself worthy of help, since I am a sinful man and need to beg God on my own, so that according to his great mercies he may grant me forgiveness of my many sins." After he received the Holy Mystery[4] he returned to his own home. This is how he regarded his infirmity—as if another's body bore the burden of praying to God through his own prodigious determination.

[Omitted: Porphyry commissions Mark to travel to Thessalonica in order to divide his family inheritance among his brothers and return with Porphyry's portion. Upon his return, he is surprised to find Porphyry's health restored. The saint recounts to Mark a vision he received in which Christ descends from the cross and entrusts the care of the cross to him. Porphyry depletes his inheritance to support the poor, the sick, and travelers, taking up the trade of leather-working in imitation of Paul the apostle.]

(10) After some time Borilios,[5] who was patriarch[6] of the Holy City, took him and consecrated him as presbyter of Holy Resurrection,[7] despite his great reluctance, making him the guardian of the venerable cross, which is the wood of our life. Then I realized, I and Saint Porphyry also, that the vision he had seen previously had been fulfilled in him, when he saw the Lord on the cross, with the

---

3. The Basilica of Constantine, part of the Holy Sepulcher complex in Jerusalem, also known as the Martyrium.

4. That is, the Eucharist.

5. Possibly Praylius. The accepted date for these events is 392, calculated by subtracting the length of Porphyry's episcopal reign from the year 420, the date of his death in the Greek version, plus three more years corresponding to his term as priest—hence 392. A serious anachronism occurs, since Praylius was actually bishop of Jerusalem 417–22, leading to the speculation that the author wrote the name Cyril (bishop ca. 350–86), whose name was scribally altered in Syriac to Borilios. In either reading, the discrepancies and the anachronisms in Greek or Georgian are difficult to reconcile.

6. The title is technically anachronistic, since Jerusalem was not formally recognized as a patriarchate until 451. The Georgian translator or later scribe appears to have updated the text using a title familiar to him in his own day.

7. That is, the Anastasis, the traditional site of Jesus's tomb, decorated with a magnificent rotunda structure as part of the Holy Sepulcher complex in the fourth century.

thief at his right side, and our Lord gave him the cross to keep. It came to pass in the very way he had seen in the vision!

The saint became worthy of the priesthood at forty-five years of age, as he confided in me. He altered his former pattern of living in no way, continuing with the same virtues of fasting, vigils, and great labors. His food was bread and a few vegetables, which he would take when the sun had gone down. But on the Lord's days, at the sixth hour, he would take bread and olives and some soaked pulses, along with a single glass of wine for the sake of his stomach illness.[8] He did not vary from this regimen and rule all the days of his life.

(11) Three years after Porphyry became presbyter, the bishop of Gaza died, whose name was Abibos.[9] He was a holy man distinguished by every virtue, who had completed an angelic lifestyle on earth. He remained in the bishopric for a few years and then died. I am unable to describe his virtues now, but I will relate them to you in another place, if the Lord wills; or I will leave it to others to tell, as it is fitting.

After this blessed Abibos died, all the Christian citizens of Gaza gathered and began debating who would be bishop over them, disputing the matter for many days. Because they were divided—some saying one thing and some another, for although there were clergy there who were holy and deserving of the honor of the high priesthood, they did not want to appoint any of them—on account of the split between them, the whole assembly finally decided unanimously to send people to Caesarea, to the city of John the Archbishop, and that he should appoint for them a worthy and holy man as bishop, whomever the Holy Spirit would reveal to him.

(12) This holy John, archbishop of the city of Caesarea, was filled with the grace of the Holy Spirit and adorned with every virtue. After the delegates from Gaza arrived at Caesarea they went in and greeted the archbishop, asking him to designate for them as bishop one who would be worthy and well schooled in doctrine so that they might refute the idol worshipers who were in Gaza. When the archbishop heard all this from them, he sent a messenger to the city, instructing them to fast and pray for three days, after which God would show him a man suitable to become chief priest over them. After three days God gave him a revelation concerning Saint Porphyry. At that very moment he wrote a letter to Borilios, patriarch of Jerusalem, asking him to dispatch Saint Porphyry to him speedily so that he might interpret for him some passages of Scripture—for through God the saint had been given the gift of interpreting the divinely in-

---

8. See 1 Tim 5:23.

9. A name derived from the Semitic *Ḥabib*. The Greek text gives the Greek name Aeneas instead.

spired Scriptures, and if there were some deep passage, the saint would explicate it easily. When the letter of John the archbishop arrived, Praylius the archbishop of the Holy City received it gladly. He summoned Saint Porphyry and read out the letter from Caesarea written by John the archbishop and ordered him to go there—but to remain there no longer than four days.

(13) When the saint heard this, he was deeply grieved, but he prayed and declared: "The will of God be done in everything." Then he called me and said: "Brother Mark, come and let us venerate the sacred sites and the wood of life and the place of the resurrection of our life-giver, for much time will pass before we get to pray in the sacred sites again."

"How so, Father?" I asked him. He answered: "This very night I saw the life-giver in a vision that came to me, telling me: 'Behold, I give you this talent[10] that you might multiply it faithfully. I wish to betroth to you a certain woman who is impoverished according to the flesh, yet she is destined to be wealthy. When you marry her, adorn her until she forgets her former poverty. Although today she is a pauper, she is no stranger to me but a beloved bride. She is not to be like on earth your wife, a manager of home and property, but a receptacle of spiritual treasures.'"

"This is what our Lord Jesus Christ told me tonight. So now I am afraid, my son. For I cannot even examine my own sins diligently. What will I do when the Lord sets me over others and entrusts me with many souls—I who have been unable to care properly for this one soul, and have never been able to fulfill the will of God!"

[Omitted: Porphyry visits the holy sites one more time, after which he and Mark and Baruk (a poor youth in Porphyry's care) travel to Caesarea.]

(16) Then Archbishop John called the people who had come from Gaza and spoke to them privately: "Prepare to take away a bishop tomorrow, a man who is holy and worthy and humble, a teacher of the divine Scriptures, adorned with every virtue, whom God has revealed to me to make ruler over you."

Next morning they took Saint Porphyry and, despite his reluctance, consecrated him bishop of Gaza. He wept profusely: "I do not deserve this laying on of hands!" Nevertheless, due to their persistent pressure—and since the thing came through God—he accepted it. After the divine office was finished and we had received the Holy Mystery, the archbishop brought us back again. We ate with him, then made preparations to depart on our journey the next day.

(17) We received a blessing from the holy man and set out the next day. We reached Lydda in the evening and lodged there. When it was morning we left for Gaza, arriving at the city after nightfall, after enduring much hardship and

10. See Matt 25:14–30.

toil. The cause of our hardship was this: the villages around Gaza were in the grip of the error of idol worship. As we went along, the devil stirred them up fiercely against us so that they filled our path with thorns and thistles and with a great deal of filth that is toxic to humans. Some people lit human excrement on fire, others made large piles of filth, to choke us. But we persevered and were delivered so that we did not perish in all this. Through great toil we were barely delivered from death, and with great effort we arrived at the city in the third watch of the night.

All this happened to us at the devil's instigation, for he was troubled by the saint's entering the city, since he had a home within it through the numerous idols there. Also, he did not want their worship to be disgraced through the saint's work (which indeed happened later). Yet the saint was not distressed, nor did he become fainthearted about it, for he knew the enemy's cunning and was not troubled in the least.

(18) We went into the bishop's residence, and the Christians received us with great rejoicing. But the idol worshipers were inflamed with malevolence and treachery toward us.

(19) The year we arrived, there was a severe drought in the city and surrounding area. The Gazaites were saying: "That holy man's arrival is a problem for us"; and the idolaters were saying: "Woe, that the foot of Porphyry has entered our city! What has become of us now?" When the months of the rainy season were done yet there was still no rainfall, the city inhabitants felt severely oppressed by the drought.

At that time the idolaters gathered at the temple of the idol Maron,[11] making a great offering and praying for rain. They were also declaring: "Maron has power over the rains." They stayed there seven days in prayer then went outside the city, for outside the city there was a house of prayer. They kept praying for a long time but got no benefit. Grieving in great anguish, they all went away to their own homes.

But all the Christian men and women assembled. They came to Saint Porphyry and began asking him to go out with them to sing hymns and to pray for rain, for they were afraid they would experience a great famine because of the drought.

(20) So the saint went out with them, proclaiming a fast and ordering all the people to assemble in the evening and keep vigil, which they did. We kept vigil,

---

11. The most prominent cult in Gaza was that of the local *ba'al*, Marnas, a storm deity that the Greeks identified with Zeus of Crete. The Temple of Marnas in Gaza was one of the wonders of the region. The Georgian uses the name Maron, a term derived from Syriac "lord." The rest of the text prefers the name Nonos.

crying and pleading with God. When morning dawned we proceeded from the church, taking with us the sign of the life-giving cross. Singing hymns, we went first to the holy church to the west of the city, the one that the holy Bishop Asklipos[12] had built—the same man who endured many trials on behalf of the true faith, whose name is written in the book of the living ones with all the saints. After praying there for a long while we left that place and went to the Church of the Holy Martyr Timothy, where the martyrs are, and prayed there with much weeping and groaning.

We returned to the city with much hymn singing, but when we got to the city gates we found them shut against us, for it was the ninth hour. The idolaters who lived there did this, trying to scatter the congregation of the flocks of Christ and to keep their prayers from being finished properly. We stood outside the gates of the city for two hours but no one opened them for us. Then God saw the groaning of his faithful people and the tears of the holy Bishop Porphyry, and he did not disregard them. All at once the sky covered over with cloud, there were lightning flashes and mighty peals of thunder, and it began to rain upon the earth as in the days of Elijah the prophet.[13] Furthermore, it did not come down like mere rain but like waterfalls. When people inside the city saw this miracle they came out rejoicing and opened the gate for us.

(21) Many of the idol worshipers believed in God and were shouting in a loud voice: "Great is the God of the Christians!" They joined us and we all went into the church. Praying for the people, Saint Porphyry made the sign of the cross and dismissed them in peace. Those who believed in Christ and were baptized in that very hour were 127 souls, men and women. Giving thanks to God, each of them went away to his own house very joyfully.

The rain kept coming down in this fierce way for two days and nights, until the people were afraid that their houses might collapse, for the buildings were made of unbaked brick. It rained for another month and the mercy of God continued to be multiplied upon us. We kept the Festival of the Theophany[14] with happy rejoicing, thanking God for the good things he had sent upon us. Many faithful souls were added to the flock of Christ.

However, the idol worshipers were filled with envy and treachery concerning the holy Bishop Porphyry and his flock, and they would not relent from making trouble for us each and every day. Whenever a magistrate would come, they would raise accusations against the Christians in order to make trouble for them,

12. Asclepas of Gaza, deposed ca. 341 due to his support for Athanasius in the Arian controversy.
13. See 1 Kgs 18:45.
14. Also known as Epiphany.

and they vexed the Christians with much mischief. But the saint mourned their foolishness and kept praying to God with much weeping, that he might convert them from their error to the correct faith in Christ our God.

[Omitted: Baruk is beaten nearly to death by a pagan in a nearby village. When Baruk's nearly lifeless body is carried back into Gaza by some Christians, a riot ensues because of the apparent violation against the custom that corpses may not be brought into the city. Porphyry revives Baruk and uses his staff to dispel a mob of idolaters. Porphyry appoints Mark and Baruk as deacons.]

(26) At that time, because of the disturbances the idol worshipers were inciting constantly toward us, both openly and in secret, Saint Porphyry decided to send me to the imperial city and petition the emperor to issue a decree for the overthrow of the idols of the city of Gaza. For they had the audacity to keep praying in the idol shrines, especially in the temple of their god Nonos.[15] He wrote letters for me to John, the patriarch of Constantinople, called John Chrysostom[16] on account of his great virtues, a man who deserves glory and honor from all the faithful.

I left the city of Gaza and after twenty days arrived at the city of Byzantium. I conveyed the letters of Saint Porphyry to the holy John Chrysostom and also recounted orally the whole business concerning which I had been sent. He sent straightaway for the chamberlain, the eunuch who was in charge of the treasury of Emperor Arcadius.[17] He summoned him and read the letters of Bishop Porphyry, after which he instructed him to attend diligently to this business himself, taking up divine zeal and seeing to it with every effort. Then the eunuch said to me: "Do not be troubled, my son, for I believe in our Lord Jesus Christ and that all your business will be administered effectively and turn out favorably."

He left and explained the matter to Emperor Arcadius. After seven days he produced documents in which was written the decree that all the idol shrines of Gaza were to be closed. The documents were entrusted to a certain man named Galaros, and he was commanded to go to Gaza and close the idol shrines within it.

(27) Then Chrysostom wrote a special letter for me, and I departed and came to Gaza. I found Saint Porphyry gripped by a fever, but after he read the Patriarch John's letter he was very happy and immediately sloughed off the fever. He said to me: "My son, my illness occurred due to the grief and anguish befalling me every day because of the idol worshipers. But from now I am convinced of the

---

15. The Georgian prefers the name Nonos for the deity, presumably following its Syriac source, where the name Maron ("lord") could be offensive due to the word's associations with Jesus Christ and the Lord God.

16. That is, "Goldenmouth." John Chrysostom was bishop of Constantinople 398–404.

17. Arcadius reigned 395–408.

ministrations of God, who does not overlook those who hope in his name and who causes them who stray to turn back to the way of truth."

After the seventh day, the emperor's emissary Galaros arrived. He assembled all the idolaters and read to them the emperor's letter, in which was decreed the closure of all the idol shrines. But secretly they gave him a large amount of gold, converting him to their side. So he deliberately left for them the temple of their god Nonos, and they kept worshiping in it. Furthermore, they did not desist at all from their malicious habits against the Christians. They continued harassing them with much evil, for they were the majority among the free inhabitants of the city.

(28) Nevertheless, many of them converted from their error to the right faith and were added to Christ. The reason for their conversion was this: there was a certain woman from among the notables of the city of Gaza who followed the law of the idol worshipers. She was pregnant. When the time of her childbearing was completed, the delivery became very difficult for her. The baby was not coming down naturally, because it had turned in the womb so that it poked out its hand, but the rest of its body was stuck and could not come out. The midwives could not find a way to help her and she was in serious trouble. Every day her pain and distress increased and the suffering got worse, up to the seventh day. Many physicians came but they were unable to be of any use to her. As a last resort they conferred and decided to cut the baby out of its mother's womb with a sword, thereby saving at least one of them from death. As they were preparing to do this, they noticed she was very weak because of her severe struggle. Then they could not bear to touch her, for they were afraid she would die in their hands, so they left her and withdrew.

Her parents and husband had been making a great many sacrifices to the idols and profane demons, yet got no help. They brought numerous enchanters but not a single one found a remedy.

(29) Now that pregnant woman had a wet nurse who was a faithful Christian. When she saw the woman's distress, she went to all the churches, praying to God for her with many tears, that he might show her mercy and deliver her from her difficulties. Now on a particular day that woman came in to pray as usual, and Saint Porphyry came in to pray at the ninth hour, and I was with him too. We saw the woman standing to one side, for she was praying to God through tears for the pregnant woman. When Saint Porphyry heard her groaning, he responded to her: "Tell me, woman, why are you groaning and weeping?" She came and fell down before the saint and began imploring him to make a prayer to God on behalf of the afflicted woman so that God might deliver her and she could survive. When the saint heard her, he burst into tears just as if she were a friend of his, for he had mercy on the afflicted.

The saint said to the wet nurse: "I have heard about their house. They are idol worshipers, and such people are scarcely able to be saved before God. Yet he is not without power for those who hope on his name and everything is possible for his many mercies. For now, depart and gather the men and women of the city and her husband and all her kin, and tell them: 'They have found a certain excellent physician, someone who is very expert concerning this kind of disease. He asked me: "If I deliver this woman from such a fierce affliction, what reward will you give me for it?"'

"Then they will promise you anything, so tell them: 'If he heals this woman, swear to me by the living God that you will not be false to what you promise, nor will you forsake him and go over to another.' Once they have promised you this, tell them to raise their hands to heaven and swear to you that they will keep unswervingly to what they have promised. When they do this, say to that woman who is debilitated by pain, in the presence of everyone: 'Let Christ, the Son of God, heal you; believe in him.'"

(30) When the woman heard this message from Saint Porphyry, she received it with conviction and went out to the pregnant woman. She found her in indescribable distress, with her family members mourning over her. She told them to be silent for a little. After they fell silent for a while, she told them: "I have found a certain excellent and very expert physician who promised me: 'I will heal your daughter.' But if he heals her, what will you give as a reward for it?" When the girl's parents and the woman's husband heard this, they were very glad, and told her: "If he wants to carry off all our possessions, let him carry them off—only please let him heal her!"

The wet nurse said to them: "Lift your hands up to heaven. Swear by the living God: 'If she is healed, we will not be false to what we promise nor will we forsake him and go over to another.'" They made the promise eagerly, raising their hands to heaven and speaking with much weeping: "All that we have, let him take it, and we will serve him all the days of our lives as slaves. For what happiness shall we have, or what consolation after her death? For there have never been offspring like her!"

Once they swore to do just what the healer wanted, the wet nurse lifted her hands and said to the pregnant girl in a loud voice in front of everyone: "The great Bishop Porphyry says to you: 'Jesus Christ, Son of the living God will heal you; believe in him.'" The girl cried out in a loud voice: "I believe in you, my lord God Jesus Christ—have mercy on me now." After she said this, at once the baby came down and was delivered alive.

(31) Then all who were with her shouted loudly: "Great is the God of the Christians, and there is no other God beside him! And great is his minister Porphyry!" The next day the girl's parents and her husband and all her kin came to

the church of the holy Bishop Porphyry. Falling down before him, they entreated him with tears to give them the light of Christ.[18] When the saint heard this, he was very glad and sealed them with the sign of Christ's cross and made them catechumens, instructing them to be as diligent about being at holy church. After a number of days he baptized them, that woman and the son that she bore, whom he both baptized and called by his own name, Porphyry. And sixty-four souls were baptized because of that woman.

(32) When the idol worshipers saw that the believers in Christ were multiplying, they were enraged and began to afflict them with great wrongdoing, like the Egyptians did when they enslaved the Israelites and treated them abusively.[19] When Saint Porphyry saw the idolaters' violence and scorn toward the Christians, he could not bear it but was incited to divine anger. He left Gaza and came to Caesarea, to Archbishop John, imploring him to let him go and withdraw into the hermit's life to which he was accustomed. He said: "I can no longer witness the wrongs that the idol worshipers are doing to the Christians in the city of Gaza." But Archbishop John tried to console him, entreating him not to leave his throne and flock.

(33) Saint Porphyry answered: "If I have found grace before your holiness, and so that I may do as you command, comply with my request for the sake of the faith of the Father and the Son and the Holy Spirit, and come with me to the imperial city. We will entreat the emperor to demolish all the shrines of the city of Gaza. Otherwise, countless souls will perish in the city, and I fear that I will be found liable to divine judgment due to my indifference and negligence." Archbishop John answered and said: "Your word is good, son, but it is not the time to go—winter has come." Saint Porphyry replied: "If the will of God is with me, and he has mercy on the assembly in Gaza so as to save them from error and convert them to the right faith, he is able to preserve us also from the winter." Then John said to him: "May the will of God be upon everyone."

[Omitted: chapters 34–62 tell the story of Porphyry's mission to Constantinople and his return. At first, Emperor Arcadius is reluctant to grant the bishop's request to order Gaza'a shrines closed, because the non-Christian citizens of Gaza were generous with their tributes and gifts. Yet with the help of Empress Eudoxia, Porphyry exploits the occasion of the baptism of the royal newborn, Theodosius I (emperor 379–95), to maneuver the emperor into sponsoring his plan. Porphyry returns to Gaza with imperial decrees and royal gifts. The emperor dispatches Count Zhenighos and a company of soldiers to enforce the decree.]

(63) After ten days, Count Zhenighos arrived with a considerable host, hav-

---

18. That is, baptism. The Georgian idiom "to receive light" denotes baptism.
19. See Exod 1:8–14.

ing been dispatched by the emperors to demolish the idol shrines. When the idolaters found out about his coming—and why he had come—many of them left the city and their homes, fleeing to other cities, and some scattered into the villages. These were principal citizens of the city and Zhenighos turned their houses into residences for the band of soldiers. Then he publicized in Gaza the decree of the emperors, for which he had been sent, reading aloud to them the emperors' document, in which it was inscribed: "All the idol shrines of Gaza shall be eradicated from their very foundations, and their idols burned with fire, without any promise or excuse."

When the idolaters heard that their idols were about to be burned with fire, they made many sacrifices before them that very day. Upon seeing this, Count Zhenighos was furious and ordered his soldiers to beat them, dispersing them amid tears and insults.

(64) Then Zhenighos and all the Christians considered together how to demolish all the idol shrines. In the city of Gaza there were eight idol houses, in which were innumerable idols. In the middle of them there was a large house, the most important of them all, called the house of Nonos. But outside the city, in the villages and their territories, there were so many idols in the countryside that no one could count them. For the devil had appropriated the Gazaites and led their hearts astray on account of their pliability, though any of them who turn away from their error are ardent and firm in their faith in Jesus Christ.

(65) Then a multitude of Christians assembled with the soldiers to demolish the idol shrines. First of all they went to the temple of the Gazaites' god Nonos in the middle of the city, in order to demolish it, yet they could not, for the priests found out about it and blocked the doors inside the temple with stones and left. They buried all the temple vessels and the ornaments of gold and silver in an underground receptacle and went out by another way, for they had an underground passage for exiting and entering, about which only they knew and not any of the attendants. Since the Christians could not get into the temple, they left it and began demolishing the other idol shrines, from their very foundations, burning the vessels they found inside. . . .

(66) Over a period of twenty days they demolished all the idol shrines, except for the Temple of Nonos. Then they conferred about its demolition, considering many different methods. Their thinking was discordant, for some would say one thing, and others something else, and they could not settle on anything.

In the end Saint Porphyry instructed them to fast and pray in the church until the ninth hour, and at the ninth hour to stop for the liturgy. A woman was there who had a small child on her shoulders. At that moment the child began to cry out using the voice and words of a grown man, speaking in the Syriac language: "I say to all you Christians—burn that temple down to the foundation with fire, in this manner: take pitch and oil and sulfur, mix them together, and put the mixture on the copper doors of the inner temple. Set fire to it and let them burn up completely. As for the surrounding courtyards, do not disturb them. Instead, when the profane inner temple is burned up, cleanse it well and build a holy church of God."

The child spoke up again: "Consider nothing else, for by no other means will you be able to demolish it, apart from what I am telling you—and it is not just I speaking, but Christ who is speaking through me."[20] All those who heard marveled and began praising God.

(67) When Saint Porphyry heard this, he raised his hands to heaven, thanking God and saying to him: "I thank you, Father of heaven and earth, for you hid this from the wise and intelligent and revealed this to infants. Yes, Father, for thus it was pleasing before you."[21] After celebrating the Holy Mystery, he called the child's mother. When she came, he took the child from her and said to the woman: "Look, I order you under oath by Christ, the Son of the living God, to make the truth known to me—did you instruct this child to say what he has said in the church, or has someone else?" The woman replied to Saint Porphyry: "I swear to you by the living God and by the altar of the Lord that I have not instructed him in any of this that he was saying in the church; neither has any other instructed him. Look, the child is in front you—admonish and interrogate him. Out of fear, he will not refuse but will confess to you directly, as a child, explaining to you the truth, whatever it may be."

When Saint Porphyry heard this, he blessed her and sent her out. Then he had the child brought. He admonished him, saying: "Quickly, explain to me: who instructed you to give the idea in the church that you told us about the Temple of Nonos?" The child was silent. Then Porphyry ordered him threatened with a beating so that he would explain the truth about who instructed him to tell this idea. The man holding the rod raised it up, showing his intention to beat him, and saying: "Confess, before you are beaten—who instructed you to speak in the church?" But the child stood speechless.

(68) Once everyone was silent, the child spoke up in Greek, saying: "Everyone, listen to what I am telling you! Burn up the inner temple with fire, for many wicked things have been done in this place and much blood has been spilled in this place. It shall be burned in just the manner that I told you through Christ." Then Saint Porphyry—along with everyone standing there—marveled at the child's intelligent speech. Again Saint Porphyry called the child's mother and asked her whether he knew how to speak in Greek. She replied: "We have never

20. See 2 Cor 13:3.
21. Matt 11:25–26; Luke 10:21.

been taught any of the Greek language; our speech is that of the Syriac language instead, as your holiness knows."

Saint Porphyry and everyone standing there were amazed at the child's exactness of speech. He gave the child's mother three drachmas, dismissing them in peace. When the child saw the drachmas in his mother's hands, he said to her in the Syriac language: "Do not take this gold, mother, for it is not right to sell the gift of God for money."[22] At that, the woman returned the drachmas, telling the bishop: "Holy father, pray for me and my son." Then she went away to her home.

(69) Saint Porphyry assembled all the members of the church. He came and explained to Count Zhenighos and his officers the miraculous sign associated with that child. Everyone unanimously affirmed the child's word, since he was speaking through the Holy Spirit. They did just as the child instructed them, setting fire to the Temple of Nonos. It burned for many days. An enormous amount of gold and silver and various furnishings that the idol worshipers had hidden in there burned up. Yet no one was able to take any of it, due to the fierceness of the blaze.

[Omitted: a crypto-pagan officer curses the Christians on account of the destruction and is slain by a blazing timber that falls on his head. The shrine burns down to its stone foundations.]

(71) Then we also searched the houses and courtyards, finding countless numbers of idols. We removed them and burned them with fire. We also found a number of the books by which they executed their lawless ritual and their profane religion. We burned it all with fire.

(72) Large crowds were abandoning their error and coming to the holy church and confessing the right faith of the Lord. Saint Porphyry welcomed them all happily, training them all for the salvation of their souls and saying: "'The one who asks shall receive; and to the one who knocks it will be opened; and the one who seeks shall find,'[23] according to the word of the Lord."

At that time some were telling Saint Porphyry: "It is not right to welcome into the holy church those who did not separate from the deceitful worship of idols of their own accord but abandoned their religion out of fear of the emperors. Their minds are still in the same error and they are just waiting for the opportunity to revert back to it."

(73) Yet Saint Porphyry answered: "The apostle says: 'Whether in falsehood or in truth, Christ is preached; I rejoice about this,'[24] for at last they will all

22. See Acts 8:20.
23. Matt 7:8.
24. Phil 1:18.

preach the truth. This is good, even if they learn righteousness out of fear, for the prophet David says: 'It is good for me that you humbled me, so that I might learn your righteousness.'[25] Even if some of these converts are uncertain today, in time wisdom will mold their minds toward serving the true God, for they will be taught many precepts and will get knowledge of the Scriptures that will convert them from their error to the holy church."

(74) From that day forward, the worship of idols was held in contempt and faith in Jesus Christ multiplied. Baptism was esteemed, and the Christians in Gaza grew bold through the help of the Lord.

(75) Once the temple of the idol Nonos was burned up, Saint Porphyry decided to build the holy church on that site, just as he had seen in a vision when he was in Constantinople, using the money he had received there from Empress Eudoxia. When Count Zhenighos and his officers set off for Constantinople, after demolishing the idol shrines, he left with Porphyry a contingent sufficient for helping with the construction of the holy church and all the rest of the business—so that none of the idol worshipers would dare cause a disruption in the city after he left, and to assist in the acquisition of stone, wood, and everything needed for the construction of the holy church.

The builders began discussing various ways of setting the foundation. Some were saying: "We should build it in the shape of the former one, as it was before the burning." For the building had been round, built in the shape of a crown, with outer colonnades set around it in the same shape; but the center rising up above all the defiled parts had burned in the fire. Others were saying: "The foundation should not match the shape of that profane temple at all, lest the name of the idol shrine remain associated with the holy church." A majority of the people followed that argument, saying: "We should not build it on the site of the foundation of the idolatrous temple."

Saint Porphyry said: "First prepare the foundation of the burnt structure, and God will reveal what sort of building will be pleasing to him." For as they prepared the site, an emissary arrived, sent from the palace by the emperors to Saint Porphyry. He had a letter from Empress Eudoxia, in which was written: "Peace and greetings from the emperors to Saint Porphyry and to all his flock. So that the emperors would not be forgotten in their holy prayers," and so forth. In that letter a plan was drawn, representing the building in the shape of the venerable cross. When the saint read the letter and saw the shape of the venerable cross, he was very glad and perceived that this instruction had come through God, remembering what is written: "The hearts of kings are in the hands of God."[26]

25. Ps 119:71.
26. Prov 21:1.

It was also written in that letter: "Look, I am sending beautiful pillars and many precious things, including many marble panels for decorating the holy church, along with all sorts of other materials befitting the holy church."

(76) Then they buried all the idol offerings and profane utensils of that temple in the ground so that no one would take any of it and be defiled. Nor did Porphyry allow people to walk upon the foul and profane utensils, so that all of it might remain in the ground.

Saint Porphyry instructed all the people to gather at the church and spend the night in sleepless prayer. Once they had done this, he instructed them all to take up iron tools for building the church.

[Omitted: a crowd carries tools to the construction site in a liturgical procession led by Baruk. An architect from Antioch named Rop'ianos (Rufinus) lays out the church according to the design specified by Eudoxia.]

(79) Once they had dug out and laid the foundation with large stones and stones salvaged from the Temple of Nonos, the saint valiantly girded his own loins and began working wholeheartedly. When they all saw him laboring this way, they began working all the more ardently, shouting so much that the sound of their rejoicing was heard outside the city, three miles away.

[Omitted: three young boys fall into a well near the construction site and are miraculously recovered unharmed. The magnificent edifice rises, resplendent with the grand pillars donated by Eudoxia. The idolater-heretic Ivliana (Juliana) arrives in Gaza, leading new converts astray by her teaching. Porphyry debates her, publicly refuting her doctrine. The demons within her are struck by God and she falls dead, causing many people to put their faith in Christ.]

(92) After five years the construction of the church was finished, for they decorated it profusely with all sorts of ornamentation. They gave it the name of Empress Eudoxia. Then Saint Porphyry celebrated the dedication of the holy church, blessing it on the day of the Lord's resurrection—that is, on Easter. He gathered a numberless throng of Christians from the city and surrounding countryside, lavishly setting a great banquet for them—for a congregation of monks was there, about one thousand men, along with bishops and countless laypeople. There was great celebration throughout the days of dedication, during which the saint exulted. The assembly was like that of holy angels, and there was so much spiritual jubilation, for they sang the praise of God and the adulation of the holy church in loud voices.

Then the hearts of the idolaters in the city began to melt with sorrow—not on account of the assembly's rejoicing, but because they saw how beautiful the finished holy church was, how very ornate and filled with faithful people was the temple of God. At one time it had been the temple of their god Nonos and had been in their hands, but now it was taken away and given to the Christians. Their grief and sorrow were magnified because of this, and although they gnashed their teeth at the Christians, they could not hurt them because they feared the people and the authorities. So they were cut to pieces with anger.

(93) There was a former time, when the saint was laying the foundation of the holy church, that the Christians told him: "You have set the foundations of the holy church exceedingly grand, Father. We are a small group of Christians and we fear we will not be equal to it." For it would have been the largest church of Palestine up to that time. But Saint Porphyry said to them: "Why are you so small of faith, my children? Remember what Scripture says: 'Unless the Lord builds the house, its builders labor in vain.'[27] For my hope is from God, that we will have him as our helper. He will cause this building to turn out favorably for us and your eyes will see it finished, and you will delight in it along with the multitude of people who will be added to this congregation. For this tiny congregation, by the power of Christ, is going to multiply, and Christianity is going to expand; and those who come into this building are going to be innumerable, until the space of this place cannot contain them."

And it was so, for during the days of the dedication the building was unable to contain them. Then the people recalled the statement Saint Porphyry had made at the laying of the foundation, and they glorified God. After the days of the dedication were over, the saint blessed the people and they departed in peace to their own regions.

(94) Saint Porphyry also built near the church a very large hostel for accommodating traveling strangers, constructing also many rooms in it for housing the sick and the poor. He put faithful and God-fearing people in it to serve the strangers and the sick, generously providing them food to provide amply for strangers and the sick. As for the poor, to some he gave gold, to others silver, and to others some money, depending on the severity of their poverty. In this way, during the principal catholic festivals a considerable amount of material support would be distributed to all the poor each day. He used to instruct his flock concerning mercy: "Chief of all virtues is mercy to the poor. Let this be the profit acquired ahead of all profits, for it leads you to the kingdom of heaven."

[Omitted: a property dispute breaks out between a Christian and a prominent pagan. In the ensuing riot, Baruk is beaten and several Christians killed. The mob assails the episcopal residence, forcing Porphyry and Mark to flee across the rooftops of the city. An orphan girl named Peace provides them with shelter. News of the tumult reaches Caesarea, and a host is dispatched to subdue the rioting idol worshipers in Gaza. Many of them are executed by imperial order. Porphyry baptizes Peace,

27. Ps 127:1.

her grandmother, and her aunt, providing for them financially. Peace chooses to remain single in devotion to her bridegroom Christ.]

(103) Having finished building the holy church and decorating it with all sorts of ornamentation, Saint Porphyry ably converted all the idol worshipers through the ordinance given to him by God. Enduring many trials, he gathered them to the holy church, making them into one flock with a single shepherd.

After the consecration of the church he lived a few years.[28] Later, he grew weak, becoming sick with the very illness by which he died. At that time he summoned the honorable priests, along with the God-loving laypeople, saying: "Behold, I am departing at the bidding of my Lord, and I do not know what sort of reception mine will be, since I have never fulfilled his will—unless perchance by his mercy he take away my sins. But you, my children, be cautious and stand fast upon the faith of our Lord Jesus Christ. Behold, your path has been cleared of stones so that the travelers will not stumble, and the thorns have been pulled out of your garden so that the workers will suffer no harm. Your wheat has been cleansed of tares so that nothing foul will befall the eaters, for your city has been cleared of idol worshipers so that your faith may remain firm. Now you also, be diligent after I am gone, guarding the right faith that was given to you by God, that you may stand blameless before your Lord." Raising his hands up to heaven and blessing all of us, he commended us to God, the ruler of all, and surrendered his spirit into the hands of his creator. Thus the saint ended his residence upon the earth like an angel.

He had remained in the episcopate twenty-five years, less one month. He died on February 26, inheriting the kingdom unseen by eyes that was promised by our Lord Jesus Christ, along with all his holy ones, by the grace of the Lord, to whom be glory, forever and ever. Amen.

28. According to calculations derived from the Greek version, the year would be 420.

ولا يجوز لاحد من المؤمنين التزوج بما من يتوج عالي الايمان ضعيف في
الامة ويتسع من محل الطبيعة يشاركها كذلك فاختلاص ترويج مطلقة قصر
وان يقول للرسول القوم يحبب اليه ويتعتبر بها حتى ما احلها الله
في الممالك فاما الممالك بلحظة من الوجه واحدة عليهم نفير نشيطه
مسطله ولا احتياج لهم رضاها ولا بوا وليس له القدرة بستهم وكلهم
اكثر ما يطلبون فاذا ذلك الا كلما ضاء الله ما قال الرسول فانا
احب يتسع الرجل المؤمن يتوفاني في نسا الجاهزين من اجمله
المرئيه والنكاح انهم من عليهم المعنو والخروج الي هذا العمل العود
اليلاه لعله لعله يسري بيات والطفا لصالح الي القيام عليهم وهذه
محمور محمد بذر تعلمه لعل الرجل يذرف امرأته ولا يسما لنف
وبات ملبك من يقر حليهم وجدهم وهما للتزوج لم اختياج
بركم وحرم وقدهم لهما ايضا الكاهر واستياق خرطا زلخيائب
القول بمواريث الامر بمواريث الامر فيها خارج على خارج دائم ومؤتمر
ورسوم ثم كل ملك كا نهار الا ليتم ووقع عليه اصطلاح خرم فبه
احراج حقوق الله سيما وأعطا المتالكين نصيبهم كأرث الرجل
في

فجمال الكركات اللذين تحوا مؤمنين بالمسيح الى الغرض في هذه الشريعة
معرفة الله وتقدسه وتمجيده واشتوا العارف كانا فعل الانصاف
والمناه وطلب البلي الباقي لاحد امر عن الانا الفاني يا اماما أتدى
ذلك من الشرائع ولحكام وماستسل لك الأحكام وفهلا مذهبا
واعتقاد ما جاحلبه على ما بد سمه رضاه الذي هناك انه عنا يقال
شيها بناما النسخ بالتقديس والنهي والتبتل البلايا البلاين
غيرها بقاله في ذلك الانا بلحيل انا تنفر بنفعها الله وانفعكم
قال امرنا على الانسان ايها يعتقد هوالكن الما يعتقد عزم قد مر
الباطميان قال لك ذلك قال انا وحل ايه قال الذي لك تا تفن
كأن ليبين ليبات ساور ورنه اذا في ذلك يرجع امرك لك دينه
جميع اصالا الادبار المخالفين لهم يتقولوا ايشا ابالا فاذا كان هذا
الجرا يسترد بناصحاب جميع الاديان بنتجم يوم على ايد ابداية
يصف الحجة الاد دخله ريس الايمان ليسله هذه لاحد بعينها
فاذا انقضا حجة الخا الفعل ولا تقبل تلك المحة من اهل الفئة
نقول ان هذا القول الكون والباطن هم بجميع الاحيان ان اعلم .

4

ARABIC

Introduction and Bibliography by John C. Lamoreaux

In the first half of the seventh century CE the initial stages of the Arab conquests were set in motion. Within one hundred years, a large portion of the world's Christians—perhaps a majority of them—found themselves living under Muslim rule. Three of the five ancient patriarchates were now under the authority of the Muslim conquerors: Alexandria, Jerusalem, and Antioch. As well, with the fall of Sassanid Persia to the Muslims, Christians living beyond the eastern borders of the Byzantine Empire were also now subject to Muslim rule. Likewise, with the expansion of the Muslim armies westward, crossing from North Africa into Spain in the early eighth century, Christians in North Africa, parts of Spain, and parts of southern Europe also soon found themselves living under Muslim authority.[1]

In the central regions of the new Muslim empire—Egypt, the Levant, and Mesopotamia—the Christians now living under Islam belonged to many of the seventh century's main divisions of Christendom: most importantly, the Eastern Orthodox, the Church of the East, the Oriental Orthodox, and the Maronites.

In the seventh century, the Eastern Orthodox under Islam were to be found mainly in Syro-Palestine and Egypt, in the patriarchates of Alexandria, Jerusalem, and Antioch. They were defined by their acceptance of the six ecumenical councils that had been held to date, and in this they were in communion with the patriarchates of Rome and Constantinople. (At the time of the Muslim conquests, it would still be many centuries before the Eastern Orthodox and Roman Catholics would split from one another.) When speaking of the early centuries of the Muslim era, it is common for these Eastern Orthodox Christians under Islam to be called

---

1. For the earliest stages of Arab conquests, see Fred Donner, *The Early Islamic Conquests* (Princeton: Princeton University Press, 1981); Hugh Kennedy, *The Great Arab Conquests: How the Spread of Islam Changed the World We Live In* (Philadelphia: Da Capo, 2007); and Robert G. Hoyland, *In God's Path: The Arab Conquests and the Creation of an Islamic Empire* (Oxford: Oxford University Press, 2015).

"Melkites," from Arabic *malik* and Syriac *melkā* ("king"), indicating that they were in communion with the imperial authorities at Constantinople. In the modern period, this name is used more narrowly, to refer to the Melkite Catholic Church.[2]

At the time of the Muslim conquests, living alongside the Eastern Orthodox there were three other Christian communions, all of which had split from the Eastern Orthodox over questions of Christology.

Living mainly beyond the eastern borders of the Byzantine Empire, in territories controlled by the Sassanids and further east, was the Church of the East. They had parted ways with the Eastern Orthodox over the Council of Ephesus (431 CE). This they rejected because they believed it to have compromised the full humanity of the incarnate Son. Historically, they have been called "Nestorians" by their opponents, after Nestorius (died after 451 CE), the patriarch of Constantinople, who had been deposed by the Council of Ephesus.[3]

In Egypt and Syria were the churches of the Oriental Orthodox. The Oriental Orthodox were united by their rejection of the Council of Chalcedon (451 CE). They believed this council to have compromised the union of the incarnate Son's

2. For a brief overview of the history of the Eastern Orthodox under Islam, see the introduction to Samuel Noble and Alexander Treiger, eds., *The Orthodox Church in the Arab World, 700–1700: An Anthology of Sources* (DeKalb: Northern Illinois University Press, 2014), 3–39; as well as the running historical narrative in the opening sections to each volume of Joseph Nasrallah's *Histoire du mouvement littéraire dans l'Église Melchite du Ve au XXe siècle*, vols. 2.2, 3.1, 3.2, 4.1, 4.2 (Leuven: Peeters, 1979–89); vol. 2.1, ed. Rachid Haddad (Damascus: Institut Français de Damas, 1996); vols. 1 and 5, ed. Rachid Haddad (Beirut: Institut Français du Proche-Orient, 2016–17). On the use of the name "Melkites" to refer to the Eastern Orthodox, see Sidney H. Griffith, "'Melkites,' 'Jacobites,' and the Christological Controversies in Arabic in Third/Ninth-Century Syria," in *Syrian Christians under Islam: The First Thousand Years*, ed. David R. Thomas (Leiden: Brill, 2001), 9–55; and Griffith, "The Church of Jerusalem and the 'Melkites': The Making of an 'Arab Orthodox' Christian Identity in the World of Islam (750–1050 CE)," in *Christians and Christianity in the Holy Land: From the Origins to the Latin Kingdom.*, ed. Ora Limor and Guy G. Stroumsa (Turnhout: Brepols, 2006), 175–204.

3. For the Council of Ephesus, see Leo D. Davis, *The First Seven Ecumenical Councils (325–787): Their History and Theology* (Wilmington, DE: Glazier, 1983; repr. Collegeville, MN: Liturgical Press, 1990), 134–69. For the history of the Church of the East, see Aziz S. Atiya, *A History of Eastern Christianity* (London: Methuen, 1968), 237–302; Wilhelm Baum and Dietmar W. Winkler, *The Church of the East: A Concise History* (London: RoutledgeCurzon, 2003); Christoph Baumer, *The Church of the East: An Illustrated History of Assyrian Christianity*, new ed. (London: Tauris, 2016); David Wilmshurst, *The Martyred Church: A History of the Church of the East* (London: East & West, 2011); and Dan King, ed., *The Syriac World* (London: Routledge, 2019), 120–23, 188–201. For the Church of the East's theology, and its relation to Nestorius, see Sebastian P. Brock, "The Christology of the Church of the East," in *Traditsii i nasledie khristianskogo Vostoka (Traditions and Heritage of the Christian East)*, ed. D. E. Afinogenov and A. V. Murav'ev (Moscow: Indrik, 1996), 159–79; and Brock, "The 'Nestorian' Church: A Lamentable Misnomer," *Bulletin of the John Rylands University Library of Manchester* 78 (1996): 23–35.

divine and human natures. While these churches have historically been called "monophysite," or more recently "miaphysite," today this body of churches is more often called the Oriental Orthodox Church, a communion of churches that encompasses a variety of geographically and culturally distinct churches: from Ethiopia, Eritrea, and Egypt, to Syro-Palestine, to Armenia, to India.[4]

In Egypt, the Oriental Orthodox who rejected Chalcedon comprised the Coptic Orthodox Church, called "Copts" from the Greek name for Egyptians (*Aigyptoi*), which entered Arabic as *Qibṭ*. After Chalcedon, the once united line of patriarchal succession in Alexandria had split into two rival hierarchies: one for the Eastern Orthodox and one for the Copts (the former being largely urban and much the smaller of the two; the latter having struck deep roots in the Egyptian countryside).[5]

In Syro-Palestine, and in regions further east, another branch of the Oriental Orthodox was to be found: the Syrian Orthodox. Historically they have been called "Jacobites," after Jacob Baradaeus (died 578 CE), who helped establish a hierarchy independent of the Eastern Orthodox. Like the Copts in Egypt, they formed a rival line of succession to the patriarchate of Antioch. It is likely that the Syrian Orthodox outnumbered their more urban Eastern Orthodox neighbors, although not to the same extent as did the Copts in Egypt.[6]

The origins of the Maronites, a third line of succession to the patriarchate of Antioch, are obscure, and until today controversial. The Maronites had their beginnings in Syria, to the south of Antioch and seem to have been closely associated with the Monastery of Saint Maron, from which they took their name.

4. For the Council of Chalcedon, see Davis, *First Seven Ecumenical Councils*, 207–57. For theological opposition to Chalcedon, see Sebastian P. Brock, "Miaphysite, not Monophysite!" *Cristianesimo nella storia* 37 (2016): 45–54; W. H. C. Frend, *The Rise of the Monophysite Movement: Chapters in the History of the Church in the Fifth and Sixth Centuries* (London: Cambridge University Press, 1972); and Dietmar W. Winkler, "Miaphysitism: A New Term for Use in the History of Dogma and in Ecumenical Theology," *Harp* 10 (1997): 33–40.

5. For the history of the Coptic Orthodox Church, see Atiya, *History of Eastern Christianity*, 11–144; Stephen J. Davis and Gawdat Gabra, eds., *The Popes of Egypt: A History of the Coptic Church and Its Patriarchs from Saint Mark to Pope Shenouda III*, 3 vols. (Cairo: American University in Cairo Press, 2004–11), esp. vols. 2–3; Lois Farag, ed., *The Coptic Christian Heritage: History, Faith, and Culture* (London: Routledge, 2013); Theodore H. Partrick, *Traditional Egyptian Christianity: A History of the Coptic Orthodox Church* (Greensboro, NC: Fisher Park, 1996); and Nelly van Doorn-Harder and Kari Vogt, eds., *Between Desert and City: The Coptic Orthodox Church Today* (Eugene, OR: Wipf & Stock, 2012).

6. For the history of the Syriac Orthodox Church, see Atiya, *History of Eastern Christianity*, 167–235; Sebastian P. Brock et al., eds., *The Hidden Pearl: The Aramaic Heritage*, 4 vols. (Piscataway, NJ: Gorgias, 2001); King, *Syriac World*; and Fergus Millar, "The Evolution of the Syrian Orthodox Church in the Pre-Islamic Period: From Greek to Syriac?" *Journal of Early Christian Studies* 21 (2013): 43–92.

According to most modern academic investigators, the Maronites were originally adherents of the Council of Chalcedon who shortly before the Muslim conquests adopted monothelitism. This was a christological comprise sponsored by imperial authorities, meant to reconcile the defenders of Chalcedon with its detractors. It affirmed that the incarnate Son had but a single divine will, and not two wills, one human and one divine. Monothelitism would later be condemned at the Sixth Ecumenical Council (681 CE).[7]

At the time of the Crusades, the Maronites began the process of entering into union with the Roman Catholic Church, such that today they represent one of the region's largest Eastern-rite Catholic churches. In later centuries, segments of the other Middle Eastern churches would also split from their parent bodies and enter into union with Rome. Historically called "uniate churches," these Eastern-rite Catholic churches include the Chaldean Catholic Church, which began to split from the Church of the East in the sixteenth century; the Syrian Catholic Church, which split from the Syrian Orthodox Church in the seventeenth century; the Coptic Catholic Church, which split from the Coptic Church in the eighteenth century; and lastly, the Melkite Catholic Church, which split from the Eastern Orthodox in the eighteenth century.[8]

Other churches and religious organizations as well have had a significant presence in the Arabic-speaking Middle East and have contributed to the growth of Christian Arabic literature, especially in the early modern and modern periods. These include the Armenian Catholic Church (which split from the Armenian Apostolic Church, an Oriental Orthodox Church, and entered into union with Rome in the eighteenth century), with a significant presence in Syria and Lebanon.[9] So too, various Roman Catholic religious orders—especially, the Franciscans, Capuchins, and Jesuits—have been and are active in the region, and

7. For the Sixth Ecumenical Council, see Davis, *First Seven Ecumenical Councils*, 207–57; and Cyril Hovorun, *Will, Action, and Freedom: Christological Controversies in the Seventh Century*, Medieval Mediterranean 77 (Leiden: Brill, 2008), esp. 53–102. For the controversy surrounding the origins of the Maronite Church, see Jack Tannous, "In Search of Monotheletism," *Dumbarton Oaks Papers* 68 (2014): 29–67; and Harald Suermann, "Maronite Historiography and Ideology," *Journal of Eastern Christian Studies* 54 (2002): 129–48. For the history of the Maronite Church, see Atiya, *History of Eastern Christianity*, 391–423; King, *Syriac World*, 731–50; and Harald Suermann, *Die Gründungsgeschichte der Maronitischen Kirche*, Orientalia Biblica et Christiana 10 (Harrassowitz: Wiesbaden, 1998).

8. For the Eastern-rite Catholic churches of the Mideast, see Alastair Hamilton, *The Copts and the West, 1439–1822: The European Discovery of the Egyptian Church* (Oxford: Oxford University Press, 2006), 49–103; King, *Syriac World*, 126–29; and Aidan Nichols, *Rome and the Eastern Churches: A Study in Schism*, 2nd ed. (San Francisco: Ignatius, 2010).

9. Georg Graf, *Geschichte der christlichen arabischen Literatur*, 5 vols (Vatican: Biblioteca Apostolica Vaticana, 1944–53), 4:82–93.

through their educational activities in particular have made important contributions to the development of Christian Arabic literature.[10] As well, since the nineteenth century, various Protestant denominations have established a small but vibrant presence in the region, with a sizable output of Christian literature in Arabic.[11]

While there were certainly Arabic-speaking Christians prior to the rise of Islam, those Christians have left few literary remains in Arabic, aside from the occasional inscription or pieces of poetry preserved in later texts (often of dubious authenticity).[12] Most likely these Arabic-speaking Christians would have known Christianity primarily through the main literary and spoken languages of their more settled neighbors: Syriac and Greek, in particular. Within about a century of the Muslim conquests, however, with the spread of fluency in Arabic among the Christians living under Islam, the various branches of Middle-Eastern Christianity began the long and halting process of adopting Arabic as a language for ecclesiastical use.

In no church would Arabic ever entirely displace the older languages of liturgy and theology. Instead, it tended to coexist alongside other, more traditional languages: Greek and Coptic in Egypt; Greek and Syriac in Syro-Palestine; Syriac in the former territories of Sassanid Persia. As one enters the early modern and modern periods, Arabic tended to play a larger role in the lives of most of the churches in the Arabic-speaking Middle East, especially as languages like Coptic and Syriac had long since ceased to be living languages. That said, it is difficult to imagine any of these churches ever adopting Arabic as their sole language: the prestige of the traditional liturgical languages remains high, and all of these churches have today grown far too geographically diverse, with growing diasporas and accelerating emigration to North America, Europe, Australia, South America, and elsewhere.

Unsurprisingly, as Christians began to adopt Arabic as their spoken language, the most urgent task was to translate the biblical and liturgical texts needed for the daily life of the church. Simultaneously, efforts were begun to convey large

---

10. Graf, *Geschichte der christlichen arabischen Literatur*, 4:169–271.

11. Dated but still valuable is Graf's discussion at *Geschichte der christlichen arabischen Literatur*, 4:272–85.

12. There is a rich literature on the history of Christianity among the Arabs prior to the rise of Islam. See Greg Fisher, Philip Wood, et al., "Arabs and Christianity," in *Arabs and Empires before Islam*, ed. Greg Fisher (Oxford: Oxford University Press, 2015), 276–372; and Theresia Hainthaler, *Christliche Araber vor dem Islam: Verbreitung und konfessionelle Zugehörigkeit: Eine Hinführung*, Eastern Christian Studies 7 (Leuven: Peeters, 2007). J. Spencer Trimingham's *Christianity among the Arabs in Pre-Islamic Times* (London: Longman, 1979) is dated, but still valuable.

parts of the massive patristic heritage into Arabic. Much effort was devoted to this task in the various centers of Christianity throughout the Muslim world: in Alexandria and Cairo, in Jerusalem, in Damascus and Antioch, in Baghdad, as well as in the larger monastic establishments of the various Christian churches. The enormity of what was accomplished by these translators is staggering and includes translations not just of liturgical and biblical texts, but also of lives of saints, works of patristic theology and exegesis, and so forth. Translated initially were works in Greek, Syriac, and Coptic. From the early modern period onward, among Eastern-rite Catholics especially, an enormous amount of Latin theological literature too was translated into Arabic, as well as religious literature from various modern European languages.[13]

Original theological compositions in Arabic took slightly longer to begin to flourish, but already by the late eighth and early ninth centuries the process had begun. The literature that was produced falls into a variety of genres: polemic and apologetic literature directed against rival churches, as well as against Jews and Muslims; scholastic theology in the Aristotelian tradition; works of canon law; hagiography; history, both local chronicles and world histories; religious poetry; homilies and hymns; catechetical literature; commentaries on Scripture and liturgical usage; and so forth.[14]

The standard work of reference for Christian Arabic literature (Georg Graf's *Geschichte der christlichen arabischen Literatur*) consists of five large, densely

---

13. The entirety of the first volume of Graf's *Geschichte der christlichen arabischen Literatur* is devoted to biblical and patristic texts translated into Arabic. As well, Nasrallah's *Histoire du mouvement littéraire dans l'Église Melchite* includes, throughout, discussions of translations of biblical and patristic literature. See also Barbara Roggema and Alexander Treiger, eds., *Patristic Literature in Arabic Translations* (Leiden: Brill, 2019); and Samuel Rubenson, "Translating the Tradition: Some Remarks on the Arabization of the Patristic Heritage in Egypt," *Medieval Encounters* 2 (1996): 4–14. For the Bible in Arabic, see Sidney H. Griffith, *The Bible in Arabic: The Scriptures of the "People of the Book" in the Language of Islam* (Princeton: Princeton University Press, 2013); *Bibliography of the Arabic Bible* (online at https://biblia-arabica.com/bibl/index .html); as well as Brill's monograph series "Biblia Arabica: Texts and Studies." Arabic versions of Latin and vernacular European theological literature are discussed throughout the fourth volume of Graf's *Geschichte der christlichen arabischen Literatur*.

14. On the earliest Christian Arabic literature, see Sidney H. Griffith, *The Church in the Shadow of the Mosque: Christians and Muslims in the World of Islam* (Princeton: Princeton University Press, 2008); Griffith, "The Monks of Palestine and the Growth of Christian Literature in Arabic," *Muslim World* 78 (1988): 1–28. The key authors and texts are discussed in vol. 2 of Graf's *Geschichte der christlichen arabischen Literatur*. For early Christian Arabic literature produced by the Eastern Orthodox, see Nasrallah, *Histoire du mouvement littéraire dans l'Église Melchite*, vol. 2.2.

packed volumes.[15] For all that, it is incomplete, as its author did his work nearly seventy years ago and had limited access to many important manuscript collections in the Middle East. To this day, the greater part of Christian Arabic literature exists only in manuscript form. It has been estimated—reasonably, I think—that as much as ninety percent of surviving Christian Arabic literature remains unedited.[16] Including both edited and unedited literature, it seems likely that the amount of surviving Christian Arabic literature in manuscript form is larger than that in Syriac and Coptic combined.

Given the scale and diversity of Christian Arabic literature, no set of selections can hope to provide an overview of the tradition as a whole, and no such attempt is made here. Instead, the selections included are intended to give just a glimpse of the tradition's richness. I tried to choose readings that are self-contained and accessible, on topics that will hopefully be of interest to nonspecialists, especially to those coming from Western Christian backgrounds. To my knowledge, none of the materials translated here has ever appeared in English before.[17]

Bibliography

Overviews of Christianity in the Middle East

Atiya, Aziz S. *A History of Eastern Christianity*. London: Methuen, 1968.

Bailey, Betty Jane, and J. Martin Bailey. *Who Are the Christians in the Middle East?* 2nd ed. Grand Rapids: Eerdmans, 2010.

Cragg, Kenneth. *The Arab Christian: A History in the Middle East*. Louisville: Westminster John Knox, 1991.

Dalrymple, William. *From the Holy Mountain: A Journey among the Christians of the*

---

15. For the Arabic literature of the Eastern Orthodox and Melkite Catholics, Nasrallah's *Histoire du mouvement littéraire dans l'Église Melchite* forms an essential supplement to Graf's *Geschichte*. Similarly, for the Arabic literature of the Maronites, Graf must be read alongside Michael Breydy, *Geschichte der Syro-Arabischen Literatur der Maroniten vom VII. bis XVI. Jahrhundert* (Opladen, Germany: Westdeutscher Verlag, 1985). For any Christian Arabic texts that have to do with Muslims, David Thomas et al., eds. *Christian-Muslim Relations: A Bibliographical History*, 13 volumes to date (Leiden: Brill, 2009–), esp. vols. 1–5, 7, 10–12, is absolutely essential and contains up-to-date bibliographies of secondary literature.

16. Noble and Treiger, *Orthodox Church in the Arab World*, 5.

17. As the present contribution was being prepared for publication, an unpublished translation of Ḥunayn's *How to Discern the True Religion* was brought to my attention; see Stephen J. Davis, "Hunayn ibn Isḥāq, On How to Discern the Truth of Religion," *Early Church Fathers: Additional Texts* (online at www.tertullian.org/fathers/sbath_20.1_Hunain_ibn_Ishaq.htm).

Middle East. New York: Holt, 1997 (with numerous reprints, including under the title *From the Holy Mountain: A Journey in the Shadow of Byzantium*).

Griffith, Sidney H. *The Church in the Shadow of the Mosque: Christians and Muslims in the World of Islam.* Princeton: Princeton University Press, 2008.

Jenkins, Philip. *The Lost History of Christianity: The Thousand-Year Golden Age of the Church in the Middle East, Africa, and Asia—and How It Died.* New York: HarperCollins, 2008.

Pacini, Andrea, ed. *Christian Communities in the Arab Middle East: The Challenge of the Future.* Oxford: Clarendon, 1998.

Roberson, Ronald, G. *The Eastern Christian Churches: A Brief Survey.* 7th ed. Rome: Orientalia Christiana, 2008 (available online at the Catholic Near East Welfare Association website).

Thomas, David. "Arab Christianity." Pages 1–22 in *The Blackwell Companion to Eastern Christianity.* Edited by Ken Parry. Oxford: Wiley-Blackwell, 2007.

On the Doctrinal Controversies Leading to the Fragmentation of Middle Eastern Christianity

Davis, Leo D. *The First Seven Ecumenical Councils (325–787): Their History and Theology.* Wilmington, DE: Glazier, 1983 (repr. Collegeville, MN: Liturgical, 1990).

Frend, W. H. C. *The Rise of the Monophysite Movement: Chapters in the History of the Church in the Fifth and Sixth Centuries.* London: Cambridge University Press, 1972.

Hovorun, Cyril. *Will, Action, and Freedom: Christological Controversies in the Seventh Century.* Medieval Mediterranean 77. Leiden: Brill, 2008.

Tannous, Jack. "In Search of Monotheletism." *Dumbarton Oaks Papers* 68 (2014): 29–67.

On the Arab Conquests

Donner, Fred. *The Early Islamic Conquests.* Princeton: Princeton University Press, 1981.

Hoyland, Robert G. *In God's Path: The Arab Conquests and the Creation of an Islamic Empire.* Oxford: Oxford University Press, 2015.

Kennedy, Hugh. *The Great Arab Conquests: How the Spread of Islam Changed the World We Live In.* Philadelphia: Da Capo, 2007.

On Christianity among the Arabs in the Pre-Islamic Period

Fisher, Greg, Philip Wood, et al. "Arabs and Christianity." Pages 276–372 in *Arabs and Empires before Islam.* Edited by Greg Fisher. Oxford: Oxford University Press, 2015.

Hainthaler, Theresia. *Christliche Araber vor dem Islam: Verbreitung und konfessio-
    nelle Zugehörigkeit: Eine Hinführung.* Eastern Christian Studies 7. Leuven:
    Peeters, 2007.
Shahîd, Irfan. *Byzantium and the Arabs.* 7 vols. Washington, DC: Dumbarton Oaks,
    1984–2009 (available online at https://www.doaks.org).
Trimingham, J. Spencer. *Christianity among the Arabs in Pre-Islamic Times.* London:
    Longman, 1979.

On the Eastern Orthodox Churches of the Mideast

Griffith, Sidney H. "The Church of Jerusalem and the 'Melkites': The Making of an
    'Arab Orthodox' Christian Identity in the World of Islam (750–1050 CE)." Pages
    175–204 in *Christians and Christianity in the Holy Land: From the Origins to the
    Latin Kingdom.* Edited by Ora Limor and Guy G. Stroumsa. Turnhout: Bre-
    pols, 2006.
———. "'Melkites,' 'Jacobites,' and the Christological Controversies in Arabic in Third/
    Ninth-Century Syria." Pages 9–55 in *Syrian Christians under Islam: The First
    Thousand Years.* Edited by David R. Thomas. Leiden: Brill, 2001.
———. "The Monks of Palestine and the Growth of Christian Literature in Arabic."
    Muslim World 78 (1988): 1–28.
Noble, Samuel, and Alexander Treiger, eds. *The Orthodox Church in the Arab World,
    700–1700: An Anthology of Sources.* DeKalb: Northern Illinois University
    Press, 2014.
Panchenko, Constantin A. *Arab Orthodox Christians under the Ottomans, 1516–1831.*
    Translated by Brittany Pheiffer Noble and Samuel Noble. Jordanville, NY: Holy
    Trinity Seminary Press, 2016 (originally published in Russian in 2012).
Treiger, Alexander. "The Arabic Tradition." Pages 89–104 in *The Orthodox Christian
    World.* Edited by Augustine Casiday. London: Routledge, 2012.

On the Church of the East, Syrian Orthodox, and Maronites

Baum, Wilhelm, and Dietmar W. Winkler. *The Church of the East: A Concise History.*
    London: RoutledgeCurzon, 2003.
Baumer, Christoph. *The Church of the East: An Illustrated History of Assyrian Christian-
    ity.* New ed. London: Tauris, 2016.
Brock, Sebastian P. "The Christology of the Church of the East." Pages 159–79 in *Tra-
    ditsii i nasledie khristianskogo Vostoka (Traditions and Heritage of the Christian
    East).* Edited by D. E. Afinogenov and A. V. Murav'ev. Moscow: Indrik, 1996.
———. "Miaphysite, Not Monophysite!" *Cristianesimo nella storia* 37 (2016): 45–54.
———. "The 'Nestorian' Church: A Lamentable Misnomer." *Bulletin of the John Rylands
    University Library of Manchester* 78 (1996): 23–35.

Millar, Fergus. "The Evolution of the Syrian Orthodox Church in the Pre-Islamic Period: From Greek to Syriac?" *Journal of Early Christian Studies* 21 (2013): 43–92.

Suermann, Harald. *Die Gründungsgeschichte der Maronitischen Kirche.* Orientalia Biblica et Christiana 10. Harrassowitz: Wiesbaden, 1998.

———. "Maronite Historiography and Ideology." *Journal of Eastern Christian Studies* 54 (2002): 129–48.

Wilmshurst, David. *The Martyred Church: A History of the Church of the East.* London: East & West, 2011.

Winkler, Dietmar W. "Miaphysitism: A New Term for Use in the History of Dogma and in Ecumenical Theology." *Harp* 10 (1997): 33–40.

On Eastern-Rite Catholic Churches and Protestantism in the Mideast

Brock, Sebastian P. "The Christology of the Church of the East." Pages 159–79 in *Traditsii i nasledie khristianskogo Vostoka* (*Traditions and Heritage of the Christian East*). Edited by D. E. Afinogenov and A. V. Murav'ev. Moscow: Indrik, 1996.

Hamilton, Alastair. *The Copts and the West, 1439–1822: The European Discovery of the Egyptian Church.* Oxford: Oxford University Press, 2006.

Nichols, Aidan. *Rome and the Eastern Churches: A Study in Schism.* 2nd ed. San Francisco: Ignatius, 2010.

Roccasalvo, Joan L. *The Eastern Catholic Churches: An Introduction to Their Worship and Spirituality.* Collegeville, MN: Liturgical Press, 1992.

Sharkey, Heather J. *American Evangelicals in Egypt: Missionary Encounters in an Age of Empire.* Princeton: Princeton University Press, 2008.

Tejirian, Eleanor, and Reeva Spector Simon. *Conflict, Conquest, and Conversion: Two Thousand Years of Christian Missions in the Middle East.* New York: Columbia University Press, 2012.

On the Translation of Patristic and Biblical Works into Arabic

Griffith, Sidney H. *The Bible in Arabic: The Scriptures of the "People of the Book" in the Language of Islam.* Princeton: Princeton University Press, 2013.

Roggema, Barbara, and Alexander Treiger, eds. *Patristic Literature in Arabic Translations.* Leiden: Brill, 2019.

Rubenson, Samuel. "Translating the Tradition: Some Remarks on the Arabization of the Patristic Heritage in Egypt." *Medieval Encounters* 2 (1996): 4–14.

Reference Works on the History of Christian Arabic Literature

Breydy, Michael. *Geschichte der Syro-Arabischen Literatur der Maroniten vom VII. bis XVI. Jahrhundert.* Opladen, Germany: Westdeutscher Verlag, 1985.

Graf, Georg. *Geschichte der christlichen arabischen Literatur.* 5 vols. Vatican: Biblioteca Apostolica Vaticana, 1944–53.

Nasrallah, Joseph. *Histoire du mouvement littéraire dans l'Église Melchite du Vᵉ au XXᵉ siècle.* Vols. 2.2, 3.1, 3.2, 4.1, 4.2. Leuven: Peeters, 1979–89.

———. *Histoire du mouvement littéraire dans l'Église Melchite du Vᵉ au XXᵉ siècle.* Vol. 2.1. Edited by Rachid Haddad. Damascus: Institut Français de Damas, 1996.

———. *Histoire du mouvement littéraire dans l'Église Melchite du Vᵉ au XXᵉ siècle.* Vols. 1 and 5. Edited by Rachid Haddad. Beirut: Institut Français du Proche-Orient, 2016–17.

Thomas, David, et al., eds. *Christian-Muslim Relations: A Bibliographical History.* 13 volumes to date. Leiden: Brill, 2009– (for Christian writings in Arabic, see esp. vols. 1–5, 7, 10–12; online from Brill).

1. *Homilies on the Gospel Readings for Holy Week*

Introduction and translation by John C. Lamoreaux

The first reading is taken from an anonymous series of Eastern Ortho-dox *Homilies on the Gospel Readings for Holy Week*. These homilies are found in *Sinai ar. 507*, folios 1r–107r, which was copied at Sinai in 1473 CE.[1] A number of folios are missing at the beginning of the text, but presumably the original title page once attributed the homilies to John Chrysostom, as do the present titles of the individual homilies. Chrysostom cannot have been their author. In the course of one homily (folio 92r), the author states that the Jews have been exiled from Jerusalem for 1,121 years, since the destruction of Jerusalem by the Romans forty years after the cruci-fixion.[2] Accordingly, the text must have been written sometime around 1191 CE, that is, just a few years after the fall of Crusader Jerusalem to the Ayyubids. The homilies are largely typological and comprised mostly of brief comments on the scriptural texts, but those comments are often interwoven with more extended theological reflections. The selections translated below are from the homily on Luke 23:32–49 (folios 83r–99r), from the section containing homilies on the Twelve Gospels, read on the evening of Holy Thursday. These selections treat the manner of human-ity's salvation from slavery to Satan, by Satan's payment of blood money (*diyah*) as his punishment for having unjustly killed Christ.

---

1. A colophon states (folio 107r) that the text was copied at Sinai by a monk named Ephrem, in Nīsān 6981 AM, that is April 1473 CE. I am unaware of other copies of this series of homilies. It does not seem to have been mentioned by Graf in his *Geschichte der christlichen arabischen Literatur*, and while Nasrallah mentions it, he seems to have known no other copies (*Histoire du mouvement littéraire dans l'Église Melchite*, 3.2:210).

2. The destruction of Jerusalem is also dated to forty years after the crucifixion at folio 20r. There too the author says that "over one thousand years have passed" since Jerusalem was destroyed by the Romans.

Homilies on the Gospel Readings for Holy Week

My brothers and my beloved, understand this: when a slave and a bondsman has been manumitted by his master and become free, and he then goes and willingly sells himself to a second master, becoming his bondsman, reduced again to the state of a slave, his first lord is unable to seize him from his new master, and if he does so, he acts unjustly.

As for Adam, God created him free, independent, able to make choices, and master of his own will, and "in the image and likeness of God," for even as God is master of his own will, so too did he create man. Saying that "he created him according to his image" means that he created him like himself: free, with the ability to make choices, and master of his own will.

As long as Adam willingly enslaves himself to his creator, he merits the greatest honor from him, because he was able not to enslave himself to him, whereas if he does not enslave himself to him, he merits the greatest dishonor from him, because he was able to enslave himself to him, but did not do so.[3]

When God created Adam and placed him in paradise, he forbade him to eat from one tree out of all the trees in paradise, making it clear to him that a dreadful punishment will befall him if he disobeys and eats, for he said to him: "If you do that, you will die." In giving this command, it was God's wish that should Adam willingly obey, he would merit being made forever unable to die, even as his creator. It was also made clear to Adam that he would die should he disobey.

Satan then said to Adam: "Your creator lied to you when he said that you will die if you eat of the tree. Rather, he knew that if you eat of it you will become like God, knowing good and evil, and thus he forbade you from eating of it. God was too miserly to allow you to become like himself, and thus he caused you to fear death to prevent you from doing this."

The wretched man thus waxed proud and lusted after divinity. He believed that his creator was a liar and a miser: a miser toward him with respect to divinity and a liar in saying that he will die. And he immediately obeyed Satan, who had deceived him, and he ate of the tree, and he straightaway became his slave—and

---

3. Omitting lines 2–4 of folio 83v (from *li-kawni-hi* up to *li-kawni-hi*). The scribe's eye skipped, and he wrote a number of lines twice.

this, of necessity, for he was free, and yet he willingly and through his own lust sold himself.

When Adam chewed and swallowed the fruit of disobedience, he caused the unclean spirit to enter into him. This spirit in truth is death, and it drags into sin anyone in whom it dwells. Through trickery and deception such as Satan perpetrated on Adam, as well as through sin, man thus merits death, for Satan is death, and sin and death come through his temptation and deception.

What God had said to Adam was thus confirmed, that he would die should he eat of the tree, for Satan, who is death, entered and dwelled in him, and came to own him, whereas the Spirit of God, who is life, who before[4] that death used to dwell in him, blessing and delighting him, went forth from him and departed from him.

The spirit of life withdrew from him, and the spirit of death came to dwell in him. So too, the spirit of death began to dwell in everyone born of human seed: from the moment they are born it dwells in them, even until they grow up and reach understanding, and find that the tempter and seducer dwells in them, leading them into every sin.

Life withdrew from the soul and death came to dwell in it. So too, the soul began to withdraw from the body, such that it dies and returns to dust, while the soul descends into hell, beneath the earth, for because it obeyed Satan an ascent to heaven was no longer possible for it.

Man came to be entirely deprived of life, for when God said to him: "When you eat of the tree, you will die," he did not also say to him: "You will be restored to life." God thus says that unceasing death came to be required of him and necessary for him, and for all his offspring, as he is the father of all.

When Iblīs[5] took ownership of Adam, he also took ownership of Adam's offspring, and it became impossible for God to take them from him by force, because of his justice.

The accursed and wicked Iblīs then boasted of his wickedness, thinking that he had overcome and conquered the wisdom of God through his own wisdom. It is as the prophet David said: "Why do you boast of wickedness, O mighty one?"[6] And again, the prophet Isaiah says that someone boasting was overthrown and that this someone says: "By the strength of my hand I shall do it and by the wisdom of my mouth I shall change the boundaries of the nations and plunder their strength. And I shall fight with the inhabited cities and I shall conquer the

---

4. Reading *qabla* for *qatala*.

5. *Iblīs* is another name for Satan in the Muslim tradition. The name is perhaps derived from Greek *diabolos* ("devil").

6. Ps 52:1.

whole world, and in my hand I shall gather it like a nest, as eggs are gathered. And there is no one who will escape from my hand and no one who will answer me in what I say or open his mouth, and no one who will talk nonsense."[7] All of this boasting here described by God pertains to him.

After Satan overcame and conquered Adam and made him his own, both him and all his offspring, the wicked one said to himself: "It is forever impossible for Adam and his offspring to be restored to life, because of God's truthfulness and his justice, for God's truthfulness and his justice will prevent them from being restored to life and from being set free from slavery to me." As for God's truthfulness, this is because he told them that they will die—but without giving any promise of life. As for his justice, this is because they were endowed with freedom.

The wicked one said: "They willingly sold themselves to me, and his justice is unable to take them from me by force." Because of this notion, the prophet says: "The sinner said in his heart: 'I shall not cease, from generation to generation, with acts of wickedness.'"[8] And again, he says: "God has forgotten the wretch, and he has forever turned his face aside."[9] Iblīs was thus assured in his heart that the salvation of human beings is forever impossible and that God is unable to save them, due to his truthfulness and his justice. It is as the prophet David said: "Many say to my soul, you have no salvation through your God."[10]

In his great mercy and wisdom, God thus contrived a plan whereby he saved them, while preserving his truthfulness and his justice, neither lying nor acting unjustly—namely, the incarnation of the Son of God and his crucifixion.

You who believe in the crucified one, listen and understand how in his great mercy and wisdom God contrived a plan to save us without lying or acting unjustly, to wit: the eternal Son of God, who is begotten of the Father before all time, who is from the Father, in the Father, and with the Father, as the rays of the sun are from its disk, true God in his hypostasis like his Father, the God of truth, even as the apostle Paul says that he is "the image of God"[11] and his likeness and "the likeness of his hypostasis,"[12] who is an incorporeal spirit, unseen and unlimited, like his father—the eternal Son of God, I say, by the will of his father and his wise plan, became incarnate and a human being.

---

7. Isa 10:12–14.

8. Ps 10:6 (9:27 LXX). The text reads *bi-l-aswā'*. It is tempting to emend this to *bi-lā sū'*, to bring the text closer to the Septuagint's *aneu kakou*, but this seems contrary to the sense of the author's argument.

9. Ps 10:11 (9:32 LXX).

10. Ps 3:2.

11. Col 1:15 and 2 Cor 4:4.

12. Heb 1:3.

He entered into the world, but without sin, and thus he did not merit death, for God imposed death on a sinful man or on those who are from the seed of the sinful Adam. He did not become a human being from the seed of the sinful Adam, but from the Holy Spirit and the Virgin Mary, he became a new man, without sin. He was not a man[13] like one born of the seed of Adam, but he was like Adam before he ate of the tree, humanity without sin. And thus, in no respect was death required of him, not with respect to God's promise of death, not with respect to the slavery of Iblīs.

In his great mercy he handed himself over to death, although death was not required of him. When he died in his humanity, his death became a ransom for all humanity, from whom his Father required death, for he freely handed himself over to death for their sakes, in order to ransom them from death and restore them[14] all to life. And by this means he and his Father[15] thus saved them through his death.

He showed himself to be truthful and he did not lie, for he who ransomed them by his death was equal to all of them, and indeed to very many more than them. He was not merely a man, such that the value of his death was minimal, but being true God become man, who although a man died a true death, his value was great, equal to and exceeding that of all men, and thus was he able to ransom them all.

By this death of his, he thus saved them from his Father's promise of death, and by it too he saved them from slavery to Iblīs, for when he appeared in the world, in his great wisdom he did not allow Iblīs to understand that he is God, nor did he permit him to understand that he is a man begotten of something other than the seed of Adam, for before he became man of the Virgin, he planned that she be betrothed to Joseph and enter into his household. When she conceived, Iblīs thus believed that she had conceived of Joseph.

Christ ensnared him through his wise plan, so that Iblīs might be put to shame—he who boasted of his wisdom and wickedness and believed that he had conceived a plot so wise that it would never be defeated. It is thus that the creator made a plan to defeat him though wisdom, not through power, so that he might never again boast, in order that he might fulfill the words of the prophetess Hannah, the mother of Samuel: "Let not the wise boast of his wisdom."[16]

Being blind of heart, Satan believed that the Virgin had conceived of Joseph. He did not reflect on the words of the prophet Isaiah, when he says that "the

---

13. Reading *al-insān* for *al-shayṭān*.
14. Reading *wa-yuʿīdu-hum* for *wa-yuʿabbidu-hum*.
15. Reading *huwa wa-abū-hu* for *min wa-abū-hu*.
16. 1 Sam 2:10 (LXX).

Virgin will conceive and bear a son, and his name will be called Immanuel,"[17] which means, God with us. Although blind of heart, had he pondered and understood this prophecy, the wise plan regarding the Son of God would not have been fulfilled. Rather, thereby, his ignorance became even more evident, since this prophecy concerned the Son and Iblīs did not understand this, although he boasted that he was wise.

Because Satan believed that Christ was a man of the seed of his slave Adam, he desired him to sin like all other men who are of the seed of Adam his slave. When Christ refused to heed him, Satan was filled with an incomparable wrath.

Because Christ was teaching human beings in his preaching that they must repent and not sin, being overcome by his great wrath, Satan compounded his wickedness, teaching it to the priests and elders, to make them envy and hate him. By this envy and hatred Satan blinded them, so that they were unable to recognize Christ's clear and manifest power, which was evident to all and in which the mass of the people believed, those whom envy and hatred had not blinded. Satan then incited them to kill him. He convinced them that they had to kill him, because otherwise he would cause the whole nation to be destroyed. The priests and elders said to themselves:

> As is clear to all, we are subject to the Romans and under their authority. Our people have proclaimed that this man is the Christ. The Romans, our masters, have heard us say and know well that we regard the Christ as a king who will make us rulers of the world and who will destroy our masters. When they hear us saying that this Christ is our king, and we flock to him, praising him and describing his great power, even as the rest of the nation now does, the Romans will quickly attack us and destroy us, because they see us behaving subversively against them with this new king from among us. If we do not make haste to destroy him, the Romans will destroy the whole nation because of him. We have but one option: we must seize him and hand him over to the Romans, telling them: "This man claims to be our king and he wants us to behave subversively against you. We do not concur with him in this, but see, we have handed him over to you." When we hand him over to them, we shall urge them to kill him, persisting in this until they kill him.

With regard to all this, it was Satan who was urging them and continually prompting them to do it.

After Christ died, he immediately seized Satan and required of him the blood money for his own death, rightfully demanding it from him. He then took all his

---

17. Isa 7:14.

property from him, as the blood money for his own death—namely, Adam and all his offspring. He justly took them from him, as the blood money for his own death. And thus by his death he saved us from the legal claim of his Father, as well as from slavery to Satan.

[Omitted: the remainder of the sermon, up to the final paragraph.]

Through his great wisdom Christ planned all his deeds and words, both before his incarnation and after it, so as to hide his divinity from Iblīs. Because Christ hid his divinity from him, Iblīs thought that he was just a man, and he then attacked him so as to kill him. And when the Lord died, he demanded blood money from him and he saved us from him through this blood money.

2. Theodore Abū Qurrah, *That God Is Not Weak*

Introduction and translation by John C. Lamoreaux

The second reading is an unpublished treatise by Theodore Abū Qurrah.[1] Living in the second half of the eighth and the early ninth centuries, Abū Qurrah was the Eastern Orthodox bishop of Haran (Ḥarrān)
and one of the first Christians to compose original works in Arabic.[2] In
his many surviving works he shows himself to be mainly a theological
controversialist, with a desire, first, to identify methods to establish which
is the true religion and, second, to find ways to prove that the Eastern
Orthodox Church is alone the true form of Christianity. Specific topics
to which he devoted his attention include the defense of the Councils
of Ephesus and Chalcedon against their Christian detractors, theological
epistemology, the refutation of Judaism and Islam, and the defense of
the veneration of icons. The present treatise is preserved—uniquely, it
seems—in *Damascus, Greek Orthodox Patriarchate 181* (according to the
numeration of the 1988 handlist; but formerly bearing the shelf mark 1616),
which was copied in 1561 CE.[3] In it Abū Qurrah argues that Christ's death
on the cross was the only way that God could save humanity from slavery
to Satan, without behaving in a manner inconsistent with his attributes of
justice, generosity, might, and wisdom. Abū Qurrah's opponents are not
specified by name, but given the monotheism he shares with them, and
the set of divine attributes he holds in common with them, they would
appear to be Jews and Muslims.

---

1. Its full title, likely assigned by a later scribe, is "The refutation of those who say that
Christians believe in a weak God, in that they say that Christ is God and that he was slapped,
struck, crucified, died and rose again." For this treatise, see Davis Thomas et al., eds., *Christian-
Muslim Relations: A Bibliographical History* (Leiden: Brill, 2009), 1:471–72.

2. For his biography and an English translation of many of his works, see John C. Lamoreaux, *Theodore Abū Qurrah*, Library of the Christian East 1 (Provo, UT: Brigham Young
University Press, 2005).

3. I wish to express my gratitude to Cyril Cairala, who some years ago kindly digitized for
me portions of this manuscript.

Bibliography

Studies

Lamoreaux, John C. *Theodore Abū Qurrah*. Library of the Christian East 1. Provo, UT: Brigham Young University Press, 2005.

That God Is Not Weak

My friends, as for what you say to us, the community of the Christians, namely, that Christ is weak because he was slapped, beaten, and crucified, and because he experienced pain, suffering, and fatigue, and that therefore he is not God—as for what you say, you have fallen into error and have not understood the reasons behind all this. Allow me to explain.

God is just, generous, mighty, and wise. Whoever does not attribute these four characteristics to God has caused him to be lacking, necessitated that he be defective, and made him to be something other than God. May he be exalted above that! What is *justice*? It is that he neither coerces those who are weak nor in his might forces them to do things, but that he deals with them equitably and wrongly seizes nothing that belongs to them, as well as that he gives them rightfully what they deserve from him. What is *generosity*? It is that when he is in a position to do something good for someone he must do so, he must grant it to him. What is *might*? It is that he has the ability to accomplish whatever he wishes and that there is nothing that he wants to do that he cannot do, as well as that he is not compelled to do anything, but that instead whatever he wants will exist, for as long as he wills it. What is *wisdom*? It is that he understands everything fully, that nothing is obscure to him, and that none of his plans can fail to be accomplished, as well as that he does not err in what he does. These are the four characteristics, and thus are they understood and interpreted by the erudite. Pay attention now as we propose a parable that will help to explain how these characteristics are joined together in God.

Imagine a king fully possessed of the four above-mentioned characteristics. This king has a friend whom he treats as well as he treats his own self. His friend stands in need of a certain shabby garment belonging to a certain impoverished beggar, one who is most weak. The friend of the king requests the garment from the beggar, who refuses to hand it over. At this, he takes the beggar to the king, and he says to the king: "I require this man's garment. Through it and it alone I shall benefit most greatly. I have asked him for it in every possible way, but he has refused me. My king, please take it from him for me." The king examines the matter in his wisdom and recognizes that his friend really and truly needs that garment, and his generosity urges him not to refuse him, in that it will be of benefit to him. It is thus his desire to give the garment to his friend. He thus says to the beggar: "Give it to him, and I shall reward you handsomely." To him the beggar[4] replies: "I shall never give it to him—unless, that is, you give me permission to slap your face while you are seated in your court in the presence of everyone."

Now then, tell me, what do you think the king[5] should do? In order to please his friend, do you think he should use force against that weak beggar with regard to his possessions? To do this, however, would be neither right nor fair. He cannot do it if in fact he is just. On the other hand, do you think that he should refuse to allow himself to be slapped, to avoid both the pain and the shame? This, too, would not be proper for him, if in fact he is generous. After all, if one who is generous refuses to undergo things that are odious when they are required of him, he would no longer be generous. If he is to do well by his friend, there is no other option—he must allow himself to be slapped.

Now then, imagine that this weak fellow goes up to the king and slaps him while he is sitting in his court with everyone looking on. What will they say? Fault will be found with this by those who are ignorant and confused, who refuse to search out the reasons and causes behind things, and they will be quick to regard the king as weak and to despise him. As for those who are wise, they will not judge precipitously, but they will reflect on matters in a considered manner, making inquiries of those in the know so as to understand the reason for this, and then they will praise the king for letting it happen, increasing yet further their admiration and high opinion of him. As for us, the Christian community, we to whom God has granted subtle minds and intellects characterized by consideration, we say that this is a parable for Christ.

That notwithstanding, you will respond. Your parable about this king is fitting, in the manner that you have exposited it, but tell us: What is it that compelled God to undertake this humble course of action and to suffer all that you Christians attribute to him?

We answer you as follows: When God created Adam, he gave him charge over himself and placed him in paradise. He showed him the path of wickedness and

4. Reading *qāla al-ṣaʿlūk* for *qāla li-l-ṣaʿlūk*.
5. Reading *li-l-malik* for *al-malik*.

carefully warned him against it, promising him death should he take that path. He had also created the angels and the devils in the same way that he created Adam, in terms of their having charge over themselves and freewill. When Iblīs saw how much beauty and felicity Adam enjoyed in paradise, he envied him for that and sought a way to deprive him of it. Because in creating Adam God had given him strength and had armed him generously with the ability to protect himself, Iblīs knew that the only way he could do this would be through deceit. He thus cunningly approached in disguise, and he said to Adam: "It was out of envy that God forbade you from this tree. He knew that if you were to eat of it, you would become like him." Adam believed Iblīs and disbelieved God, considering him to be a liar. He then took of the tree and ate, acting in enmity against God. At this, he was subject to the consequences[6] of death, and he lost his strength and became weak and sick with regard to his mind and his ability to exercise the freedom of his will. Now that he was in this state, Satan was able to vanquish him and take him as a slave. It was then that Adam recognized his error and that he was now subject to affliction in being a slave to Satan.[7] He thus threw himself down in sadness and began to call on God, beseeching him to save him from his error, to forgive him, and to rescue him from Iblīs.

In his mercy God thereupon desired to save Adam. If he were to go ahead and save him from Satan by force, however, he would transgress the limits of justice and only increase Iblīs's just claim, who would then open his foul mouth and say: "God cannot[8] save Adam from my hands without becoming unjust. If God acts unjustly in some matter that he wants to do, it is not right that I be blamed for causing Adam to slip[9] when I wanted to enslave him." As for Satan, there was no way that he would ever willingly release Adam. As for God, because he is just, he would never use force against Satan with regard to Adam. As for Adam, he was locked up in the possession of Satan, with no way being known for his deliverance from him.

You now, you should show us some clever stratagem by means of which Adam might be delivered from that into which he had fallen. You know no such clever stratagem, however, for you do not believe in Christ, our Lord and our God. Listen to us, then, and we shall explain to you the clever stratagem that we learned from the Holy Spirit—and perhaps your hearts will soften and the holy faith will take root in them.

---

6. Reading *tawābi'* for *s.w.a.y.q.*
7. The language here (*wa-massa-hu al-ḍurr*) is reminiscent of Qur'ān 7:95; 10:12; 30:33.
8. Reading *mā qadara Allāh* for *mā qadara Allāh mā qadara*.
9. For the language here (*fī izlālī li-Ādam*), cf. Qur'ān 2:36.

Here is an analogy for understanding this: with regard to what took place between God and Iblīs, God resembles a mighty king, one for whom nothing is difficult because of his strength,[10] but one who is also just. He sets his soldiers at liberty in a field, but establishes boundaries for them, saying: "Take care not to cross this boundary, and know that whoever crosses it will become a slave to the person who causes him to cross it." As for Satan, he resembles yet another man, one who is weak, and who is the first to cross that boundary, not because he is deceived by another, but because he yields to his own desire, and thus becomes a slave to desire. Like some beast or animal, he acts precipitously in that to which his desire stirs him, with difficulty restraining his desire. Thus does he renounce obedience to the king and become the leader of error and obduracy. He then begins to deceive those at liberty in that field, making use of their desires, by the likes of which he himself had been deceived and had crossed that boundary. He overcomes all of them, leading them forth from that field and taking possession of them. As for the mighty king, because of his justice he does not wish to use force against them. He thus makes use of a clever stratagem.

The king has a son, one like him in might, justice, majesty, and every other matter. He has his son disguise himself by taking on the appearance of those soldiers formerly at liberty in the field. When that wicked man sees him, he supposes him to be one of those soldiers, and he wishes to lead him astray even as he had led his companions astray. He applies himself to this task with all his strength, but he is unable to deceive him or to lead him astray as he had led his companions astray. When the rogue sees that this man will not submit to him and do as he wishes, he uses force against him: he attacks him and kills him without cause, committing an outrage against him, in that the king's son had not pledged himself to him as his companions had pledged themselves.

As for the king's son, he willingly allows himself to be killed by him, so that his father might regard it as justly permissible to reclaim his soldiers, whom that wicked man had overcome and enslaved. After the wicked man kills him, his father, the mighty king, accosts this accursed man, saying: "Did you not lead astray and enslave all whom I set at liberty in this field? And yet, did I use force against you with respect to any of them?" He says: "No." The king then says: "What of this man who stuck by me and remained in my domain? On what grounds did you kill him?" It is thus that the just claims of that weak and depraved man are annulled.

The mighty king then says: "As for this man, he is my son. You have acted unjustly in killing him. All the other men that you possess are not equal to him,

10. Reading *al-ṭāqah* for *al-laṭāfah*.

nor would an innumerably greater number of other men be equal to him. And so it is that you have now forfeited[11] your ability to use force." The mighty king then turns to the slaves of that weak man and saves them from his hands, and yet still he has not taken vengeance on him for the killing of his son, nor will he ever be able to do so, for there is nothing equal to the king's son.

It is in a similar manner that we speak of Christ's crucifixion and everything else that befell him. That is, he is the Son of God and he disguised himself from Satan. He clothed himself from the Virgin Mary in a body like our bodies, with a soul like our souls and a mind not different from our minds. He then went forth from her and walked about in the world. Satan thought him to be like one of us, and so he yearned to possess him and he desired to overcome him, even as he had overcome us. He was unable to do this, however. When Christ had thwarted his efforts, Satan flew into a rage and made bold to kill him. Because Satan had killed his Son, God was justly entitled to save us from slavery to him, as well as from its consequences, such as death and the like.

Do not think that when he was killed death touched his divinity. Far be that from him! No, death only touched his human clothing. As for all the other trials that befell him, each reached only so far as it had the ability and capacity to reach.

This then is proof that Christ was not weak when he suffered what is mentioned in the gospel, but that he did this out of his goodness and as a clever stratagem, for the sake of our salvation.

11. The manuscript reads *kh.s.n.t* or *ḥ.s.n.t*, which I tentatively emend to *khasirta*.

3. The Disputation of Abraham of Tiberias

Introduction and translation by John C. Lamoreaux

This text is taken from what purports to be the account of a theological disputation that occurred in Jerusalem at the court of Emir 'Abd al-Raḥmān al-Hāshimī (late eighth–early ninth centuries).[1] The main protagonist is a monk named Abraham of Tiberias (Ibrāhīm al-Ṭabarānī), who debates in turn three Muslims, besting them all, before finally performing a number of wonders and winning some converts, only to be thrown into prison but then released by the emir. If not wholly fictional, the text is at best a fictionalized account of an actual disputation. It is not known who its author was. He seems to have been Eastern Orthodox and to have lived sometime in the second half of the ninth century or in the tenth century. Whoever he was, he was well acquainted with both the Qur'ān and the details of Muslim religious law (sharī'ah). He was also a graceful stylist in Arabic. To judge from the number of copies surviving in manuscript form, the disputation was quite popular with Arabic-speaking Christians. It exists in two recensions: an earlier and a later, expanded version. The selections translated here are from the earlier recension, which is edited by Giacinto Būlus Marcuzzo.[2] These selections treat a variety of topics: why and how Christ became incarnate and willingly submitted to crucifixion; how Christ's miracles are superior to those of the prophets and confirm the incarnation; that Christ was truly crucified, contrary to the Qur'ān; and that the apostles' testimony about Christ was confirmed by miracles and the earliest manner of Christianity's spread.

1. On this text, see Graf, *Geschichte der christlichen arabischen Literatur*, 2:28–30; Nasrallah, *Histoire du mouvement littéraire dans l'Église Melchite*, 2.2:34–36; Thomas, *Christian-Muslim Relations*, 1:876–81. For an overview of Christian Arabic disputation texts with Muslims, a genre that was widely cultivated, see Sidney H. Griffith, "The Monk in the Emir's *Majlis*: Reflections on a Popular Genre of Christian Literary Apologetics in Arabic in the Early Islam Period," in *The Majlis: Interreligious Encounters in Medieval Islam*, ed. Hava Lazarus-Yafeh et al. (Wiesbaden: Harrassowitz, 1999), 13–65.

2. Giacinto Būlus Marcuzzo, *Le dialogue d'Abraham de Tibériade avec 'Abd al-Raḥmān al-Hāšimī à Jérusalem vers 820*, Textes et études sur l'Orient Chrétien 3 (Rome: Pontificia Universitas Lateranensis, 1986). The selections translated here (§§233–322 = pp. 372–411 in Marcuzzo's edition) were not included in the partial translation by Krisztina Szilágyi in Noble and Treiger, *Orthodox Church in the Arab World*, 90–111.

Bibliography

Texts and Studies

Marcuzzo, Giacinto Būlus. *Le dialogue d'Abraham de Tibériade avec 'Abd al-Raḥmān al-Hāšimī à Jérusalem vers 820*. Textes et études sur l'Orient Chrétien 3. Rome: Pontificia Universitas Lateranensis, 1986.

TRANSLATION

The Disputation of Abraham of Tiberias

The Muslim said:[3] "Tell me, monk, was God unable to execute his own commands while sitting on his throne, such that he needed to choose this man,[4] as you say?"

The monk said:[5] "I wonder at how poorly you understand the methods of rational theology."

[Omitted: a brief digression (from the latter half of §234 to §239) where the author compares the Son's residing in Christ to God's sitting on his throne.]

"Let us return to your question: 'Was God unable to execute his own commands?' Surely he has the ability, power, and capability to do so. Nevertheless, his essence remains invisible, indescribable, and incomprehensible, and he is neither reckoned nor regarded to be a created being whose words can be heard and who can be seen, even as Moses, the prophets, and the apostles informed us. Thus, when God saw that human hearts had become corrupt and that their inner selves were becoming still more wicked and were even more persistently opposing the truth, such that they were deviating yet more from the faith in him to which he had called them, the eternal God clothed himself in humanity and appeared. He then guided human beings with his wisdom, grace, and mercy, delivering them from the error and unbelief to which they were subject because of their worship of Iblīs and leading them to the truth. God the Word

---

3. Speaking here is Manẓūr Ghaṭafān al-ʿAbsī, one of the three Muslim interlocutors in the disputation.
4. That is, Christ.
5. That is, Abraham of Tiberias.

did not appear in his essence, however, nor did he depart from his essence. He did not descend from his abode to an abode where he was not. The throne was not deprived of him. The heavens and the earth and what lays between them were not deprived of him. The lowest habitation and the highest habitation were not deprived of him. He did this by being transcendent-not-immanent and immanent-not-transcendent—in a manner that is without description, limit, mixture, and separation."

The Muslim said: "The people did not obey Christ. Instead, they humiliated him with the cross, as you yourselves claim."

The monk said: "By my life, he was received by those whom he chose, those on whom he had mercy, those whom he made to understand his ways and to become obedient to him. As for those who did not receive him, they are the Jews, who are accursed unbelievers. Consider Christ's hidden plan for our salvation, how he performed signs and wonders among them. That is to say, he did not venture to summon people to anything, without first presenting them with proofs, through the signs and wonders he performed among them. He thus showed them very clearly that all his deeds were the deeds of God, until at last they confessed that he is the Son of the living God. Because of the great wickedness of the Israelites, the corruption of their hearts, and their envy, they paid no attention to his deeds, nor did they reflect on the divine Scriptures, but instead they rejected him, as we have said. He did not surrender himself into their hands because he was incapable or weak, but he did this out of his wisdom and mercy, willing it for the sake of the plan for our salvation, neither did he cause the Jews to be punished immediately, as he knew that they would not escape punishment."[6]

The Muslim said: "You Christians exalt Christ only because he brought the dead to life. The prophets Elisha and Ezekiel, as well as other prophets, however, also brought the dead to life.[7] One must not take everyone who with the permission of God brings the dead to life to be a god and a lord worthy of worship."

The monk said: "We do not take Christ to be God solely because he brought the dead to life. Rather, he brought the dead to life, and then he said: 'I am the Son of God,'[8] 'I am the light of the world,'[9] 'I am the good shepherd,'[10] 'I bring death and I bring life,'[11] 'I am the judge of the final judgment,'[12] and 'I forgive

---

6. The author alludes here to the Roman destruction of Jerusalem in 70 CE.
7. 2 Kgs 4:18–37 and Ezek 37:1–14.
8. Matt 27:43 and John 10:36.
9. John 8:12.
10. John 10:11, 14.
11. Cf. Deut 32:39 and 1 Sam 2:6.
12. Cf. John 5:22 and Acts 10:42.

whom I will and I punish whom I will.'[13] Christ performed signs by his own effective authority, without needing to offer prayers and supplications, as is the case with the prophets. If a man acts as Christ acted, it is right that any claims he makes about himself or others be accepted. As for what you mentioned concerning the prophets, I do not deny this, but how great is the difference between the signs performed by the prophets and those performed by Christ. When a prophet wanted to do something, he would fast and pray, he would offer supplications and petitions, he would devote himself intensely to his prayers, and only then would he intercede. As for Christ, however, he did not behave like this, but he used to walk about in the markets among the people and perform signs and marvels by his own effective authority. Again, the prophets were unable to perform signs at all times, whereas Christ performed signs whenever he wished: whether bringing the dead to life, or opening the eyes of the blind, or healing the sick, or feeding thousands of hungry people with a few loaves. And all this happened through an authority that was intrinsic to him. Again, my Muslim friend, you should know that the prophets did not comprehend the unseen or what is found within the heart, whereas Christ used to tell people about the innermost thoughts of their hearts and used to know what lay hidden and to tell people about what was and what will be. Again, were the prophets to say to the people: 'We are sons of God,' the people would have been right to accept their claim, because of the marvels they were performing. They would not lie, however, and would not lay claim to what does not pertain to them. Rather, they said: 'We are the servants of God,' whereas Christ said: 'I am the Son of God.' Christ and the prophets both spoke truly."

The emir said:[14] "How insolently do you speak against God, monk, when you say that Christ is the Son of God and then you say that he was crucified. Do you think that God would hand his Son over to be crucified? God forbid! Rather, that 'was made to appear to them.'"[15]

The monk said: "I can imagine that the crucifixion might be doubtful to the deviant Jews. But how could it be doubtful to the apostles, the helpers of God? If God had 'made that to appear' to the apostles, then the error could only have come from God. God forbid! For the apostles said that they saw him undergo crucifixion, that he tasted death and was buried, that he arose after three days, that he came to them numerous times after his resurrection and spoke to them, that he remained on earth for forty days after his resurrection, and that he ascended into heaven before their very eyes. How could it be that this was 'made

---

13. Cf. Rom 9:18.
14. That is, 'Abd al-Raḥmān al-Hāshimī, in whose court the disputation takes place.
15. Qur'ān 4:157.

to appear to them'? Or do you accuse the apostles of lying,[16] even though your own prophet testifies that they are 'the helpers of God'[17] and that they spoke only what they were taught by the Holy Spirit who was sent to them by God?[18] Or do you think that God would speak something false to them, so as to lead his servants astray? God forbid! You should not speak disparagingly of Christ. You should not call his apostles liars."

The Muslim said: "By my life, I do not disparage Christ, but I honor him even more than do you, and I am many times more worthy to lay claim to him than are you."

The monk said: "My Muslim friend, please understand that you do indeed persistently disparage him. Should you call a sovereign king a slave or deny that a well-born man is his father's son, then you will have disparaged them in the extreme. Notwithstanding your testimony that Christ is 'the Word of God'[19] and 'his Spirit,'[20] you say that he, like all other human beings, is but a humble slave, and you refuse to say that he is the Son of God, even though the Scriptures testify to us that this is clearly so."

The Muslim said: "What you say is only to be found in your corrupt gospel and your corrupt Scriptures. As for the original gospel, it is in our possession. We received it from our prophet,[21] whereas John and his companions lost the gospel after Christ's ascension into heaven and they instead composed what they wished. Of this we were informed by our prophet Muḥammad."

The monk said: "If the matter is as you claim, then produce this gospel and these authentic Scriptures, to which you have compared our Scriptures, such that you are now so certain that ours are corrupt. Do this, and we shall accept the authentic Scriptures and reject the corrupt Scriptures. Moreover, how can you claim that your prophet informed you of this, when he himself testified that the apostles are 'the helpers of God' and that they were given revelation by God? Further, you should explain to us how it was that kings and all manner of people came to accept this forged book from John and his companions, who were themselves responsible for forging it, as you claim? Perhaps you will say that they were covetous of the apostles' wealth, or that they were wary of their many armies, or that they feared the edge of their swords, or that they were looking for a way to make their precepts and laws less burdensome.[22] If you make such

---

16. Reading *aw tattahimu al-rusula bi-l-kadhib* for *aw yuttahamu al-rusulu bi-l-khadhib*.

17. Cf. Qurʾān 3:52; 61:14.

18. Cf. Qurʾān 2:87, 253.

19. Qurʾān 3:39, 45.

20. Qurʾān 4:171.

21. Evidently what is meant here are the words attributed to Jesus in the Qurʾān.

22. That is, that the message of the apostles was accepted because it offered a less burdensome ethic.

claims, people well know how the apostles lived and what they commanded, whether renunciation, or humility, or meekness, or the sharing out of one's possessions. The apostles must accordingly have had some remarkable power, which they manifested to these kings and commoners, such that they accepted their Scripture and their religion. You must know, however, that it was not because they desired the apostles' wealth, or because they were wary of their armies, or because they feared[23] their swords, or because they wished for less burdensome religious obligations, that these kings and commoners accepted this religion and the gospel from John and his companions. Rather, they furnished these kings and commoners with proofs, such that only then did they accept this Scripture from John and his companions—namely, the signs and wonders that they performed, such as raising the dead, driving out demons, and healing various kinds of illness. Come then, you who lays these false accusations and charges against the holy and divine gospel, compare this gospel that you claim to have been forged with your so-called original gospel. Consider which of them is more just and which of them is more authentic in its precepts and deeds: your precepts and deeds or their precepts and deeds, such as fasting, prayer, alms, the renunciation of all pleasures, and the sharing out of one's possessions to the poor and needy. Do this, and you will come to understand the light that is pure, and thereby its superiority over that to which you and the rest lay claim will become clear to you. Finally, do you not claim—and how strange!—that in all the books of his prophets and messengers God said that he will bring forth from the offspring of Adam, from the seed of Abraham, from the family of Israel, and from the loins of David, a man whom God will cause to redeem and save his servants and to serve as an intermediary between him and his servants? Ceaselessly we awaited that man, generation after generation, until the days in which he was to appear were fulfilled. After he appeared and performed signs, and the books of the prophets were fulfilled by his confirmation of their words, you yourselves denied him. Nor were you pleased until you set yourselves up in opposition to all who believe in him, claiming that Muḥammad is mightier and more honorable in God's sight than he."

The emir said: "Woe to you, monk! Do you not know that Muḥammad is mightier and more honorable in God's sight than Christ, or even than Adam and all his progeny?"

The monk said: "No, by God, this I do not know. But I do know that the heavens are more honorable and more noble in God's sight than the earth, and that the inhabitants of the heavens are more honorable and more noble in God's sight than human beings. You should know that Christ is in the highest heaven, while

---

23. Reading *faza'an* for *faraqan*, with variant cited in apparatus.

Muḥammad and all the other prophets are beneath the ground, that heaven is the throne of God and his seat, and that Christ is seated on the throne of might, on the right hand of the Father, above the angels and heavenly servants. How then is one who is beneath the ground more honorable in God's sight than one who is in heaven on the throne of might?"

The Muslim said: "Do you not claim that Christ knows what is secret and the inner thoughts of human hearts? How is it then that when his disciples asked him when the day of the resurrection will occur, he told them that God alone knows this?"

The monk said: "No, he knew when it will occur, but he did not want to reveal the day to anyone. As for your words 'God alone knows this,' what he actually said is that 'only the Father knows this.'[24] And what he said is true: God is truly his Father and no one other than he knows this, though there is no division or disagreement between Christ and his Father."

The Muslim said: "I shall not accept what you say until you supply me with something to confirm it."

The monk said: "Do you not know that when Adam disobeyed his Lord in the garden, and his private parts became evident and so he hid himself, God cried out to him: 'Adam, Adam, where are you?' and he answered: 'I am here.' Could it be that God did not know where he was?"

The Muslim said: "Yes, surely he knew."

The monk said: *[Omitted: §§317–19, which disrupt the logic of the argument, and may have originated as a marginal comment, perhaps by a scribe hostile to the author's argument here.]*

"You should understand that even as God knew where Adam was, and yet he still cried out to him, so too Christ knew when the day of the resurrection will occur. And how could he not know when it will occur, when he had informed them what that day will be like, as well as about the signs that will take place during it and before it? And behold, we shall see these signs with our own eyes."

24. Matt 24:36.

4. Ḥunayn Ibn Isḥāq, *How to Discern the True Religion*

Introduction and translation by John C. Lamoreaux

The fourth reading comes from the pen of Ḥunayn Ibn Isḥāq (died 873), a member of the Church of the East who spent much of his life in Baghdad.[1] Fluent in Greek, Syriac, and Arabic, Ḥunayn is remembered today mainly for his hundreds of translations of Greek philosophical and scientific texts into Syriac and Arabic.[2] He was also the author of original compositions on those same topics, as well as of a handful of theological treatises. One of these theological treatises is translated here: *How to Discern the True Religion*. In this small treatise, by examining the reasons that cause people to accept religions, Ḥunayn seeks to identify a methodology that will allow one to adjudicate the claims of the various religions, both past and present, and to identify which is the true religion. This work exists in two different versions: an independent treatise and a shorter version that has been incorporated into a longer letter by Ḥunayn. It remains unclear which recension is the more primitive. The independent treatise is translated here, from the excellent edition by Samir Khalil Samir.[3]

Bibliography

Text and Editions

Samir, Samir Khalil. "Maqālat Ḥunayn b. Isḥāq fī Kayfīyat idrāk ḥaqīqat al-diyāna." *Al-Mashriq* 71 (1997): 345–63.

---

1. On this treatise, see Thomas, *Christian-Muslim Relations*, 1:775–79; and Graf, *Geschichte der christlichen arabischen Literatur*, 2:122–32.

2. On his life and his translations of medical works, see my *Ḥunayn ibn Isḥāq on His Galen Translations* (Provo, UT: Brigham Young University Press, 2016).

3. Samir Khalil Samir, "Maqālat Ḥunayn b. Isḥāq fī Kayfīyat idrāk ḥaqīqat al-diyāna," *Al-Mashriq* 71 (1997): 345–63. For earlier editions and translations into Italian and French, see the entry in Thomas, *Christian-Muslim Relations*.

How to Discern the True Religion

How can a man know that his own profession of faith is true, while what others profess is false? He might argue that it is true because he inherited it from his ancestors, or because he got it from some Scripture or from some prophet who proffered inspired verses,[4] or because it is founded on his own investigation (i.e., when he investigated his own religion, he was satisfied that it was valid). But should he argue in this manner, all the adherents of religions that contradict his own would be able to argue similarly.

Since all the adherents of the various religions will respond in this same fashion, whoever bases the acceptance of his own religion on such arguments will of necessity have to accept every other religion, insofar as they can be justified by these exact same arguments. If, on the other hand, he rejects these arguments when they are offered by those who adhere to religions that contradict his own, then they too will rightly reject these arguments when they are offered by the adherents of his own religion.

To those who would argue in this fashion, we also say the following: whether a religion is true or false can be discerned only from the reasons that initially summoned people to accept it. Moreover, the reasons whereby what is a lie is accepted are not the same as those whereby what is true is accepted.

There are six reasons that lead a man to accept what is a lie: the first of these is when he is unwillingly compelled by force to accept what is proffered. The second is when he willingly flees from a state of constraint and hardship: being unable to bear this state, he thus transfers himself from it to one wherein he hopes for ease and abundance. The third is when he prefers might to lowliness, honor to humiliation, and power to weakness, and he thus abandons his religion and converts to another. The fourth is when the man propounding the religion is cunning and crafty in his manner of speaking, such that he misleads and deceives those whom he summons to it. The fifth is when he takes advantage of the ignorance and the lack of education of those whom he summons. The sixth is when there is a natural bond of affinity between the man being summoned and

---

4. As miracles are argued below to confirm a religion, it does not seem that *āyāt* here can mean "miracles." Ḥunayn seems rather to be obliquely referring to Islam, as the verses of the Qur'ān are called *āyāt* (literally, "miracles").

someone else, such that, not wishing to severe this bond of affinity, he comes to agree with him with respect to his religion.

As for the reasons whereby what is true is accepted, of these there are four: the first of these is when the man who accepts the religion sees signs that surpass human ability. The second is when the outward observances of that to which he is being summoned are an indication bearing witness to the truth of its aspects that lay hidden.[5] The third is a logical demonstration whose acceptance is necessary. The fourth is when the thing's end is in agreement with its beginning, and the foundation of what comes later is something about which there can be no doubt because of the validity of what came before.[6]

What we have said should be sufficient for us to begin to consider how it is that we can know that all other religions were accepted solely because of these six characteristics, whereas the one true religion was accepted because of these four characteristics.

It would be tedious for me to recount here every single religion: whether those that are ancient, which are false because that on which they were founded is false, or those that are more recent, whose foundation is no different from those that are false, for to the extent that we know that their foundation is false, they too are false, just as the religions that preceded them are false.

If someone wishes to understand for what reasons his religion was originally accepted—whether it was for the reasons whereby what is false is accepted or for the reasons whereby what is true is accepted—he must examine who at the present time accepts that religion and for what reasons they accept it—whether it is for the reasons whereby what is true is accepted or for the reasons whereby what is false is accepted. Should he do this, based on why these religions are accepted at the present time, he will understand why they were originally accepted. He will also see that what is true is accepted on its own merits, while what is false requires certain inducements to be persuasive in the eyes of those who accept it.

Whoever employs this methodology will thereby be able to see which religion is true and which religions are false. For my part, I shall forgo the examination of all the other religions, and restrict myself to examining my own religion,

---

5. As is made clear below, Ḥunayn is here (ẓāhir mā yadʿū ilay-hi al-dāʿī) referring to the rigor of the ethical demands on the Christian believer.

6. I suspect that the text is partly corrupt, with two glosses having made their way from the margin into the body of the text: the first, a gloss on "foundation" (al-aṣl) (wa-huwa al-ṣaḥīḥ—"namely, that it is valid"); the second, a gloss added at the end of the paragraph, by a scribe who reverses the sense of Ḥunayn's argument (fī-mā yaḥduthu taṣḥīḥ mā qad salafa—"in what comes later there is a confirmation of what came before."). Both glosses are omitted from the translation.

showing that it was accepted solely because of the reasons whereby what is true is accepted: whether because of all of these reasons or because of just some of them. I argue as follows.

It is impossible to believe that people accept some particular religion apart from one of the reasons whereby every religion is accepted. It is also impossible to conceive of any reasons other than the ten characteristics that we have already enumerated: the six whereby what is false is accepted and the four whereby what is true is accepted. If it is established that the reason for accepting the religion is *not* one of the reasons whereby what is false is accepted, then it follows of necessity that the reason for accepting it *must be* the four reasons whereby what is true is accepted: either all of them or just some of them. Should it be discovered that the religion to which we adhere was accepted, not for the reasons whereby what is false is accepted, but rather for reasons that are as opposite as it is possible to be, then its validity will be all the more firmly established and compelling. And thus shall we find that the matter is.

A consideration of each of the reasons.

As for the first, this religion was not accepted through the might of some king or through compulsion at the hands of some prince. Rather, all the kings and princes of the earth showed themselves hostile to it and sought to drive everyone from it, with every manner of torment and dreadful death, exiling them from the very face of the earth. And yet, it overcame all those rulers and it came to be firmly established.

Second, this religion did not summon its adherents to abandon a state of constraint and hardship for one of abundance and ease. Rather, it summoned them from states that were full of every abundance and ease to a state full of every constraint and hardship, a state that was most detestable. And yet, it was readily accepted.

Third, this religion did not summon its adherents from lowliness to renown or from self-abasement to might. Rather, it summoned them from might to self-abasement. And yet, it was so readily accepted that its followers used to prefer death to life for its sake.

Fourth, this religion was not received from people who were full of cunning and crafty in their manner of speaking. Rather, it was received from men who were ignorant, incapable of expressing themselves, and by trade fishermen, indeed, men who were more mute and more incapable of expressing themselves than are fish (as the saying holds).[7]

Fifth, those who accepted this religion were neither ignorant nor foolish,

---

7. Seemingly an allusion to the Greek idiom ἰχθύων ἀφωνότερος ("muter than fish"), attested in Classical Greek and Patristic Greek, as well as in the works of Galen.

nor were they members of the vulgar rabble, nor were they barbarians. Rather, they were the best logicians and philosophers in the entire world, possessed of discernment and the scholarly arts, surpassing all other men in their wisdom.

Sixth, those who accepted this religion did not thereby join themselves to their friends and acquaintances. Rather, in accepting it, they used to sever themselves from all those to whom they were tied by bonds of affinity, whether from their relatives or from their friends.

Should you wish to add a seventh characteristic, then apply your mind with consideration to the following: there was nothing more demanding than what the apostles preached regarding this religion, as touching its outward observances.

Since all these matters are so, there is thus no room left[8] for anyone to deny that our religion was accepted because of the appearance of signs and wonders. This is impossible, except for someone with a hostile disposition who proposes it in his frenzy.[9] If you say this, you should demand from yourself, on behalf of your own religion and the other religions, something similar to what we have described to you with respect to our religion. You will then immediately recognize that there is no comparison between us and them.

---

8. Tentatively reading *yattasiʻu* for *yanbaghī*, with the personal recension.
9. Tentatively reading *bi-junūni-hi* for *bi-khibrati-hi*, with the variant cited by Samir.

5. Miracles of Saint George

Introduction and translation by John C. Lamoreaux

The fifth reading comes from an unedited Eastern Orthodox collection of miracle stories about Saint George, a martyr who was and is
widely venerated throughout the Arabic-speaking Mideast. A great deal
of literature about Saint George was both translated into Arabic and composed in Arabic, by all branches of Christianity. Little of this literature has
been studied or even properly cataloged.[1] It is not known who complied
the present collection: while some of the miracle stories are known in
Greek and may be translations, others seem to be original compositions
in Arabic. Some of the stories are associated with Saint George's famous
shrine in Diospolis (Lydda, modern-day Lod, some ten miles southeast of
Tel Aviv). Some are set in the early Islamic period, others in the tenth and
eleventh centuries. For the three miracle stories translated here I mainly
follow *Sinai ar. 507*, folios 150r–156r (1273 CE), noting where appropriate
differences in *Mingana Chr. Arab. 83 [no. 44]*, folios 209r–216r (1255 CE),
and *Balamand 157*, folios 25v–30v (seventeenth century CE). The first
story recounts the healing of the mother of one Būluṣ Ibn Hibah (Paul the
son of Hibah), a Christian administrative secretary (*kātib*) from ʿAmmān,
in the employ of the Jarrāḥids. The second tells how Saint George saved a
Muslim merchant traveling to Egypt. The third is a story told by a certain
Abba Simeon, from the Monastery of Saint George in Daphne, a suburb
of Antioch, about how Saint George saved a Muslim merchant from Damascus, as he was returning from a business trip to Constantinople.[2]

---

1. Graf, *Geschichte der christlichen arabischen Literatur*, 1:502–4, compiled a list of texts
about Saint George that were known to him, without worrying much about their contents.

2. For another miracle story from this same collection, see my chapter on hagiography in
Noble and Treiger, *Orthodox Church in the Arab World*, 115–17, 128–34.

Miracles of Saint George

Concerning an old woman on the point of death, she being the mother of one of the administrative secretaries of the Arabs

Again, a certain devout Christian reported to us that he heard about the follow-ing miracle of the excellent and holy Mar George from Būluṣ Ibn Hibah, who had the teknonym Abū al-Layth,[3] one of the administrative secretaries (*kuttāb*) of the Arabs, the Banū Jarrāḥ.[4]

Abū al-Layth said that he was in al-Kḥ.ll.ḥ(?),[5] in the service of the emir, when a messenger came to him and told him that his mother had fallen ill and there was little hope that she would survive, and that if he did not travel in haste, he would not be able to see her before she died. He thus set out immediately and came to the city of 'Ammān, where his residence was located. He entered the house and saw that his mother was laying still on her bed amid her family, unable to utter a word to anyone.

After many days had passed with her in this condition, without her eating or drinking and without her speaking, they prepared a shroud for her, as well as whatever else was required for her burial and interment. One of her children (i.e., the aforementioned Abū al-Layth) sat at her side awaiting the departure of her soul, in order that with his own fingers he might close her eyes.

As he was sitting there, in a state of inattention, somewhere between sleep and wakefulness, he saw as if he were in the shrine of the holy Mar George, in a place known as Ṣalkhad,[6] in the district of Hauran,[7] and that he was leaning

---

3. This man seems to be otherwise unknown.

4. More commonly known as the Banū al-Jarrāḥ. They were a Bedouin dynasty that exer-cised varying degrees of control in Palestine and the Transjordan in the late tenth century and the first half of the eleventh; see *Encyclopaedia Islamica*[2], 2:482–85, s.v. "Djarrāḥids."

5. The Sinai manuscript has *al-kh.ll.h*, with the *tashdīd* clearly marked. The Mingana manu-script reads *al-ḥ.l.h*. The Balamand manuscript instead reads "in a certain place" (*fī maḥallah*). While it might be tempting to take this as the Iraqi city of al-Ḥillah, located some sixty miles south of Baghdad (see *Encyclopaedia Islamica*[2], 3:389–90), it was only founded in 1102 CE, too late to overlap with the Jarrāḥids. From the context, moreover, one expects a city or village located in southern Syro-Palestine.

6. Ṣalkhad is a town in southern Syria, near the modern border of Syria and Jordan, some forty miles east of Dar'ā; see *Encyclopaedia Islamica*[2], 8:994–96.

7. For an overview of the Hauran and its Christian remains, see Warwick Ball, *Rome in the East: The Transformation of an Empire* (London: Routledge, 2000), 238–43.

on one of its walls. A young man in white clothes then appeared to him and said to him: "If you wish that your mother not die, then take an oath and make a vow to the holy Mar George, the master of this shrine, and she will live and not die." He replied to him: "My lord, all my possessions belong to the holy Mar George. Whatever he wants, I shall give it to him. From him I have never kept anything back."

Thereupon, returning to himself, he said to those sitting around him: "My mother will not die of this illness. Of this you can be certain, because I just now saw something that convinces me that she will receive healing. Glory be to you, my God! How great is your mercy!" The next day, in the morning, the grace of the saint manifested itself in his mother, and she was healed of her illness.

"After relating to her what I had seen, I took her, and we went to Ṣalkhad, to the shrine of the holy Mar George. And we there offered prayers and litanies, and fulfilled the vow, giving glory to God, to whom be praise forever and ever. Amen."[8]

What the holy Mar George did for a Muslim merchant from the east

Once there was a certain merchant from the lands of the east who wished to journey to Egypt, there to live out the rest of his life. He had a great deal of possessions, as well as herds and slaves. He departed from his house together with a large caravan, to make his way to Egypt.

Satan entered his slaves, and they conceived a desire to kill their master and seize his property, as he was an old man and he had no children. They were watching for a place suitable for their wicked plan but were unable to find one. They then decided among themselves that this would not be possible for them to do until they reached the middle of the desert. As they continued traveling, they eventually reached a certain desolate place, far from human habitation.

They avoided preparations for departure, as if they were unaware that the caravan was departing, until they were left there alone and were able to accomplish their purpose. When they had done this and the caravan had departed, morning dawned, and their owner woke up. On seeing that the caravan had departed, and that he was left there alone with his slaves, he shouted to them, and they pretended like they had just been roused from sleep.

He then said to them: "How could you have committed this great blunder? Why did you not wake us when the caravan departed during the night?" They said: "Sleep overcame us and we were unaware of its departure." He said to them:

---

8. While the switch to the first person here is clumsy, it is clear that Būluṣ Ibn Hibah is meant to be the speaker.

"Saddle your camels and let us travel in haste, and perhaps we can overtake our companions and not end up lost in this desolate desert."

Each of them then began to look at his companion, to see which of them would leap up and begin to kill him. When he saw them behaving as they had never behaved before, he refused to believe what they were doing, and he said to them: "Tell me what you are up to, for you have disquieted me and grieved my heart." One of them answered him, saying: "We have decided to kill you and seize your property, and it is for this reason that we delayed our departure. We are determined on this."

He answered them, saying: "You are welcome to all that I have. As for killing me, however, this will neither benefit you nor is it lawful for you. I have done nothing to merit this. I have done you no wrong, at any time, such that I deserve this. Take these goods then and go your way, letting me live and leaving me here by myself. Do not stain yourself with my blood. Do not sin by killing me."

They answered him: "You are a danger to us, and we shall not be secure should you reach a city and tell the governor what we have done, for he will expend every effort to find us, wheresoever we are, and he will seize from us all that we have seized from you, and in the end he will sentence us to death. If we kill you, however, you will not be a danger to us and we shall be secure, with no need to fear you laying charges against us."

When he saw that they were determined to kill him, and seeing no way to escape, he lifted his eyes to heaven and wept, saying: "God of the Christians, through the intercession of the holy Mar George, the noble martyr, on whom those in distress call for help, whatever the matter, whatever the need, on land and at sea, have mercy on me and send him to save me, so that I might celebrate his name in every land and every country, and share my possessions with him, visiting his shrine all the days of my life."

As he uttered these and other such words in his heart and in the depths of his soul—Glory be to you, my God! How great is your mercy!—he suddenly saw a horseman hastening toward him from the distant desert. When he had verified this, his heart was strengthened, and he regained his confidence.

In the blink of an eye, the horseman arrived in their presence and greeted them, and then he said: "Why did you allow yourself to get left behind by the caravan? It has halted, and it is waiting for you to depart." Dismounting his horse, he then began to rebuke the slaves for being remiss and for not getting underway. As great dread overcame the slaves, the merchant's fear disappeared.

They saddled the camels unwillingly and reluctantly, and their master mounted and set out. And in less than half an hour they found themselves in the midst of the caravan. (The distance traversed was very great.)[9]

9. The Sinai manuscript here adds "about four stages (*burud*)," a phrase that is not found in

The man turned to the horseman who had saved him, in order to thank him for his kindness and reward him for what he had done, but he did not see him. He then began to ask everyone in the caravan about him, but none of them could give him any information about him.

When he reached Egypt, he made inquiries about the shrine of the holy Mar George. After they pointed it out to him, and he had entered it, he asked the priest there to show him the image of the lord of the shrine. On seeing it, he prostrated himself to it, recognizing the image as being the man who had appeared to him.

He then told the priest and those present in detail all that had happened to him, saying to them: "This is precisely the man who saved me, and gave me my life and all that I possess. I have no doubt or hesitation in this matter, as this is the exact image of the man whom I saw. I am thus obligated to discharge my debt and present to him what I have vowed. Were it not that I fear the people of my own religious community, I would abandon my religion and join that of the Christians."

He then produced the most valuable of his tapestries and precious cloth, and with them he adorned that shrine dedicated to Mar George, as well as other shrines dedicated to the name of the exalted and holy Mar George, who does not reject the requests of those who invoke him, whether on land or at sea, whether on a mountain or on a level plain, who does not inquire about the size of the gift, but looks to the excellence of the intention.

[Omitted: a concluding invocation of Mar George.]

Concerning a Muslim commercial agent[10] from Damascus, and how he was saved from drowning and imprisonment

Again, Abba Joseph the monk, the abbot of the Monastery of Mar Palladius,[11] reported to me the following story, which he heard from Abba Simeon the monk of Antioch.[12]

---

the Mingana or Balamand manuscripts. As a single *barīd* (plural *burud*) is equivalent to some six or twelve miles, this is hardly consistent with a journey of half an hour.

10. The *wakīl* ("commercial agent") fulfilled a number of functions, including acting as representative for foreign merchants, banker, attorney, and manager of warehouses. See S. D. Goitein, *Studies in Islamic History and Institutions* (Leiden: Brill, 2010), 345–48.

11. The Monastery of Palladius is located in the village of 'Imm, some twenty-five miles from Antioch, on the road to Aleppo. Elsewhere in the text (*Sinai ar. 507*, folio 156v), this same Abba Joseph, who appears to be otherwise unknown, transmits another story about Saint George from a Muslim in Ramla.

12. This Abba Simeon is below said to be from the Monastery of Saint George, in Antioch.

Abba Simeon decided to go to Jerusalem, to worship at the Holy Sepulcher, the source of life, and to receive blessings from the holy places. After setting out, he arrived at Jerusalem, where he prayed and fulfilled his purposes. As he was returning, he passed through the city of Damascus, and while crossing through the Fabrics Market,[13] a Muslim commercial agent called out to him. When the monk did not answer him, the Muslim adjured him by his religion and his baptism to come back and speak with him.

Abba Simeon came to him and greeted him. The commercial agent then said to him: "Where are you from, monk?" He said to him: "I am from the city of Antioch, from a monastery named for the holy Mar George." The Muslim then said to him: "Since you are from a monastery dedicated to the likes of this great saint and this mighty horseman, sit and I shall tell you about the mighty miracle that he did for me." When the monk took a seat, the Muslim began to tell him the following story:

One year I traveled to the city of Constantinople, regarding certain merchandise that I had. After I had sold it and had realized my profits and gains, I purchased as much brocade as I could, it being forbidden to purchase more. I also purchased with the proceeds of my sale some very beautiful cloth, for three *ratls* of gold.[14] I then set out by sea.

When we had reached a certain disagreeable place, the winds began to rage against us, until we were certain that we would be wrecked and drown. Each of the passengers began to beseech God for help and to ask him for deliverance. As for me, however, I besought Saint George: if he delivers me from drowning, that fine gilded cloth will belong to his shrine, whatever shrine that is.

As I was making this request, I saw a young man astride a white horse, and he was circling the ship on his horse and supporting it from every side. And immediately, the waves subsided and the winds grew quiet, and we reached the harbor of one of the cities located on the shores of that sea. After setting foot on dry land, and unloading our merchandise, we laid it out in the sun, in that we had been soaked with water.

On the Monastery of Saint George in Daphne, just south of Antioch, see Sebastian P. Brock, "Syriac Manuscripts Copied on the Black Mountain, near Antioch," in *Lingua restituta orientalis: Festschrift für Julius Assfalg*, ed. Regine Schulz and Manfred Görg (Wiesbaden: Harrassowitz, 1990), 62.

13. For the Fabrics Market (*Sūq al-Bazz*), which was located on Straight Street, directly south of the Umayyad Mosque, see Nikita Elisséeff, "Corporations de Damas sous Nūr al-Dīn: Matériaux pour une topographie économique de Damas au XIIe siècle," *Arabica* 3 (1956): 61–79 at 74 (no. 47) and 72 (map).

14. The *ratl* was a measure for weight, equivalent to approximately fifteen ounces.

I then began to make inquiries about the shrine of the holy Mar George, in order that I might fulfill my vow to him, and I was informed that there was a shrine of Saint George not far from the harbor. Before I had even entered the shrine, I saw an image of the person whom I had seen save us from drowning, painted on the door of the shrine, in the exact same form and likeness. On seeing it, I rejoiced greatly, giving much thanks to God for this wonderful miracle.

I entered and found an elderly monk in the service of the shrine. I greeted him and told him all that had happened. I then brought out the cloth and spread it out there, in the holy shrine. And after I received blessings from that place, I departed.

Word of what had happened then spread abroad in that city. When the governor heard about it, he summoned me, and he said to me: "You are a Muslim and this city belongs to Islam, and yet I see you exalting the religion of the Christians. By doing this you have brought not a little ruin on yourself." He then gave orders that I be thrown into prison. He also sent to the monk and seized the cloth from him.

When I reached the prison, I reflected on how suddenly both I and my property had been brought to ruin, and once again I began to beseech the holy Mar George for help, saying: "Just as you saved me from calamitously drowning in the sea, so too save me from this dark prison." And then, being so sad, I fell asleep.

When I awoke, I saw that some lamps had been kindled, and I said to the man who was beside me: "My brother, who has kindled this great light in the prison?" He answered me, saying: "My brother, this is no prison, as you assert. This is the shrine of the holy Mar George."

As I was looking at those lamps, I suddenly saw the holy monk, the one who served the shrine of the holy Mar George, and I said to him: "My lord, I do not understand what has happened to me—only that yesterday the governor threw me in prison, and I asked Saint George to save me from my distress. And now suddenly, the saint has looked on me in his mercy, and he has saved me and brought me to his shrine. As for you, elder, know that this miracle is even greater than the first that he did for me." The monk then brought me some food, which I ate, and some water, which I drank.

When it was morning, and the governor looked for me in the prison but did not find me, I heard the heralds crying out in search of me. After the governor learned where I was, he sent and seized both me and the elderly monk. On our arrival in his presence, he began to question me, saying: "What act of sorcery have you done in order to get out of prison, without the doors even having been opened." I said to him: "Your honor, all that has happened to me is wondrous, but there is nothing of sorcery in it." And I told him in detail what had happened to me.

When the governor heard what I had to say, he was seized with fear and trembling, and he gave orders for the cloth, that gilded brocade, to be brought—this he had seized from the shrine of Mar George—and he commanded them to wrap me up in that cloth and to throw me into the sea.

When they had brought the cloth into his presence, he looked at it, and behold, it looked differently than it had when he first saw it. He then said to his slave: "This is not the cloth that we seized from the monk." He rebuked the slave and argued with him, but the slave said to him: "My master, this is the only cloth that we have here." And then suddenly, at that very moment, the whole of it came to be covered with crosses of gold.

The governor began to ask me questions about the cloth, and I said to him: "As for the cloth, this is it. As for these crosses of gold, however, they were not on it." The monk too told him something similar, as did the slave who had taken charge of it.

When the governor came to understand that this was a divine wonder, and that the form and likeness of the cloth had been transformed, he marveled still more and grew yet more fearful, and he said: "I ask you, sir, to depart from our city this very day. Do not even spend the night here, lest you propagate and spread these stories among the Muslims, and there befall you something that will not please you." The governor then returned the cloth to that elderly monk, saying to him: "Take it and return it to the shrine of George."

I then immediately departed, and setting out by sea with all my possessions, I arrived at this my city, safe and sound. I do not believe, monk, that among your prophets there is any saint greater than this one.

When the monk heard his words, he wondered greatly at what the Muslim had told him, and he gave glory to God, who "works miracles among his saints."[15]

15. Ps 68:35 (LXX).

6. *Commentary on the Pentateuch*

Introduction and translation by John C. Lamoreaux

The sixth and final reading is taken from a Syrian Orthodox *Commentary on the Pentateuch*. This commentary is an original composition in Arabic, which seems to have been compiled in the thirteenth or fourteenth century, quite likely in Iraq.[1] It incorporates a diverse variety of sources: Christian traditions, both Syriac and Greek (the latter via earlier translations into Syriac or Arabic),[2] Jewish and Muslim exegetical traditions, as well as local folklore. These sources the compiler weaves together, sometimes with little regard for consistency. The commentary on Genesis was edited by Paul de Lagarde in 1867.[3] His edition is not without problems, and in the notes to the translation I suggest a number of corrections and emendations, partly based on the copy of the commentary found in *Paris ar. 17* (1661 CE). All deviations from the printed edition are noted. Translated here are portions of chapters 15 and 16 of the commentary on Genesis,[4] where the compiler retells the story of Cain and Abel, expanding the bare narrative of Genesis in a kind of midrash.

Bibliography

Text and Editions

de Lagarde, Paul. *Materialien zur Kritik und Geschichte des Pentateuchs.* Vol. 2. Leipzig: Teubner, 1867.

---

1. On this work, see Graf, *Geschichte der christlichen arabischen Literatur*, 2:284–89.

2. Many of the sources cited in this work are likely being derived at secondhand, or even thirdhand, from earlier exegetical compilations.

3. Paul de Lagarde, ed., *Materialien zur Kritik und Geschichte des Pentateuchs*, vol. 2 (Leipzig: Teubner, 1867).

4. Lagarde, *Materialien zur Kritik und Geschichte*, 48–54.

Commentary on Genesis

(15) Adam lays with Eve, and Cain and Abel are born

The Torah says: "Adam lay with his wife, and she conceived and bore Cain, and she said: 'I have gotten a man with God's help.' And again, she bore his brother Abel. Abel was a keeper of sheep, and Cain used to till the ground."[5] As for the interpretation of what God said here, it is as follows: John Chrysostom and Epiphanius the bishop of Cyprus[6] said that God drove Adam and Eve from paradise at the ninth hour, on Friday, and he caused him to dwell east of paradise, on a lofty and tremendously tall mountain. (This mountain is located among the inner mountains of the Indians.)[7] God commanded Adam to dwell in the Cave of Treasures, both he and his wife Eve.[8] (When Adam left paradise, he took along three things, namely, the myrrh, the frankincense, and the cassia.[9] Some scholars say that the gold too was taken from paradise by Adam.)[10]

After Adam had taken up residence in the Cave of Treasures with his wife, on seeing the beauty of Eve his wife he was tormented by animal lust, as she was beautiful and a delight to the eyes. God thus commanded Adam to lay with his

---

5. Gen 4:1–2.

6. While works by John Chrysostom (died 407) and Epiphanius of Salamis (died 403) were available in Syriac and Arabic versions, the compiler of the present text is dependent throughout on later biblical commentaries and seems to invoke the names of patristic authors more to lend the authority of their names to his work, than to indicate his actual sources. For the Arabic translations of works by Chrysostom and Epiphanius, see Graf, *Geschichte der christlichen arabischen Literatur*, 1:337–54, 356–58.

7. That is, *fī jibāl al-Hinduwān al-dākhilah*. Elsewhere, commenting on Gen 4:17 (Lagarde, *Materialien zur Kritik und Geschichte des Pentateuchs*, 1:56, starting at line 30), the anonymous compiler says that Cain built the first city in Delhi, which is located in "the inner lands of the Indians."

8. Reference is here made to the legends of the *Cave of Treasures*, a late-antique Syriac apocryphal text. In recounting the history of the world from Adam to the crucifixion, it tells how Adam and his righteous successors, after their expulsion from paradise, dwelled in the so-called Cave of Treasures, in the foothills of the Mountain of Paradise. There too the future gifts of the magi were stored. The *Cave of Treasures* was widely circulated in the various languages of the Christian East and was well known in Arabic; see Graf, *Geschichte der christlichen arabischen Literatur*, 1:198–200.

9. Omitting the gloss *wa-hiya al-mayʿah* ("that is, storax"), with *Paris ar. 17*.

10. That is, the gold brought by the magi to Bethlehem.

wife Eve, and she conceived and bore a son, whom she named Cain. She also bore a daughter along with Cain, whom she named Arzūn.[11] Cain and his sister were twins.[12] Cain was fair of complexion, hirsute, with dust-colored[13] and disheveled hair. He had leprous-colored spots on his face and blue eyes, and he was tall of stature. His sister Arzūn had a dark complexion and black eyes. (Cain and his sister are a symbol of murder and hubris, and of the persistent spread of sin on the earth. They were the first cause of murder and envy.) Again, Adam lay with his wife Eve, and she conceived and bore a son and a daughter. She named the boy Abel and the girl Awbar.[14] Abel and his sister were twins. Abel was of medium stature, handsome in appearance, with a fair face, black eyes, and a white complexion. In his beauty and appearance, Abel resembled his father Adam. His sister was dark and swarthy of complexion, short of stature, with dark-blue eyes, and yellow hair. (Abel was the first person on earth to be killed unjustly, while his sister was the first to be hated among the race[15] of women.) Cain was a tiller of the soil, who sowed and reaped, while Abel used to keep sheep on the plains below the Cave of Treasures. Cain was haughty and proud, while Abel was humble, calm, and magnanimous. Because of his humility, the scholars have likened him to Christ.

The Torah said: "In the course of time Cain made an offering to God of the fruit of the ground, and Abel too made an offering of his firstborn and fat sheep. And God received Abel and his offering, but for Cain and his offering he had no regard."[16] Mar Ephrem the Syrian and Mar Jacob the bishop of Serugh said:[17] Why did Cain and Abel make offerings when there was no question of sin? Offerings are made only because of sin, and Cain and Abel had never sinned. We say: God commanded Adam to separate the brothers from their sisters and to marry them to one another, marrying Cain's sister to Abel and Abel's sister to Cain. Adam thus gathered his sons before him and told them what God had said,

11. The vocalization of the name is uncertain.

12. A marginal comment from a later scribe follows: "In an old copy [of a different work? of the present work?] we found that Cain's sister was named Salmīth, while Abel's sister was named Labūd." (The vocalization of both names is uncertain.) Lagarde sets this passage off with square brackets. In *Paris ar. 17* it is preceded by *ḥāshiyah* ("marginal comment" or "note").

13. Reading *aghbar* for *aghbar aghbar* and ignoring the square brackets in Lagarde's edition, with *Paris ar. 17*.

14. The vocalization of the name is uncertain.

15. Reading *jins* for *ḥusn*, with *Paris ar. 17*.

16. Gen 4:3–5a.

17. Ephrem the Syrian (died 373) and Jacob of Serugh (died 521) are the two greatest poets of the Syriac tradition, both equally renowned for their exegetical labors. Their works were widely circulated in their original Syriac, as well as in Arabic translations. See Graf, *Geschichte der christlichen arabischen Literatur*, 1:421–33, 444–52.

but Cain was displeased with this apportionment, because his sister was more beautiful than the sister of Abel his brother. It was thus that Cain was displeased with this apportionment. Adam then commanded his sons to bring offerings, so that the Lord's will regarding their marriages might be made known. He said to them: "Let each of you bring an offering to God, from your fields and from your flocks." Cain and Abel then went out from the presence of their father Adam. Abel went to his sheep and from them he chose yearlings that were fat, choice, and large, the best there were among his flock, and he brought these sheep to his father Adam. As for Cain, he went to his field and walked among his crops, and from them he began to select ears of wheat that were unhealthy, the paltriest there were among his crops, and he brought these ears of wheat to his father Adam. The next day their father Adam commanded them to ascend the lofty mountain and present their offerings before God.

[Omitted: a discussion of the moral dispositions of Abel and Cain as they ascended to make their offerings.]

When Cain and Abel departed and presented their offerings, God selected the offering of Abel and was pleased with it, and fire descended and consumed his offering, but God was displeased with Cain's offering. Why did God accept Abel's offering, but reject Cain's offering? We say: In the case of Abel, this was because of the purity[18] of his heart, his upright thoughts, and his excellent offering. As for Cain, God rejected his offering because he had offered the most worthless[19] of his crops and had treated his father's words with disdain, as well as because of his lack of reverence[20] for God and his unclean thoughts regarding the murder of his brother. It is thus that God rejected it. When Cain and Abel presented their offerings, Cain set the ears of wheat that he had brought from his crops on the shoulders of Abel's sheep, secretly hoping thereby that God would accept his offering before that of his brother Abel. How wicked was his plan! Immediately, Abel's sheep turned and ate all of the crops that Cain had brought. And thus, Cain grew angry at his brother Abel, and from that moment, Satan possessed him, and he resolved to murder his brother.

Suppose someone asks: Why does the Torah say that Cain and Abel presented their offerings on the mountain, and then descended to the plain where Cain killed Abel? We say: Cain and Abel did not present their offerings on just one day, but for three months they continued each day to present their offerings, and God used to receive the offering of Abel and reject the offering of Cain his brother. Whenever Cain would ascend to present his offering, Satan used to make sug-

---

18. Reading *wa-naqāwah* for *wa-t.q.a.w.h*, with *Paris ar. 17*.
19. Emending *anḥas* (which is also the reading of *Paris ar. 17*) to read *abkhas*.
20. Reading *wa-qillat makhāfati-hi* for *wa-qillat mukhālafati-hi*, with *Paris ar. 17*.

gestions to him about killing his brother Abel, in order that he might have his sister Arzūn. We also say: It was at the suggestion of Abel that they continued each day for three months to present their offering, for Abel had become sad for his brother, how God would not receive his offering, and he used to hope that God would eventually receive his brother's offering. As for Cain, however, he used to ascend the mountain[21] and descend from it with his unclean thoughts. It is thus that God chose Abel and his offering, but hated Cain and his offering.

[Omitted: the discussion of Gen 4:5b–7, which is mainly moralistic in tenor.]

(16) How Cain murdered Abel his brother on the plain, and on God's dreadful curse of Cain

The Torah said: God said that,[22] and then "Cain said to Abel his brother: 'Let us cross to the plain.' And after he went to it, Cain rose up against Abel his brother and killed him. The Lord God then said to Cain: 'Where is Abel your brother?' He said: 'I do not know. Am I my brother's keeper?'"[23]—that is, his "guardian."[24] As for the interpretation of what God said here, it is as follows: Cyril the patriarch of Alexandria[25] and Mar Jacob the bishop of Serugh said: Cain and Abel crossed to the plain, not because of enmity, but because the plain was wide and spacious. On seeing that the two brothers were in a state of concord, Satan attacked and began to suggest evil thoughts to Cain, reminding him how God had received Abel's offering and rejected his own offering. And he incited him to do evil, ordering him to kill Abel his brother.

Regarding what Scripture says: "Cain rose up against Abel his brother, and he killed him," we say: Cain did not kill his brother on the day they made their offerings, but only after a substantial period of time had passed. Had Adam and Eve known this, they would not have let them go down to the plain, because of the enmity that Satan had sowed between them when they presented their offerings before God.[26] Mar Ephrem the Syrian said: when Satan possessed Cain and took control of his wicked thoughts, he killed his brother, and he thought to himself

---

21. Reading *al-jabal* for *li-l-jabal*, with *Paris ar. 17*.

22. The reference is to Gen 4:6–7.

23. Gen 4:8–9.

24. The author here glosses the scriptural *nāṭūr* ("keeper") as *raqīb* ("guardian").

25. Works by Cyril of Alexandria (died 444) were widely circulated in Syriac and Arabic translations. For the Arabic tradition of his works, see Graf, *Geschichte der christlichen arabischen Literatur*, 1:358–65.

26. Emending *quddām Ādam* (which is also the reading of *Paris ar. 17*) to read *quddām Allāh*.

that the whole world would be his, not knowing that God had determined to appoint someone else as his deputy[27] on the earth. The scholars disagree on the means of Abel's murder. Some say that Cain killed his brother with a staff. Others say that he strangled him with a rope. Yet others say that Cain knelt on his chest and murdered him. We say that Cain threw a rock at his brother, which instantly killed him. While Cain was standing there perplexed as to what he should do with him, or where he should hide him, Satan entered his heart and instructed him to dig a hole in the ground and bury him. After he had dug a hole in the ground and buried him, he ascended to his father Adam and his mother Eve, to the Cave of Treasures, and his father and his mother asked him: "Why did your brother Abel and his flocks not ascend with you?" Cain said to his parents: "From afar I saw my brother Abel, and he was ascending to paradise, and the cherubim were rising before him." Cain lied before God and his parents. As for his parents, they believed his words, but God reproached him for his lie.

Regarding what Scripture said: "The Lord said to Cain: 'Where is Abel your brother?' He said: 'I do not know. Am I his keeper?'" Mar Ephrem the Syrian said: we say that God did not ask this of Cain on the day he killed Abel his brother, but it was two days later that he asked him: "Where is your brother Abel?"

[Omitted: a discussion of four reasons that led God to ask Cain where his brother was.]

When Satan saw that Cain had been exposed for what he had done, and that he regretted having murdered his brother, he made suggestions to him, instructing him to deny murdering his brother and not to confess his sin before God. Regarding what Cain said before God: "Am I my brother's keeper?" We say: When God asked him, Cain denied it, lying before God and presuming that God did not know where his brother is. He lied in what he said before the Lord, but he was concealing the secret in his heart and saying in regret: "Would that I had been my brother's keeper and that I had not killed him!" Had Cain openly confessed before God to the murder of his brother, God would have forgiven him, for Cain had not known what he was doing. After Cain confessed to his parents that he had murdered Abel his brother, Adam and Eve grieved for Abel for one hundred years, and they remained in sadness until the birth of Seth.

Scripture said: "And God said to Cain: 'Why have you done this? The cry of your brother's blood is beseeching me from the ground. And you are cursed by the ground, which has opened its mouth to receive your brother's blood from your hands.'"[28] Mar Ephrem the Syrian said: as for what God said to Cain: "Why

---

27. Emending *yakhluq* (which is also the reading of *Paris ar. 17*) to read *yukhallif*. The reference is to Seth.

28. Gen 4:10–11.

have you done this?" this was to reprimand him and mock him and to show disdain for his ignorance. Regarding what he said to Cain: "Your brother's blood is beseeching me," we say: It was his soul that was crying out against the murderer of his body. As for the blood, it is the reason the murderer must die,[29] when it cries out on being shed unjustly. As for what the scholars record about the blood of Abel, some of them say that after two days the blood of Abel became a red worm, which ascended the mountain into the presence of God, to complain against Cain. Others say that his blood became a rivulet flowing in the plain. Other fathers and scholars said: When God cursed Cain and cursed the ground, which opened its mouth and received the blood of Abel, the earth immediately sent forth[30] the pomegranate tree, whose leaves are green, symbolizing that it is from the ground, while its blossoms are red, resembling blood. (The philosophers call these blossoms *al-jullanār*.)[31] When the pomegranate tree rose up, it carried the blood of Abel in the cups of its blossoms. These it averted from God,[32] out of fear of his wrath.

[Omitted: a discussion of the seven curses Cain earned by killing his brother Abel.]

As for the mark that God placed on Cain, whenever Cain wanted to go somewhere, he would tremble and turn back, and whenever he would strengthen his resolve to go, his eyes would grow wide in terror, and in whatever direction he used to wish to go, a corpse would appear in front of him, lying there stained with blood.[33] The wild animals of that land used to snarl at him, wherever he went, and to attack him, in an effort to eat him. God thus put a mark on Cain. No man could harm him, nor could wild animals or beasts of prey eat him. He could not be drowned in water, or even sink in it. Fire could not harm or burn him. Many times Cain threw himself into the water to gain release from his toils and misery, but the water did not harm him, nor would his body even sink.

[Omitted: remainder of the chapter, with its comments on Gen 4:12.]

---

29. Cf. Gen 9:5–6.

30. Emending *anba'at* (which is also the reading of *Paris ar. 17*) to read *anbatat*.

31. Derived from Persian, *al-jullanār* is the normal word in Arabic for pomegranate blossoms.

32. Seemingly with reference to how the blossoms incline downward, toward the ground.

33. Reading *mukhaḍḍab* for *m.kh.ṭ.b*, with *Paris ar. 17*.

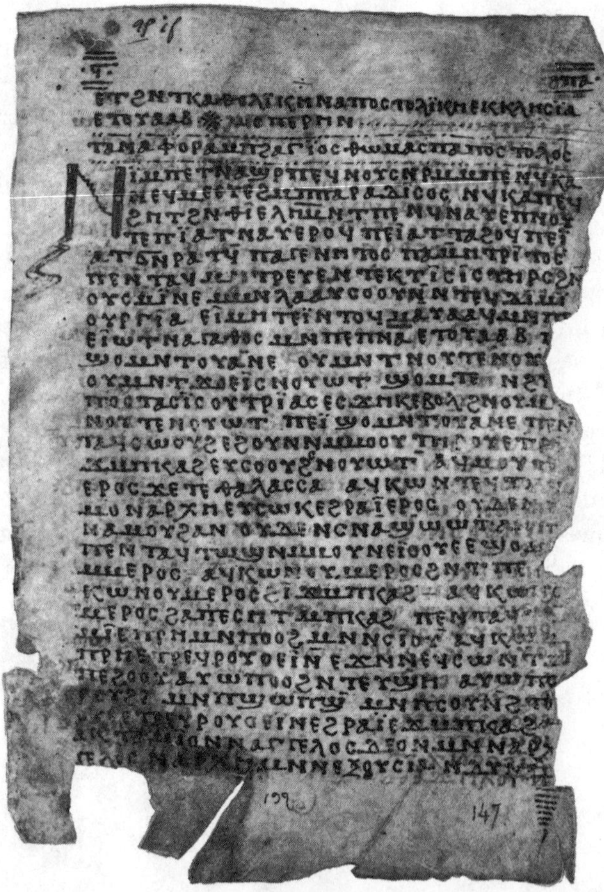

5

COPTIC

Introduction and Bibliography by Mary K. Farag

C optic" refers to a script developed in Egypt during the first three centuries of the common era, the very period during which the Christianization of Egypt also began.[1] The script consists of the Greek alphabet
supplemented with select signs derived from Demotic (the antecedent script for
producing texts in the Egyptian language) for phonemes of the Egyptian language that have no correspondent in the Greek alphabet.[2] The Egyptian language
as represented by the Coptic script is also known as Coptic. Over one dozen
dialects of the Coptic language are attested, but the majority of extant early
manuscripts are written in the Sahidic dialect, medieval ones in Bohairic.[3]

Coptic was developed and used in a thoroughly bilingual environment.[4] In
the first seven centuries CE, Greek literary culture maintained elite status in
this bilingual environment. For this reason, among others, Greek literary culture heavily pervades every aspect of Coptic usage, including script, vocabulary,

---

1. I would like to express my gratitude to Stephen Emmel for his comments on a draft,
which have greatly improved the introductory content and bibliographical references in this
contribution. Research for this piece was supported in part by the Patricia Crone Fund during
my membership in Near Eastern Studies at the Institute for Advanced Study in Princeton, NJ
(academic year 2019–20).

2. Bentley Layton, "Introduction: The Coptic Language," in Layton's *Coptic Grammar
with Chrestomathy and Glossary* (Wiesbaden: Harrassowitz, 2000), 1–4; and Stephen Emmel,
"Coptic Language," in *Anchor Bible Dictionary*, ed David N. Freedman (New York: Doubleday,
1992), 4:180–88.

3. Emmel, "Coptic Language," 182–84.

4. A multilingual environment, in fact, as the extent of Latin usage and competence has
yet to be fully evaluated. For contributions regarding these matters, see Arietta Papaconstan-
tinou, ed., *The Multilingual Experience in Egypt, from the Ptolemies to the 'Abbāsids* (New York:
Routledge, 2016), originally published in 2010 by Ashgate. See also Jean-Luc Fournet, "The
Multilingual Environment of Late Antique Egypt: Greek, Latin, Coptic, and Persian Doc-
umentation," in *The Oxford Handbook of Papyrology*, ed. Roger S. Bagnall (Oxford: Oxford
University Press, 2009), 418–51.

and literary convention, to the point that it has proven impossible to generate decisive criteria for determining whether a Coptic literary text was originally produced in Coptic or translated from Greek. In fact, some scholars continue to insist that there are hardly any original Coptic literary productions of which to speak. Instead, so they claim, most, if not all, extant Coptic literary texts are translations of Greek originals, the only texts produced in Coptic being those of everyday life, such as letters (see no. 5).[5] Most scholars, however, consider this highly improbable. Though most of the earliest extant productions do appear to be translations of Greek originals, literary texts began to be produced in Coptic by the fourth century, such as the life of the founder of cenobitic (communal) monasticism, Pachomius (see no. 1). The selections below consist of Coptic texts for which no corresponding Greek text is known or generally hypothesized to have existed (though the possibility that nos. 3, 4, and 7 were translated from Greek originals remains open).

It was Shenoute of Atripe (no. 2) who brought a high level of rhetorical sophistication to Coptic literary production. What Pushkin is thought to have been for Russian literary culture, Shenoute is thought to have been for Coptic. Whereas French had been the language of literary production in Russia, Russian began to be used for this purpose in the eighteenth century. Alexander Pushkin in the nineteenth century is credited with bringing rhetorical sophistication to the project of making Russian a literary language in its own right.[6] Similarly, whereas Greek had been the language for literary production in late antique Egypt, Coptic began to be used for this purpose in the fourth century, and Shenoute is credited with bringing rhetorical sophistication to the project of making Coptic a literary language in its own right. In fact, scholars notice that Shenoute showed such a high level of rhetorical dexterity that his successors were not able to carry the project forward.[7] In other words, there was no Coptic Nikolai Gogol to succeed the Coptic Pushkin at the White Monastery.

5. Enzo Lucchesi, "La langue originale des commentaires sur les Évangiles de Rufus de Shotep," *Orientalia*, n.s., 69 (2000): 86–87. See also Jacques van der Vliet, "The Embroidered Garment: Egyptian Perspectives on 'Apocryphity' and 'Orthodoxy,'" in *The Other Side: Apocryphal Perspectives on Ancient Christian "Orthodoxies,"* ed. Tobias Nicklas, Candida R. Moss, Christopher Tuckett, and Joseph Verheyden (Göttingen: Vandenhoeck & Ruprecht, 2017), 177–92 at 178–79.

6. Derek Offord, Vladisklav Rjéoutski, and Gesine Argent, *The French Language in Russia: A Social, Political, Cultural, and Literary History* (Amsterdam: Amsterdam University Press, 2018); and Joe Andrew, "Alexander Pushkin," in Andrew's *Writers and Society during the Rise of Russian Realism* (London: Macmillan, 1980), 1–41.

7. Stephen Emmel, "Coptic Literature in the Byzantine and Early Islamic World," in *Egypt in the Byzantine World, 300–700*, ed. Roger Bagnall (Cambridge: Cambridge University Press, 2007), 83–102 at 94–97.

From the small number of original Coptic writers whom we know from She-noute's immediate successor Besa until several bishops who were in office around the beginning of the seventh century, we have only a small number of texts, which mostly consist of orations, especially encomia (nos. 3 and 7) and homilies, such as the one by Bishop John of Paralos (no. 6). Other examples include Rufus of Shotep, who produced allegorical commentaries on the Gospels of Matthew and Luke;[8] Stephen of Hnēs (Heracleopolis Magna), who produced encomia in praise of the martyr-saint Elijah and Apollo, archimandrite of the Monastery of Isaac;[9] and Constantine of Sioout, who produced encomia on Athanasius, Shenoute, and others,[10] some of them surviving primarily, or only, in Arabic translation.[11] Most other orations, however, are attributed pseudonymously to earlier figures (nos. 3 and 7). One salient characteristic of such texts is that compositional units were sometimes repurposed in still other textual productions, such that a story in one text reappears reworked in other texts centering on the same character. Scholars designate these corpora "cycles."[12]

Four descriptors characterize some significant aspects of Coptic literary production as we know it: non-Chalcedonian, monastic, liturgical, and fragmentary. I treat each of these descriptors in turn.

The most elite metropolis in Roman and Byzantine Egypt was Alexandria in the delta region of the north. As the Roman Empire was Christianized and ecclesiastical institutional structures were established, Alexandria held a high position and was considered a great see, second only to Rome until Emperor Constantine founded an eastern capital in the fourth century, eponymously called Constantinople. Major figures of the early Christian movement were trained and/or trained others in Alexandria, such as Clement, Origen, Didymus the Blind, Athanasius, to name only a few. Two successive patriarchs of Alexandria, Cyril and Dioscorus, played leading roles in the christological controversies of the

8. J. Mark Sheridan, *Rufus of Shotep: Homilies on the Gospels of Matthew and Luke: Introduction, Text, Translation, Commentary* (Rome: CIM, 1998).

9. K. H. Kuhn, ed. and trans., *A Panegyric on Apollo, Archimandrite of the Monastery of Isaac, by Stephen Bishop of Heracleopolis Magna*, CSCO 394–95, Scriptores coptici 39–40 (Leuven: Secrétariat du CSCO, 1978).

10. Tito Orlandi, ed. and trans., *Constantini Episcopi Urbis Siout Encomia in Athanasium Duo*, CSCO 349–50, Scriptores coptici 37–38 (Leuven: Secrétariat du CSCO, 1974); Orlandi, *Elementi di lingua e letteratura copta* (Milan: La Goliardica, 1970), 100–102.

11. René-Georges Coquin, "Constantine, History," and Samir Khalil, "Constantine, Writings," both in *The Coptic Encyclopedia*, ed. Aziz S. Atiya (New York: Macmillan, 1991), 2:590–93. Many Coptic literary productions survive solely in translation, not only in Arabic, but also Syriac, Armenian, and Ethiopic.

12. Following Tito Orlandi, "Cycle," in *The Coptic Encyclopedia*, ed. Aziz S. Atiya (New York: Macmillan, 1991), 3:666–68.

fifth century, each being appointed by Emperor Theodosius II to preside over ecumenical councils, both in Ephesus, that of Cyril in 431 and that of Dioscorus in 449. Both councils were highly controversial. The former resulted in two rival councils and even the imprisonment of patriarchs.[13] The latter would be repealed by the extremely divisive council held in Chalcedon in 451. Juvenal of Jerusalem was the only bishop of high rank to have attended all three ecumenical councils as a bishop.[14] Juvenal's decisions in 451 were perceived as a downright nefarious betrayal of Dioscorus and the then-deceased Cyril (no. 3). Egypt became the stronghold of resistance to Chalcedon's decisions and adherents from 451 onward. Emperor Justinian and his successors made such an effort to quell this resistance that many extant Coptic texts display in some form or another rejection of imperial decisions and responses to Chalcedonian propaganda. These are not at all confined solely to expressions of non-Chalcedonian Christology, but include also conflicts over the administrative decisions of Chalcedon, such as the administration of the holy places (churches, monasteries, etc.).[15] To our knowledge, no Chalcedonians engaged in Coptic literary production.

However, it is important to note that Coptic literary production was not thereby the sole property of non-Chalcedonians, who designated themselves Orthodox. Other varieties of Christianity produced Coptic texts as well, such as those known by the names Gnostic, Manichean, or Melitian.

Almost all Coptic literary productions have been transmitted through the archives and libraries of monastic milieus. Archival documents have been found through the archeological study of monasteries in Egypt and the study of artifacts sold to proprietors outside of Egypt. For example, in western Thebes, the documents of the Monastery of Apa Phoibammon and the Monastery of Epiphanius continue to be studied.[16] Scribal centers produced high-quality, ornate manuscripts for monastic libraries. One such scribal center was located in Tuton in the Fayyum Oasis. The well-preserved ninth- and tenth-century manuscripts of the library of the Monastery of Phantoou in the Fayyum (now owned by the Morgan Library and Museum in New York; no. 7) were produced in Tuton. Likewise, it seems that a significant number of the manuscripts of the White Monastery,

13. George A. Bevan, *The New Judas: The Case of Nestorius in Ecclesiastical Politics, 428–451 CE* (Bristol, CT: Peeters, 2016), 149–204.

14. Ernest Honigmann, "Juvenal of Jerusalem," *Dumbarton Oaks Papers* 5 (1950): 209–79.

15. Mary K. Farag, "Relics vs. Paintings of the Three Holy Children: Coptic Responses to Chalcedonian Claims in Alexandria," *Analecta Bollandiana* 137 (2019): 261–76; and James E. Goehring, *Politics, Monasticism, and Miracles in Sixth Century Upper Egypt: A Critical Edition and Translation of the Coptic Texts on Abraham of Farshut* (Tübingen: Mohr Siebeck, 2012).

16. Martin Krause, "Coptic Texts from Western Thebes: Recovery and Publication from the Late Nineteenth Century to the Present," in *Christianity and Monasticism in Upper Egypt*, ed. Gawdat Gabra and Hany N. Takla (New York: American University in Cairo Press, 2010), 2:63–78.

much further south along the Nile River in the vicinity of Panopolis, were also produced at the scribal center in Tuton.[17]

Such high-quality, ornate manuscripts were produced for liturgical use. They often contain collections of scriptural lectionaries, prayers, hymns, homilies, and/or hagiographies (stories of saints' lives). For example, the Great Euchologion of the White Monastery contains eucharistic prayers (see no. 4 for one of them), unction prayers, marriage prayers, and so on.[18] Robert Huntington saw a lectionary in four volumes at the Monastery of Apa Macarius in Scetis in the seventeenth century. Unfortunately, this lectionary, like many Coptic manuscripts, survives today in a dismembered state.[19]

The dismemberment of the Coptic literary heritage has severely hampered and slowed the study of Coptic literature by comparison to other literary cultures of the East. As Walter Ewing Crum, who compiled *A Coptic Dictionary*[20] (which remains the definitive lexicon), remarked in 1905: "The classification and description of such material as almost wholly constitutes the extant remains of Coptic literature—remains quite without parallel among the literatures of the Christian East in their fragmentariness and dilapidation—must be a task of slower progress than where the manuscripts to be dealt with lie ready for description in book form."[21] Much has been accomplished since Crum's time. For example, Stephen Emmel reconstructed the manuscripts that transmit Shenoute's literary corpus.[22] However, still a great deal more work of this sort remains to be done. What Crum noted more than a century ago now continues to be the primary desideratum for the study of Coptic literature.

Bibliography

Atiya, Aziz S., ed. *The Coptic Encyclopedia*. 8 vols. New York: Macmillan, 1991 (online, with updates and new entries, at Claremont Colleges Digital Library).

17. Stephen Emmel, "The Library of the Monastery of the Archangel Michael at Phantoou (al-Hamuli)," in *Christianity and Monasticism in the Fayoum Oasis*, ed. Gawdat Gabra (New York: American University in Cairo Press, 2005), 63–70.

18. Emmanuel Lanne, "Le grand euchologe du monastère blanc," *Patrologia Orientalis* 28 (1958): 269–407.

19. H. G. Evelyn-White, *The Monasteries of the Wadi 'n Natrûn* (New York: Metropolitan Museum of Art, Egyptian Expedition, 1926), 1:xxxi–xxxiii.

20. W. E. Crum, *A Coptic Dictionary* (Oxford: Clarendon, 1939).

21. W. E. Crum, *Catalogue of the Coptic Manuscripts in the British Museum* (London: British Museum, 1905), xxi–xxii.

22. Stephen Emmel, *Shenoute's Literary Corpus*, 2 vols. (Leuven: Peeters, 2004).

Bagnall, Roger, ed. *Egypt in the Byzantine World, 300–700*. Cambridge: Cambridge University Press, 2007.

Behlmer, Heike. "Research on Coptic Literature (2004–2008)" and "New Research on Coptic Literature 2008–2012." Vol. 1/pp. 19–48 and 303–34 in *Coptic Society, Literature, and Religion from Late Antiquity to Modern Times: Proceedings of the Tenth International Congress of Coptic Studies, Rome, September 17th–22th, 2012, and Plenary Reports of the Ninth International Congress of Coptic Studies, Cairo, September 15th–19th, 2008*. Edited by Paola Buzi, Alberto Camplani, and Federico Contardi. Orientalia Lovaniensia Analecta 247.1. Leuven: Peeters, 2016.

Boud'hors, Anne. "The Coptic Tradition." Pages 225–38 in *The Oxford Handbook of Late Antiquity*. Edited by Scott Fitzgerald Johnson. Oxford: Oxford University Press, 2012.

Emmel, Stephen. "A Report on Progress in the Study of Coptic Literature, 1996–2004." Pages 173–204 in *Huitième congrès international d'études coptes (Paris 2004)*. Vol. 1, *Bilans et perspectives 2000–2004*. Edited by Anne Boud'hors and Denyse Vaillancourt. Cahiers de la bibliothèque copte 15. Paris: Boccard, 2006.

Fournet, Jean-Luc. *The Rise of Coptic: Egyptian versus Greek in Late Antiquity*. Princeton: Princeton University Press, 2020.

Goehring, James E., and Birger A. Pearson, eds. *The Roots of Egyptian Christianity*. Philadelphia: Fortress, 1986.

Orlandi, Tito. "Coptic." In *The Oxford Handbook of the Literatures of the Roman Empire*. Edited by Daniel L. Selden and Phiroze Vasunia (online at https://www.oxford handbooks.com/view/10.1093/oxfordhb/9780199699445.001.0001/oxfordhb -9780199699445-e-30).

Zanetti, Ugo. "Bohairic Liturgical Manuscripts." *Orientalia Christiana Periodica* 61 (1995): 65–94.

1. Life of Pachomius

Introduction and translation by Mary K. Farag

Various versions of the *Life of Pachomius* have been transmitted in various languages (Coptic, Greek, Latin, and Arabic). Pachomius (287–347) is considered the founder of cenobitic (based on the Greek phrase *koinōnos bios*) monasticism in the fourth century, in which monks live together communally in a highly organized fashion. What is here translated is the text of a Sahidic manuscript assigned the number 7 by its editor, L. T. Lefort, who dates the manuscript to sometime between 820 and 850. Unfortunately, the extant remains of this manuscript begin in midsentence and consist of the end of the life. Significantly, S[7] is one of the few versions of the *Life of Pachomius* that ends with his death, whereas the others continue to provide an institutional history narrating the lives also of Pachomius's successors.

Bibliography

Text and Editions

Lefort, L. T. *S. Pachomii Vitae Sahidice Scriptae.* CSCO 99–100, Scriptores coptici 9–10. Leuven: Durbecq, 1952.
Veilleux, Armand. *Pachomian Koinonia.* Vol. 1, *The Life of Saint Pachomius and His Disciples.* Kalamazoo, MI: Cistercian, 1980.

TRANSLATION

Life of Pachomius (according to the extant text of S[7])

. . . wearing a haircloth all the time and eating nothing but bread and water only. But whenever a brother would give him pain, he would hate him and would continue to be bound with him in wrath, with the result that he repaid evil in return for evil.

And it happened once, when our father Pachom fell asleep and was taken to the other age, as we said earlier, he saw the young, simpleminded servant, who had spent four months practicing asceticism, in great joy and gladness. And when he saw our father Pachom walking with the angel, who was showing him the beauty of the other age, he ran to him and urged him, saying: "Come and see my property, which the Lord gave me on account of your good doctrines, which you taught me to walk in, O my holy father." And he showed him his spiritual gardens and their incorruptible fruit, and he showed him his entire dwelling place and the building built for him and its indescribable beauty full of the glory of the Lord. When he showed him his entire dwelling place, the man of God rejoiced over him with great joy. Afterward, when they went out a bit from the paradise of delight, they saw the elder ascetic in a place that was scorching hot, and he was fastened like a dog to a tree laden with fruit. He lived from its fruit without having the means to release himself from that tree. And as for him, when he saw them, he put his head down, being ashamed, until he was brought forward. And when they saw him, they looked at him with great pain. And the simpleminded brother said: "Our father Pachom, you have seen the elder ascetic, whom you labored to teach. He did not obey you to walk in humility. Now see what he is like. It is his desire that the Lord has given to him in return for his evil disobedience."

It also happened one day that our father Pachom became sick. He did not tell any of the brethren that he was sick, nor did he believe he was sick according to his habit, but rather in his firm strength he went out with them to the harvest because the brethren were harvesting in those days. And while he was harvesting, he fell down upon his face in their midst. And the brothers were troubled and ran to him and stood him up on the ground. They found him with a great fever in his body from the illness. And they walked with him until they brought him to the monastery. He cast himself upon the ground while bound with his girdle. And the brothers thought it fit, since he would be faint on account of the fever, that he sleep on a bed like all the ill brethren. But he did not obey them in this [matter], but rather he lay on the ground and stayed [that way]. And one remained to cool him with his hood. And as [it happened], many succumbed to sickness in those days. For it was a difficult illness and a plague, the illness that caught them. And one of those visiting said to the brother who was cooling him with his hood: "Did you not find a fan with which to cool him?" And when he heard, he was not able to respond to him in the heavy illness that was upon him, but rather with the signal of his finger, he said: "Will this entire ill crowd find a fan for each one and so find one for me as well?" And he remained ill.

And those days were the Holy Forty of the Holy Pascha. And it happened at the end of the week of the Forty Days of the Pascha of the Lord that all the brothers of the monastery gathered at Pboou to celebrate the Pascha with each other. An angel of the Lord came to him and said: "Prepare yourself, O Pachom, because the Lord will take a great sacrifice from your house on the day of the feast." And he thought to himself: "Perhaps the Lord will visit [me] on the day of the Sabbath of the feast of the Lord." And he spent the four days of the Pascha without eating, while grieving and groaning to himself that the bond of the Koinōnia would not be dissolved.

And on the evening of the Preparation—the third day without eating—he gathered all the brethren to him. He spoke with them like Samuel did when he spoke with the people at that time, telling them all the decrees. He spoke with them saying:

I think, O my brethren and my sons, that my time has been completed and I will go the way of all the earth like all my fathers. For you know my entire way of life, how I walk with all humility and renunciation in your midst. For you know that I did not seek after my relief at all from anyone among you in anything in this holy place. For the Lord is a witness to my conscience that I did not say anything in vanity nor pride. For I would not speak with you in the matters that I did openly among you so as to persuade you, but rather I would speak with you in matters that were not apparent so that your heart would be relieved by this, because I did not leave you any impediment before God and men. In addition, the Lord knows that I laid down every word of the law for you to follow and do and complete and see no place of rest for your souls. I say this because I do not know what will befall us. For the Savior commands us in the Gospel, saying: "Watch because you do not know the day nor the hour when the Son of Man is coming."[1] For you know my aim, since I did not ever punish any one of you, even though I had the authority [to do so], unless [it were] for the salvation of his soul. Nor did I move any of you from place to place or from one occupation to another, unless I knew that it was to his benefit according to God for whom I did it. Nor did I ever repay someone evil in return for evil; nor did I curse someone, if ever he cursed me impatiently and wrathfully, but rather I patiently taught him not to sin against God, saying to him: "If you sin against me, I am a man of your kind, only guard yourself from sinning against the God who made you." Nor did anyone ever truly upbraid me. Even if it were a junior[2] person who upbraided me, I would not be displeased, but rather I would take his criticism to myself on account of God, as it is the Lord who upbraids me. Nor did I ever come and enter a place or a monastery and say, as though I had authority: "Give me a donkey for me to mount," but rather, I would gratefully and humbly walk on my feet. If one among you ran after me with a donkey, after I started walking, so that I would mount it, once he reached me on the road and

1. Matt 25:13.
2. Literally, "small," but referring to someone with little responsibility.

I knew that my body was ill and needed the thing, I would take it from him, but if I knew that I was free from illness, I would not take it. Concerning food and drink and unction and other reliefs of the body, you are not unaware of each of these [matters], as I have already told you.

As he said these things, Theodore sat at a small distance with his face down against his knees, crying. And many of the brethren were also crying, knowing the service that he did at all times without ceasing and his great humility by which he served each one of them in the fear of God. As Paul said: "We became like subordinates among you. As a nurse comforts her children, so also we desired you, approaching to give you not only the gospel of God, but also even our souls, so that you would become beloved to us."[3]

As for our father Pachom, after he uttered all these things to the brethren, he lay down ill, and it was the third day of him not eating. All were crying because of the misery that would beset them when the Lord would visit him. Apa Papnoute, the steward of the entire monastery [and] the brother of Apa Theodore, was also ill. And it was the evening of the Sabbath of the feast of the Lord when he reposed. At that time, our father Pachom recalled the word of the angel saying to him: "A great sacrifice will be taken from your house on the day of the feast."

Many of the brethren lay down with that illness, such that one lay down one day, two on another day, three or four on still another day. The visitation came to all the monasteries of brethren by the command of the Lord. Many even of the leaders of the monasteries lay down from that illness. At the hour when the fever beset them, at that time their color would change and their eyes would fill with blood, and it was like persons who choke to the point that they can no longer breathe. Apa Papnoute, the steward of the great monastery of Pboou (the brother of Apa Theodore), and Apa Sourous, the steward of the monastery of Phnoum, and Apa Kōrnēlios, the steward of the monastery of Tmouneshons, reposed from that illness. As for all those who died from that illness, there were perhaps 130 people who died in Pboou.

Our father Pachom remained ill. Theodore served him. He spent forty days lying ill in the place where all the ill brothers were, and he was being served just like all the brethren in every matter, there being no difference between him and them in any matter, according to the order that he gave to them at the start. And his body became very weak in the duration of the illness, but his heart and his eyes were like a strong fire. He said to Theodore: "Please get an old cloak and cover me with it because this [one] is too heavy and I cannot bear it. Look, it has been forty days since I became ill, but I give thanks to our Lord." And at that

3. 1 Thess 2:7–8.

time, Theodore went and took a good, light cloak from the steward and brought it and covered him. When our father Pachom saw the difference in the cloak, he was angry with Theodore and said to him: "What great violence you have done, Theodore! Or did I wish that you would leave a scandal for the brethren after me? They would say: 'Apa Pachom took his relief in his life compared to all the brethren.' I will be tied up for judgment before the Lord! Now then, take it from me. I am content to go to the feet of the Lord in any way." Theodore took it from him and brought another, a ragged garment worse than that of all the ill brothers, [and] covered him with it.

He remained ill during the days of the Pentecost, and three days before he would lie down, he sent and gathered to himself all the seniors[4] among the brethren. He spoke with them, saying: "Look, I will go to the feet of the Lord who created us and gathered us together to do his will. Now then, as for you, say together who it is that you would like to become father to you." As for them, they continued to cry. Out of grief, no one answered him, thinking about the misery that would befall them after he left their hands, like sheep taken from the hands of their shepherd. After these things, he repeated to Apa Horsiesios for a second time: "Speak with them and see who wishes to become father to them." And they responded to him together: "If this is how it will be, we do not know anyone besides the Lord and you. What you decide for us, we will do." He responded to them: "The person among you whom the Lord revealed to me would edify your souls in the fear of God is Petronios, the father of the monastery of Smeine. For through the purity of his heart, he sees revelations many times and he is competent in everything. I think that he also is ill, but, at the same time, if he lives, he is your father." At that time, he called some of the ancients [and] sent them to him to ask if he was alive.

For, indeed, shortly before he had gathered the brethren to him and spoke with them, saying: "Look, I will go in the way of all the earth," they had all gone together to the synaxis and spent three days praying and crying to the Lord, so that he might keep him for them a little while [longer] on the earth. And after three days, our father Pachom sent Theodore to them, saying: "Cease crying. For the command is from the Lord concerning me that I go to the feet of all my fathers." And the brethren returned to the place where he was lying down. They continued to cry about him with a deeply broken heart.

Afterward, he turned to Theodore and said to him: "If the Lord visits me, do not leave my body in the place where it will be buried." He responded to him in grief: "I will do as you say." Afterward, he grasped his belt and lay upon his breast a second time: "Theodore, watch. Do not leave my body in the place where it

---

4. Literally, "great ones," but referring to those who have great responsibilities.

will be buried." He replied to him again: "My lord father, I will gratefully do everything that you will bid me to do." And Theodore thought to himself: "He said this to me many times with great command, lest some will take his body to steal [it] and a martyrion be built for him, as is done for the holy martyrs," because he heard him many times find fault with those who do such things, since everyone who does so becomes a dealer in the bodies of the holy ones. Afterward, he grasped his belt again for a third time [and] said to him: "Theodore, pay heed to fulfill the word that I told you with haste"; and also: "If the brethren take interest, then awaken them in the law to God." As for Theodore, he thought to himself: "What is this thing that he told me: 'If the brethren take interest, then you should awaken them in the law of God'? Is he saying that after a time the brethren will be entrusted to me? I do not know." As he pondered these things in his heart, our father Pachom replied to him: "Do not become doubtful or have two hearts. For because it is not only what I say to you, but also about what you think in your heart."[5] Theodore replied to him, while crying: "Alright."

And after he said these things, he slept a little. He did not speak with anyone. Afterward, he signaled with his hand three times. At that moment, he opened his mouth and gave [up] his spirit on the fourteenth of the month of Pashons at the tenth hour of the day and a great fear befell that place at that hour such that it trembled three times. Many of the ancients, who saw revelations many times, said: "We saw many angels, who made announcement after announcement to each other, looking at him." Afterward, they sang before him with great zeal until they took him to his place of repose, with the result that the place in which he had reposed diffused a fragrance for many days. Theodore [put] his hands over his eyes to close them, like Joseph, about whom the Lord spoke to Jacob: "Do not be afraid to leave Egypt. For I will make you a great nation in that place, and I will come to Egypt with you and bring you up from there, and Joseph will lift his hands over your eyes."[6] And all the brethren ran to him crying [and] kissed his mouth and his entire holy body and they spent the remainder of the day and the entire night reading around him before the altar. After they performed the synaxis at the first hour, they prepared his holy body for burial like all the brethren. And they lifted up the *prosfora*[7] over him. Afterward, they sang psalms before him until they brought him to the mountain and buried him on the fifteenth of the same month, Pashons. The brethren returned to the monastery with a deeply broken heart and humility. Many of them said to the others: "Truly, we have be-

5. There seems to be something lacking here; see L.-T. Lefort, *S. Pachomii Vitae Sahidice Scriptae*, CSCO 99–100, Scriptores coptici 9–10 (Leuven: Durbecq, 1952), 94n4.

6. Gen 46:3–4.

7. The eucharistic gifts.

come orphans today." And after they came down from the mountain, Theodore took with him three other brothers on that night and took him up from the place in which he had been buried. They disinterred him along with Apa Papnoute, the brother of Apa Theodore, the accountant of the Koinōnia. And no one knows the place in which he is until today.

All the days of his life amount to sixty years. He lived as a monk for twenty-one years. And in his thirty-ninth year, he became a monk. Indeed, the Lord saw him, how he crucified his flesh in every matter until he did his will. He was pleased and gave him repose [and] received him. He did not leave him to live a long life to reach the feebleness of the body, as [was] his wish.

Title

This is the life of our holy father Apa Pachom, the archimandrite, the one who was the first to build up the Koinōnia or the legislation of the monks, who reposed on the fourteenth of the month of Pashons. May his holy blessing be with us all. Amen.

Scribal note (copied from the Antigraph)[8]

Pour forth joy and gladness and merriment and righteousness and cheer, my holy fathers, my father Apa Damianos and my father Apa Apaioulei and my father the Deacon Ammōne and the rest of our brethren, each one by their name, and those whose names I do not know. This is a plant among you, my holy fathers. Amen.

Scribal note

Pray for me, too, my holy fathers. I am the poor sinner, the Deacon Diōscōros, the son of the blessed[9] Deacon Timōth[eos]. The readers of the holy Theodore, the humble scribes, bore fruit from my state of apprenticeship. I wrote according to the antigraph. Amen.

8. "Antigraph" is the technical term for the manuscript from which the scribe copied the text to produce a new copy.
9. Meaning "deceased."

2. Shenoute of Atripe, *I Have Been Reading the Holy Gospels*

Introduction and translation by Mary K. Farag

Shenoute of Atripe (ca. 348–465) was, to our knowledge, the most prolific Coptic writer. He composed and edited nine volumes entitled *Canons* and eight volumes entitled *Discourses*. He served as the leader of a federation of three monasteries in southern Egypt, known today as the White Monastery, the Red Monastery, and the Women's Monastery. Through his writings, we learn his perspective on his relationship with the leaders of the Women's Monastery, monastic morality, persecution of pagans, among many other topics.

Bibliography

Text and Editions

Coquin, René-Georges. "Le Traité de Šenoute 'Du Salut de l'âme humaine.'"
    Journal of Coptic Studies 3 (2001): 1–43.
Moussa, Mark. "*I Have Been Reading the Holy Gospels* by Shenoute of Atripe
    (*Discourses* 8, Work 1): Coptic Text, Translation, and Commentary." PhD
    diss. Catholic University of America, Washington, DC, 2010.

TRANSLATION

I Have Been Reading the Holy Gospels (Discourse *8.1*)

Title

A *logos* [homily] that our father Apa Shenoute delivered, teaching about the salvation of the soul of the human. In the peace of God. Amen.

Excerpt

And I will tell you again what I have told you many times: God does not need a work from us. Rather, he wishes that we do small [things], in order that he might give us even greater [things], immeasurable in the face of those whom he will make worthy of them. For it is written: "You do not need my good [works]."[1] The Lord of the servant waits for him to do his works, and the God of all, Jesus, waits for his servants to prepare themselves to receive the kingdom of heaven through good works.[2]

For the sun does not need the light of ten thousand lamps. Rather, what it wishes from those who are lit is eyes that see through its light. So also, the God of all and his Christ do not need us to do works for him. Rather, what he wishes from us is what causes the eyes of our heart to receive light within it.

And we know that what he awaits from the pious is truly "to inherit the kingdom that he has prepared for them since the foundation of the cosmos."[3] And if he promised it [the kingdom] to those on his right on account of six works that they did,[4] then how much will he promise to those who have fulfilled every good [work] in all purity and modesty?[5] Who have sown blessings—and not sparingly—so that they might reap also blessings?[6] Who pray at all times?[7] Who do not become saturated with the love of God?[8] In whom all his wishes are more delightful than any good upon the earth?[9] To whom he gives power to worship him in spirit and truth,[10] that we may submit to him and entreat him[11] and not envy those who are evil or the workers of lawlessness, since they are like fodder that quickly withers and like fresh herbs that quickly fall?[12] You see the portion

1. Ps 16:2 (15:2 LXX).

2. There is an untranslatable wordplay in this paragraph. The word *ahe* is used in the first sentence transitively to mean "need," while in the last sentence it is used intransitively to mean "wait." God does not need (*ahe*) our works, but he does wait (*ahe*) for us to do them.

3. Matt 25:34.

4. Matt 25:35–36 lists six works as the reasons why the king welcomes those on the right into the kingdom: "[1] I was hungry and you gave me food, [2] I was thirsty and you gave me drink, [3] I was a stranger and you welcomed me, [4] I was naked and you clothed me, [5] I was sick and you visited me, [6] I was in prison and you came to me" (RSV). To these six works, Shenoute adds six more from various books of the Scriptures in what follows.

5. Cf. 2 Tim 3:17.

6. Cf. 2 Cor 9:6.

7. Cf. 1 Thess 5:17.

8. Cf. Eph 3:19.

9. Cf. Sir 23:27.

10. Cf. John 4:23–24.

11. Cf. Ps 37:7 (36:7 LXX).

12. Cf. Ps 37:1–2 (36:1–2 LXX).

of those who are evil that their end is destruction.[13] But blessed are those who abide in the Lord and keep his way for it is they whom he will exalt to inherit the earth.[14]

What is greater than the command of God, the Christ, the Son of God? Or what other good work will befit man more than what the Savior Jesus commands? For the Lord is exalted over everyone and his command is also exalted over every command, crying out at all times, commanding those who listen to "enter through the narrow gate."[15] It is not a wonder that many are those who enter through the wide gate, but rather the wonder altogether is that few are those who will enter the narrow gate. If there are truly wise persons, they are those who walk on the narrow path. For wisdom is not among those who run on the wide [path]. Why? Because death is on it or rather inside it. But life is on the narrow one or rather inside it. Is it not a good [thing] that relief should meet a person after [his] toil on the narrow path and after [his] entrance through the narrow gate rather than that toil should meet him after [his] relief on the wide path?

There are two narrow gates. One is on the outside of the other. The first leads into the second. "Those who have forcibly taken them"[16] entered through the first [and] their toil has ceased, having passed by; for they will enter relieved through the second without pain at all or distress. This saying[17] refers to "those who will keep the commands of the Lord God and cleave to his covenant and choose what he wishes,"[18] according to the Scriptures, as well as [those who] invoke Christ the Savior, the lover of the human, the altogether sweet one so that he might "open to them the gates of righteousness and they enter them,"[19] while they are yet in the body and showing forth to him every kind of piety—the prayers, the purities, the mercies, and all the other holy virtues—which they would have "forcibly taken"[20] for themselves, to do them during the days of their life while they were

13. Cf. Ps 37:9 (36:9 LXX).
14. Cf. Ps 37:34 (36:34 LXX).
15. Matt 7:13.
16. I believe that Shenoute is here referring to Matt 11:12 in which Jesus refers to people who take the kingdom of heaven by force. This is supported by the next sentence referring to "this saying." Shenoute is making a distinction between the narrow gate that must be passed in this life and the narrow gate to be passed after death. The former is crossed forcibly, through the laborious acquisition of the virtues and practice of pious works. If the former is crossed with great toil, the latter is crossed easily. Shenoute posits two narrow gates in order to explain how the kingdom of heaven can be taken by force as per Matt 11:12.
17. Matt 11:12. See the previous footnote.
18. Isa 56:4.
19. Cf. Ps 118:19 (117:19 LXX).
20. Matt 11:12.

yet in this dwelling place. Their toil has ceased, truly passing by along with their distress. They will enter through the gate of the kingdom of heaven without toil or pain. But as for those who will still complete their impiety while in this dwelling place—idol worship, iniquity, mercilessness, fornication, monstrosity, and the rest of the wicked [deeds]—[and] who die without being forgiven, they will find Amente[21] prepared for them and waiting to swallow them.

Hearing these things, is it not fitting for us to love what belongs to the path and the gate of life and to hate what belongs to the gate of destruction and not to set our feet upon its path? Or if we have already set our foot, then to turn it away, as it is written: "I have kept my feet from every evil way"[22] or, if we are not compelled: "Turn your foot away from every evil path"?[23]

What painful work is being taught to us from the Scriptures? What oppressive [thing] have we been commanded? Have burdens been set upon us since it has been said: "Hate what is evil and love what is good"[24] and "withdraw yourself from what is evil and do what is good"?[25] As for those who are ordered to cut stones, the work manifests that the command is oppressive, since the work is also oppressive and difficult. But as for the command of the Scriptures, how is it oppressive? If the ordinances of the Lord are not oppressive, truly his other works are also light. Is there another saying more true than what God the Christ says: "My yoke is sweet and my burden is light"?[26] For "the paths of the Lord are straight. The righteous will walk on them at the right time relieved, but the impious will become weak on them."[27] This is manifest, since we do not ever hear in the Scriptures that the works of righteousness are oppressive upon us, but rather [we hear the Scriptures] saying as follows, the sins "have pressed upon us like an oppressive burden."[28] For truly the burden of our sin is oppressive, but its judgment is even more oppressive and its punishment unbearable.

The work is also fitting for the Holy Forty Days, so that we bring it to the narrow gate and the narrow path in order that we may complete the contest, each according to his power, [and] might receive blessings from Christ Jesus, to whom belongs every blessing. For he does not force anyone beyond his power nor does he wait at all for those who do perfect works, but rather he pays heed

---

21. "Amente" literally means "[the] western [place]," but it refers to the land of the dead (like the Greek term "Hades").

22. Ps 119:101 (118:101 LXX).

23. Prov 4:27.

24. Amos 5:15.

25. Ps 34:14 (33:14 LXX).

26. Matt 11:30.

27. Hos 14:9 (14:10 LXX).

28. Ps 38:4 (37:4 LXX).

to everyone who acts according to their power. For this [reason], he set up stadia that are different from each other, so that each one may run according to his power, in order that the one who cannot give one hundred may give sixty, and, again, the one who cannot give sixty may give thirty.[29] The great, perfect measure is good, which is prayer without ceasing, and everything good, including also fasting. Good also is the just measure, on account of the powerless, which is to keep the days holy and the prescribed fasts and the virtue of marriage. For the gospel has assigned three stadia as follows: one stadion that is very long, which is the one who has given one hundred; another that is a bit short, which is the one who has given sixty; and another that is very short, which is the one who has given thirty, wishing that the powerless not look at the path that is long and be scared, with the result that he does not register his name at all, since there is no racetrack for his weakness. For many of those who do not steer straight have caused many to be scared away. Not only do they turn their face away from the path, but they remove themselves altogether, so that they do not return to go on it, like a beast of burden that has fallen on the path, since it was overburdened.

You see the goodness of the true umpire, Christ, who wishes that we, all of us, go about seeking the works of our salvation. So then, let us not be careless, we who are least in the work, since the Lord does not upbraid us with the strong and perfect in the works. For he will not find fault with the one who has sixty for not performing one hundred acts of mercy, nor the one who has thirty for not performing sixty acts of mercy, but rather he will condemn us for doing nothing at all after all these prescriptions and just measures. Now then, let us not make ourselves unworthy of the works of our salvation, we the poor in piety. Instead, let us exert ourselves according to our power, and I believe that he will not separate us from those who have done these great feats.

I will demonstrate this to you through an example. There was a person who had children. They went up to the trees to harvest some fruit. One's [harvest] produced thirty measures, and another's produced twenty, another's produced fifteen, another ten, still another produced five or three or two or even only one. And because they were not strangers to each other, but brothers, children of the same person, through the goodness of the father and the wish of the children, they cast them all upon each other. Just as they were not separate in their heart, they also did not separate the other goods. For the wise ones have already apprehended what we have said.[30]

---

29. Cf. Matt 13:8 and 1 Cor 9:24–27.
30. Cf. Matt 13:24–30 and Mark 4:26–29, where Jesus likens the kingdom of heaven to a harvest.

We will recite still another example. There were some men who went to a bridal chamber and were of the same kin. Some slayed calves and prepared wine and many goods; others, each according to his power, what pertains to the sheep and the goats and that which was available from what they had and from what they had been able to prepare. They cast them upon each other all at once and as one people. Also the other preparations for the bridal chamber they did as one. I have said previously that the wise have already understood what we are saying.[31]

31. Cf. Matt 22:1–14, where Jesus likens the kingdom of heaven to a marriage banquet.

3. Pseudo-Dioscorus of Alexandria, *Encomium on Macarius of Tkōou*

Introduction and translation by Mary K. Farag

The editor of this text, David W. Johnson, considers it pseudonymous. The text purports to be the oration that Dioscorus of Alexandria (died 454) delivered in praise of the deceased Macarius, bishop of Tkōou. The text is highly polemical and offers an early non-Chalcedonian perspective on the immediate aftermath of the Council of Chalcedon from 451 onward. The excerpt translated here concerns the resistance of a lawyer named Paul, a presbyter named Silas, and unnamed others to the return of Bishop Juvenal to Jerusalem.

Bibliography

Text and Editions

Johnson, David W. *A Panegyric on Macarius Bishop of Tkôw Attributed to Dioscorus of Alexandria*. CSCO 415–16, Scriptores coptici 41–42. Leuven: Secrétariat du CSCO, 1980.

TRANSLATION

Encomium on Macarius of Tkōou 7.1–8.16

Title

An encomium that the holy Patriarch Apa Dioscorus, archbishop of the city Rakote, delivered for the holy Apa Macarius, the bishop of the city Tkōou, at the time when Marcian the king had exiled him [Dioscorus] to the island Gangra. When Apa Papnoute went to visit him, he informed Apa Dioscorus that Apa Macarius died in Rakote as a confessor. He delivered this encomium, while a crowd of the clerics and many monks sat before him, [who] had come to visit him in exile, with Peter and Theōpistos the deacons taking down shorthand. In the peace of God. Amen.

Excerpt

(7.1) Moreover, listen, and I will tell you the entire story about what happened after we were exiled to this island. Some persons, who belonged to us and were entrusted with the truth, informed us about what happened.

Once the synod of the *pneumatomachoi*,[1] that of Chalcedon, was adjourned, the assembly of the orthodox in each city and the assembly of monasteries in each place henceforward stood against the bishops who had subscribed to the contemptible tome. They were not permitted to enter their cities again.

(7.2) And the persons of the Holy City [Jerusalem] stood against Juvenal the contemptible one [and] did not permit him to enter into Zion. For he had neither the permission nor the lot in it [Zion]. And they showed him great contempt, saying: "O transgressor,[2] Juvenal, you left full and came empty. Cast out Judas! He has no lot with Christ or his disciples! You left as a shepherd and returned as a wolf. You left as a fisherman, catcher of persons,[3] and came as an ibis, catcher of unclean fish. Cast out this unclean ibis, lest he seize the good fish that have been purified in Christ's [baptismal] font. Cast out this wicked fox, lest he destroy the Lord of Sabaoth's vineyard."

(7.3) When the impious Juvenal heard them, he was very angry. He said: "What have I done to you, so that you say all these things against me and cast me off of my throne?" They said to him, through a *scholastikos*[4] whose name was Paul: "Rightly have you spoken. Tell us the truth: In what manner do you believe? In the manner with which you stood before us before you left to the synod or not? You destroyed the faith [and] received another faith alien to the

1. Literally, "fighters against the Spirit," a polemical label formerly used in fourth-century disputes concerning the divinity of the Spirit. In this context, it is applied to the bishops who assented to the proceedings of the Council of Chalcedon in 451.

2. There is an untranslatable double entendre here because *parabatēs* can mean "the one who stands beside" (i.e., a deputy) or a "transgressor." Juvenal was Dioscorus's deputy at the ecumenical Council in Ephesus of 449, and the first business of the Council of Chalcedon in 451 was to put the judges of the 449 council on trial. Since Juvenal did not stand up to the Council of Chalcedon with Dioscorus, Dioscorus's supporters considered this former "deputy" now a "transgressor." *Parabatēs* carries both meanings.

3. Mark 1:17.

4. The title of an advocate, lawyer, or legal advisor.

Christ. Confess the truth to us: Are you numbered with us? Are you numbered with those who oppose us?" And Juvenal said: "I believe in the manner of my fathers." Paul the *scholastikos* said to him: "If your faith is sound, why has Dioscorus condemned you?" Juvenal said: "Dioscorus stained the faith. We cast him out of the council. He was angry [and] condemned us." Paul said to him: "Well, if your faith is sound, why did you not condemn him first, before he condemned you? Instead, according to your speech, it is you who has stained the faith. For this reason, you are the servants of sin. Next, recite your creed: in what manner do you believe?" Juvenal said: "I believe in the manner of my fathers."

(7.4) Paul the *scholastikos* said to him: "As the Lord lives, you will not enter the gate of this city nor will you sit upon your throne until you inform us of your entire creed written in your own hand and make an oath to God the ruler of all and the throne of the kings before your signature." Juvenal said: "I believe in the Father and the Son and the Holy Spirit and the humanity of the Lord." Paul said: "[People] of Jerusalem, help! This dog has blasphemed! He made the Trinity a quaternity! His body is being torn into four pieces and dispersed into the four winds of heaven! Cast out Judas from our city! Do not let this Samaritan enter our city! Do not let death enter into your windows!"[5] And as Paul was saying these things, they ran after Juvenal [and] chased him [and] did not let him enter the city, but rather they removed him, saying: "Go and do not return, you unclean one!"

(7.5) And that lawless Juvenal left to the king in anger, and the king sent him with a decurion,[6] saying: "Do whatever Bishop Juvenal tells you." And he went forth from the king with the decurion. He crossed over the Jordan before the sun set. They walked all night until they came to Jerusalem at the dawn of the twenty-first of Tōbe[7] before anyone knew. And the entire city was gathered in the Holy Mary in the Valley of Josaphat, performing the synaxis. And the soldiers surrounded the church. Juvenal, the one whose gray hair will be burned in Gehenna, moved hastily and mounted his cathedra. He cried out in a great voice: "Bring Paul to me, this guilty one who has hindered me until now."

(7.6) And they were reciting the trisagion at that hour: "*Agios o theos, agios eischuros, agios athanatos, o staurōthis diēmas eleēson ēmas,*"[8] which means: "Holy God, holy mighty, holy immortal, who was crucified for us, have mercy upon us." And the holy Paul was himself reciting the trisagion with them. When he heard that the impious one was summoning his name, he came forward at once. The impious one said to his soldiers: "Take him and kill him because he spoke against

5. Jer 9:21.
6. The commander of a certain number of soldiers.
7. January 16 on the Gregorian calendar.
8. Here the trisagion verse is given in Greek, followed by the Coptic translation.

his shepherd." Paul responded: "Until today, you were my shepherd, but now you have become a wolf, predator to souls. Until today, you were my teacher, but now it is you who needs my teaching and that of others." Having said these things and as the soldiers threw him outside, he cried out: "Holy Virgin, Mary, mother of the king of life, do not make me a stranger today, for they are about to pour out my blood in your midst. Let my blood cry out like that of Abel[9] over Juvenal, for they are about to pour out my blood violently." And as he was yet saying these things, the soldiers beheaded him.

(7.7) And the crowd in the church cursed Juvenal and the lawless king saying: "The Lord destroy you with the spirit of his wrath and the steam of his anger!" And as the impious Juvenal heard these things and as the crowd was proclaiming them, he immediately ordered the soldiers to shut the door of the church and kill the orthodox. And they began to kill them. They were crying out: "You who took flesh from the holy Virgin, Mary, have mercy on us and accept our souls unto yourself, O Lord, and we will not cease to confess you and your good Father and the holy life-giving Spirit as a consubstantial Trinity, as well as your mother the Virgin, who brought you forth, you being God and man. Your divinity did not part from your humanity for a single moment.[10] Anathema to Juvenal and everyone who thinks in his manner!" And hearing these things, Juvenal adjured the soldiers: "Kill them quickly!"

(7.8) O how great was the agony of the orthodox at that time that a person should have brought his children to the holy feast of the church [and] suffered the soldiers to kill them, giving them courage, saying: "My beloved children, prepare yourselves to be slain before us and then we as well. We send you as gifts before us!" A person with his children, a mother with her children, a friend with his friend, everyone in general was running toward the soldiers, braced over each other, wishing to commune. And the soldiers did not want to kill them.

(8.1) There was a presbyter at that hour named Silas, standing at the altar, celebrating over the holy *prosfora*.[11] His eyes opened and he saw the Savior upon the holy altar and Mary his mother and the army of angels. And the Savior was saying to the angels: "Take the souls of the martyrs. Bring them to the altar, and I will give them my body and blood before I take them to the heavens with me. For they gathered here today for this reason. Look, I will go back to the heavens to my Father with those who loved me. I will leave behind my city Jerusalem, the [city] in which I endured all my sufferings, and leave their house desolate.[12] For they blasphemed my

9. Cf. Gen 4:10.
10. Cf. 1 Cor 15:52.
11. Eucharistic gifts.
12. Cf. Matt 23:38 and Luke 13:35.

divinity. As for you, O holy presbyter, complete your sacrifice. For you will be the last of all these. Afterward, you too will die." And the soldiers killed the holy ones and [*eight letters, only four of which are legible*] died. The angels took them before the altar and crowned them according to their rank and the Savior kissed them.

(8.2) And the holy virgin was saying to her son: "My Lord and my God and my son, behold, my sacrifice. I have lifted it up to you upon your holy altar on the day of my commemoration, on which I died.[13] Glory to you and your good Father and the Holy Spirit forever and ever. Amen." And when the presbyter saw these things, he fell upon the ground. He was half-dead. Immediately, God the good one sent his angel to raise him up and take the fear away from him.

(8.3) Once he completed the holy sacrifice according to the command of the Lord, he joined the rest of the clerics serving with him. They turned their face over the altar [and] did not see any of the Lord's body on the altar and did not find his blood in the chalice: "It is on account of our unworthiness that you have hidden your holy body and blood from us. For we have not become martyrs with our confessing brethren. O God the good one, do not hide this work from us. If not, tell us as the contest is divided and the stadion is prepared."

(8.4) While they were yet saying these things, behold, an angel of the Lord appeared to them on the altar. He said to them in a voice full of adjuration: "Why have you ceased from your prayer? Have you not fragmented [the sacrifice] for the crowd of the orthodox, who set their heart to commune before they went to the Lord and before they enjoyed this [the sacrifice] in the body? Their souls came out of the body weeping because they did not partake of the body of Christ, but the Savior did not leave them distressed about this. Instead, he gave them his holy body and blood before they were received before him in heaven. This is why they did not find the body on the table or the chalice: because those who had been killed all communed." (8.5) When they heard these things, they were fully assured that those who had been killed received a crown of honor. For those who had been killed on that day were five thousand souls. And so they recited the doxology.

And Juvenal hastily [stepped] down from the cathedra. When he heard the clerics reciting the doxology, he came over to the altar with great vanity. He said to the clerics: "Why did you not invite me to give you communion? Instead, you communed without your bishop." The holy Silas said to him: "Just now you were so busy pouring out the blood of the holy ones and you say: 'I will give you communion'? Anathema against you, you lawless one! Anathema to whoever hails you! Anathema to whoever communes with you in this age and the one to come!" (8.6) Juvenal said to him: "Lord Silas, it is you who deserves to remain under every anathema because you have risen up against your bishop and you

13. As mentioned in 7.5, Tōbe 21 is the feast day of Mary's dormition on Egyptian liturgical calendars.

are the one who anathematized me. For it is written: 'You shall not speak evil against the leader of your people.'"[14]

The holy Silas said to him:

It is also written: "Honor God and king."[15] Do you not revere God? Have you no fear of him? Instead, you have betrayed his faith. Am I to imitate your betrayal on this occasion? I who came with you to Ephesus?[16] Were it not for the holy Cyril, archbishop of Rakote, you would have already betrayed the faith on that occasion. Or have I forgotten the time when Candidian the *comes* tempted you, while you were in the storehouse for wheat, while his [Candidian's] storehouse was dark?[17]

(8.7) Patriarch Cyril himself was sitting beside you, and you did not know [it] because of the darkness. And you stumbled, thinking that the Patriarch Cyril could not hear you when you said: "What is my job now that I am counted in but my judgment is scorned, even if ten thousand people speak with me? Patriarch Nestorius knows a multitude of good things compared to everyone else." The holy Cyril immediately hastened up to your side and said to you: "Papas Juvenal, [*three letters, only one of which is legible*] the devil has found a place to settle in you. Why have you stumbled? Because you have been confined[18] before you taste even one blow for the faith? If you were taken to the court like my fathers the apostles, if they were walking with you when they were cast down from the wing of the temple like James the brother of the Lord, if you had seen the fuller's club in his hand as the blow was coming down upon you like him [James the brother of the Lord], would you have said: 'I never saw Jesus'?[19] If they set up a cross for you like James the son of Cleopa, if you had seen the nails piercing him like him [James the son of Cleopa], would you have said: 'I will raise a libation up to your idols'?[20] If you were cross-examined like Judas called Kyriakos, would you have really seized the idols and given a kiss on their mouth?"[21]

---

14. Acts 23:5 quoting Exod 22:28.

15. Cf. 1 Pet 2:17.

16. The ecumenical Council of Ephesus in 431, over which Cyril of Alexandria was scheduled to preside. Due to the late arrival of many bishops, two rival councils were held, one over which Cyril presided and another over which John of Antioch presided.

17. This suggests that Juvenal was placed in a storehouse of wheat under confinement.

18. In a storehouse of wheat. See the previous footnote.

19. For references to these traditions regarding James ("brother of the Lord"), see D. W. Johnson, *A Panegyric on Macarius Bishop of Tkôw Attributed to Dioscorus of Alexandria*, CSCO 416, Scriptores coptici 42 (Leuven: Peeters, 1980), 45n82.

20. For references to these traditions regarding James ("son of Cleopa"), see Johnson, *Panegyric on Macarius*, 45n83; and Samuel Moawad, *Untersuchungen zum Panegyrikos auf Makarios von Tkōou und zu seiner Überlieferung* (Wiesbaden: Reichert, 2010), 126n284.

21. For references to these traditions regarding Judas called Kyriakos, see Moawad, *Panegyrikos auf Makarios von Tkōou*, 126n286.

(8.8) Are these not the admonishments that the thrice-blessed Cyril the archbishop gave you beside your throne in front of the bishops? Were you not likened to another one of them? Indeed, were it not for the holy Celestine,[22] since he had sent you to the synod as his representative, you would have already received your deposition since that time like the impious Nestorius. Did not the holy Apa Shenoute of the jurisdiction of non-Greek Egypt say that he would condemn you, were it not that the holy Cyril prevented him? Did he not cry out to all the bishops saying: "Holy fathers, there is bitterness in this brother bishop. Separate yourselves from him because he is not sound in his thoughts"?

(8.9) When Juvenal heard these things, he was very angry. He said to the holy Silas: "I have said one word to you [asking] why you did not come down and invite me to give you communion. Behold, you reply to me with a multitude of words that the entire cosmos cannot bear! Behold, I am like a bolt-smith's sack under the weight of your words! Take the throne upon which I sit. I will treat you according to your bravado and teach you what it is to despise your bishop."

Immediately he ordered that the holy Silas be seized and bound, one of his feet to one pillar of the sanctuary and the other [foot] to the other [pillar], and be left suspended upside down. (8.10) And the holy one charged the soldiers by the king's health: "Do not strip me of my liturgical vestments, but let my blood be poured out upon them!" [*six illegible letters*] After he said these things, he cried out saying: "My Lord, Jesus Christ, son of the holy Virgin Mary, whose feast we celebrate today, accept my soul to yourself for I am about to be killed violently!" Immediately, the soldiers struck him until he was divided in the middle and split in two.

And he had the soldiers surround the rest of the clerics with swords and axes [and] slay them until their blood flowed forth in the church like water until it reached the ankles of the soldiers. For they killed five thousand persons that day along with Paul the *scholastikos* and Silas the presbyter and all the clerics there.

Furthermore, they also said that after all these things the impious Juvenal did not cease from his mania but added to his evil. (8.11) And it happened that, after the soldiers withdrew, the women came to take the bodies of their men, as did the virgins from the Mount of Olives to take the body of the holy ones. Each one was lifting the body of their men, looking for their children and their husbands to take them to their homes and bury them. And when the godless Juvenal became cognizant of these things, he told the soldiers: "Rise, come, and seize the women and sleep with them." (8.12) Then the soldiers began to seize the

22. Bishop of Rome.

women. And the wife of the holy Silas the presbyter went, she and her two virgin daughters, wishing to take the body of her husband. And they were thinking about how they would bring his holy body down. Now, the soldiers were seizing the women who had come first [and] corrupting them. And the wife of the holy Silas the presbyter looked this way and that as to where she might hide herself and her two virgin daughters who had come to the age of puberty. And the wise daughters clung to their mother, embracing her, because they saw the violence that was occurring to the women.

(8.13) And she, their mother, raised up her eyes [and] saw the destruction of the limbs of her husband. She wept bitterly, saying:

> My lord presbyter who has become a martyr for the faith of Christ, let this be a sign to me that you have been counted with the chorus of martyrs and let this be for me the firstfruit of your supplications, if you have found grace before God. I know that you have found [grace], my lord. Although you were not found to be inferior, they did these things to you. And it is not that you went to war and were overthrown, but rather you contended for the faith of the Son of God. Now then, save me today and your two virgin daughters and do not let them defile my prudence and [let] others mount the bed upon which you have mounted. (8.14) Cut off the force surrounding me now, my lord, for since the time I came forth from my mother, no man has known me but you, nor did I ever look at one of your fellow clerics and say they were superior compared to you. Since the time I was taken to you when you were a reader, I showed reverence before you, calling you "my lord" and obeying you like God. Do not let the trust that I forged with you dissolve. (8.15) As God the Christ lives for whose sake you endured all these sufferings, if you save me from this force that surrounds me, I will maintain with you my covenant that I forged with you until the day of my death. Do not let those who rejoice over my frailty say: "Look, Silas was killed and the soldiers corrupted his wife and his daughters." My lord, do not let this happen!

And while Silas's wife was uttering these things, she looked at the altar [and] saw two angels in the form of soldiers. They took her hand and her two virgin daughters. They brought them out of the midst of the soldiers. No evil befell them. (8.16) And when she came to her house, she found the body of the holy one on his bed, and she glorified the God in whom they hope.

See, we have related these things concerning what happened in Jerusalem.

4. *The Anaphora of Saint Thomas the Apostle*

Introduction and translation by Mary K. Farag

The following is the only extant portion of the *Anaphora of Saint Thomas*, a characteristically Egyptian eucharistic prayer. Its inclusion in the Great Euchologion of the White Monastery may indicate that the anaphora was in use for some time at the church of the White Monastery. In any case, the prayer fell out of use. The one leaf of the Great Euchologion is our only witness to this eucharistic prayer. That the priest's parts are in Coptic (and written with black ink), while the diaconal and congregational parts are in Greek (and written with red ink), attests to the bilingual Coptic-Greek liturgical usage, which in fact continues in all the rituals of the Coptic Orthodox Church to this day.

Bibliography

Text and Editions

Farag, Mary K. "The Anaphora of St. Thomas the Apostle: Translation and Commentary." *Le Muséon* 123 (2010): 317–61 (translation used here with permission).

Lanne, Emmanuel. *Le Grand Euchologe du Monastère Blanc.* Patrologia Orientalis 28.2. Paris: Firmin-Didot, 1958.

Zentgraf, Käte. "Eucharistische Textfragmente einer koptisch-saidischen Handschrift." *Oriens Christianus* 41 (1957): 67–75; 42 (1958): 44–54; 43 (1959): 76–102.

The translation of the *Anaphora of Saint Thomas* was previously published in "The Anaphora of St. Thomas the Apostle: Translation and Commentary," *Le Muséon* 123, nos. 3–4 (2010): 317–61.

The Anaphora of Saint Thomas the Apostle
(extant text in the Great Euchologion of the White Monastery)

Priest: Who can make his mind heavenly and place his thoughts in paradise and place his heart in the heavenly Jerusalem and see God the invisible, the incomprehensible, the unattainable, the uncreated, the immeasurable? As for he who accurately measured the entire creation, his workmanship no one comprehends, except he himself and [his] good Father and the Holy Spirit. [These] three are one, a single divinity, a single lordship, three hypostases, a perfect Trinity in a single divinity. (81.16) These three are one: he who collected all the waters that were upon the earth into a single gathering and called it the sea and established the four river-branches flowing into it, (a sea that) can neither become overfilled nor lack (for water); he who bounded the waters in three parts and placed one part in heaven, one part upon the earth, and one part under the earth; he who created the sun and the moon and the stars and appointed the sun to shine upon his creations by day and the moon by night, the evening [star] and Arcturus and the morning star to shine upon the earth. (81.31) And you also created the angels and the archangels, the principalities and the authorities, the powers and all the powers that are in the heavens. And by your hands, along with your good Father and the Holy Spirit, you also created man according to your image and according to your likeness. And you also created paradise and placed the man whom you had created in it to cultivate it and to praise you, you whom the angels praise, you whom the archangels worship,

Deacon: Those who are seated stand.[1]

Priest: You whom the powers hymn, you whose holy glory the authorities sing, you to whom the thrones sing the doxology of victory,

Deacon: Look toward the east.[2]

Priest: You before whom stand your two honored creatures, the cherubim and the seraphim, each of them with six wings, with two wings they cover their faces

---

1. This diaconal line is in Greek.
2. This diaconal line is in Greek.

on account of the great glory of your divinity, and with two they cover their feet on account of the great fire emanating from around your throne, O God, the creator,

Deacon: Let us attend.[3]

Priest: and with two they fly, while hymning and praising you, glorifying you with unwearying mouth and unceasing tongue and never-silent lips, hymning you, glorifying you, saying,

Congregation: Holy holy holy, Lord Sabaoth. Heaven and earth are full of your holy glory.[4]

Priest: Holy are you, holy are you, holy are you, Lord Sabaoth. Truly heaven and earth are full of your holy glory. Fill now this sacrifice also with the joy of your Holy Spirit. You placed the man whom you had created in the paradise of delight and commanded him that from every tree in. . . .

3. This diaconal line is in Greek.
4. This congregational line is in Greek.

5. Christophoria, *Letter to the Comes Mena*

Introduction and translation by Mary K. Farag

U nfortunately, very few writings of women have been transmitted to us in Coptic. Below is one of three extant letters composed by Christophoria, who was probably the head of a woman's monastery. It is addressed to the monastery's benefactor the Comes (Count) Mena and was composed sometime between the sixth and eighth centuries. This letter is the only complete one; the other two are fragmentary. Nothing is known of Christophoria aside from what can be gleaned from her three letters. This letter was found in Hermopolis.

Bibliography

Text and Editions

Bagnall, Roger S., and Raffaella Cribiore with contributions by Evie Ahtaridis. *Women's Letters from Ancient Egypt, 300 BC–AD 800*, Ann Abor: University of Michigan Press, 2006.
Crum, W. E. *Catalog of the Coptic Manuscripts in the British Museum*. London: British Museum, 1905.

TRANSLATION

Letter to the Comes Mena (P.Lond.Copt. 1.1104)

God will fully assure your filial lordship that, except that there is this concern of your body, we have no care save the wish to see you from time to time practically and to know of your good health. Besides the care of our sins and that your body attain health, we have not had in mind to pray for anything else. Now, although the circumstances and cares that currently lie spread upon us are very great, we have cast them all aside, only because of the great suffering of yours, upon us as though our own eye were suffering. So, reply to us with your honored letters: whether you are relieved or how you are. For this, our heart is troubled daily on your account. Believe my own meanness and your least prostrators, all the brethren pray for your health every day. And it is about this great matter that we have sent, so that you might inform us how you are [doing], and if God has granted the grace that you should be able to rise, we wish to see you, your "pain turned to joy"[1] for us. As the Word who became flesh commanded the paralytic: "Take your mat and walk,"[2] may he heal your body so that you may "go from strength to strength"[3] and his help henceforth strengthen you. Be well in the power of the holy Trinity.

The beloved, glorious lord, son, lover of Christ, the Comes Mena.

Christophoria the least.

---

1. John 16:20.
2. Matt 9:6.
3. Ps 84:7 (83:7 LXX).

6. John of Paralos, *Homily on the Archangel Michael and the Blasphemous Books of the Heretics*

Introduction and translation by Mary K. Farag

John of Paralos was a monk of the Monastery of Apa Macarius in Scetis under the leadership of Daniel (around 485–575) and became a bishop of renown during the patriarchate of Damian (577–ca. 606). His homily below is not completely preserved, and it is the only one of his works to have been transmitted in Coptic. He warns against the danger he perceives in certain books read out in the villages and cities of Egypt. In general, John of Paralos is remembered in later works as someone who fought against heresies and converted heretics to orthodoxy.

Bibliography

Text and Editions

Jenott, Lance. "The Investiture of the Archangel Gabriel: A New Translation and Introduction." Vol. 2/pp. 559–564 in *New Testament Apocrypha: More Noncanonical Scriptures*. Edited by Tony Burke. Grand Rapids: Eerdmans, 2020.

van Lantschoot, Arnold. "Fragments coptes d'une homélie de Jean de Parallos contre les livres hérétiques." Vol. 1/pp. 296–326 in *Miscellanea Giovanni Mercati*. Vatican: Vatican Library, 1946.

Homily on the Archangel Michael and the Blasphemous Books of the Heretics (extant text as codicologically reconstructed by Arnold van Lantschoot)

A *logos* [homily] of our holy father, honored in every way, Apa John, the bishop of Paralos, which he delivered concerning the holy Archangel Michael and the blasphemous books of the heretics, which are read in the orthodox churches. In the peace of God. Amen.

It is certainly necessary for those who desire to take in the ray of the true, unapproachable light of the holy Trinity to abominate all the discourses written in the blasphemous books, which those workers of lawlessness[1] publish, who are darkness in the darkness of their father, the devil. As the tongue of the incense, Paul, said: "And what is the friendship of light with darkness? And what is the share of a believer with an unbeliever? And what is the unity of the temple of God with Beliar?"[2] For this reason, I myself am willing to tell you, disciples of piety or rather "children of the light and children of the day,"[3] about the aforesaid who have dared to blaspheme God, the creator of everything.

For truly their blasphemies are greater than those of the Jews and the unclean, lawless pagans. For they have written books of every blasphemy as follows: that which they entitle "The Appointment of Michael," and "The Kerygma of John," and "The Laughter of the Apostles," and "The Teachings of Adam," and "The Counsels of the Savior," and all the discourses of blasphemy that they have written. And they leave behind the light of the holy writings of the prophets and the apostles and all the fathers, the teachers of the church, by whom the orthodox faith was strengthened and who were able with all virtue to please God. For the wicked heretics dare to declaim compositions that are full of curses and bitterness, which, when the simple recite them in the villages and cities of Egypt, some of the *spoudaioi*[4] hear them and think that their discourses that they hear from them are true. And when I was told about this by men, servants of God, namely that they read from books of this sort, they did not recognize the destruction that is in them.

The situation then compels me to inform you, O servants of God, concerning the polluted discourses written in the rejected books of those [people], so that

---

1. Cf. 1 Macc 3:6 and Luke 13:27.
2. 2 Cor 6:14–15.
3. 1 Thess 5:5.
4. Literally, "the zealous ones," but referring to an organized group.

your hearts may not perish in the unclean share of theirs, as I recall that fearful voice speaking through the prophet Ezekiel: "As for you, son of man, I made you a watcher of the house of Israel and you will hear a discourse from my mouth and threaten them from me. If you do not tell the lawless: 'You will die a death,' and if that lawless one does not turn away from his wickedness and he from his wicked way and he dies in his lawlessness, I will seek after his blood from you. And if you tell the lawless one and he does not turn away from his lawlessness, you will save your soul[5] because I do not desire the death of the sinner, but that he turn and repent, says the Lord, the Pantocrator."[6] James the apostle also says: "He then who knows to do good and does not do it, to him it is sin."[7] Therefore, it is necessary for us to inform you about the matter firmly, and as for you, [it is necessary for] you [to] listen to the matter attentively. For the Holy Scripture seeks after two ranks, a wise teacher and an understanding listener, so that the labor of the teacher might not become vain through the negligence of the hearers, and instead, we keep the saying of the tongue of the incense, Paul the apostle of Christ, who said: "Remember your great ones who spoke the word of God to you";[8] and also: "Heed your great ones and be subject to them; for they are the ones who give day and night for your souls, since they do this joyfully and do not groan. For this is [to] your advantage. Pray for us."[9] Therefore, it is necessary for us, O servants of God, not to have you declaim from the blasphemous books, but rather [to have] you flee from them.

Now, O brethren, declaim from the pious books and be glad in the joy of the Holy Scriptures, which are full of salvation and light, and respond with one voice, saying: "The holy Trinity is uncreated and existent from eternity before all things." [The holy Trinity] is the one who made all the innumerable ranks of angels and archangels, the cherubim and seraphim, the four creatures who are many eyed, the powers and the dominions, and all the innumerable ranks, which the Scripture did not name, but rather the following is what we have been told: that they are multitudinous, innumerable names in the heavens. For this reason, the blessed Paul says about the Christ: "He is exalted above every principality and every authority and every power and every dominion, and every name that is named, not only in this age but in the one to come."[10] Therefore, the myriads of myriads of holy ones who serve the Trinity exist in the heights long before the cosmos came to be in light that befits those who love Christ gloriously.

For God is living light. He is incomprehensible. And those who serve God exist in this sort of light in holy glory, and they do not release their hands at any

---

5. Ezek 33:17–19. Cf. 3:17–19.
6. Ezek 33:11.
7. Jas 4:17.
8. Heb 13:7.
9. Heb 13:17–18.
10. Eph 1:21.

hour from giving glory and worshiping openly the true divinity. Those who are there neither sleep nor do they rest. They neither hunger nor thirst. They do not eat at all. For they are luminous spirits. Indeed, it is never night there or day. There is no star, no moon, no sun, no cold, no heat. For all these came to be at the end of time when God wished to make the cosmos. For even heaven and earth came to be in these six days along with everything that exists in them. Indeed, since that time until now when we have written these discourses, we know the years, as we find them in the genealogies of the Holy Scriptures. Therefore, through this he truly reveals, before God made the cosmos, other great [amounts of] time, which cannot be reckoned.

God created the entire incorporeal nature, which is the holy angelic powers and the glory and the entire power and the heavens, which receive light from the light of his holy *kenosis* and the glory of his exalted divinity, with joy and gladness full of spiritual rejoicing. They are well fed by the sight of the true *kenosis* of the holy Trinity, not in a separated sight, but rather in a sight that is humble and a double myriad pure according to the ability of each rank. As it is written: "The chariot of God is a double myriad; thousands are they who are glad."[11] For the sight of the true knowledge of the divinity of the holy Trinity is not limited. The ranks, whom we named at first, upon seeing the glory of that radiance, become greater, also shining forth light. And they bubble up springs of living water, which are holy, spiritual praises and odes. And in this way the entirety responds with an exalted response, all the more greatly exalting the holy Trinity. In truth, holy lights are alive in the presence of the light of the divinity that exists among them. For this reason, they become more divine, as it is written: "Declare the God of gods, declare the Lord of lords for his mercy is forever."[12]

Concerning the making of these holy, angelic powers, [nothing] was written, since the thought of men was not complete in the glory of God at that their time. Indeed the blessed Moses did not write about them; for he was well suited [to the task] and knew that the thought of man was not complete. Therefore, he did not speak of them, but rather the making of the cosmos alone is what he spoke about. As for those who spoke before the six days about the making of the powers that are in the heights, he did not speak about them.

For the devil fell from heaven in his great glory, even though he himself was an angel, but his thought was exalted in blasphemy and the evil of his iniquity, having said in his heart: "I will go up to heaven and establish my throne in the midst of the stars and become those exalted like God."[13] Because of these wicked

---

11. Ps 68:17 (67:17 LXX).
12. Ps 136:2–3 (135:2–3 LXX).
13. Isa 14:13–14.

thoughts, he fell in a very great fall. For this reason, God gave his authority to those who love his divinity to become a derision of him, namely the devil who had become an apostate and an enemy to God.

For this reason also, God made his servants to trample upon him and all his power. And on what occasion did the devil fall? The Scriptures did not tell us about it, nor did it tell us about their countless names, who are the archangels and the entire multitude of servants of God. But rather, it told us the name of those three archangels alone, which are Michael and Gabriel and Raphael.

Yet one will say to me: "In which place did the Scriptures say this to you?" Listen, and I will tell you: when he wrote in the book of Daniel the prophet about Michael and Gabriel, as he said: "Michael, the great leader, is the one who guards over the children of your people";[14] and also he said: "The man Gabriel came to me"[15]; and also: "Gabriel taught me the vision";[16] and he wrote also about Gabriel in the holy Gospels. Concerning the third archangel, namely Raphael, search the book of Tobit and Tobias his son, and you will recognize the precise revelation concerning him, the good president for the entire race of men and good announcer to the mysteries of God.

We also make remembrance of these archangels, who were chosen in the goodness of God, to have mercy on us and release us from our sins and our trespasses according to the greatness of his compassions. I honor also the churches built in the name of these holy archangels. We know that God—along with his angels and their dispatch in his mercy over the entire inhabited world over them [i.e., the churches]—the God of everyone exists in every place built in his name, and he purifies them, blessing them on the day of their provision of bread. And these exist through the entreaty of the Archangel Michael and the servant of the holy archangels.

Therefore, we make remembrance of these holy archangels, not by remembering their creation on the occasion when it happened. We do not suggest that on the twelfth of Hathōr Michael was appointed as an archangel according to the discourse of those who have gone astray. It did not happen in this way, but rather before day or evening or month were given name, Michael was an archangel along with his other countless friends. After the devil fell from heaven in his great glory, he gave his evil thoughts to the heart of those who claim that on the twelfth of the month of Hathōr Michael the archangel was appointed in place of the devil. After they, along with those who are prone to fall, say that the devil

14. Dan 12:1.
15. Dan 9:21.
16. Dan 8:16.

was cast out on the twelfth of that month, namely Hathōr, Michael himself was established on the twelfth of this same month Hathōr.

As for us, we respond to those who say these things in the following way: "You have gone astray, and you do not know the Scriptures or the power of God."[17] For our fathers the teachers who existed before us did not say any of these things. Those who say that on the twelfth of Hathōr the devil was cast out or Michael was appointed in his place, those of this sort have been led astray from the knowledge of God. For they blaspheme the great Archangel Michael, to whom they give a blow, and they do not consider both his great honor and glory to be anything, as they say in their heart worthy of excommunication: "If the devil had not fallen from heaven, Michael would not have become an archangel, but [*two illegible lines*]." For we believe that the holy Archangel Michael is honored in front of the holy Trinity, and he is the leader of all the armies of heaven before the devil fell at all.

Then, others do not find glory in these things, but say that "at the hour when man was made, God told all the angels to worship Adam" and "the angels worshiped Adam, except the devil only." Then they say that "the devil said to God: 'I will not worship [. . .].'" [*To our knowledge, the rest of the homily has not been transmitted*]

17. Matt 22:29.

7. Pseudo-Cyril of Alexandria, *Encomium Interpreting Part of the Apocalypse of John the Apostle of Christ Jesus*

Introduction and translation by Mary K. Farag

This homily attributed to Cyril of Alexandria, but probably not written by him, offers a verse-by-verse commentary on Revelation 4 and 7–12. It is unique for two reasons. First, verse-by-verse commentaries are a rare find among extant Coptic texts. Second, very few commentaries on Revelation were produced in late antiquity. Translated here for the first time into English is the section on Revelation 12:1–5. The woman described in 12:1–2 is variously identified by late antique and medieval exegetes as Mary the Theotokos, the church, or the anti-Theotokos. The critical issue centers on the woman's pain in travail. Here, however, the homilist quotes a version explicitly stating that the woman did not have pain, thus obviating objections to the identification of the woman as Mary.

Bibliography

Text and Editions

Hyvernat, Henri, ed. *Codices Coptici Photographice Expressi: Bibliothecae Pierpont Morgan.* Vol. 25. Rome: n.p., 1922.

Orlandi, Tito. *Omelie copte: Scelte e tradotte, con una introduzione sulla letterature copta.* Turin: Società editrice internazionale, 1981.

TRANSLATION

Encomium Interpreting Part of the Apocalypse of John the Apostle of Christ Jesus

Title

An encomium that Apa Cyril, the archbishop of Rakote, delivered, interpreting part of the Apocalypse of John the Apostle of Christ Jesus. In the peace of God. Amen.

Excerpt (from Coptic pp. 57–59)

"A woman clothed with the sun, the moon under her feet, also twelve stars were a crown upon her head, being pregnant, in travail though not [*sic*] having pain, shouting to give birth."[1] Who is that woman whose name it partly named? She is the one who has known within herself the [names] that belong to her. She is also the one who has cleansed those round about us, having appeared to accept the middle into our hands and the Lord of all, through whom the entire inhabited world received light according to the testimony of the twelve stars (which are the sun and the moon and the stars and their cosmic force) to the mystery that he revealed. Their voice went forth equal to one another like the other lights. For I call the apostles "light." For truly in light, their light spread forth over the entire inhabited world.[2] Now then, let us come to the woman. For our mouth is not needed to beautify her. For which person knows her? And which mouth can approach her? We will not be able to think about it. City or appointed time? Virgin or with child? Nurse or mother? Abiding or at rest? Place of light or place of appearance? Mother of Christ or pure treasure? For she is the holy Theotokos, Mary, who gave birth to the great light of the entire inhabited world, our Lord Jesus Christ and our God, our Savior.

And also, he said: "Another great sign appeared in heaven, a great red dragon, having seven heads and ten horns and seven diadems upon his horns."[3] And also, he said: "he drew the twelve stars down with his tail. He cast them down to the earth, and the dragon stood up to the woman, so that, when he would

1. Rev 12:1–2.
2. Cf. Ps 19:4 (18:4 LXX).
3. Rev 12:3.

see her give birth to her child, he might eat him. And she gave birth to a male child, who would give pasture to all the nations with an iron staff."[4] But he did not give the means to this one [the male child] because it was not yet his time to mount the cross and be crucified for our race, so that we might speak freely and our nations would marvel at us. He [the dragon] is the one who plotted against our race through a multitude, to which he gave the instrument. Although they knew that no one could do him evil, all the nations followed. He gave them pasture with an iron staff and no evil would befall him, since he is the Son of God. Because of this, "he was seized to God,"[5] since he came forth from God, and he is his only begotten.

4. Rev 12:4–5.
5. Rev 12:5.

6

ETHIOPIC

Introduction and Bibliography by Aaron M. Butts

T he ancient Kingdom of Aksum, which was centered on what is now Eritrea and northern Ethiopia, was considered one of the great world powers in late antiquity.[1] The *Kephalaia* of the third-century prophet Mani, for instance, go so far as to list the Kingdom of Aksum as one of the four great kingdoms of the world alongside those of Babylon and of Persia, the Romans, and the Chinese. The prominence of the Aksumite Kingdom during late antiquity derived at least in part from its port city, Adulis. Strategically located on the western side of the Red Sea, Adulis was an important stop on the Indian Ocean trade routes that spanned from the Roman Empire to India and beyond. The port of Adulis, thus, brought significant wealth to the Aksumite Kingdom and connected it to the broader Mediterranean world.

Christianity reached the Aksumite Kingdom by the reign of King ʿEzana in the middle of the fourth century. This can be established by one of ʿEzana's inscriptions, written in Greek, that begins: "In the faith of God and in the power of the Father, Son, and Holy Spirit, who saved the kingdom for me, in the faith of his Son Jesus Christ, who helped me and who always helps me, I, ʿEzana, king of

1. This publication was supported by the Andrew W. Mellon Foundation Fellowship for Assistant Professors at the Institute for Advanced Study in Princeton, NJ. I would also like to thank the following people for their help: Glen Bowersock, Jeremy Brown, Peter Brown, Leah Comeau, Paul Dilley, Ted Erho, Simcha Gross, Reese Hartmann, Christopher Jones, Steven Kaplan, Dawit Muluneh, Meseret Oldjira, Janet Timbie, Lucas Van Rompay, and James Walters. For additional information on most topics related to Ethiopia, including Ethiopian Christianity, the reader is directed to S. Uhlig, ed., *Encyclopaedia Aethiopica*, vol. 1: *A–C*; vol. 2: *D–Ha*; vol. 3: *He–N*; vol. 4 (with A. Bausi): *O–X*; A. Bausi, ed., vol. 5 (with S. Uhlig): *Y–Z, Supplementa, Addenda et Corrigenda, Maps, Index* (Wiesbaden: Harrassowitz, 2003–14), where state-of-the-art entries, often with extensive bibliographies, can be found. In addition, a number of foundational articles in the field are collected in A. Bausi, ed., *Languages and Cultures of Eastern Christianity: Ethiopian* (Surrey: Ashgate, 2012).

the Aksumites . . ." (*RIÉ* 271).[2] Further evidence for 'Ezana's Christianity derives from numismatics: in addition to coins with a pagan crescent and moon as well as coins without a religious symbol, a Christian cross is found on some of the official coinage of 'Ezana. Hagiographic accounts of the conversion of an Aksumite king also exist, first attested in the *Ecclesiastical History* (10.9–10) of the Latin church historian Rufinus (died 411), which was transmitted into Ethiopic as the *Homily on Frumentius*, but it remains uncertain whether these hagiographic accounts contain reliable historical information.[3]

Apart from the scant information that can be distilled from coins and inscriptions, little is known about Christianity in the Aksumite Kingdom.[4] There are Christian church buildings in Adulis already from the fourth century. In addition, an Aksumite building, which archeologists identify as a fourth-century Christian basilica, was recently discovered at Betä Säma'ti, a village located over forty kilometers northeast of Aksum.[5] In general, however, there is little material evidence for Christianity in the Aksumite Kingdom before the sixth century, when remains of other church buildings and Christian structures are first widely attested.[6] Around this same time, the traveler Cosmas Indicopleustes (ca. 550) reported that there were a large number of churches in the Aksumite Kingdom as well as numerous bishops, martyrs, and monks. It is also known that the sixth-century Aksumite King Kaleb sent a military expedition to Ḥimyar in the Arabian Peninsula in order to quell the persecution of Christians in the city of Najran. This event would be widely remembered not only in Ethiopic sources but also across the broader Mediterranean world, where it was recounted in Greek, Syriac, Arabic, and other languages.[7] Apart from occasional exceptions

---

2. A full translation of this inscription is given below in no. 1.

3. A translation of the Ethiopic *Homily on Frumentius* is given below in no. 2, where additional discussion of its historical reliability is found. I am writing a fuller study of this topic, tentatively entitled *Ezana: The First Christian African King*.

4. In general, see H. Brakmann, *ΤΟ ΠΑΡΑ ΤΟΙΣ ΒΑΡΒΑΡΟΙΣ ΕΡΓΟΝ ΘΕΙΟΝ: Die Einwurzelung der Kirche im spätantiken Reich von Aksum* (Bonn: Borengässer, 1994).

5. M. J. Harrower et al., "Beta Samati: The Discovery and Excavation of an Aksumite Town," *Antiquity* 93.372 (2019): 1534–52. This is the initial publication, and some scholars are awaiting additional data before accepting the dating as well as the interpretation as a Christian basilica.

6. For the archeology of the Aksumite Kingdom, see D. W. Phillipson, *Foundations of an African Civilisation: Aksum and the Northern Horn, 1000 BC–AD 1300* (Suffolk: Currey, 2012); for the churches in particular, see D. W. Phillipson, *Ancient Churches of Ethiopia: Fourth–Fourteenth Centuries* (New Haven: Yale University Press, 2009), 37–50.

7. See G. W. Bowersock, *The Throne of Adulis* (Oxford: Oxford University Press, 2013); with more detail in J. Beaucamp, F. Briquel-Chatonnet, and C. J. Robin, eds., *Juifs et chrétiens en Arabie aux Vᵉ et VIᵉ siècles* (Paris: Association des amis du Centre d'histoire et civilisation de Byzance, 2010).

such as these, however, most of what we know about Ethiopian Christianity is mediated through later periods.[8]

The Christianity of the Aksumite Kingdom was miaphysite: it professed "the one incarnate nature [*physis*] of God, the Word" in the footsteps of Cyril of Alexandria (seated 412–44), rejecting the two-nature (dyophysite) Christology held by Nestorius and other Antiochene theologians, which was condemned at the Council of Ephesus (431), as well as rejecting the Christology accepted at the Council of Chalcedon (451), which professed "two natures, without confusion or change, without division or separation." Thus, the Christianity of the Aksumite Kingdom was allied with the other miaphysite Christians who would ultimately become known as the Oriental Orthodox churches, including the Coptic, Armenian, Syriac Orthodox, and others. Among these, Ethiopian Christianity has throughout its history had especially close ties with the Coptic Christianity of its northern neighbor Egypt.

During the Aksumite period, a sizable number of texts were translated from Greek into the Ethiopic language, which is also known as Gəʿəz. This includes the Greek Bible (both the Septuagint and the New Testament) as well as a number of parabiblical texts, such as *Enoch, Jubilees, Paralipomena Baruch* (*Fourth Baruch*), and the *Ascension of Isaiah*. Parabiblical texts such as these may have been considered authoritative by Ethiopian Christians in the Aksumite period.[9] In addition to biblical and parabiblical texts, other Greek texts were also translated into Ethiopic during the Aksumite period, such as the body of theological texts known as *Qerəllos* (i.e., Cyril of Alexandria) and the more-recently discovered group of texts now referred to as the *Aksumite Collection*, to name only two.[10] Native Ethiopic compositions from the Aksumite period are, however, far less certain. A number of liturgical texts, above all the *Daggʷa*, are, for instance, attributed to the Ethiopian Saint Yared, purportedly active in the sixth century.[11] There is, however, no definitive evidence that these liturgical texts

8. See P. Piovanelli, "Reconstructing the Social and Cultural History of the Aksumite Kingdom: Some Methodological Reflections," in *Inside and Out: Interactions between Rome and the Peoples on the Arabian and Egyptian Frontiers in Late Antiquity*, ed. J. H. F. Dijkstra and G. Fisher, Late Antique History and Religion 8 (Leuven: Peeters, 2014), 329–50; and, more emphatically, A. M. Butts, "Mind the Gap: Sources for Late Antique Aksum" (forthcoming).

9. For a nuanced approach to thinking about authoritative texts in earlier Ethiopian Christianity, see T. Erho, "The Shepherd of Hermas in Ethiopia," in *L'Africa, l'Oriente mediterraneo e l'Europa: Tradizioni e culture a confronto*, ed. P. Nicelli, Africana Ambrosiana 1 (Milan: Biblioteca Ambrosiana/Rome: Bulzoni, 2015), 97–117.

10. For the latter, see A. Bausi and A. Camplani, "The *History of the Episcopate of Alexandria* (*HEpA*): *Editio minor* of the Fragments Preserved in the *Aksumite Collection* and in the *Codex Veronensis* LX (58)," *Adamantius* 22 (2016): 249–302, with further references.

11. A hagiographic account of Yared is translated below in no. 3.

extend back to the Aksumite period, not to mention that the figure of Yared seems legendary, with his hagiography appearing only many centuries after he is said to have lived.[12]

Regardless of whether any native compositions from the Aksumite period survive, there is still a sizable body of Ethiopic literature from the Aksumite period consisting of translations from Greek. It must, however, be stressed that texts stemming from the Aksumite period are almost exclusively transmitted in manuscripts dating to a much later period. Most Ethiopic manuscripts date to after 1500, with a smaller number dating between the thirteenth and fifteenth centuries. There are, however, a few possible earlier exceptions. The earliest Ethiopic manuscripts are two gospels from ᵓInda Abba Gärima (I and III). These manuscripts include Ethiopic translations of the Four Gospels, along with other prefatory texts, as well as an impressive illumination program.[13] Though there is general consensus about their relative dating as the earliest Ethiopic manuscripts, scholars disagree about their absolute dating. Most scholars date them between the ninth and thirteenth centuries. Recently, however, a much earlier date, ranging from 330 to 650, has been proposed based on radiocarbon dating. There is not yet, however, a consensus in the field regarding the validity of the radiocarbon dating—a problem exacerbated by the results never having been published in full. If the Abba Gärima gospels do, however, go back to late antiquity, they would be precious evidence for the Aksumite period of Ethiopian Christianity.

By the seventh century, the Aksumite Kingdom was in decline, and it would eventually collapse, probably by around 900. This was at least partly due to changing trade patterns along the Indian Ocean trade routes in the wake of the expansion of Islam. Another factor was the depletion of natural resources, including but not limited to land degradation. Little is known about the time period from the collapse of the Aksumite Kingdom to the beginning of the Solomonic period around 1270—to which we turn shortly. During this intermediate period, local leaders seem to have vied for power, but they left little trace in the written record. Aksumite literature must have, however, continued to be copied and transmitted during this time. In addition, some of the hypogeum, or rock-hewn, churches, especially those of the Gärʿalta region (the so-called

12. For Yared through history, in text, art, and music, see M. E. Heldman and K. K. Shelemay, "Concerning Saint Yared," in *Studies in Ethiopian Languages, Literature, and History: Festschrift for Getatchew Haile, Presented by his Friends and Colleagues,* ed. A. C. McCollum, Äthiopistische Forschungen 83 (Wiesbaden: Harrassowitz, 2017), 65–93.

13. See J. S. McKenzie and F. Watson, *The Garima Gospels: Early Illuminated Gospel Books from Ethiopia* (Oxford: Manar al-Athar, 2016), for a recent study, which is, however, not without problems.

églises de vallée, "churches of the valley"), could possibly date to this intermediate period, though both earlier and later dates have been proposed.[14] Thanks to recent scholarship, more is known about the dynasty immediately prior to the Solomonic: the Zag^we.[15] During the Zag^we Dynasty, power shifted away from the northern highlands to the central regions of what is now Ethiopia. A new capital was established around Lalibäla, named after the most famous king of the Zag^we, where spectacular monolithic church buildings were carved into rock.

Around 1270, Yətbaräk, who would be the last king of the Zag^we, was killed by Yəkunno Amlak. This event would later be remembered as inaugurating a new era: the Solomonic. According to the new rulers, the accession of Yəkunno Amlak restored the Solomonic dynasty that had connected the earlier Aksumite rulers with the biblical Solomon via his son Menelik, who was conceived by Makəda, the Queen of Sheba, and who became the first ruler of Ethiopia in time immemorial. One of the classic formulations of this narrative is told in the *Kəbrä Nägäst*, or *Glory of the Kings*.[16] The Solomonic dynasty would last from Yəkunno Amlak in ca. 1270 until 1974 with the rise of the Marxist Derg. Christianity would flourish during the Solomonic period—with the occasional interruption, such as the conquests of Grañ discussed below—throughout what is now Ethiopia and Eritrea. During the medieval period, Ethiopian Christians would also venture outside of their homeland, especially throughout Egypt as well as to Jerusalem and beyond.[17]

In contrast to the earlier Aksumite period, much more is known about the Solomonic period of Ethiopian Christianity.[18] Perhaps most famously, hundreds of thousands—and perhaps even a few million—Ethiopic manuscripts are likely to be extant. Again, it should be stressed that the vast majority of these manuscripts date to after 1500, with a smaller number dating between the thirteenth and fifteenth centuries. Many of these manuscripts contain locally produced art,

---

14. For discussion, see Phillipson, *Ancient Churches of Ethiopia*, 86–107, 184–87.

15. See especially M.-L. Derat, *L'énigme d'une dynastie sainte et usurpatrice dans le royaume chrétien d'Éthiopie du XIᵉ au XIIIᵉ siècle*, Hagiologia: Études sur la sainteté et l'hagiographie (Turnhout: Brepols, 2018).

16. See the selection translated below in no. 4.

17. S. Kelly, "Medieval Ethiopian Diasporas," in Kelly's *A Companion to Medieval Ethiopia and Eritrea* (Leiden: Brill, 2020), 425–53.

18. See Taddesse Tamrat, *Church and State in Ethiopia, 1270–1527* (Oxford: Clarendon, 1972); S. Kaplan, *The Monastic Holy Man and the Christianization of Early Solomonic Ethiopia* (Wiesbaden: Steiner, 1984); M.-L. Derat, *Le domaine des rois éthiopiens, 1270–1527: Espace, pouvoir et monarchisme* (Paris: Publications de la Sorbonne, 2003); and most recently Kelly, *Companion to Medieval Ethiopia and Eritrea*. For the broader African context, see F.-X. Fauvelle, *Le rhinocéros d'or* (Paris: Alma, 2013), with English translation as *The Golden Rhinoceros: Histories of the African Middle Ages*, trans. Troy Tice (Princeton: Princeton University Press, 2018).

some of very high quality. In addition, these manuscripts preserve a huge body of Ethiopian Christian literature of various genres, including hagiography, liturgy, homilies, and chronicles. Most of the Ethiopic literature of the Solomonic period consists of translations of Christian Arabic texts that were circulating in Egypt, and some of these Christian Arabic texts were themselves translated from other traditions, such as Syriac.[19] Many of the Ethiopic translations of Arabic texts are attributed to the circle of Abba Sälama (active in the fourteenth century), though translations from Arabic into Ethiopic took place before and after this time as well. In addition to translation literature, there are also native compositions in Ethiopic from the Solomonic period, though they are admittedly fewer.

One of the most prominent patrons of native Ethiopic literature was King Zär'a Ya'əqob (born 1399). Zär'a Ya'əqob ruled the Solomonic dynasty from around 1434 until his death in 1468. In addition to being the political ruler, he also played an outsized role in the leadership of Ethiopian Christianity at this time. Under his auspices, for instance, a large number of texts were produced, both native compositions as well as translations. Much of the literature associated with Zär'a Ya'əqob concerns religious controversies—and related reforms—during his times. Zär'a Ya'əqob proved to be especially influential in institutionalizing the veneration of Mary—a trait for which Ethiopian Christianity continues to be known today. The following paragraphs explore in more detail the literary production associated with Zär'a Ya'əqob in order to provide a glimpse of the richness, diversity, and complexity of Ethiopian Christianity in the early Solomonic period.

When Zär'a Ya'əqob came to power, Ethiopian Christianity was gripped by a controversy over whether Saturday should also be celebrated as a Christian Sabbath. More recent Ethiopian rulers and the Coptic patriarchs, under whose authority Ethiopian Christianity was at the time, opposed this, whereas a monastic group called the Ewosṭateans, who were based at the monastery of Däbrä Bizän, vehemently argued for the two-Sabbath position, in line with traditional Ethiopian practice. This conflict became so intense that the Ewosṭateans refused

19. For the Syriac connection, see A. M. Butts, "Syriac Contacts with Ethiopic Christianity," in *GEDSH*, 148–53, and with more detail Butts, "From Syriac to Arabic to Ethiopic: *Loci* of Change in Transmission," in *Circolazione di testi e superamento delle barriere linguistiche e culturali nelle tradizioni orientali*, ed. R. B. Finazzi, F. Forte, C. Milani, and M. Moriggi, Orientalia Ambrosiana 7 (Milan: Biblioteca Ambrosiana–Centro Ambrosiano, 2020), 21–57. In this regard, it should be noted that most scholars have now abandoned the previous hypothesis of a "second Christianization" of Ethiopia according to which Syriac Christians heavily influenced Ethiopian Christianity in the Aksumite period. See A. Brita, *I racconti tradizionali sulla seconda cristianizzazione dell'Etiopia: Il ciclo agiografico dei Nove Santi*, Studi Africanistici: Serie Etiopica 7 (Naples: Università degli Studi di Napoli "L'Orientale," 2010).

ordination from the Egyptian metropolitan—a practice that seems to have been well established at the time and that continued for centuries later (until 1948 in fact). Zär'a Ya'əqob was sympathetic to the view of the Ewosṭateans, and their position was accepted at the council of Däbrä Məṭmaq (1450), a council over which Zär'a Ya'əqob himself personally presided. Zär'a Ya'əqob marked the occasion by giving extensive land grants to the Ewosṭateans, but he also bestowed favors on the opposition group, many of whom were based at the important monastery of Däbrä Libanos. In this way, Zär'a Ya'əqob was ultimately able to appease both sides. The decision of the council is recorded in the *Book of Light*, a voluminous work outlining Zär'a Ya'əqob's view on a number of theological topics. The two-Sabbath position is also promoted in other works attributed to Zär'a Ya'əqob, such as his collection of hymns entitled *The Lord Reigns*.

Zär'a Ya'əqob adopted a less conciliatory approach in a conflict with a different monastic group, the Stephanites, who were based in the monastery of Gundä Gunde. Following their leader Ǝsṭifanos, the Stephanites were critical of Zär'a Ya'əqob's innovative promotion of the cult of the cross and especially of the cult of Mary. In response, Zär'a Ya'əqob had Ǝsṭifanos tortured and imprisoned, where he eventually died. Zär'a Ya'əqob also persecuted the followers of Ǝsṭifanos, labeling them "enemies of Mary" and *Ayhud*, or "Jews."[20] In defense of Zär'a Ya'əqob's innovative views on the veneration of Mary and of the cross, a number of texts were composed, such as the *Book of the Trinity* and the *Book of Nativity*, polemical treatises that specifically engage the Stephanites.[21] He also promoted the *Miracles of Mary*, incorporating their reading into the liturgical cycle.[22] In addition, Zär'a Ya'əqob was a patron of visual art in support of the veneration of Mary and of the cross.[23] It is, thus, no coincidence that one of the most-accomplished Ethiopian painters, Fərē Ṣeyon, was active during the reign of Zär'a Ya'əqob, when he painted devotional images venerating Mary. A fine example survives, which has a legend identifying the painter and mentioning Zär'a Ya'əqob by name.[24]

20. *Ayhud* here is a polemical label. Zär'a Ya'əqob adopts the well-established practice of Christians' mapping their theological opponents onto "Jews"; for earlier antecedents, see A. M. Butts and S. Gross, "Introduction," in *Jews and Syriac Christians: Intersections across the First Millennium*, ed. A. M. Butts and S. Gross, Texts and Studies in Ancient Judaism 180 (Tübingen: Mohr Siebeck, 2020), 12–18, esp. n60. Thus, Zär'a Ya'əqob's *Ayhud* should be strictly distinguished from the so-called Ethiopian Jews, or Betä Ǝsra'el; for which, see n. 29 below.

21. A selection is translated below in no. 6.

22. One of the *Miracles of Mary* is translated below in no. 5.

23. S. Kaplan, "Seeing Is Believing: The Power of the Visual Culture in the Religious World of Aṣe Zär'a Ya'eqob of Ethiopia (1434–1468)," *Journal of Religion in Africa* 32 (2002): 403–21.

24. See M. E. Heldman, *The Marian Icons of the Painter Frē Seyon: A Study in Fifteenth-Century Ethiopian Art, Patronage, and Spirituality* (Wiesbaden: Harrassowitz, 1994),

Mention should also be made of Zär'a Ya'əqob's campaign to eradicate magic. An entire treatise on this topic is attributed to him, the *Epistle of Humanity*. In addition, a number of passages in the *Book of the Pearl* also seem to be motivated by a desire to eradicate magic. In these works, Zär'a Ya'əqob condemns various types of magicians, preferring instead his particular version of institutional Christianity.[25] It is tempting to connect Zär'a Ya'əqob's condemnation of magic with the Christian prayer amulets—often called "magic scrolls"—that survive today.[26] Though all surviving examples—there are thousands and thousands—probably date to the last couple of centuries, the practice of such Ethiopic prayer amulets likely goes back much earlier. Thus, some of Zär'a Ya'əqob's polemic in the fifteenth century may be directed specifically against such prayer amulets. This provides an interesting perspective on Zär'a Ya'əqob's vision for Christianity: his is a top-down approach that seeks to regulate the practices of the common Christian.[27] There is also perhaps a gendered aspect to this. While it cannot be denied that the Ethiopian prayer amulets are used by men, the vast majority of surviving amulets are for women. One wonders if the same dynamics are not at play with Zär'a Ya'əqob: do we see with Zär'a Ya'əqob a male Christian hierarchy dismissing a religious practice associated primarily with women as non-Christian magic?

These paragraphs provide just a brief, selective overview of the religious activity of a single—even if important—figure of Ethiopian Christianity in the Solomonic period. So much more could be said about Zär'a Ya'əqob, not to mention about the broader Solomonic period of Ethiopian Christianity in which he participated. There were, for instance, important authors before Zär'a Ya'əqob, such as Giyorgis of Sägla, who wrote numerous works, none more important than his voluminous theological treatise the *Book of Mysteries* (written in 1424). After Zär'a Ya'əqob, mention could be made of the Muslim convert 'Ənbaqom (ca. 1470–1560), who translated a number of Arabic works into Ethiopic as well as wrote several treatises of his own, including the *Gate of Faith*. This is not even

---

though note that her attribution of other paintings to Fəre Ṣeyon is difficult to maintain on stylistic grounds.

25. S. Kaplan, "Magic and Religion in Christian Ethiopia: Some Preliminary Remarks," in *Studia Aethiopica: In Honor of Siegbert Uhlig on the Occasion of His 65th Birthday*, ed. V. Böll et al. (Wiesbaden: Harrassowitz, 2004), 413–22.

26. A representative Ethiopian prayer amulet is translated below in no. 7. In general, see B. Burtea, *Zwei äthiopische Zauberrollen*, Semitica et Semitohamitica Berolinensia 1 (Aachen: Shaker, 2001).

27. See A. M. Butts, "Rethinking 'Magic' in Ancient Christianity and Judaism: A View from Ethiopian Prayer Scrolls" (forthcoming).

to mention that Christian literature continued to be written in Ethiopic through the period of the House of Gondär (1560–1770) and in fact continued after this, even until today, though on a more limited scale.

Two events in the sixteenth century would have a lasting impact on Ethiopian Christianity. Starting in the 1530s, Ethiopia came under attack from the Muslim leader Aḥmad b. Ibrāhīm al-Ghāzī, or Grañ as he is more commonly known. Victorious in a number of battles, Grañ was able to conquer many regions of Ethiopia. Both Ethiopic Christian and Muslim Arabic sources speak of the destruction of a large number of Ethiopian churches and monasteries during this period. In addition, a number of Christians converted to Islam. Grañ was ultimately killed in battle in 1543, after which time the Muslim conquest of Ethiopia came to a halt. Not too long after the fall of Grañ, the Portuguese sent a number of Jesuit missions to Ethiopia. Though resisted at first, the Jesuits ultimately were able to convert two Ethiopian kings, Zädəngəl (ruled 1603–4) and Susənyos (ruled 1607–32), to Roman Catholicism. The Ethiopian people, however, rebelled, and Zädəngəl was killed in battle, whereas Susənyos was ultimately forced to abdicate the throne, transferring power to his son Fasilädäs (ruled 1632–67). During Fasilädäs's reign, Ethiopian Christianity would again become dominant.

Today, Ethiopia is home to the largest number of Oriental Orthodox Christians in the world. According to the 2007 national census of Ethiopia, over 32 million Ethiopians—or 43.5% of the population—identified with the Ethiopian Orthodox Täwaḥədo Church, as it is known today.[28] This does not include the several million adherents of the Eritrean Orthodox Täwaḥədo Church, which has been autonomous since Eritrea gained its independence from Ethiopia in 1993. In addition, 13.6 million Ethiopians identified as Protestant in the 2007 census, with a much smaller number of Catholics (slightly over 532,000). Islam is the second largest religion in Ethiopia, with over 25 million Muslims counted in the 2007 census (33.9% of the population). Mention should also be made of the much smaller number of "Ethiopian Jews," or Betä ᵓƎsra'el (also called Fälaša), most of whom immigrated to the modern State of Israel after its establishment in 1948.[29] A relatively large number of Ethiopian Christians live in diasporas throughout the world, with the greatest number in the United States. Tens if not hundreds of thousands of Ethiopians are, for instance, estimated to live in the broader Washington, DC, metropolitan area. Ethiopian Christianity has also spread beyond

---

28. The Ethiopic word *täwaḥədo* means "being one, united," referring to the confession of one nature of Christ: Greek *mia physis*.

29. For the Betä ᵓƎsra'el, see S. Kaplan, *The Beta Israel (Falasha) in Ethiopia* (New York: New York University Press, 1992). For their literature, see W. Leslau, *Falasha Anthology* (New Haven: Yale University Press, 1951); S. Kaplan, *Les Falāshās* (Turnhout: Brepols, 1990).

the Ethiopian people themselves, most notably being a major influence on the Rastafari movement that developed in Jamaica in the 1930s and became world famous with the reggae singer Bob Marley (1945–81).

Bibliography

Bausi, A., ed. *Languages and Cultures of Eastern Christianity: Ethiopian.* Surrey: Ashgate, 2012.

Bausi, A., and A. Camplani. "The *History of the Episcopate of Alexandria (HEpA): Editio minor* of the Fragments Preserved in the *Aksumite Collection* and in the *Codex Veronensis* LX (58)." *Adamantius* 22 (2016): 249–302.

Beaucamp, J., F. Briquel-Chatonnet, and C. J. Robin, eds. *Juifs et chrétiens en Arabie aux Vᵉ et VIᵉ siècles.* Paris: Association des amis du Centre d'histoire et civilisation de Byzance, 2010.

Bernand, É. *Recueil des inscriptions de l'Éthiopie des périodes pré-axoumite et axoumite.* Vol. 3, *Traductions et commentaires.* Part A, *Les inscriptions grecques.* Paris: Boccard, 2000.

Bernand, E., A. J. Drewes, and R. Schneider. *Recueil des inscriptions de l'Éthiopie des périodes pré-axoumite et axoumite.* Vol. 1, *Les documents.* Vol. 2, *Les planches.* Paris: Boccard, 1991.

Bezold, C. *Kebra Nagast: Die Herrlichkeit der Könige.* Munich: Franz, 1905.

Bowersock, G. W. *The Throne of Adulis.* Oxford: Oxford University Press, 2013.

Brakmann, H. *ΤΟ ΠΑΡΑ ΤΟΙΣ ΒΑΡΒΑΡΟΙΣ ΕΡΓΟΝ ΘΕΙΟΝ: Die Einwurzelung der Kirche im spätantiken Reich von Aksum.* Bonn: Borengässer, 1994.

Brita, A. *I racconti tradizionali sulla seconda cristianizzazione dell'Etiopia: Il ciclo agiografico dei Nove Santi.* Studi Africanistici, Serie Etiopica 7. Naples: Università degli Studi di Napoli "L'Orientale," 2010.

Budge, E. A. W. *The Book of the Saints of the Ethiopian Church.* Cambridge: Cambridge University Press, 1928.

———. *Legends of Our Lady Mary the Perpetual Virgin and Her Mother Ḥannâ.* London: Medici Society, 1922.

———. *The Miracles of the Blessed Virgin Mary.* London: Griggs, 1900.

———. *One Hundred and Ten Miracles of Our Lady Mary.* London: Medici Society, 1923.

———. *The Queen of Sheba and Her Only Son Menyelek (Kĕbra Nagast).* Oxford: Oxford University Press, 1932.

Burtea, B. *Zwei äthiopische Zauberrollen.* Semitica et Semitohamitica Berolinensia 1. Aachen: Shaker, 2001.

Butts, A. M. "The Ethiopic Homily on Frumentius: A Critical Edition." Forthcoming.

———. *Ethiopic in 20 Lessons*. Leuven: Peeters. Forthcoming.

———. "From Syriac to Arabic to Ethiopic: Loci of Change in Transmission." Pages 21–57 in *Circolazione di testi e superamento delle barriere linguistiche e culturali nelle tradizioni orientali*. Edited by R. B. Finazzi et al. Orientalia Ambrosiana 7. Milan: Biblioteca Ambrosiana–Centro Ambrosiano, 2020.

———. "Mind the Gap: Sources for Late Antique Aksum." Forthcoming.

———. "A Plea for a Medieval Reading of Ethiopic Manuscripts: The Case of the Homily on Frumentius." Forthcoming.

———. "Rethinking 'Magic' in Ancient Christianity and Judaism: A View from Ethiopian Prayer Scrolls." Forthcoming.

———. "Syriac Contacts with Ethiopic Christianity." Pages 148–53 in *The Gorgias Encyclopedic Dictionary of the Syriac Heritage*. Edited by Sebastian P. Brock et al. Piscataway, NJ: Gorgias, 2011 (online at https://gedsh.bethmardutho.org).

Butts, A. M., and S. Gross. "Introduction." Pages 1–26 in *Jews and Syriac Christians: Intersections across the First Millennium*. Edited by A. M. Butts and S. Gross. Texts and Studies in Ancient Judaism 180. Tübingen: Mohr Siebeck, 2020.

Cerulli, E. *Il libro etiopico dei Miracoli di Maria e le sue fonti nelle letterature del medio evo latino*. Rome: Bardi, 1943.

Colin, G. *Le livre éthiopien des miracles de Marie (Taamra Mâryâm)*. Paris: Cerf, 2004.

———. *Le synaxaire éthiopien: Mois de Genbot*. Patrologia Orientalis 47.3. Turnhout: Brepols, 1997.

Derat, M.-L. *Le domaine des rois éthiopiens, 1270–1527: Espace, pouvoir et monarchisme*. Paris: Publications de la Sorbonne, 2003.

———. *L'énigme d'une dynastie sainte et usurpatrice dans le royaume chrétien d'Éthiopie du XIᵉ au XIIIᵉ siècle*. Hagiologia: Études sur la sainteté et l'hagiographie. Turnhout: Brepols, 2018.

Dobberahn, F. E. *Fünf äthiopische Zauberrollen: Text, Übersetzung, Kommentar*. Walldorf-Hessen: Orientkunde, 1976.

Drewes, A. J. *Recueil des inscriptions de l'Éthiopie des périodes pré-axoumite et axoumite*. Vol. 3, *Traductions et commentaires*. Part A, *Les inscriptions sémitiques*. Revised by Manfred Kropp. Edited by Manfred Kropp and Harry Stroomer. Äthiopistische Forschungen 85/De Goeje Fund 34. Wiesbaden: Harrassowitz, 2019.

Erho, T. "The Shepherd of Hermas in Ethiopia." Pages 97–117 in *L'Africa, l'Oriente mediterraneo e l'Europa: Tradizioni e culture a confront*. Edited by P. Nicelli. Africana Ambrosiana 1. Milan: Biblioteca Ambrosiana/Rome: Bulzoni, 2015.

Fauvelle, F.-X. *The Golden Rhinoceros: Histories of the African Middle Ages*. Translated by Troy Tice. Princeton: Princeton University Press, 2018.

———. *Le rhinocéros d'or*. Paris: Alma, 2013.

Getatchew, Haile. "The Homily in Honour of St. Frumentius, Bishop of Axum." *Analecta Bollandiana* 97 (1979): 309–18.

Harrower, M. J., et al. "Beta Samati: The Discovery and Excavation of an Aksumite Town." *Antiquity* 93.372 (2019): 1534–52.

Heldman, M. E. *The Marian Icons of the Painter Frē Seyon: A Study in Fifteenth-Century Ethiopian Art, Patronage, and Spirituality.* Wiesbaden: Harrassowitz, 1994.

Heldman, M. E., and K. K. Shelemay. "Concerning Saint Yared." Pages 65–93 in *Studies in Ethiopian Languages, Literature, and History: Festschrift for Getatchew Haile, Presented by His Friends and Colleagues.* Edited by A. C. McCollum. Äthiopistische Forschungen 83. Wiesbaden: Harrassowitz, 2017.

Kaplan, S. *The Beta Israel (Falasha) in Ethiopia.* New York: New York University Press, 1992.

———. *Les Falāshās.* Turnhout: Brepols, 1990.

———. "Magic and Religion in Christian Ethiopia: Some Preliminary Remarks." Pages 413–22 in *Studia Aethiopica: In Honor of Siegbert Uhlig on the Occasion of His 65th Birthday.* Edited by V. Böll et al. Wiesbaden: Harrassowitz, 2004.

———. *The Monastic Holy Man and the Christianization of Early Solomonic Ethiopia.* Wiesbaden: Steiner, 1984.

———. "Seeing Is Believing: The Power of the Visual Culture in the Religious World of Aşe Zär'a Ya'eqob of Ethiopia (1434–68)." *Journal of Religion in Africa* 32 (2002): 403–21.

Kelly, S. *A Companion to Medieval Ethiopia and Eritrea.* Leiden: Brill, 2020.

———. "Medieval Ethiopian Diasporas." Pages 425–53 in *A Companion to Medieval Ethiopia and Eritrea.* Edited by S. Kelly. Leiden: Brill, 2020.

Leslau, W. *Falasha Anthology.* New Haven: Yale University Press, 1951.

Lifchitz, D. *Textes éthiopiens magico-religieux.* Paris: Institut d'ethnologie, 1940.

Marrassini, P. *Storia e leggenda dell'Etiopia tardoantica: Le iscrizioni reali aksumite.* Brescia: Paideia, 2014.

McKenzie, J. S., and F. Watson. *The Garima Gospels: Early Illuminated Gospel Books from Ethiopia.* Oxford: Manar al-Athar, 2016.

Mercier, J. *Art That Heals. The Image as Medicine in Ethiopia.* New York: Museum for African Art, 1997.

———. *Rouleaux magiques éthiopiens.* Paris: Seuil, 1979.

Phillipson, D. W. *Ancient Churches of Ethiopia, Fourth–Fourteenth Centuries.* New Haven: Yale University Press, 2009.

———. *Foundations of an African Civilisation: Aksum and the Northern Horn, 1000 BC–AD 1300.* Suffolk: Currey, 2012.

Piovanelli, P. "Reconstructing the Social and Cultural History of the Aksumite Kingdom: Some Methodological Reflections." Pages 329–50 in *Inside and Out: Interactions between Rome and the Peoples on the Arabian and Egyptian Frontiers in*

Late Antiquity. Edited by J. H. F. Dijkstra and G. Fisher. Late Antique History and Religion 8. Leuven: Peeters, 2014.

Six, V. "Kategorien der äthiopischen Zaubertexte." *Zeitschrift der deutschen morgenländischen Gesellschaft* 139 (1989): 310–17.

Strelcyn, S. *Prières magiques éthiopiennes pour délier les charmes (maftəḥe šəray)*. Rocznik orientalistyczny 18. Warsaw: Państwowe Wydawnictwo Naukowe, 1955.

Taddesse Tamrat. *Church and State in Ethiopia, 1270–1527*. Oxford: Clarendon, 1972.

Uhlig, S., ed. *Encyclopaedia Aethiopica*. Vol. 1, *A–C*. Vol. 2, *D–Ha*. Vol. 3, *He–N*. Vol. 5 (with A. Bausi), *O–X*. A. Bausi, ed., vol. 6 (with S. Uhlig): *Y–Z, Supplementa, Addenda et Corrigenda, Maps, Index*. Wiesbaden: Harrassowitz, 2003–14.

Ullendorff, E. *The Ethiopians: An Introduction to Country and People*. 3rd ed. Oxford: Oxford University Press, 1973.

Villa, M. "Frumentius in the Ethiopic Sources: Mythopoeia and Text-Critical Considerations." *Rassegna di studi etiopici* 48 (2017): 87–111.

Wendt, K. *Das Maṣḥafa Milād (Liber Nativitatis) und Maṣḥafa Sellāsē (Liber Trinitatis)*. CSCO 221–22, 235–36. Leuven: Secrétariat du CSCO, 1962–63.

1. Select Inscriptions of 'Ezana

Introduction and translation by Aaron M. Butts

Despite conflicting arguments in the earlier secondary literature, there is now general consensus that 'Ezana is the first Aksumite king to present himself as a Christian. As noted above, this can be shown by the Christian cross found on some of the official coinage of 'Ezana as well as the trinitarian language in one of 'Ezana's inscriptions, written in Greek (*RIÉ* 271). This documentary evidence (both inscriptions and coins) for the Christianity of 'Ezana is corroborated by a letter attributed to Constantius that is embedded in Athanasius's *Apology to Constantius* (written in 356). This letter clearly implies that 'Ezana (along with one Sazanes)[1] is Christian, and it also discusses Frumentius, who is found in various hagiographic sources.[2] Thus, there is no question that 'Ezana presented himself as a Christian in the fourth century. Nevertheless, not all of 'Ezana's inscriptions have Christian language. Some invoke traditional deities, such as "the invincible god Ares (= Greek Ἄρεως [genitive], Ethiopic MḤRM)" (*RIÉ* 185 II = 185 bis II and parallels). Other inscriptions, such as *RIÉ* 189, employ what has been called "undifferentiated monotheistic" language, with references to the "Lord of heaven," the "Lord of the land," and the "Lord of all."[3] To account for these disparate data, scholars typically propose a linear conversion narrative of 'Ezana, whereby he moved from pagan to "undifferentiated monotheist" to Christian. This linear development is said to be paralleled by numismatic evidence, given the existence of 'Ezana's coins with disc and crescent, with no religious symbol, and with Christian crosses. This linear narrative of 'Ezana's conversion is not, however, without problems, and other interpretations of the data are possible and perhaps even preferable. The distinct self-presentations

---

1. For whom, see n. 11 below.

2. This includes the Ethiopic *Homily on Frumentius*, which is translated below in no. 2, as well as its ultimate source, the *Ecclesiastical History* (10.9–10) of the Latin church historian Rufinus (died 411).

3. Similar language is found in Old South Arabian inscriptions from the Arabian Peninsula starting in the second half of the fourth century, at almost exactly the same time as 'Ezana.

of 'Ezana may, for instance, have been motivated by different aims and intended audiences.[4]

Bibliography

Text and Editions

Bernand, É. *Recueil des inscriptions de l'Éthiopie des périodes pré-axoumite et axoumite*. Vol. 3, *Traductions et commentaires*. Part A, *Les inscriptions grecques*. Paris: Boccard, 2000.

Bernand, É., A. J. Drewes, and R. Schneider. *Recueil des inscriptions de l'Éthiopie des périodes pré-axoumite et axoumite*. Vol. 1, *Les documents*. Vol. 2, *Les planches*. Paris: Boccard, 1991.

Drewes, A. J. *Recueil des inscriptions de l'Éthiopie des périodes pré-axoumite et axoumite*. Vol. 3, *Traductions et commentaires*. Part B, *Les inscriptions sémitiques*. Revised by Manfred Kropp. Edited by Manfred Kropp and Harry Stroomer. Äthiopistische Forschungen 85/De Goeje Fund 34. Wiesbaden: Harrassowitz, 2019.

Studies

Marrassini, P. *Storia e leggenda dell'Etiopia tardoantica: Le iscrizioni reali aksumite*. Brescia: Paideia, 2014.

---

4. This is developed further in a monograph currently in progress, which is tentatively entitled *Ezana: The First Christian African King*.

TRANSLATION

RIÉ 185 I = 185 bis I (Ethiopic language in Old South Arabian script, with parallels)[5]

'Ezana, king of Aksum, of Ḥimyar, of Raydan, of Ḥabasha,[6] of Saba', of Ṣal-ḥen, of Ṣəyamo, of Kasu, and of Bəga,[7] king of kings, son of Ares,[8] who is not conquered [by his enemies],[9] after the people of Bəga revolted, we sent our brothers[10] Sazanes[11] and Ḥadifa to make war with them. After they arrived in the land, six kings along with their troops submitted. After they submitted, they led them away from their land with their children, their women, their troops, and their livestock—the number of people of the six kings was 4,400 along with 3,012 cattle, 5,224 sheep and goats, and around 677 animals[12]—supporting them from the day that they led them out of their land, each day, with 20,020 loaves of spelt bread and meat sufficient for them and giving them beer and wine to drink until satiated, for four months. When they arrived in Aksum, before us, we clothed them—the full extent of their people—and we adorned their kings.

5. The full notation of this multilingual series of inscriptions is *RIÉ* 185 I = 185 bis I / 185 II = 185 bis II / 270 = 270 bis. The text is written twice in Ethiopic language, once in the Old South Arabian script and then again in unvocalized Ethiopic script; there is also a Greek version of the text—giving two total languages and three total scripts. If this is not already complicated enough, it is all then doubled, with each script/language combination extant in duplicate. That is, there are two copies of the Greek (*RIÉ* 270 = 270 bis), two copies of the Ethiopic language in unvocalized Ethiopic script (*RIÉ* 185 II = 185 bis II), and two copies of the Ethiopic language in Old South Arabian script (*RIÉ* 185 I = 185 bis I). The translation here focuses on the Ethiopic language in Old South Arabian script, though variants in the other scripts/languages are occasionally mentioned, but far from systematically.

6. In the Greek version, this is "Ethiopia."

7. So *RIÉ* 185 I. This list of toponyms/ethnonyms varies slightly in the other versions and their duplicates.

8. So the Greek version. In the Ethiopic-language versions (both in Old South Arabian script and in Ethiopic script), this is MHRM. So also below.

9. Not found in *RIÉ* 185 I or in the Greek, which has "invincible."

10. This could be biological brothers, but it does not necessarily have to be; for instance, "brothers-in-arms" or the like is also possible.

11. This is the same person addressed as one of the rulers (*tyrannoi*) of Aksum, along with 'Ezana, in the letter attributed to Constantius embedded in Athanasius's *Apology to Constantius*.

12. The numbers throughout this translation derive from *RIÉ* 185 II = 185 II bis. The Greek version in its two copies (*RIÉ* 270 = 270 bis) has similar numbers but with some minor variation, whereas only blank spaces are found in the two inscriptions in Ethiopic language in Old South Arabian script (*RIÉ* 185 I = 185 bis I).

We sent them to live in the region of Matlia,[13] within the border of our land. We have taken care to support them there, and we apportioned to each of the kings 4,190 cattle, (which is) for the six kings (a total of) 25,140 cattle. We offered to Ares, who begat us, in thanks one statue of gold, one of silver, and three of bronze. We wrote this inscription, and we erected it, and we offered to Ashtar,[14] to Bəher,[15] and to Ares, who begat us. If anyone destroys this stela,[16] may he, his family, and his children be blinded and (?),[17] may they be driven from this land, and may they be cut off from the beer (?).[18] As we have erected (this stela) for them, may it be profitable for us and for our city forever. [We offered to Ares, to SWT, and to BDḤ.][19]

RIÉ *189 (Ethiopic language in Ethiopic script)*

By the power of the Lord of heaven, who is in heaven, and (of) earth,[20] who is victorious for me, I, 'Ezana, son of Ǝlle 'Amida, man of Ḥalen, king of Aksum, of Ḥimyar, of Raydan, of Saba', of Ṣalḥen, of Ṣəyamo, of Bəga, and of Kasu, king of kings, son of Ǝlle 'Amida, who is not conquered by his enemies. By the power of the Lord of heaven, who has given me (power), the Lord of all, in whom I have believed, the king who is not conquered by enemies, may no enemy arise before me, and may no enemy follow after me.

By the power of the Lord of all, I have made war against Noba, when the people of Noba rebelled and acted arrogantly. "He will not cross the Täkäzi," said the people of Noba. When they oppressed the people of Mängurto, of Käsu, and of Barya,

---

13. The location of this place is unknown.

14. This deity is absent in *RIÉ* 270, whereas *RIÉ* 270 bis has "to heaven."

15. This is the word for "land." *RIÉ* 185 II has MDR, which means "earth," and "to earth" is also found in *RIÉ* 270 bis. *RIÉ* 270 does not have either.

16. Literally, "stone."

17. The interpretation of the word is uncertain.

18. *RIÉ* 270 bis has a slightly different curse formula phrased in the active voice with "the God of heaven and of earth" as the subject. No curse formula is present in *RIÉ* 270.

19. Present in neither *RIÉ* 185 I = 185 bis I nor *RIÉ* 270.

20. This is the Ethiopic word *mədr*, just as occurs in one place in *RIÉ* 185 II (see n. 15 above). So also below. Also note that the syntax here is ambiguous: it could mean "the Lord of heaven . . . and earth" as two separate entities: "the Lord of heaven . . . and the Lord of earth"; with ellipses and again two separate entities: the "Lord of heaven . . . and of earth" as one entity; or even the "Lord of heaven who is in heaven and on earth."

and (when) black made war on red,[21] and when they destroyed their oath a second and a third time, and when having no mercy they were killing their neighbors, and when they plundered our emissaries and messengers, whom I had sent so that they could hear (from me), and when they pillaged them of their possessions and stole their spears (?), and when they did not listen to me after I had sent (again) and they refused to cease and (?),[22] (only) then did I go to war and arise.

By the power of the Lord of the land,[23] I killed at the Täkäzi, at the bank of the Kəmälke. Then, they fled and did not arise, and I followed those who had fled for twenty-three days, killing, taking captive, and plundering booty wherever I halted, while my troops who had gone to the countryside brought back captives and booty. While I was burning their villages, both those of stone and of straw, (my troops) pillaged their cereals, their brass, their iron, and their (?). They were destroying the form of their houses and their barns of cereals and cotton. They were hurling them down into the Seda River, and it is many who died in the water—their number is unknown.

While (my troops) sank their boats full of people, both women and men, I captured two officers who had come as spies, riding on camels, whose names were Yəsäka and Butale, as well as a noble (named) ʽƎngäbenawe. Those officers who died were Dänokwe, Dägäle, Anäkwe, Ḥaware, Kärkara, and their priest. (My troops) . . . and took from him a silver crown (?) and a gold ring (?).[24] Those officers who died were five as well as one priest.

I arrived at Kasu, killing them and taking captives at the confluence of the Sida and Täkäzi rivers. On the second day, I arrived and sent into battle the regiment of Mäḥaza as well as the regiment(s) of Hara, of Dämäwä, of Fälḥa, and of Səra' up the Sida, to the villages of stone and of straw—the names of their stone villages are Alwa and Däro. (My troops) killed, took captive, and hurled into the water, and safely they returned home, having terrified their enemies and having conquered them by the power of the Lord of the land.

After that, I sent the regiment of Ḥalen, the regiment of Luken, as well as the regiment(s) of Säbärat, Fälḥa, Səra' down the Sida, to the four straw villages of Noba, to the village of Nəgwäse, to Täbito the stone village of the Kasu, which the Noba had taken, and to Fərtoti. My troops penetrated as far as the area of the Red Noba, and safely they returned home having taken captives, killed, and plundered by the power of the Lord of heaven.

21. This may be a merism to refer to the whole, i.e., "they all went to war."
22. The interpretation here is uncertain.
23. This collocation will ultimately become the typical word for "God" in Ethiopic.
24. The exact objects are uncertain.

I set up a throne at the confluence of the rivers Sida and Täkäzi in front of the stone village on this island.

The Lord of heaven has given me the following: prisoners men 214, prisoners women 415, total of 629. Killed men 602, killed women and children 156, total of 7[58]. Total prisoners and killed 1,387. Plunder: cattle 10,5[6]0, sheep and goats 51,050.

I set up a throne here in Sado by the power of the Lord of heaven, who has helped me and has given me the kingdom. May the Lord of heaven strengthen my kingdom. Just as today he has conquered for me my enemies, may he conquer for me wherever I go. Just as today he conquered for me and has made my enemies submit to me, (I will reign) in justice and truth, not wronging people. I have placed this throne, which I have established, under the protection of the Lord of heaven, who has made me king, and under the protection of earth,[25] who bears it. If anyone uproots it, destroys it, or removes it, may he and his family be eradicated and uprooted from the land. May he be eradicated! I have established this throne by the power of the Lord of heaven.

RIÉ 271 (Greek)

In the faith of God and in the power of the Father, Son, and Holy Spirit, who saved the kingdom for me, in the faith of his Son Jesus Christ, who helped me and who always helps me, I, 'Ezana, king of the Aksumites, of the Ḥimyarites, of Raydan, of the Sabeans, of Ṣalḥen, of Kasu, of Bəga, of Ṣəyamo, man of Ḥalen, son of Ǝllä 'Amida, a servant of Christ, give thanks to the Lord, my God. I am unable to tell the extent of his favor, because my mouth and my mind are unable (to tell) all the favor that he had done for me, for he has made me strong and powerful, and he bestowed upon me a great name through his Son, in whom I have believed. He has made me the guide of all my kingdom because of the faith of Christ, by his will and by the power of Christ, because he guided me. In him I have believed, and he has become a guide for me. I went out to make war with Noba, because the Mangartho, the Kasu, the Atiaditai, and the Bareotai cried out against them, saying: "The Noba have crushed us. Help us! For, they

---

25. Or MDR (as at n. 15 above). The syntax here is less ambiguous than at the beginning of the inscription (see n. 20): MDR ("earth") seems to be a separate entity from the "Lord of heaven."

have oppressed and killed us." I arose in the power of God, Christ, in whom I have believed, and he guided me. I arose from Aksum, on the eighth day of Magabit,[26] a Saturday, by the faith of God, and I came to Mambaria, and there I procured provisions.[27]

26. The Ethiopian month of Mäggabit falls from March to April.

27. The inscription ends here abruptly, and so it seems that only the first part survives, with the remainder presumably continuing on a different stone. On the reverse side of *RIÉ* 271 is *RIÉ* 190, a quite damaged inscription written in Ethiopic language in Old South Arabian script that also deals with a campaign against Nubia (no king is found in the surviving words). Given that both inscriptions deal with a campaign against Nubia, and given their physical proximity, some scholars, though certainly not all, consider *RIÉ* 190 to be the bilingual counterpart to *RIÉ* 271. In this regard, it should be noted that *RIÉ* 190 does not use the same overtly Christian language as *RIÉ* 271 but rather "Lord of the land" (or "God"; see n. 23 above) as well as "Lord of heaven."

2. *Homily on Frumentius*

Introduction and translation by Aaron M. Butts

The Ethiopic *Homily on Frumentius* presents a story about the conversion of an Aksumite king to Christianity at the hands of a certain Frumentius. This story is first found in the *Ecclesiastical History* (10.9–10) of the Latin church historian Rufinus (died 411), from which the Ethiopic *Homily on Frumentius* certainly derives, likely via Socrates's Greek *Ecclesiastical History* (1.19). From the *Homily on Frumentius*, this story spread elsewhere in Ethiopian Christianity, including into the *Synaxarion* (see the next selection), where the main protagonist is no longer Frumentius but one Abba Sälama. Previous scholars tended to accept the historicity of the *Homily on Frumentius*, seeing it as a narrative account of the conversion of the fourth-century Aksumite King ʿEzana. There are, however, many historical problems with this. Thus, more recent scholarship questions the historicity of the *Homily on Frumentius*, preferring to focus on the promulgation of the story in fourteenth- and fifteenth-century Ethiopia as a response to the Ewosṭatean movement (mentioned above), which refused ordination from the Egyptian metropolitan.[1]

Bibliography

Text and Editions

Butts, A. M. "The Ethiopic *Homily on Frumentius*: A Critical Edition." Forthcoming (critical edition that takes account of all five known manuscript witnesses).

Getatchew, Haile. "The Homily in Honour of St. Frumentius, Bishop of Axum." *Analecta Bollandiana* 97 (1979): 309–18 (a handwritten edition, based on a single manuscript, with English translation).

---

1. See A. M. Butts, "A Plea for a Medieval Reading of Ethiopic Manuscripts: The Case of the *Homily on Frumentius*" (forthcoming) as well as a monograph currently in progress, tentatively entitled *Ezana: The First Christian African King.*

Studies

Villa, M. "Frumentius in the Ethiopic Sources: Mythopoeia and Text-Critical
Considerations." *Rassegna di studi etiopici* 48 (2017): 87–111.

Homily of the Holy and Blessed Frumentius, Bishop of Aksum

The story about the way in which the interiors of Ethiopia arrived at Christianity

It is expedient for me to tell you how your land, the land of the Ag'azi,[2] became
Christian, as we found written, in that all of your lands became Christian. A man
from the Roman Empire, whose name was Meropius, a philosopher, came and
was eager in his heart to see the land of the Ag'azi. He brought with him two
children from his family, whose names were as follows: one was Frumentius,
and the other was Edesius. He arrived by boat at the border of the land of the
Ag'azi at the shore of the sea, and he saw everything that he wanted in the land
of the Ag'azi. From there he determined to return to his land, and he arrived at
the harbor where his boat was. Three enemies arrived and killed that man and all
those who were traveling with him, except for the two children from his family,
whom they mercifully did not kill, because they were young. They brought them
as a gift to the king of Aksum, Ǝllä Aläda.[3] When the king saw those children, he
was very pleased with them, and he appointed the one whose name was Edesius
as steward of his house, and he appointed Frumentius as keeper of the law, that
is, the scribe of Aksum.

After a little while, the king died and left a young son with his mother, making
Ǝllä Azg\u02b7ag\u02b7a[4] king and freeing the children. Seeing to the rule of her young son,
the wife of the king asked the two children, Frumentius and Edesius, to watch

---

2. Ag'azi (literally, "free people") seems to refer to the Aksumite population.

3. A King Ǝllä Aläda is not known from the Aksumite coins and inscriptions. In the Aksumite inscriptions 'Ezana's father is named Ǝllä 'Amida (see, e.g., the translation of *RIÉ* 271 above).

4. Again, a King Ǝllä Azg\u02b7ag\u02b7a is not known from the Aksumite coins and inscriptions, nor
is 'Ezana ever called by this name.

over her son until he was old enough, just as they had served his father, so also that they might watch out for him until he was old enough. "As soon as he reaches adulthood, you will return to your lands," she told them. They stayed watching over the king and being entrusted with him. The administration of the property fell especially to Frumentius.

Eagerly, he set about the task to seek and to enquire about the faith and about Christians from among those who were at the market,[5] and he found some. He began to tell them everything that had happened, and he was asking them to go to a quiet place where they could chant the Psalms. Little by little, they passed the days teaching, and they built a place of prayer. Instructing and teaching many, they gathered to themselves many from the people of the Agʿazi.

After that king arrived at adulthood, those associated with Frumentius handed over all their administration, and they asked that they might return to their lands. Though the king and his mother were begging them to stay, they were unable to convince them, because they wanted to see their lands. Edesius, on the one hand, desired to go to the land of Tyre so that he might see his father and his family. Frumentius, on the other hand, after having arrived in Alexandria to Patriarch Athanasius[6] in his new appointment, told him everything about himself: how he had traveled, how he had been captured, how he had found favor with the king, and how the land of the Agʿazi had the hope of believing in Christ. Frumentius asked the Patriarch Athanasius to appoint bishops and priests and to send them to the land of the Agʿazi. Begging him, he said: "Do not overlook them with regard to Christ so that they might find their salvation!" Patriarch Athanasius thought that it was best to appoint Frumentius himself as bishop, saying: "We will not find anyone more suitable than him." Frumentius was appointed, being worthy of the episcopate. Immediately, he returned to the land of the Agʿazi, and he became a preacher for the faith of Christ. He set up many places of prayer, and he was worthy of favor with God. He worked many miracles, he healed the sick, and God healed the weak and afflicted through his hand.

All of this, someone whose name was Rufinus narrated about Abunä Frumentius, having heard it from Edesius, his companion, (who) narrated all of this.

This is Abunä Frumentius, the first bishop for the land of the Agʿazi. In the land of the Roman Empire, we found in books that he is the first appointed for the land of the Agʿazi, and here in the diptychs,[7] we have found him inscribed as the first. This is the good yeast who came to the land of the Agʿazi. This is the

---

5. Possibly the *emporium* in Adulis.

6. That is, Athanasius of Alexandria, whose intermittent episcopacy spanned from 328 to 373.

7. The diptychs consist of a list of saints, living on one side and deceased on the other, who are proclaimed by the deacon during the liturgy.

one who first illuminated the land of the Ag'azi. This is the one whom God sent as an apostle to the land of the Ag'azi. This is the first leader of the faith for the land of the Ag'azi.

Therefore, my brothers, let us honor the day of his remembrance. All of you, from small to great, be diligent about the date of remembrance of the blessed and holy Abunä. Let us make his commemoration a great feast so that his prayer may arrive at us. Be diligent about the day of his passing, on the eighteenth of Taḫśaś.[8] He passed away in Jesus Christ our Lord—praise and glory be to him with his Father and with the all-Holy Spirit, both now and always, forever and ever, amen.

8. The Ethiopian month of Taḫśaś falls from December to January.

3. *Synaxarion* on Yared

Introduction and translation by Aaron M. Butts

T he *Synaxarion* is a hagiographic collection consisting of short vitae arranged according to the calendar year. The Ethiopic *Synaxarion* was translated from the Arabic *Synaxarion* of the Coptic Church sometime in the fourteenth century by Simon from the Monastery of Saint Antony in Egypt. Between 1563 and 1581, the Ethiopic *Synaxarion* was revised, producing a second recension, to which were added many Ethiopian figures who were not found in the original translation. Several decades later, a revision of the second recension was produced that appended concluding poems to most of the entries. The following translation consists of the entry on the Ethiopian Saint Yared, who is alleged to have lived in the sixth century and to whom is traditionally attributed the authorship of a number of liturgical texts, including especially the *Degg*ᵘ*a* (see above).

Bibliography

Text and Editions

Budge, E. A. W. *The Book of the Saints of the Ethiopian Church.* Vol. 3/pp. 875–77. Cambridge: Cambridge University Press, 1928 (English translation).

Butts, A. M. *Ethiopic in 20 Lessons.* Leuven: Peeters. Forthcoming (edition of the earliest layer of the Ethiopic *Synaxarion* for Yared, which is the basis of the present translation).

Colin, G. *Le synaxaire éthiopien: Mois de Genbot*, pp. 50–53. Patrologia Orientalis 47.3. Turnhout: Brepols, 1997 (Ethiopic with French translation).

Synaxarion on Yared

On this day,[1] also Yared, the melodist, the image of the seraphim, passed away. This Yared was from the family of Abba Gedewon, from the priests of (the church of) Askum, which is the first church that was built in the land of Ethiopia, in which the faith of our Lord Christ—praise to him—was preached, and which was sanctified in the name of our Lady, the twofold holy Virgin, Mary, Mother of God. When this Abba Gedewon began to teach the Psalms to the blessed Yared, he was unable to memorize them for many days. So, Abba Gedewon beat and afflicted him, and he fled to the wilderness. He cast a shadow on a tree, and he saw a caterpillar climbing up the tree. After reaching halfway up, the caterpillar would fall to the ground. Many times it did this, and with great difficulty it finally reached the top of the tree. When the holy Yared saw the determination of this caterpillar, he repented in his soul, and he returned to his teacher. He said: "Forgive me, O Abba, and do with me what you want." His spiritual teacher accepted him. After he asked God with weeping, his mind was opened, and he learned in a single day the books of the Old and New Testament. Then, he was appointed as a deacon.

At that time, there were not songs of *qəne*[2] in a loud liturgical chant but only whispering. Wanting to establish for him a memorial, God sent to him three birds from the garden of Eden, and they spoke with him in the language of humans. They carried him away with them to the heavenly Jerusalem, and there he learned the songs of the twenty-four priests of heaven. When he returned to himself, he entered the holy church of Gäbäzä Aksum[3] in the third hour, and he cried out in a loud voice saying: "Hallelujah to the Father, hallelujah to the Son, hallelujah to the Holy Spirit. As the first Zion, he established heaven, and in the second, he showed Moses how to construct the tabernacle." He called this song *Aryam*.[4] When they heard the sound of his voice, the king and queen, along with the bishop, priests, and royal officials, ran and waited, listening to him. He arranged a song for each time of the year: for summer, winter, spring, and fall; for

1. That is the eleventh of Genbot, the Ethiopian month that falls from May to June.
2. A type of religious poetry.
3. Gäbäzä Aksum is one of the names of the central church of Aksum, which is also called Aksum Zion and Maryam Zion.
4. Literally, "the heights."

festivals and sabbaths; for angels, prophets, martyrs, and saints; in three modes, that is, *gəʿəz*, *ʾəzəl*, and *araray*. Nothing surpasses these three modes, whether the speech of humans or the sounds of birds and animals.

One day, Saint Yared was singing, stationed under the legs of King Gäbrä Mäsqäl.[5] As he listened to his voice, the king stabbed the staff of his spear into the foot of Saint Yared until a lot of blood flowed forth. Saint Yared did not notice this until he had finished the song. When the king saw this, he was terrified and removed the staff from his foot. He said to him: "Ask me what you want as remuneration for this blood of yours that has spilled." Saint Yared said to him: "Swear to me that you will not refuse me." When the king had sworn to him, Saint Yared said to him: "Send me to become a monk." When the king heard this, he was very sad, along with all his court, but he feared breaking his oath. After entering the church, Saint Yared stood before the ark[6] of Zion. When he had said: "Holy, sacred, praised, blessed, honored, exalted" until the end, he was lifted up from the ground about one cubit.

Then, he went to the wilderness of Sämen,[7] and he resided there in fasting and prayer. He greatly mortified his body, and he completed his *gädl*[8] there. God gave a covenant to anyone who invokes his name or celebrates his memorial. Then, he passed away in peace. His burial place is not known until this day.

5. Gäbrä Mäsqäl is traditionally understood to be the son and successor of the Aksumite King Kaleb (first half of the sixth century), though he may well be entirely legendary; see Butts, "Mind the Gap."

6. The Ethiopic word here is *tabot*. The *tabot* is among the most important and sacred components of an Ethiopian church building: it is kept in the enclosed sanctuary and visible only to priests. The *tabot* mentioned here is especially important, since it is the one in the church of Aksum: according to tradition, the *tabot* of the church in Aksum is the biblical ark of the covenant brought back by Menelik from the Jerusalem temple—a story recounted, among other places, in the *Glory of the Kings*, a selection of which is translated next.

7. A highland region south-southeast of Aksum.

8. The Ethiopic word *gädl* can mean both "spiritual struggle/fight" and the genre of literature associated with this, i.e., a saint's *Vita* (*Life*).

4. *Glory of the Kings* (*Kəbrä Nägäśt*)

Introduction and translation by Auron M. Butts

The *Kəbrä Nägäśt*, or *Glory of the Kings* (better: *Honor of the Kings*), is often considered the national epic of Ethiopia. As one prominent scholar puts it, the *Glory of the Kings* is "the repository of Ethiopian national and religious feelings, perhaps the truest and the most genuine expression of Abyssinian Christianity."[1] Among its many purposes, the *Glory of the Kings* first and foremost seeks to legitimate the Solomonic dynasty, against the previous Zagʷe (see above). Despite its importance (or perhaps because of it), much remains unknown about the *Glory of the Kings*. This includes when it was written: many but not all scholars think that the current form of the text dates to the beginning of the Solomonic period (ca. 1300), even if the text contains earlier layers, whereas other scholars propose earlier—sometimes even much earlier (sixth century)—dates. In addition, the original language of the text remains disputed. A colophon states that the text was translated from Coptic to Arabic and then into Ethiopic. Some scholars accept this, but others see it as nothing more than a literary device.

The following translation consists of only a short excerpt from the much longer text: the story of how Solomon and Makəda, the Queen of Sheba, conceived Menelik, the mythical first ruler of the Solomonic dynasty of Ethiopia. The excerpt begins with Makəda in ancient Israel with Solomon. After a lavish banquet, Solomon sets a trap for Makəda by which Menelik is conceived. Solomon then has a dream in which the sun leaves Israel to reside forever above Ethiopia—an all-too-obvious metaphor for the transfer of the Solomonic dynasty from Israel to Ethiopia. After some time, another sun—a metaphor for Jesus—appears in Judah, where it is rejected, but it ultimately shines for the entire world.

---

1. E. Ullendorff, *The Ethiopians: An Introduction to Country and People*, 3rd ed. (Oxford: Oxford University Press, 1973), 139.

Bibliography

Text and Editions

Bezold, C. *Kebra Nagast: Die Herrlichkeit der Könige*, pp. 22–26. Munich: Franz, 1905 (Ethiopic text).
Budge, E. A. W. *The Queen of Sheba and Her Only Son Menyelek (Kĕbra Nagast)*. Oxford: Oxford University Press, 1932 (English translation, though not always accurate).

TRANSLATION

Glory of the Kings (Kǝbrä Nägäśt)

King Solomon said to the queen (i.e., Makǝda): "Since you have come here, why would you go before seeing the law of the kingdom, how dinner is prepared for the chosen of the kingdom in the manner of righteous ones, and how the peoples are driven out in the manner of sinners? From this, you will find wisdom. Follow me, and you will sit in my splendor in the tents. I will complete wisdom for you, and you will learn the law of the kingdom. For, you love wisdom, and it will reside with you until your end and forever." A prophecy is apparent in this speech.

The queen replied: "When I was a fool, I became wise in following your wisdom. When I was rejected by the Lord of Israel, I became a chosen one because of the belief that is in my heart. From now on, I will worship only him. In what you have said, you want to increase for me wisdom and honor, and I will come as you want."

Solomon rejoiced on account of this. He had the chosen ones get dressed, he added a second portion to the table, and he commanded that the entire order of his house be arranged. All day, while the house of King Solomon was being made ready, he prepared it with great honor, joy, peace, wisdom, and mercy, along with all humility and modesty. Then, the table of the king was arranged according to the law of the kingdom. The queen entered through a path in splendor and honor, and she sat behind him where she could see, perceive, and observe everything. She was greatly amazed at what she saw and at what she heard. She was praising in her heart the Lord of Israel, and she was in awe at the palace that she saw. She could see, but no one could see her, as Solomon had arranged for her in his wisdom. He had made her seat beautiful, having spread out fine linen, having laid out carpets, having provided musk, alabaster, and precious stones, having sprayed perfumes, having sprinkled myrrh and cassia, mixed with myrrh-oil and frankincense.

When they arrived at that seat, its smell was so wonderful, and the taste of its scent satiated them before they ate food. They brought to her thirst-inducing food in cunning and in wisdom, as well as acidic drinks, fish, and peppery dishes. This Solomon did, and he gave to the queen so that she might eat from it. When the table of the king was finished, three courses and then seven courses, and when the administers, counselors, young men, and servants had retired, the king arose and went to the queen. When they were alone, he said to her: "Be comforted here on account of love until morning." She said to him: "Swear to me by your Lord, the Lord of Israel, that you will not do violence to me. If I stray from the law of the people—being a young girl—I will go down the path to strife, pain, and tribulation."

Solomon answered her: "I will swear to you that I will not do violence to you, but you swear that you will not do violence to anything in my house." The queen laughed and said to him: "Being wise, why do you speak like a fool? Will I steal or rob anything from the house of the king that the king has not given me? May it not seem to you, my lord, that I have come here out of love of possessions. My kingdom is rich by your grace, and nothing is lacking to me from what I want. Rather, I came here seeking wisdom." He said to her: "If you make me swear, then swear to me. Indeed, an oath is fitting for two so that neither is wronged. If you do not cause me to swear, then I also will not cause you to swear." She said to him: "Swear to me that you will not do violence to me, and I also will swear that I will not do violence against your possessions." He swore to her, and he made her swear.

The king got up on his bed on one side of the room, and for her they prepared a bed on the other side. The king said to a servant boy: "Wash a bowl and set out a pitcher of water while the queen is watching you. Then, close the doors and go to sleep." He said this to him in another language that the queen did not know. The boy did as he was told, and he went to sleep. The king, however, did not yet go to sleep, only laying his head down as if he were asleep but watching carefully. The palace of King Solomon was as bright in the night as it was in the day, because wisely he had made shining pearls like the sun, the moon, and the stars on the ceiling of the palace.

The queen slept a little while. When she awoke, her mouth was parched with thirst, because in wisdom Solomon had given her thirst-inducing food.

Her mouth was very parched and dry, and she felt around in her mouth but could not find any saliva. She thought about drinking the water that she saw, and she watched and carefully observed Solomon, and he seemed to be sleeping heavily. He was not, however, asleep, but he was waiting for when she would take and steal the water for her thirst. She got up without making any sound with her feet, went to that water in the bowl, and raised it to drink, but Solomon seized her by the hand before she could drink. He said to her: "Why have you transgressed the oath that you swore not to do violence against anything in my house?" She answered fearfully: "Is the oath really transgressed by drinking water?" The king said to her: "Have you seen anything more beneficial than water under the sun?" She said: "I have wronged myself. You are free from the oath. Let me drink the water for my thirst." He said to her: "Am I by chance free from the oath that you made me swear?" The queen said: "Be free from the oath, and let me drink water." He let her drink water. After she drank the water, he did what he wanted, and they slept together.

After he fell asleep, a bright sun appeared to King Solomon. It descended from the heavens, and it shone brightly over Israel. Then, after having tarried, suddenly it withdrew and flew to the land of Ethiopia. It shone brightly there forever, because it wanted to reside there. I waited for it to return to Israel, but it did not return. Then, after having waited, a light dawned, and a sun came down from heaven to the land of Judah, and it shone brightly here as previously. Israel, however, declared the sun evil because of its flame, and they did not walk in its light. That sun disregarded Israel, and they were jealous of it. Peace was not possible between them and the sun. Israel raised their hands against it with rods and knives, and they wanted to extinguish the sun. They darkened the entire world with earthquakes and fog, and it seemed to them that the sun would not dawn for them again. They destroyed its light. They attacked it, and they guarded the tomb in which they put it. But, it came forth from where they did not look for it. The sun shone for the entire world, especially for the first land and for the last land, for Ethiopia and for Rome. Israel, however, the sun greatly disregarded, and it ascended to its ancient throne.

When King Solomon saw this vision while asleep, his soul was terrified, and his mind was carried off like lightening. He awoke terrified.

5. Miracles of Mary

Introduction and translation by Aaron M. Butts

The *Tä'ammərä Maryam*, or *Miracles of Mary*, is among the most well-attested texts in Ethiopian manuscripts, with hundreds, if not thousands, of extant exemplars. Its extensive manuscript attestation speaks directly to the importance of the *Miracles of Mary* as one of the most prominent pieces of Ethiopian Christian literature. The *Miracles of Mary* is not a single, standardized text but rather a fluid collection of individual miracles said to have been performed by Mary, whether during her lifetime or after her death. More than seven hundred individual miracles are known. Some manuscripts contain only a few miracles, or sometimes even just one, whereas others contain several hundred. The earliest kernel of the *Miracles of Mary* can be traced back to twelfth-century France, from where it spread throughout much of medieval Europe. In the thirteenth century, a collection of the *Miracles of Mary* was translated into Arabic, and the Arabic version was in turn translated into Ethiopic at the end of the fourteenth century during the reign of Zär'a Ya'əqob's father, Dawit II (ruled 1379/1380–1413). As part of his systematic program to increase the veneration of Mary, Zär'a Ya'əqob made the recitation of the *Miracles of Mary* part of the liturgical cycle as well as sponsored the production of numerous manuscripts of the *Miracles of Mary*, which were then spread throughout his kingdom. This intervention by Zär'a Ya'əqob led to the widespread copying and use of the *Miracles of Mary* in Ethiopian Christianity from the fifteenth century until today. The following translation is of a single miracle, that of Hildephonsus, bishop of Toledo (656–67), who is said to have written a work on the miracles of Mary, thereby initiating the genre.

Bibliography

Text and Editions

Budge, E. A. W. *Legends of Our Lady Mary the Perpetual Virgin and Her Mother Ḥannâ*. London: Medici Society, 1922 (English translation).
———. *The Miracles of the Blessed Virgin Mary*. London: Griggs, 1900 (Ethiopic).

————. *One Hundred and Ten Miracles of Our Lady Mary*. London: Medici Society, 1923 (English translation).

Colin, G. *Le livre éthiopien des miracles de Marie (Taamra Mâryâm)*. Paris: Cerf, 2004 (French translation).

Studies

Cerulli, E. *Il libro etiopico dei Miracoli di Maria e le sue fonti nelle letterature del medio evo latino*. Rome: Bardi, 1943.

TRANSLATION

Miracles of Mary

The first miracle of our Lady, the holy Virgin, Mary Mariham, mother of God.[1] May her intercession be with us. Amen.[2]

It is said that there was in the church of the city of Toledo a bishop whose name was Daqsis.[3] He was a blessed and good man who loved our Lady, the holy Virgin, Mary Mariham, with all his heart and who was serving her with all his ability. From the flame of his love for her, he made and gathered a book, *Her Miracles and Her Praises*,[4] about her glory. When he completed the book of her miracles, our Lady, the Virgin, Mary Mariham, the crown of the believers, appeared to him. She took the book in her hand, and said to him: "O my beloved, Daqsis, I am pleased with you, and I extol you, since you have made this book for me." Then, she was hidden from him.

When the bishop saw this in a vision, out of love of our Lady, the holy Virgin, Mary Mariham, he was overjoyed, and his heart burned like a fire in his love for her. He was contemplating what he would do to enhance and increase her glory. He made a Festival of the Annunciation, which was previously impossible for people to do at that time because of the fast, and he set it on the eighth day before

1. This is the Ethiopic equivalent of Greek *theotokos*.

2. This translation is based on MS EMML 9002, which dates to the time of Dawit II, who is specifically mentioned throughout the manuscript.

3. A corruption of (Hil)dephonsus, which must have involved Arabic given the interchange of *ph* and *q*.

4. The Latin title of Hildephonsus is *De Virginitate Mariae contra tres infideles*.

the Festival of Nativity. It has been established from his episcopacy until today. When the people celebrate this festival, they rejoice greatly.

Our Lady, the Virgin, Mary Mariham, the friend of the good and beautiful, appeared to him, and in her hands there was a garment of glory, and she said to him: "O my beloved, Daqsis, my steadfast minister. I extol you; I rejoice in you; and I am pleased with your work. Just as you have rejoiced in me and have made for me a Festival of the Annunciation of Gabriel, the angel who announced the good news to me, and you made all people rejoice concerning me, I also want to reward and honor you in this world before all people, just as you have honored me. Behold, I bring to you this garment to wear and to be yours. No one will be able to wear it apart from you after you, and no one will be able to sit on your throne apart from you. Whoever transgresses this that I tell you, I will punish." After she said this, she was hidden from him.

When the days of his life were completed and he departed from this world to the mercy of God Almighty, they placed that garment in the treasury of the church in great honor and purity.

When another bishop had been appointed after him, he wanted to wear that garment and to sit on that throne of Bishop Daqsis. The priests and elders of the church conveyed to him the glory of that garment, and they told him: "On account of God, do not do this!" He replied to them: "Am I not a human like he was a human? Am I not a bishop like he was a bishop? I want to wear this garment and to sit on his throne." They were unable to prevent him. When he put on that garment and sat on that throne, immediately he fell from that throne in front of all the people in the church, and he died a most wicked and accursed death. All the people in the church were amazed at the miracle that occurred. They praised God, praiseworthy and almighty, and they extolled our Lady, the holy Virgin, Mary Mariham, for what she did. They feared her, and they increased her cult and her glory. May the prayer and the blessing of our Lady, the holy Virgin, Mary Mariham, be with King Dawit,[5] forever and ever, amen, amen, and amen, may it be, may it be, may it be.

5. This is Dawit II (ruled 1379/80–1413), father of Zär'a Ya'əqob.

6. Zär'a Ya'əqob, *Book of the Trinity*

Introduction and translation by Aaron M. Butts

The following selection comes from the *Book of the Trinity* attributed to Zär'a Ya'əqob. The *Book of the Trinity*, which is also called the *Gate of the Sun*, is intertwined in the longer—and potentially later—*Book of Nativity*. This particular passage focuses on Christology with polemics directed explicitly against the Stephanites. It is difficult to glean much, if anything, about the position of the Stephanites from this polemical passage, but it does give a good sense of the broader theological landscape in fifteenth-century Ethiopia, especially Zär'a Ya'əqob's place within it. A number of other interesting themes also appear in this excerpt. For instance, mention is made of the biblical canon of eighty-one books, which is likely a reform of the more expansive and fluid situation of earlier periods. Relatedly, it is interesting to see what written authorities are adduced: there are direct quotations from Genesis, Psalms, Gospel of John, and Pauline Epistles, along with allusions to other biblical texts, as well as quotations from the *Synodos* and the *Didascalia*, both of which are included in the traditional eighty-one-book canon of Ethiopian Christianity. On a different theme, at the very end of the passage, the text rebukes magicians, calling them the children and messengers of Satan—a polemic developed more fully in other works attributed to Zär'a Ya'əqob, especially the *Epistle of Humanity*, as mentioned above.

Bibliography

Text and Editions

Wendt, K. *Das Maṣḥafa Milād (Liber Nativitatis) und Maṣḥafa Sellāsē (Liber Trinitatis)*. CSCO 221–22, 235–36. Leuven: Secrétariat du CSCO, 1962–63 (Ethiopic with German translation).

TRANSLATION

Book of the Trinity

We believe in this great *Book of the Trinity*, which is called the *Door of the Sun*—the sun is Mary, the mother of Adonai, whom she conceived and gave birth to in virginity of mind and in virginity of flesh, without sin. O Christlike, gospel-like Christian, chosen from the people of the world, worship his nativity in pure belief of the Trinity and bow down to it in a belief of thanks. First, believe in the birth of Christ from God, the heavenly Father, and second (believe) in his birth from Mary, the twofold Virgin, daughter of Judah and of Levi. . . .

Again, rejoice, O Christian, in the Trinity, the Father, the Son, and the Holy Spirit, because the foundation of Christianity is belief in the Trinity. Thus, believe in the Father, in his person, his image, and his substance; also believe in the Son, in his person, his image, and his substance; and also believe in the Holy Spirit, in its person, its image, and its substance. The Word of the Father and of the Holy Spirit[1] is the Son, and that speaking one speaks from himself where he wants. It is not called two words or three words but one Word, who is the Son, just as the apostles taught us in their *Canons*:[2] "The believers hold these Scriptures, and these are their names, which we command to the believers: Christ is from the old and from the new, and he is the book of the message, which came down from God the Father and from the Holy Spirit, that is, the canon of eighty-one books with the book of the *Synodos*,[3] which we proclaimed to Clement. The old speaks of the later, and later is the fulfillment of the first. There is a witness for this: One! From one Word and one speech act, God, the crafter and creator, (created) by his Word and his Spirit." The apostles and the Scriptures do not say: "God, the creator, (created) in his words and his spirits." Rather, they say: "One! From one Word and from one speech act, God, the crafter and creator, (created) by his Word and his Spirit." There are some Christians who say the following: "The Father exists with his word and his spirit; the Son exists with his word and his spirit; and the Spirit exists with its word and its spirit." We, however, say to them: "From three words and from three spirits, who created all creation? Tell me! If it is impossible for you to say, then believe that (it is) one Word, one

---

1. Some manuscripts include "Son" but probably incorrectly.
2. The *Canons* mentioned here are part of the Ethiopic *Synodos*; see the next footnote.
3. The Ethiopic *Synodos* was the most important canonical-liturgical collection of Ethiopian Christianity in the Solomonic period.

speech act, and one Spirit. When the Father speaks in his word, do you think that it is possible for you to say that the Son and the Holy Spirit do not speak? When the Son speaks in his word, do you think that it is possible for you to say that the Father and the Holy Spirit do not speak? When the Holy Spirit speaks in its word, do you think that it is possible for you to say that the Father and Son do not speak?"

Again, the apostles say in their *Synodos*: "Rejoice, our children! Hallelujah, which is to say: We praise the one who is God, the worshiped and praised, who laid the foundation of the entire world with one Word." See, O Christian, that the Word of the Father and of the Holy Spirit is one, and the Son is himself the Word of the Father and the Word of the Holy Spirit. The Word, which the Son is called, is the first Word of the Father, just as John, the son of thunder, said: "In the beginning was the Word, and the Word was with God; the Word was God. Thus, in the beginning and from the beginning he was with God. All things came to be through him, and without him nothing came to be. Everything that came to be on account of him is life, and life is the light of people. The light shines and makes visible in the darkness, and the darkness does not overcome or draw near to it."[4] See, O Christian, how John, the son of thunder, spoke: "All things came to be through him, and without him nothing came to be." This is what John said about the Father, who created all creation through his Son, Jesus Christ, who is the Word of the Father and the Word of the Holy Spirit. He is called the Word of the Father and the Word of the Holy Spirit, that Son, Jesus Christ, the one Word. When you make into three, you make a scattering of the Trinity. When you make the Holy Spirit into three, you make a scattering of the Trinity.

Again, the apostles say in the *Didascalia*:[5] "Gather in the church, evening and morning. Praise, sing, and recite the 62nd and 140th psalms of David. Especially on the Sabbath of the Jews and on Sunday, the Sabbath of the Christians, which is (the day of) his holy resurrection, offer up praise, thanksgiving, and honor to God, who created everything through his Son, Jesus Christ." See, O Christian, that God the Father created through his Son and through his Spirit all creation. He did not create any of creation except by his Son and by his Spirit. He created nothing without his Son and his Spirit, just as David said: "By the word of God he formed the heavens, and by the breathing of his mouth all their hosts."[6] "By the word of God" is meant the Father, "his word" the Son, and "by the breathing of his mouth" the Spirit.

---

4. John 1:1–5.

5. The Ethiopic *Didascalia* is a work of canon law, corresponding to the first seven books of the *Apostolic Constitutions*.

6. Ps 33:6.

Tell me, O heretic, how is it that God created by his Son and by his Spirit? If you fail to answer "the Word," then I will tell you that "by his Son he created" means "by his Word he created." The Word of the Father is his Son, Jesus Christ, just as the Octateuch[7] said: "In the beginning, God created the heavens. The earth existed from of old, but it was not visible and was incomplete. Darkness was over the deep, and the Spirit of God hovered over the water. God said: 'Let there be light, and there was light.'"[8] All of these and the like created things, which are innumerable, the awesome and fear-inspiring God the Father created: he created through his Word, which is his awesome and fear-inspiring Son, and he created through his one Spirit, which is the awesome and fear-inspiring Holy Spirit. The Father created all created things through his one Word and through his one Spirit, just as the apostles wrote in their *Synodos*: "This, God, the crafter and creator, (created) by his one Word and his one Spirit." The Word is not three, and the Spirit is not three. The Word is one, and the Spirit is one. All created things, the Father created by his one Word and by his one Spirit. Paul said: "All of us drink one Spirit."[9] Whoever teaches three words and three spirits establishes three gods and cannot say one Lord and one God, because one God is called by one Word and one Spirit. We worship God the Father, the Son Jesus Christ, who is his Word, and the Holy Spirit, the Paraclete—one Father, one Word, and one Spirit, believing and worshiping: this is the unity of the Trinity.

Listen, O accursed Stephanite, who is submerged in the sea of heresy, who says: "I do not venerate Mary," while also saying: "Three words and three spirits."[10] We say: one God the Father, one Word who is his Son, and one Spirit that is the Paraclete. This is the uniting of the Trinity. There is a difference between creators and creatures. If God Almighty bestows one spirit, the spirit of created people, on ten thousand people, then their word is one, and their thought is one. When one of their spirits dies, then all ten thousand people die. When one lives, then all live. When one of their spirits becomes sad, all become sad. When one of their spirits rejoices, all rejoice. But, I worship the Trinity, the Lord who resides in the heights.

Listen, O Christian: when you establish the Father with his word and his spirit, the Son with his word and his spirit, and the Spirit with its word and its spirit, you render void the unity of the Trinity. You liken the Trinity to creatures

---

7. Collection of the biblical books of Genesis, Exodus, Leviticus, Numbers, Deuteronomy, Joshua, Judges, and Ruth.

8. Gen 1:1–3.

9. 1 Cor 12:13.

10. As mentioned in the introduction, one should be cautious in understanding this polemical rhetoric as the actual position of the Stephanites, but the Stephanite *Acts of Abba ʿEzra* seems to maintain that each person of the Trinity speaks with its own word.

like Abraham, Isaac, and Jacob. Abraham was created with his word and his spirit, Isaac was created with his word and his spirit, and Jacob was created with his word and his spirit. All humans have been created in this way. When Abraham speaks, it is not said that Isaac speaks. When Isaac speaks, it is not said that Jacob speaks. When Jacob speaks, it is not said that Abraham and Isaac speak. That which Abraham thinks, Isaac does not know. That which Isaac thinks, Jacob does not know. That which Jacob thinks, Abraham and Isaac do not know. For, their word is three, and their spirit is three. So, Abraham does not know the thought of Isaac, Isaac does not know the thought of Jacob, and Jacob does not know the thought of Abraham and Isaac. For, their spirit is like the spirit of all people. Again, you liken the Trinity to Ananya, Azarya, and Mishael, who made the belly of flames into a door.[11] These three children had three spirits. Ananya did not know what Azarya was thinking. What Azarya was thinking, Mishael did not know. What Mishael was thinking, Ananya and Azarya did not know. But, if their spirit was in the power of God, then their heart and thought would be one.

Hear, O Christian, do not say that the Word of God is three, and the Spirit of God is three. When you say this, you fall from the rank of Christian, and you become a child of the devil Satan. We believe in one God. We believe in one Word, which is the Son, as the Word of the Father and of the Holy Spirit. We believe in one Holy Spirit, who is the Holy Spirit, as the Spirit of the Father and the Son. The Son of God was born from God the Father, and the Holy Spirit God proceeded from God the Father, just as the apostles, the spiritual doves, have taught us. You, O Christian, believe in the Father, in his person, his image, and his substance; also believe in the Son, in his person, his image, and his substance; and also believe in the Holy Spirit, in its person, its image, and its substance. We believe and worship three persons, three images, and three substances. Know, O Christian, the Father does not wear our flesh. The Spirit does not wear our flesh. But the Son does wear our flesh, which he took from Mary, our Lady. In that flesh and in the Trinity, we take refuge so that our Lord might save us from the hand of Satan, our enemy, and from the hand of his children, the magicians, who are his messengers, forever and ever, amen and amen, may it be concerning the flesh and blood of Christ, may it be, may it be!

---

11. The "belly of the flames" here refers to the story of Shadrach, Meshach, and Abednego (Dan 3:19–23), which is understood to be a door for Christ.

7. Prayer Amulet: MS Duke Ethiopic 15

Introduction and translation by Aaron M. Butts

Ethiopian prayer amulets take the physical format of a roll. They are often made of three pieces of parchment sewn together, ranging from five to fifteen centimeters in width, with their length often the same as the height of a person. Ethiopian prayer amulets contain an assortment of prayers intended to protect the patron against diseases and/or the evil spirits responsible for them. The texts of the amulets can be divided into two broad categories.[1] First, there are narrative and/or literary texts, including but not limited to biblical texts. The texts in this first category are relatively stable, though variations—sometimes significant—occur frequently. The second category is a less-homogenous group consisting of phrases that occur with a great deal of variation. They can be strung together in various combinations; different elements can be adapted, combined, or repeated; and they often seem to occur more or less as filler material. The second category is the main place that the so-called *asmat*, or names, appear in the amulets. The *asmat* are the names by which the invocations are believed to become efficacious. The texts of the amulets are broken up by colorful talismanic images, often three in number, of various themes, such as angels, stars, crosses, and demons. The amulets—at least in modern times—are made by a *däbtära*, a member of the clergy responsible for chanting the psalms and hymns during the liturgy. As mentioned above, all surviving Ethiopian prayer amulets probably date to the last couple of centuries; the practice, however, may go back much earlier, since the formulas are at home in the magical traditions of late antiquity, including Coptic.

Bibliography

Text and Editions

Burtea, B. *Zwei äthiopische Zauberrollen.* Semitica et Semitohamitica Berolinensia 1. Aachen: Shaker, 2001.

1. See V. Six, "Kategorien der äthiopischen Zaubertexte," *Zeitschrift der deutschen morgenländischen Gesellschaft* 139 (1989): 310–17.

Dobberahn, F. E. *Fünf äthiopische Zauberrollen: Text, Übersetzung, Kommentar.* Walldorf-Hessen: Orientkunde, 1976.

Lifchitz, D. *Textes éthiopiens magico-religieux.* Paris: Institut d'ethnologie, 1940.

Strelcyn, S. *Prières magiques éthiopiennes pour délier les charmes (maftǝḥe sǝray).* Rocznik orientalistyczny 18. Warsaw: Państwowe Wydawnictwo Naukowe, 1955.

Studies

Mercier, J. *Art That Heals: The Image as Medicine in Ethiopia.* New York: Museum for African Art, 1997.

———. *Rouleaux magiques éthiopiens.* Paris: Seuil, 1979.

TRANSLATION

Prayer Amulet (MS Duke Ethiopic 15)

In the name of the Father, the Son, and the Holy Spirit, one God, the prayer of Saint Susenyos concerning the disease of those who are nursing at the breast of their mother. It is also useful for the woman by the help of the almighty and glorious one. Let her write, and it will be useful to her by the help of the almighty and glorious one forever and ever, amen. May he save her from Wǝrzǝlya, *šätolay, mäggañña,* pleurisy, the evil eye *zar, zarit, tǝgǝrtya, sǝqsǝqat, nägärgar,* who comes like a shadow and dream, accident, demon, *qätr,* who destroys in day and at night. Save your servant Wälättä Maryam.[2] There once was a man whose name was Susenyos. He married a woman and begat male and female. With his first child, Wǝrzǝlya came and killed the child. His mother wailed and cried bitterly. When Saint Susenyos heard the crying of the mother, he said to her: "O woman, what is making you cry?" She said to him: "(It is) because Wǝrzǝlya came and killed the child!" He said: "Where is Wǝrzǝlya?" She said: "She went to the garden, where she was in the beginning." He mounted his horse, took his spear in his right hand, and went to her. He found the old woman with many demons surrounding her. When he saw Wǝrzǝlya, he dismounted his horse and turned his face toward the east. He stretched out his hands and prayed to God, saying: "O my Lord, Jesus Christ, God of the Christians and King of Israel, kill Wǝrzǝlya

---

2. This is the name of the client, a woman named Wälättä Maryam.

for me! If I kill her, after she has fallen under my hands, I will be a witness to your holy name." A voice came from heaven saying: "O Susenyos, your prayer has been heard and answered, and the power has been given to you from God to take Wərzəlya and to do anything that you want." He went to her and pierced her side. Wərzəlya said to him: "O Susenyos, my lord, I adjure you by the seven archangels Michael, Gabriel, Surafel, Kirubel, Ruphael, Uruel, and Aguel, these are the ones who stand around the throne of God at all times forever and ever, amen." Wərzəlya swore, saying: "O Susenyos, my lord!" By the name of my Lord, may the prayer and the blessing of Saint Susenyos save from Wərzəlya, *šätolay*, *mäggañña*, tremors, *təgərtya*, bleeding, *barya*, who causes blood to flow and kills children, remove and expel all the demons from your servant Wälättä Maryam. In the name of the Father, the Son, and the Holy Spirit, one God, prayer concerning *šätolay* and *šätolawit*, who kill infants and cause bleeding. I bind you, I bridle you, I adjure you, I scourge you, I bind you, I adjure you, you, *šätolay* and *šäto-lawit*, so that you do not kill infants and so that you do not cause bleeding from the belly of your servant Wälättä Maryam. I seal you with the seals of the Father, the Son, and the Holy Spirit, one God. Again, I bind you with the binding of the *asmat*: *mä'ağən, mä'ağən, mä'ağən, fäqağən, fäqağ, fäqağ, qälağəmo, qälağəmo, qäğəmäl, qäğəmäl, mä'ağ, mä'ağ, ğämo, ğämo, a a a, čä čä čä*, by the power of these *asmat*, remove, expel, and crush this demon whose name is *šätolay*, so that it is far away, withdraws, and is not near your servant Wälättä Maryam. I believe in the Father, I believe in the Son, I believe in the Holy Spirit, one God, three persons, one Godhead, so that you *šätolay* and *šätolawit* neither draw near to me nor touch me. May your poison be ineffective, may your bones be crushed, by these *asmat*: *himağ, himağ, himağ, himağ, himağ, foloğ, foloğ*. I adjure you, I anathematize you, you *šätolay* and *šätolawit*, so that you do not draw near to the soul or body of Wälättä Maryam. *Kon, bərkoni, lušädqan, mäsṭeṭ, 'əlwan, mənatir, äbyatir, äqyatir*, Jesus Christ, Son of the living God, and by the Father, burning of fire, so that all of the evil spirits, the black *barya*, the red *barya*, *dask*, *lägewon, mäggañña, gʷəsəmt*, the evil eye, chest pain, colic, headache, *mətat*, slap in the face, *məč, tälawaš*, slap in the face, *fera, nədad*, nausea, *zar(i)t*, tremors, rheumatism, hand, foot, rib, back, any part of the body, *buda*, blacksmith, work-man, artisans, plague, *nägärgar, dədəq*, demon of the night, *ğinn*, and *wəllağ* are extinguished by all these names of yours. I adjure you, I anathematize you, so that you do not draw near to the soul or body of the servant of God, Wälättä Maryam. In the name of the Father, the Son, the Holy Spirit, one God, prayer for the coagulation (of blood): *säntəm, qätnəm, qäntəm, ağər, mägər, mägər*, by *duhämo* you are bound, by *duhämo* you are expelled, you, *barya* and *legewon*, who bring forth blood and kill infants. After you have released, go to enclose *duradir* by the power of these names of yours, congeal the blood of your servant

Wälättä Maryam, and may her body no longer be ill. *Sadär* the n(ail), *aladär* the n(ail), *danat* the n(ail), *adera* the n(ail), *rodas* the n(ail). By these nails of the cross of our Lord, Jesus, who stopped the devil, similarly stop the blood of your servant Wälättä Maryam, and may her body no longer be ill. Prayer for the co-agulation of blood: # # # # # # # # * * * * * * * * * * @ @ @ @ @ @ @ @ @ @ ^ ^ ^ ^ ^ ^ ^ ^[3] *šä šä šä šä šä šä šä šä šä šä,* by this talisman and by these names, coagulate and stop the blood of the womb of Wälättä Maryam. O my Lord, Jesus Christ, just as you gave (children) to Sarah and Elizabeth, so also give seed so that your servant Wälättä Maryam may bear male and female children, and con-geal her blood. In the name of the Father, the Son, and the Holy Spirit, one God, prayer for the coagulation of blood: *susulame, susulame, sulame, bäṣäbaləyos, bäṣäbaləyos, bäṣäbaləyos, čäčä'al, čä'al,* by the power of these *asmat* of yours, may a child dwell and grow strong in the womb of your servant Wälättä Maryam, and may her menstrual blood congeal. Prayer for the coagulation of blood: God sent to Eve twelve angels of mercy, twelve angels of compassion, twelve angels of light, and twelve angels of Zion, so also strengthen the menstrual blood of your servant Wälättä Maryam. O my Lord, Jesus Christ, who took it from the side of man into the stomach of woman, and it is fertile in the soft uterus. When he,[4] she coagulates it and places it in the . . . ,[5] so also place the child in the womb of your servant Wälättä Maryam. Prayer for the coagulation of blood. Gospel of Mark.[6] When the Lord Jesus was walking in the flesh in the cities of people, a woman whose blood had been flowing for twelve years came. She was in great pain and had spent all her possessions for protection against magic. All her pos-sessions were exhausted, and she did not improve but grew worse. Having heard that the Lord Jesus had come, she went to him, and she stood among the people and touched the edge of his clothing. Immediately her blood stopped. She herself was surprised, and she lived. So also make alive and congeal the blood of your servant Wälättä Maryam. *lis, aflis, iliyab, səlyab,* your *asmat* and the name of your divinity, flame of fire, *mi, səlwanos, zozälon, zäzälma'el, bägädgäd, ṣəlmutan, anfär'i'i,* strong hail, by our Lord and by the power of these names of yours, congeal the blood of your servant Wälättä Maryam and strengthen the fruit of her womb. In the name of the Father, the Son, and the Holy Spirit, one God, the prayer of *nädära,* which is the eye of *barya.* When the Lord Jesus was going to the Sea of Tiberias, his twelve disciples came, and they saw the form of an old

---

3. The characters here resemble those of the Ethiopic script but are not actually letters: such *caractères à lunettes,* or talismanic writing, are found relatively frequently in the Ethiopian prayer amulets.

4. The text here is corrupt.

5. The text here is difficult to understand.

6. Mark 5:25–28.

woman. She was exceedingly frightening for her eyes were flashing like red gold, and her hands and feet were like chariot wheels, and flames of fire were coming from her mouth as high as sixty cubits. The disciples of our Lord Jesus said to him: "What is this?" (He answered them:) "This is the wicked and accursed evil eye. Whenever she sees a boat going (to sea), she overturns it. Whenever she sees a horse running, she casts it down along with the one who is riding it. Whenever she sees a cow being milked, its milk ceases to flow. Whenever she sees a woman carrying her child, it dies. This is the accursed evil eye." He consumed her in fire so that the memory of the evil eye would be erased from your servant Wälättä Maryam.

CONTRIBUTORS

General Editor

J. Edward Walters, Syriac Manuscript Cataloger at the Hill Museum & Manuscript Library

Section Editors

Arabic—John C. Lamoreaux, associate professor in the Department of Religious Studies at Southern Methodist University

Armenian—Jesse S. Arlen, doctoral candidate in Near Eastern Languages and Cultures at the University of California, Los Angeles

Coptic—Mary K. Farag, assistant professor of Early Christian Studies at Princeton Theological Seminary

Ethiopic—Aaron M. Butts, associate professor in the Department of Semitic and Egyptian Languages and Literatures at the Catholic University of America

Georgian—Jeff W. Childers, Carmichael-Walling Professor of New Testament and Early Christianity in the Graduate School of Theology at Abilene Christian University

Syriac—J. Edward Walters, Syriac Manuscript Cataloger at the Hill Museum & Manuscript Library

Individual Contributors

Philip Michael Forness, postdoctoral researcher in late antique Christianity in the Near East at Goethe-Universität Frankfurt am Main

Jeanne-Nicole Mellon Saint-Laurent, associate professor in the Theology Department at Marquette University

Erin Galgay Walsh, assistant professor at the Divinity School of the University of Chicago

Jeffrey Wickes, associate professor of theology at the University of Notre Dame

INDEX OF SUBJECTS

INDEX OF SCRIPTURE
AND OTHER ANCIENT TEXTS